Bruno Maderna

Contemporary Music Studies

A series of books edited by Nigel Osborne, London, UK

Volume 1
Charles Koechlin (1867–1950) His Life and Works
Robert Orledge

Volume 2
Pierre Boulez — A World of Harmony
Lev Koblyakov

Volume 3
Bruno Maderna
Raymond Fearn

Additional volumes in preparation

Hanns Eisler
David Blake

Stefan Wolpe
Austin Clarkson

Bruno Maderna

By

Raymond Fearn

University of Keele, UK

harwood academic publishers
chur · london · paris · new york · melbourne

Harwood Academic Publishers

Post Office Box 197
London WC2E 9PX
United Kingdom

Post Office Box 786
Cooper Station
New York, New York 10276
United States of America

58, rue Lhomond
75005 Paris
France

Private Bag 8
Camberwell, Victoria 3124
Australia

Cover photograph: Bruno Maderna
(Photograph: Pit Ludwig)

Library of Congress Cataloging-in-Publication Data

Fearn, Raymond, 1944-
    Bruno Maderna / Raymond Fearn.
    p. cm. -- (Contemporary music studies, ISSN 0891–5415 : v.3)
    Includes bibliographical references
    ISBN 3–7186–5011–8
    1. Maderna, Bruno--Criticism and interpretation. I. Title. II. Series
ML410.M174F4 1990   780'.92--dc20

Contents

Introduction to the Series

The rapid expansion and diversification of contemporary music is explored in this international series of books for contemporary musicians. Leading experts and practitioners present composition today in all aspects — its techniques, aesthetics and technology, and its relationships with other disciplines and currents of thought — as well as using the series to communicate actual musical materials.

The series also features monographs on significant twentieth-century composers not extensively documented in the existing literature.

NIGEL OSBORNE

List of Plates

(Between pp. 168 and 169)

1. (Cover Photograph: Bruno Maderna, Darmstadt, 1960. (Photograph: Pit Ludwig)
2. Bruno Maderna, Darmstadt, 1952. (Photograph: Pit Ludwig)
3. International Summer School, Darmstadt, 1956: (Left to Right) Pierre Boulez, Bruno Maderna, Karlheinz Stockhausen. (Photograph: Hans Kenner)
4. Bruno Maderna, Darmstadt, 1958. (Photograph: Hans Kenner)
5. Darmstadt, 1959: (Left to Right) Kasimierz Serocki, Nuria Nono-Schoenberg, Luigi Nono, Bruno Maderna. (Photograph: Hella Steinecke)
6. Darmstadt, 1960: (Left to Right) Bruno Maderna, Earle Brown, Wolfgang Steinecke, Severino Gazzelloni, Pierre Boulez. (Photograph: Hella Steinecke)
7. Darmstadt, 1960: (Left to Right) Bruno Maderna, Earle Brown. (Photograph: Hella Steinecke)
8. Bruno Maderna, Darmstadt, 1961. (Photograph: Hans Kenner)
9. International Chamber Ensemble, Darmstadt, 1961: rehearsal of Earle Brown's *Available Forms I*: conductor Bruno Maderna. (Photograph: Hans Kenner)
10. Bruno Maderna, Darmstadt, 1962. (Photograph: Pit Ludwig)
11. Bruno Maderna and Severino Gazzelloni (flute), Darmstadt, 1964. (Photograph: Pit Ludwig)
12. Bruno Maderna in performance of Varèse: *Ionisation*, Darmstadt, 1966. (Photograph: Pit Ludwig)

In memory of my mother and father . . . . *'l'Amor che move il sole e l'altre stelle'*.

Preface

The present work attempts to give a picture of the compositional work of Bruno Maderna, an attempt which has not so far been made in English, and one which is long overdue. Maderna's activities as a conductor were pursued with an almost incredible intensity, particularly during the last decade of his life, and his championing of the work of countless contemporary composers tended to overshadow his own composition, to which he was already rarely able to devote as much time and energy as he would have wished. Nevertheless, one has only to glance at the number and the variety of the works which he produced in his fifty-three years to be amazed that one lifetime was sufficient for such an enormous activity; add to this his activities as a teacher, editor and transcriber, and it becomes clear that he was no ordinary musician, but one of a remarkable creativity.

My own work on Maderna grew from a chance event. A few years ago, while passing some hours in Milan awaiting a train to bring me home from a vacation in Italy, I wandered into Ricordi's music-shop (partly, it must be admitted, to escape from the heat of the Piazza del Duomo), and I picked up Massimo Mila's little book *Maderna: Musicista Europeo*. I had at that time only a scanty knowledge of Maderna's music, but the little book seemed a useful way of passing the hours of the train journey back to England. I finished the book on the train, and felt immediately inspired to delve further into Maderna's music: if the truth be told, I felt also that there were many gaps in Mila's portrait of the composer (a judgment with which, as I discovered on a visit to Massimo Mila shortly before his death, he completely concurred) and decided that, if it were possible, I would like to take on the task of a deeper critical study of Maderna's work.

Obstacles lay in the path of such a plan. Many of the scores of Maderna's works remain in a poor state, many others rely on materials that are not readily available, and the whole enterprise of research seemed doomed from the start. What I had not, of course, counted on was the reaction of those who had known and worked with Maderna: on my frequent visits to Italy and elsewhere in pursuit of assistance in my task, the number of those willing, indeed anxious, to help grew almost daily. Maderna had touched in a quite remarkable way many of those who had the good fortune to encounter him, and on one occasion my hesitant greeting of one of his colleagues evoked tears of joy that the task of re-evaluating the composer was being undertaken.

Such overwhelming enthusiasm on the part of those who knew and loved Maderna is, of course, both inspiring and at the same time daunting to one who only began to discover his music after the composer's death, and who never saw him conducting any of his concerts. It is only to be hoped that the present study, which does not attempt to discuss all of his works, but rather to describe some which represent the main tendencies of his composition, will go some way towards justifying the faith of those who gave assistance to me in the enterprise.

Ultimately, the persuasiveness of the music itself must be its own advocate, and those conductors, such as Pierre Boulez, Luciano Berio and Lucas Vis, who have taken on the task of bringing before the public the most important works of Maderna, will eventually present to us the full measure of Maderna's originality, inspiration and expressivity.

Acknowledgements

To acknowledge fully all the assistance given to me in my work, whether materials, information, guidance or simply encouragement, would be an impossibility, but I must nevertheless attempt to do so, even in the full knowledge of my inadequacy. First of all, I must thank the Paul Sacher Foundation in Basel, where the manuscripts, sketches and other documents relating to Maderna are housed in conditions that any artist would regard as ideal. Those who have charge of the material there, Hans Jörg Jans, René Karlen, Lukas Handschin, Harriet Leander and Sabine Stampfli, as well as the Foundation's indefatigable secretary Ingrid Westen, made my stay in Basel in the spring of 1988 pleasant as well as instructive.

I was enabled to visit Basel through the help of a research grant from the British Academy, without which it would have been impossible, and I am indebted to the Academy for the help that they gave to me.

I was fortunate that during one of my visits to Italy, I was put in touch with Rossana Dalmonte and Mario Baroni, and the discussions I was able to have with these two musicians, together with the opportunity to view some materials in the Fondo Maderna that they have assembled in the University of Bologna, pointed me in directions that might otherwise have been more obscure. Their organization of the Maderna Conference in Bologna in the spring of 1983 resulted in an inspired and inspiring event, to which the book *Bruno Maderna: Documenti* bears witness.

I am also indebted to various individuals and organizations for their help or advice in specific matters: the BBC Archives Department in Caversham Park, Reading; NOS Television in Hilversum, Holland; Hans Heg, film producer in Amsterdam; Marino Zuccheri of the Studio di Fonologia Musicale in Milan; the National Sound Archive in London; Wilhelm Schlüter and Friedrich Hommel of the International Music Institute in Darmstadt, West Germany; Lotte Thaler of the West German Radio in Frankfurt-am-Main; the Discoteca di Stato in Rome.

Finally, I must thank Hans Keller, Reginald Smith Brindle, Joachim Noller, Patricia Pitts, Roger Marsh and Stephen Banfield for their help at various stages of the enterprise, and my wife for endless encouragement and guidance in what at times threatened to take over our lives.

The following publishers and copyright holders kindly gave me permission to quote from the material indicated:

Suvini Zerboni: Maderna's interviews and lectures; *Concerto for Two Pianos; Tre Liriche Greche; Composizione No. 2; Composizione in tre tempi; Studi per 'Il Processo' di Kafka; Serenata No. 2; Quartetto in due tempi; Musica su due dimensioni; Honeyrêves; Don Perlimplin; Aria.* Dallapiccola: *Cinque Frammenti di Saffo;* Nono: *Polifonica-Monodia-Ritmica.*

Ricordi: *Quadrivium; Grande Aulodia; Venetian Journal; Aura; All the World's a Stage.*

Salabert: *Satyricon; Oboe Concerto No. 3.*

Bruzzichelli: *Oboe Concerto No. 1.*

Boosey and Hawkes: Bartok: *Sonata for Two Pianos and Percussion.*

Paul Sacher Foundation, Basel: sketches of Maderna's works, *Alba;* photograph of sketch of *Musica su due dimensioni.*

Cristina Maderna, Darmstadt: *Fantasia per due pianoforti.*

EDT (Edizioni di Torino): from Enzo Restagno (Ed.): *Nono.*

ERI (Edizioni RAI): from Leonardo Pinzauti: *Musicisti d'oggi: venti colloqui.*

Marion Boyars, London: from *Luciano Berio: Two Interviews.*

Einaudi, Torino: from Massimo Mila: *Maderna: Musicista Europeo.*

Secker and Warburg: from Kafka: *'The Trial'.*

Mondadori, Milano: from Quasimodo: *Lirici Greci.*

Roberto Leydi, Milano: from text of *Ritratto di Città*

Mentor Books (New American Library): from *Petronius: Satyricon* (translated by William Arrowsmith).

Ernst Eulenburg and Faber and Faber: from Pierre Boulez: *Conversations with Célestin Deliège* and fom Karl H. Wörner: *Stockhausen: Life and Works* and from Pierre Boulez: *Orientations.*

International Music Institute, Darmstadt: for the supply of photographs used in the book, and to the photographers named in each case.

Chapter 1

Studies with Pedrollo, Bustini and Malipiero — Alba — Fantasia and Concerto for two pianos — the influence of Hermann Scherchen — Tre Liriche Greche — first visit to Darmstadt in 1950.

It is perhaps inevitable that the name of Bruno Maderna should be linked with Darmstadt: not only was he actively involved, as composer and conductor and later as teacher, with the Darmstadt 'Ferienkurse' from 1950 onwards, but he also made his home in that city from about the mid-1950s, and the performances of the Darmstadt Chamber Ensemble for New Music which he directed in many parts of Europe strengthened this link. However, there never was a 'Darmstadt School' of composers, even during the early 1950s when composers of an avant-garde inclination needed Darmstadt as a focal-point, if a temporary one, in their struggles for recognition and in their desire for the companionship of those of some common attitude to themselves. There were of course some shared beliefs, approaches and aims, but a School needs more than a couple of weeks each year for its true foundation, and in any case the diversity of the music produced by Boulez, Nono, Stockhausen, Pousseur, Berio and the others of the younger generation who went to Darmstadt during the 1950s is sufficient to counter any such easy classification.

Maderna himself was temperamentally opposed to the idea of a School just as much as he was opposed to the idea of a 'zero-year', a mythical starting-point for the New Music of the post-war generation: his own background, education and personality led him towards the highest degree of individuality in musical creation, as well as towards a keen sense of the continuity of musical history. For him, old and new, 'traditional' and 'avant-garde', were equally expressions of this continuity, as the programmes for the concerts which he conducted amply testify.

It was in fact as a conductor that Maderna had first appeared before the public: billed as 'Brunetto', he had directed many concerts of music from the Classical and Romantic repertoire from the age of twelve in many parts of Italy, being used by the Fascist authorities as a means of propaganda. His formal studies of music really began in 1933, when he was admitted to the Benedetto Marcello Conservatoire in Venice. When in the following year the insecurity of his family circumstances was finally resolved,[1] and he was given into the care of a Signora Irma Manfredi in Verona, she took it upon herself to suggest a period of study with Ildebrando Pizzetti in Milan, but this came to nothing when she realised that she would not be able to keep him with her in Verona if this were realised, and so a more favourable plan was made for Arrigo Pedrollo,[2] a composer from Vicenza who regularly passed through Verona on his way to Milan, to take charge of Maderna's musical tuition, which lasted from 1934 to 1937. Pedrollo was a figure of some significance at that time: he had written a *Symphony in D Minor* whose première had been given by Toscanini in 1900, and he was also a pianist and conductor of some distinction. Although the roots of his musical outlook were embedded in the styles of Verdi and Puccini, he was also open to wider influence, particularly from Richard Strauss, Fauré and Debussy. The 57-year-old composer appears, however, to have lacked the qualities necessary for an adequate teacher of the *bambino prodigio* who was put in his care, and in 1973 Maderna gained only a poor result in the examinations he entered privately at the Milan Conservatoire. Pedrollo had nevertheless introduced Maderna to the art of accompaniment-writing and fostered his studies of harmony (from his earliest years, 'Brunetto' had already composed or arranged music for the dance-band — The Happy Grossato Company — run by his father, in which he also played violin).

Signora Manfredi, aware by now of Pedrollo's limitations, arranged in 1937 that her adopted son should begin study with a more severe master, Alessandro Bustini,[3] Vice-President of the Santa Cecilia Academy in Rome; Bustini examined the work Maderna had accomplished with Pedrollo, declaring that although he had been well-taught in harmony and counterpoint, the 17-year-old musician was ill-prepared in fugue. He admitted Maderna to his class in Fugue in that autumn, and the composer therefore moved into a lodging in Rome. Bustini as a composer had contributed to the re-birth of instrumental music in Italy, and had published a book *The Symphony in Italy* in 1904, and although he had provided great encouragement to younger composers, he had gained little esteem as a composer himself. His powers as a teacher of composition were however considerable, and Maderna had to undergo a very rigorous training in all musical forms in Bustini's class. The recruits of this were evident when he gained the highest result in the Diploma examinations at the Santa Cecilia Academy in 1940, and the rigour of this training was always evident in Maderna's work throughout his life.

Maderna, during these years of study with Bustini, continued to conduct many concerts, gradually including works from a wider repertoire of Italian music from the nineteenth and twentieth centuries (his programmes between 1933 and 1941 included music by Donati, Faccio, Martucci, Pizzetti, Pilati and Respighi), but his return to Verona from his studies in Rome in 1939 created something of a crisis: he was no longer the *bambino prodigio* who had been able to rely on his tender years to create opportunities to conduct. However, an event occurred which was to prove crucial in his development as a musician: late in 1940, he met Gian Francesco Malipiero, then Director of the Conservatoire in Venice, and a member of the so-called 'generazione dell 'Ottanta', that group of Italian composers born around 1880 which also included Ildebrando Pizzetti, Ottorino Respighi and Alfredo Casella[4]; Maderna was to remain in close contact with Malipiero from 1940, although there is no evidence of any formal study with him until 1942–3.

A quite important composition which is to be found amongst the Basel collection probably dates from the period of Maderna's study in Rome (1937–40) and consists of a setting for contralto and string orchestra of the poem *Alba* (Dawn) by Vincenzo Cardarelli (1887–1959):[5] this composition, consisting of some 78 bars (a passage marked *Lento con stanchezza* is followed by one marked *Calmo*) is in a youthful and highly expressive style, with some intricacy in the polyphonic writing for the strings. The composer evidently spent some time in the revision of the work before its final version was made, and it displays a great sensitivity to the atmosphere of the text, which had been published only in 1934 in Rome. [Ex. 1.1]

During the years of his first acquaintance with Malipiero, a considerable re-orientation of Maderna's musical horizons took place, and is discernible not least

Ex. 1.1: Maderna: *Alba*: 1–17

Ex. 1.1: *Contd*

in the programmes of the concerts he directed: a clear movement towards older music becomes a feature of these concerts from 1941 (works by Bach, Monteverdi, Caldara, Galuppi, Vivaldi, Marcello and Purcell come to the fore, in place of works of the Romantic-Modern repertoire of his earlier concerts). Meanwhile, the composer had been conscripted into the army in 1942, but for a while he continued to live in Verona and to pursue his musical activities, attending the Venice Conservatoire for advanced study of composition.

The clearest imprint of Malipiero's musical outlook on the younger composer is to be seen in Maderna's involvement in the editing and performing of older, particularly Venetian, music, an element which was to remain an essential facet of his musical interests throughout his life. Luigi Nono was later to recall how, during the period of his own studies with Maderna, the two composers along with some others spent a great deal of time in the Biblioteca Marciana in Venice, searching amongst the library's rich fund of musical manuscripts, studying both compositions and theoretical treatises from the Medieval and Renaissance periods, in order to uncover the real nature of musical history through an examination of musical sources.[6]

The compositions which Maderna attempted during this period of study with Malipiero included a *Concerto per pianoforte e orchestra* which was performed in 1942 in Venice and an *Introduzione e passacaglia 'Lauda Sion Salvatorem'* also composed in 1942: the former work has remained in only a partial state (it was performed by Gino Gorini in Venice in 1942); the latter was given its only performance, conducted by Maderna, in Florence in 1947, and has been presented to the Maderna Nachlass housed now in Basel.

It must inevitably be asked at what point Maderna became fully aware of the possibilities offered by the serial 'method' of composition, and whether Malipiero was to any extent influential in this direction; it was in 1941–2 that Camillo Togni[7] had composed the first serial pieces in Italy, and Dallapiccola had felt the influence of Webern's music as early as 1935.[8] In an interview Maderna gave with George Stone and Alan Stout for WEFM Radio in Chicago in 1970, the composer was asked about this with reference to a *Requiem* he had composed immediately after the war:

Q: Had you already begun to compose serial music at that time?

A: Yes, but the *Requiem* was a work of transition. You see, before the war, we Italians didn't know the music of the Vienna School very well, but we still knew it better than the Germans did. In fact Mussolini had a great friend, the futurist Marinetti; Mussolini himself was not very intelligent, but he listened enough to Marinetti who drew him towards modernity and progress in all the arts. By this means, we were not completely separated from the rest of Europe: composers such as Dallapiccola and Petrassi, the generation before ours, kept in touch with the music of Bartok, Stravinsky and the Viennese, certainly more than was possible for German composers . . .

Q: During your period of study with Malipiero, did your teacher interest himself in the new techniques?

A: Certainly, Malipiero was a personal friend of the Viennese; he used to say that they were too complicated, but he would also say how much he respected them . . .

Q: Tell us something about your work with the serial technique. Did Malipiero encourage you in this, even if he himself did not like to employ it?

A: Certainly, he was a truly open person and did not pay a lot of attention to someone's personality. He always said to me 'I don't like this system *for me*, but I have great respect for the Viennese group and it would please me if *you* worked in this direction.'[9]

From the beginning of 1943 until the end of the war, Maderna's life was completely absorbed in the events of the conflict (he joined the Partisans after the Armistice) but it is not without some significance that the last concert he directed before events overtook his musical activities, in Milan in December 1943, included the *Variations for Orchestra op. 30* by Webern, alongside works by Purcell and Mendelssohn; he was only to resume his conducting activities in 1946.

When Maderna returned from his work with the partisans to the house of Irma Manfredi in 1945, the problem of his material existence urgently needed solution: his activities as a conductor could not be resumed immediately but he did set about the re-organisation of the musical life of Verona as director of the Società Musicale Pietro Marconi. He also began to compose music for films, including *Sangue a Cà Foscari* and *Il fabbro del convento*, both directed by Max Calandri, and this activity continued sporadically for some years. He was invited by Malipiero to teach some classes at the Venice Conservatoire, a post he held from 1947 until 1952, but it was on the strength of his ability as an editor of earlier music, rather than as a composer, that this appointment was given.

Maderna had begun his work of editing or transcribing earlier music by contributing six Vivaldi *Concertos* to the edition of this composer's works made under the auspices of the Istituto Italiano Antonio Vivaldi between 1947 and 1949, and it is clear that Malipiero had been the prime mover in Maderna undertaking this task. However, Maderna's involvement in such editorial or transcriptive work was to continue throughout his life, largely but by no means exclusively in tandem with his conducting activity. During subsequent years, he was to produce versions of works (some published, others in manuscript form) by Pérotin, Josquin, Petrucci (*Odhecaton*), G. Gabrieli, O. Vecchi (*L'Anfiparnaso*), Monteverdi (*Orfeo*), D. Belli (*Orfeo Dolente*), Viadana, Ziani, Stradella, Lotti, Bach, Marini, Galuppi, Gluck, Schubert (*Five Dances* for piano in orchestral transcription), as well as pieces from the *Fitzwilliam Virginal Book* transcribed in *Music of Gaity*. Maderna's more than casual acquaintance with and involvement in such earlier music, an involvement which he shared with his friend Berio, may be judged from the interview with Christoph Bitter which is reproduced in the Appendix.

His composition, however, was resumed immediately on his return from the war; it is known that he composed a *String Quartet* in three movements at some point in this period, but he omitted this work from the list of his works which he made in later years. Of the *Requiem* for soloists, chorus and orchestra which he probably composed between 1945 and 1946, only fragments remain and this, like the *String Quartet*, has remained unpublished and unperformed. Luigi Nono saw the score of the *Requiem* at the time of its composition and his memory of a work in which fugal writing held pride of place would seem natural for Maderna during this period.[10]

A *Serenata* which he wrote in 1946 was, however, performed at the first Venice Biennale Festival of the post-war years, in a concert of music by the younger generation of Italian composers held at La Fenice: the other works in this programme were by Riccardo Malipiero (*Piccolo Concerto* for piano and chamber orchestra), Valentino Bucchi (*La dolce posa*), Guido Turchi (*Trio* for flute, clarinet and viola), and Camillo Togni (*Variazioni* for piano and orchestra). Some problems regarding this work of Maderna's cannot be adequately resolved: it is not known whether the work may be identifiable as the *Concertino* (also listed by Maderna in a catalogue of his music made in 1946, and also for 11 instruments), and in any case the *Serenata* has been lost. What is certain is that this work is in no way identifiable with the *Serenata No 2* which he composed in 1954/7: this early work was divided into four movements (*Allegro sostenuto, Lento, Andante, Allegro energico*), and we can only ponder about its precise nature. Maderna himself, in the program-note for the concert, wrote that:

> 'The composer wishes to re-forge links with the baroque and classical tradition of chamber-concertos, and specifically of divertimentos, serenades and entertainment-music. Memories of seventeenth-century and neo-classical attitudes (which are never parodied) come together freely in the polyphonic writing of the piece.'[11]

It would seem, therefore, that Maderna's allegiance at this stage was to a form of 'neo-classicism', and it is interesting to note that in the same programme the works of Riccardo Malipiero (nephew of Gian Francesco) and of Camillo Togni reflected, in contrast, their composers' growing attachment to serial methods of composition.

Maderna's orientation towards serialism occurred in fact only in 1948, and can be dated to his first encounter with Hermann Scherchen.[12] It was Scherchen who was to encourage Maderna to undertake his first journey to Darmstadt in the following year, but the immediate result of their acquaintance was to lead the Italian composer towards the music of the Viennese serialists. Although Maderna had given one of the earliest Italian performances of Webern's music, as we have seen, in 1943, he had not up to this point adopted serial writing for himself. Scherchen, with a long background of work with all three of the Viennese composers, was the ideal person to reveal to Maderna the possibilities of this kind of writing, and in fact Scherchen may be said to have occupied a position in the development of Italian music in the immediate post-war years similar in some ways to that occupied by René Leibowitz in France.[13]

If we are fully to understand the ease with which Maderna adopted the serial approach to composition in the years 1948–9, it is essential that we observe closely the sequence of his compositional activity during this period, which included his first meeting with Hermann Scherchen. Two works were composed during this year, both involving the use of two pianos: *Concerto per due pianoforti e strumenti* and *Fantasia per due pianoforti*, and his first composition employing serial techniques, *Tre Liriche Greche*. The *Concerto* was given its first performance in Venice in September 1948; the Fantasia was performed during the Darmstadt Summer School in the summer of 1949 (with the title *B.A.C.H. Variationen für zwei Klaviere*): according to Giordano Montecchi[14] the score of *Fantasia* appeared to have been lost, but my own research in the library of the Internationales Musikinstitut in Darmstadt brought to light a score of a work bearing the date 1948 and the title:

Concerto per due pianoforti e strumenti

This score bears no resemblance to the score of the *Concerto* published by Suvini Zerboni, and the incorporation in the work of countless variants of the B.A.C.H. motif leads to the conclusion that this score is without doubt the 'lost' *Fantasia*[15] The striking-out of the latter part of the title of this work (' . . . *e strumenti*') and its naming as 'Concerto' appear puzzling: it might perhaps be that Maderna, at some later date, inadvertently gave the 'wrong' title to this score of some years earlier. It is certainly because of this wrong naming of the score that it was catalogued in Darmstadt as though it were of the *Concerto*, and also for this reason that it had been overlooked previously.

The layout of the work for two pianos alone is perfectly self-sufficient, despite some suggestions in the sketches of the composer for a full-scale orchestration of the B.A.C.H. material. The date 1948 given also in the title-page would indicate a work written at about the same time as the *Concerto* in this work's original form: it is possible that the composer wished to compose an orchestral work on the B.A.C.H. material, but was eventually led to restrict the work to the more practical medium of two pianos, perhaps because he knew that it could thus be more easily performed in this instrumentation.

What, then, is the style of this work from the period of Maderna's life immediately before his adoption of serial techniques of composition? Its form, that of a 'traditional' Fantasy and Fugue on B.A.C.H., obviously links the work with the many examples in which composers of the past had involved this pregnant musical motif in their work, composers as diverse as J.S. Bach himself (notably in Contrapuncti XI and XIX of *The Art of Fugue*), J.C. Bach, Schumann, Liszt, Rimsky Korsakov, Reger, Casella and Busoni. The most significant of these previous works was perhaps that of Busoni, whose *Fantasia Contrappuntistica* would without doubt have been known by Maderna in its solo piano version, if not in the version which Busoni made of the work for two pianos. In the same tradition as these works, Maderna's *Fantasia* was intended as an homage to the greatest contrapuntist, an homage to the musical past. We should, however, also attempt to understand the *Fantasia* as a work which in some senses is equally a step towards the future for Maderna: at this crucial stage in his evolution of a personal musical language, the work, using traditional contrapuntal techniques for a searching, rigorous and chromatic exploration of the possibilities offered by the B.A.C.H. motif for musical development, allows us to catch a glimpse of Maderna moving to some extent in the direction of a serial approach in a natural and logical manner.

Maderna was already aware at this point of Webern's music, which was at that time beginning to be discussed and circulated, and it is therefore very likely that he was aware of Webern's employment of the B.A.C.H. motif as a cell from which the series of his *String Quartet opus 28* is derived.

However, the nature of Maderna's use of the motif does differ in important respects from Webern's: whereas Webern had constructed a whole series from transpositions of the pitch-group Bb-A-C-B, employing each cell thus created in strict rotation, Maderna here uses only two transpositions of the cell (excluding for the moment the pitches Bb-A-C-B, which will appear 'dramatically' at the opening of the *Allegro Vivace* section in bar 29), and the rhythmic freedom which Maderna employs here contrasts with the relative rigour in the melodic dimension.

Right from the start of the work, in the *Molto Lento* section, the reliance of all the material upon the B.A.C.H. motif is very clear: the single melodic line with which the work opens, whose repetition of pitches gives it a certain 'cantus firmus' character, extends for all of 21 bars. [Ex. 1.2]

The extremely slow tempo of this opening melodic line was to become something of a feature of many of Maderna's later works, the opening passage of *Composizione No 2* for orchestra, for example, and the piccolo melody with which *Serenata No 2* begins. There is clearly a purpose behind such slow and relaxed opening passages: Maderna appears to wish to present the basic material of the work in as leisurely a manner as possible, and also to give a certain 'improvisatory' quality to this presentation of material.

Ex. 1.2: Maderna: *Fantasia*: 1–21

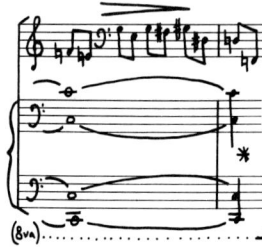

Ex. 1.2: *Contd*

The presentation of the basic material of the work at the beginning of the *Fantasia* is however of a certain logical as well as improvisatory kind. Maderna constructs the main melodic line in first piano from the two transpositions of the basic cell and then incorporates the second piano's octaves into this: the extension of the melody over the subsequent bars is a free melodic sequence, but still limited to the eight pitches already set out. The pedal-note C# over which the melody here comes to rest may in some senses be understood as a 'tonal centre' for the first part of the work as a whole: this impression is confirmed also by passages in which C# is a focal-point in the harmony, and in particular by the reversal of the whole melodic line which occurs in bars 116–133 over a pedal-C#, leading to the entry of the fugue.[Ex. 1.3]

Ex. 1.3: Maderna: *Fantasia*: 117–134

Ex. 1.3: *Contd*

At the beginning of the *Allegro Vivace*, the B.A.C.H. motif itself, now encompassing these actual pitches for the first time, is spread between the two piano-parts, and becomes the germ of a melodic phrase whose Bartokian character is emphasised by the ostinato-figures in the accompaniment. [Ex. 1.4.]

Ex. 1.4: Maderna: *Fantasia*: 29–35

This B.A.C.H motif not only employs notes which had been meticulously avoided in the opening passages of the work (their introduction now paving the way for that chromaticism which becomes explicit in the melodic figuration already alluded to in the *Allegro Vivace*) but the *intervallic shape* B.A.C.H is also here employed for the first time.

The fugue which forms the central part of the work, is as we noted earlier introduced by a reversal of the opening melody of the work; the reliance of the fugue's subject on the B.A.C.H motif and the melodic material already shown earlier in the work is obvious from the start [Ex. 1.5.] The feature of this fugue, however, which is perhaps of greatest interest lies in the intricacy of the manner in which the composer organises both the element of pitch and that of rhythm

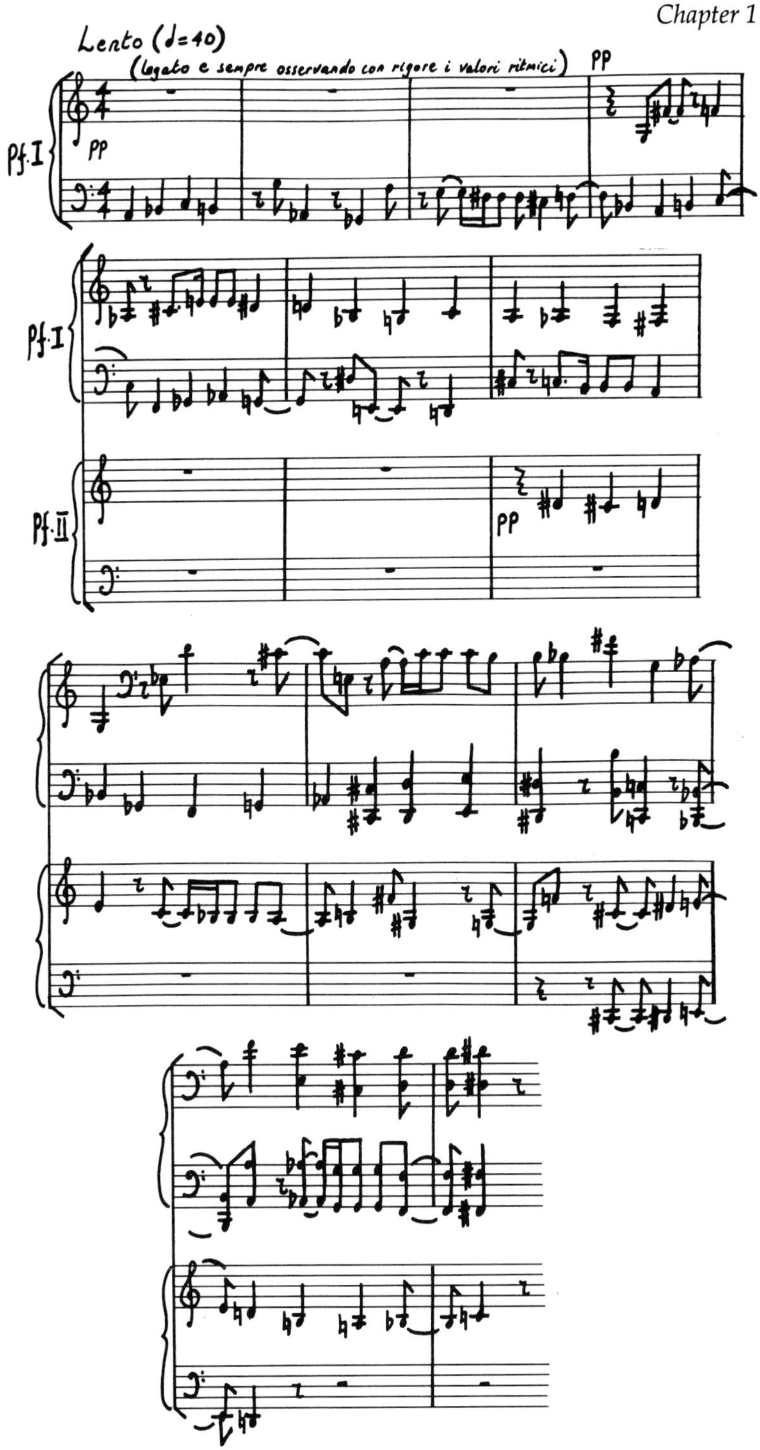

Ex. 1.5: Maderna: *Fantasia*: 135–144

Pitch-Cells

Rhythm-Cells

Ex. 1.6: Maderna: *Fantasia*: Fugue: Pitch- and Rhythm-Cells

within this contrapuntal web. Each four-note 'cell' (numbered A–F in the example) is constantly varied in internal shape in successive appearances, at first (up to bar 146) maintaining a consistent order in the appearance of the cells within each 'voice', thereafter becoming freer in order as the fugue progresses; the rhythmic shape which each 'cell' possesses is, meanwhile, subject to a constant variation revolving around a group of four 'rhythmic cells' (numbered a–d in the example). [Ex. 1.6]

However, he reserves one final element for the last bars of the work, as a further homage to Bach: he places above the fugal stretto the Chorale *Vor Deinem Thron tret'ich hiermit,* its placement giving it great prominence over the strongly chromatic material. [Ex. 1.7] One is clearly tempted here to recall the second movement of Berg's *Violin Concerto,* and the influence of the Berg model is certainly obvious. However, one might also make a distinction in the manner of approach in the two works, the Chorale *Es ist Genug* in the *Concerto* arising from the previous material in a natural manner, whilst in Maderna's *Fantasia* the Chorale *Vor Deinem Thron* being rather imposed upon the Fugue in high relief, rather as an 'Homage to Bach' than in terms of Berg's expressive allusion to the death of Alma Mahler's daughter which had given rise to the composition of the *Concerto*.

Ex. 1.7: Maderna: *Fantasia*: 321–324

The final 'resolution' of the work leaves a considerable degree of openness at the ending. While the second piano brings the Chorale-harmony to a resolution in a G major chord, the first piano, employing al the remaining chromatic notes, unfolds into distant registers, creating an effect of harmonic tension between the two halves of the texture, similar in some ways to that created by Berg in the final (or rather, 'encircling') harmony at the end of *Wozzeck*, which is similarly grounded in G major harmony. [Ex. 1.8]

The *Fantasia* as a whole has a similar double-aspect; whilst in many respects it is a work whose roots and techniques lie in the past (the contrapuntal and fugal procedures, and the formal layout as a Fantasy and Fugue on B.A.C.H.), some other aspects seem to look towards the *future* (particularly the chromatic language, the employment of 'pre-serial' devices such as retrogradation, and the often percussive piano-writing which Maderna had without doubt assimilated from a study of Bartok). It certainly could not be claimed that the work shows a fully individual and

Ex. 1.8: Maderna: *Fantasia*: 337–340

characteristic style, but the insight into Maderna's musical origins which it gives to us is of some importance in our understanding of the development of Maderna's musical thinking encompassed within the three works composed in 1948–49.

We have already noted that the *Fantasia* appears to have been composed at about the same time as the *Concerto per due pianoforti e strumenti*, and that the latter was given its first performance in Venice in September 1948. We cannot, therefore, expect to see a dramatic change of style between the two works, nor indeed, between these works and the *Tre Liriche Greche* composed also during that same period. What we do see, however, by comparing the *Fantasia* and the *Concerto*, is to some extent a *refinement* and also a greater degree of *differentiation* of texture amongst the various episodes of the latter work.

The original form of the *Concerto* was as a three-movement work (*Allegro moderato ed energico – Vivace; Grave – Tempo di siciliano; Lo stesso tempo – sempre animando – Allegro*) and it was in this form that the work was given its first performance in Venice in September 1948 by the duo Gorini-Lorenzi. Maderna made a new version, however, before the work's publication in 1955, removing the first two movements and adding 29 bars of new material to the opening of the remaining movement, as well as enlarging the final six bars by the addition of parts for percussion. He had submitted the work in its earlier form to Dallapiccola for his comments, and he evidently took to heart Dallapiccola's advice that a single-movement work would be more effective, but not until the original version had been performed.

This single-movement form, one which was to be greatly favoured by Maderna throughout his life, is articulated through the various episodes of which it is comprised as one of gradually increasing excitement and energy, with the final six bars *Maestoso* bringing a final repose and radiance to the work in a manner perhaps analogous to the final bars of the *Fantasia*.

In the opening episode, comprising the 29 bars of *Grave* which the composer added to the final movement of the earlier version, we can see a texture which, whilst it retains the closely-worked 'note-cell' nature of the opening of the *Fantasia*, adds to this a further stylistic dimension, that of a Webernesque canonic statement, with widely-spaced melodic shapes and a gradual building-up of harmonic units through accumulation. [Ex. 1.9.]

This opening maintains a strict canon between the two piano parts up to the beginning of bar 20, setting out the seven pitches on which it is based (the tritonal group A-Eb) in fixed register at first until, from bar 11, the pitches begin to spread over the whole piano register. It will be observed that, like the B.A.C.H motif on which the *Fantasia* was based, the pitches enclose a semitonal group: this arrangement is not accidental, nor is the group of pitches to be treated in any strict serial manner, but nevertheless we can see that Maderna, at this crucial stage in his development, was already inclining towards basic material which contained a high degree of chromaticism and potential for harmonic density. It was perhaps natural that, from the four-note cell of the *Fantasia*, and the seven-note cell in this work, he should be led to the total chromatic employed in his next work, the *Tre Liriche Greche*, probably composed shortly afterwards. As in the *Fantasia*, in which the actual pitches B.A.C.H. were reserved for a dramatic entry at the faster section of the work, so here similarly the remaining pitches only begin to make an appearance later in the work.

The chromatic nature of much of the writing in the Concerto, allied with imitative polyphony, brings some passages very close to the style of Bartok's *Sonata for Two Pianos and Percussion*, then heard only recently for the first time in Italy. This can be seen at the opening of the *Andante* from bar 30, in which Maderna employs a pedal-note D to give some stability to the free chromaticism of the other parts, a device which had also appeared in the *Fantasia* (see Ex. 1.3). The steady quaver-motion of this passage, allied with imitative chromatic figurations, bring it close to the Bartok model. [Ex. 1.10 (a), (b)]

Another feature of the work which, together with the chromatic writing and the use of imitative polyphony, shows some influence from Bartok, is to be found in its rhythmic aspect. In the *Concitato* episode from bar 75, for example, the throwing into relief of syncopated rhythms of 3/4 metre against 6/8 clearly derives from the cross-rhythms to be found in Bartok's *Sonata for Two Pianos and Percussion*. [Ex. 1.11. (a), (b)]

Ex. 1.9: Maderna: *Concerto*: 1–9

Ex. 1.10(a): Maderna: *Concerto*: 30–36

We have already noted how Maderna added to the original version of the work the initial 29 bars of *Grave*, and that the final six bars of this original version were also transformed by the inclusion of other instruments alongside the two pianos. On the basis of the work as it finally came to be published, it is in fact reasonable to infer that Maderna had originally conceived the work for two pianos alone, since the other instruments only begin to appear from bar 52, and the material assigned to them is clearly secondary to the basic material of the work which lies in the two piano parts. The final bars may therefore be seen as a widening of the instrumental coloration: the harps and pitched percussion add a shimmering brilliance to this ending, based upon repetitions in the piano parts of a figure heard earlier in the work which is now spread out over a wide register, accompanied by ostinati and repeated harmonies, giving to the final bars a suggestion of whole-tone 'openness'. Thus, the openness of the work's ending is achieved by harmonic means, as in the *Fantasia*, but with a somewhat different harmonic perspective. [Ex. 1.12]

In the two works now examined, therefore, we may observe an important stage in the evolution of Maderna's musical formation. He had absorbed, as we have

I

Ex. 1.10(b): Bartok: *Sonata*: 1–8

© 1942 by Hawkes & Son (London) Ltd.

Ex. 1.11(a): Maderna: *Concerto*: 75–81

Ex. 1.11(a) *Contd*

seen, a certain influence from Bartok in the percussive writing for piano, and also in the chromatic and often canonic polyphony; at the same time, we might detect a certain influence from Webern's use of melodic 'cells' as generative elements in the polyphony of the *Concerto*. Maderna attempted to forge from these disparate influences a personal and characteristic musical language which, in its rigorous exploration of the possibilities for development inherent in motivic material of a closely-knit chromatic kind, begins to approach serial methods of composition by way of contrapuntal elaboration. Maderna, therefore, did not abandon the polyphonic approach which had characterised his previous composition, but rather, brought to it the influences from the 'moderns' whose music he was at this point beginning to study with great fervour. The serialism which began to appear in the *Tre Liriche Greche*, composed at about the same time, was thus a logical extension of the approaches which he had already made in the two-piano works which immediately preceded it.

As we have already noted, it was under the influence of his study with Hermann Scherchen that Maderna adopted serial methods of composition. He attended Scherchen's advanced course for conductors held at the Venice Conservatoire in the summer of 1948, and the friendship of the two musicians was to last right up to Scherchen's death in 1966. It was not, however, a matter of a formal period of study of composition with the older musician, but rather that Scherchen's very broad acquaintance with, and sympathy for, the Viennese serialists had a profound effect on Maderna's thinking.

Ex. 1.11(b): Bartok: *Sonata*: 23–28
© 1942 by Hawkes & Son (London) Ltd.

Maderna regarded this adoption of the serial approach as a very logical and natural move on his part, and repudiated the idea of any 'lingua franca' on the part of the younger European composers at that time:

> 'In my case — as for all the young Italian composers — it was a logical thing; it is impossible to compose without meeting this way of thinking. One begins by studying polyphony, then the polyrhythms of Stravinsky and Bartok, then, as one looks around, one finds the Viennese and their way of thinking . . . Any theory which cannot grow is dead: one must always modify and adapt it to one's own needs. For example: an Italian and an American have experienced different things, different movements of thought, and do not have the same ethical and aesthetic points of view as those from which Expressionism arose . . . '(16)

Maderna appears, in these comments, to be drawing a thumb-nail sketch of his own development as a composer: beginning with his study of polyphony under the guidance of Malipiero, through the absorption of influences from Stravinsky and Bartok, and then the Viennese serialism which began to be a major influence

Ex. 1.12: Maderna: *Concerto*: 336–341

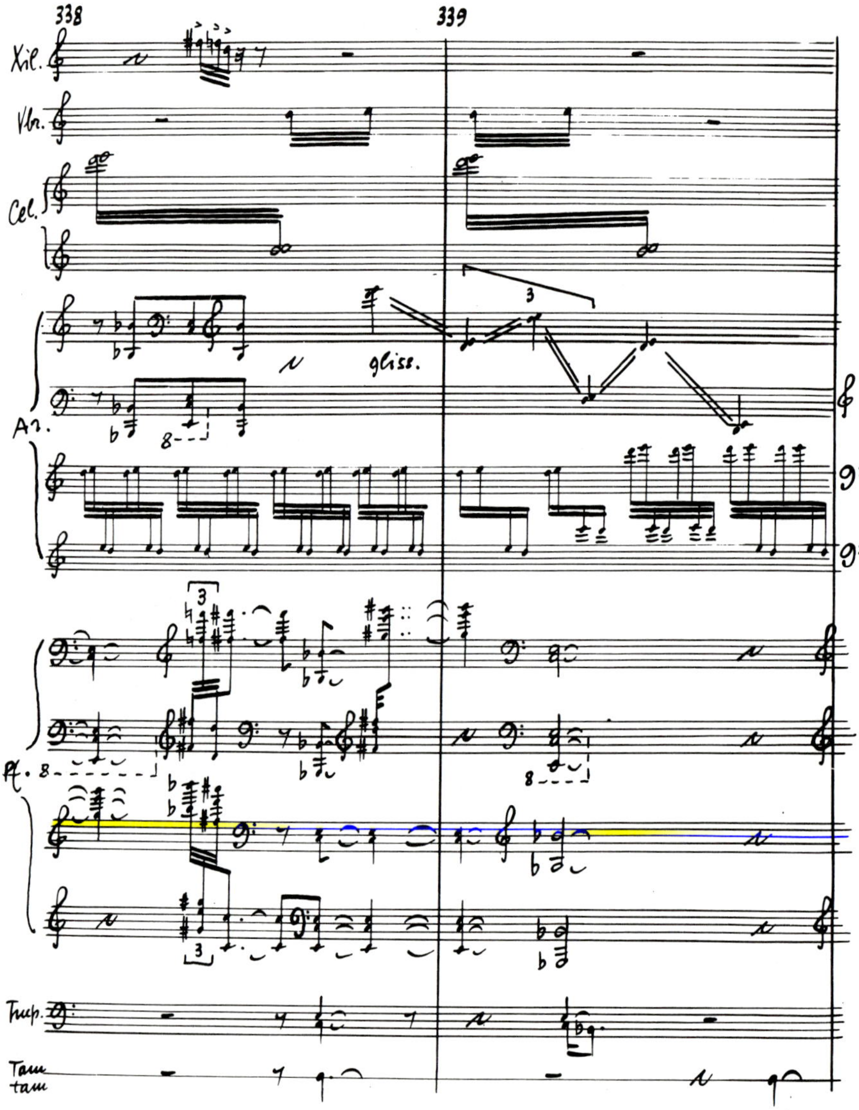

Ex. 1.12: *Contd*

Ex. 1.12: *Contd*

on his composition from 1948 onwards. But he is careful to stress the *individuality* which must be a characteristic of any serial approach. He set out this individuality in these terms:

> 'Personally, I thought that serialism offered musicians more possibilities than the, let's say, 'traditional' technique. But I never really felt like poor old Leibowitz (a very kind, civilised person, to be sure, well in touch with the world), nor yet like Dallapiccola, enclosed within his rock-crystal'[17]

Maderna's statement that he 'never felt like . . . Dallapiccola, enclosed within his rock-crystal' will be worth bearing in mind as we examine the *Tre Liriche Greche*. Given that Dallapiccola, who had made for himself a very personal variety of serialism in the previous few years, and who had himself composed a group of works taken from the same textual source with the overall title *Liriche Greche*, we must inevitably ask whether Maderna was not in some way influenced by this model from a composer whom he greatly admired. However, the immediate impulse towards the composition of the Greek poems came from a source which has only recently been clarified by Luigi Nono:

> 'In 1948, when Scherchen was holding his conducting course, there arrived in Venice a group of thirty Brasilians who came from a school founded by Kollreuter, a German composer and conductor who had left Germany after 1933. Amongst these Brasilians there was a very talented pianist and composer, a woman called Eunice Catunda. She was half-Indian from the Mato Grasso, and Scherchen fostered a friendship between her, Bruno and myself. Those were the years of the Popular Front, a time of violence and deep division, and Catunda was a Communist. Bruno and I were to join the Communist Party only in 1952, but we were already involved with it. We therefore shared a great identity of outlook with Catunda, and it was from her that we first heard about the rhythms of the Mato Grasso, information which to some extent anticipated what we were to learn later from Varèse. The most extraordinary thing which we all experienced was, however, the discovery of Lorca, whose work was well-known to Catunda. Scherchen asked us to write some songs: Bruno chose those Greek poems in Quasimodo's translation, Catunda chose Lorca, and I took a bit of each. What most attracted our attention was not so much the 'Gypsy' Lorca as the metaphysical or surreal Lorca, something which put us in touch with other worlds.
>   We found ourselves busy with the study of Lorca, with the rhythms of the Mato Grasso and those of Andalusia. Bruno had a book which contained a special study of Gypsy rhythms, not Gypsies in a folk sense but the Arab Gypsies of the Muezzin, whose songs use fourths and octaves. In this way, my first *Epitaph* came into being, and it is worth noting that this work, like *Polifonica-Monodia-Ritmica*, is based upon a Brasilian song . . . '[18]

Nono gives us here a fascinating glimpse into the explorations which the two Italian composers were undertaking at that time, explorations which were prompted at least in part by the personality of Scherchen. He points to some of the characteristics of his own early works: *Polifonica-Monodia-Ritmica* (1951) and

Epitaph auf Federico Garcia Lorca (1952–3), which had some roots in Spanish, Brasilian and Gypsy rhythms and melodies, with the pervading influence of the poet Lorca. Nono hints also, perhaps, at a certain Lorca-inspired 'Spanish Gypsy' element to be found in the *Tre Liriche Greche* of his friend and teacher Maderna, and this may be detected above all in the second song of the set, in which we hear an *ostinato* timpani-figuration accompanying the song in which the poet evokes the wildness of the life of the Danaïds and their searching for hypnotic herbs. Might we not hear in this 'hypnotic' *ostinato*-figuration an echo of the foot-stamping of the Andalusian Gypsy?

> 'They had seen neither form of men nor that of women: they trained in racing-chariots naked through the woods; and often in the quarry they gladdened their minds hunting for resin in trees of incense and fragrant dates of cassia — the tender seeds of Syria'. [Ex. 1.17.]

The texts which Maderna set in the *Tre Liriche Greche* were all taken from the translations which Salvatore Quasimodo had made of Greek poetry just a few years earlier and published in *Lirici Greci* in 1940. All of the texts chosen are of a highly evocative nature, and offered the composer possibilities of contrast between each song of the set: the first presents a picture of pastoral simplicity, the second evokes the contrastingly frenetic and passive aspects of the life of the Danaïds, the third, merely a single phrase, describes the brilliance of the starry heavens. Dallapiccola had based his own *Liriche Greche* (consisting of three works, *Cinque Frammenti di Saffo*, *Due Liriche di Anacreonte* and *Sex Carmina Alcaei*) on the same textual source, and composed these works during the war-years, at a time when he was in hiding from the authorities; all three works were heard for the first time shortly after the war. Luciano Berio, who was then a student at the Milan Conservatoire with Paribeni and Ghedini, wrote his own *Tre Liriche Greche* for voice and piano in 1946 (Maderna did not meet Berio until 1953, so it is likely that the two composers did not have a chance to see each others' works until about that time). Dallapiccola's *Sex Carmina Alcaei* had been dedicated to Webern on his 60th birthday (3 December, 1943) and the composer asked Suvini Zerboni, their publisher, to send a copy of all of the *Liriche Greche* to 'the master I love and admire most, Arnold Schoenberg' (letter of Dallapiccola to Suvini Zerboni, 14 December, 1949.)[19] We have evidence that Maderna knew at least some of these works from a letter he wrote to Dallapiccola on 22 July, 1949:

> 'It is now almost thirty years since Schoenberg brought about his re-evaluation of the means of expression and opened up marvellous and limitless horizons, yet there are still people who cannot get used to it, who will not admit the validity of his work.
> My friend Nono and I think that it would be impossible not to recognise in your recent works, and especially in the *Sex Carmina Alcaei*, the precious contribution you have made to the evolution of those principles, and their undoubted beauty . . . '[20]

In recognising that dodecaphonic principles began to enter into play for the first time in Maderna's work in the *Tre Liriche Greche*, we must equally recognise that for him, as the quotation given earlier indicated, dodecaphonic techniques were a *possibility* for the organisation of musical material, rather than an overriding and all-pervasive *method* to be used consistently. He by no means abandoned in this work the principles (particularly the canonic and polyphonic approaches) which, as we have seen, had governed his musical thinking in the two works for two pianos which we earlier examined. The serial approach, which had been revealed to Maderna in full by Scherchen, was employed in the *Tre Liriche Greche* in an idiosyncratic, and by no means consistent, manner.

In the first song of the set, the text which Maderna employs is of an engaging simplicity and directness of expression:

Morning Song

Gilded birds with shrill voices, make a confused lament freely through the lonesome wood to the tops of the pines; one begins, another delays, another calls towards the mountains: and the echo, unending and friendly in the void, repeats it from the depths of the valley.

Despite Maderna's later statement to the contrary, he *does* in fact appear in this song to be approaching in some ways what he was to describe as the 'rock-crystal' manner of Dallapiccola: Dallapiccola himself was later to make a setting of this same text and that of the third of Maderna's set (in the *Cinque Canti* of 1956), but the technique employed by Maderna approaches more closely that used by Dallapiccola previously in the first of his *Cinque Frammenti di Saffo* (1942), in which Dallapiccola had constructed an expressive melodic line from the basic set in the soprano's opening phrase. [Ex. 1.13.] This series is treated canonically by the flute, whilst the remaining instruments of the small ensemble employ portions of it in combination with other series. The evocation of a pastoral and primordial 'greenness' in the text which Maderna sets leads him to employ a somewhat similar canonic approach at the opening of his piece, with a series given by the solo soprano and echoed in canon by the second flute, whilst the first flute, placed at a distance from the other two performers, combines fragments of each of the other voices. A prominent feature of this writing is the use of unisons, either simultaneously or in close proximity, which together with the avoidance of semitonal harmony, gives a certain mellifluousness to the passage. [Ex. 1.14 (a), (b)]

Ex. 1.13: Dallapiccola: *Cinque Frammenti di Saffo*: vocal opening

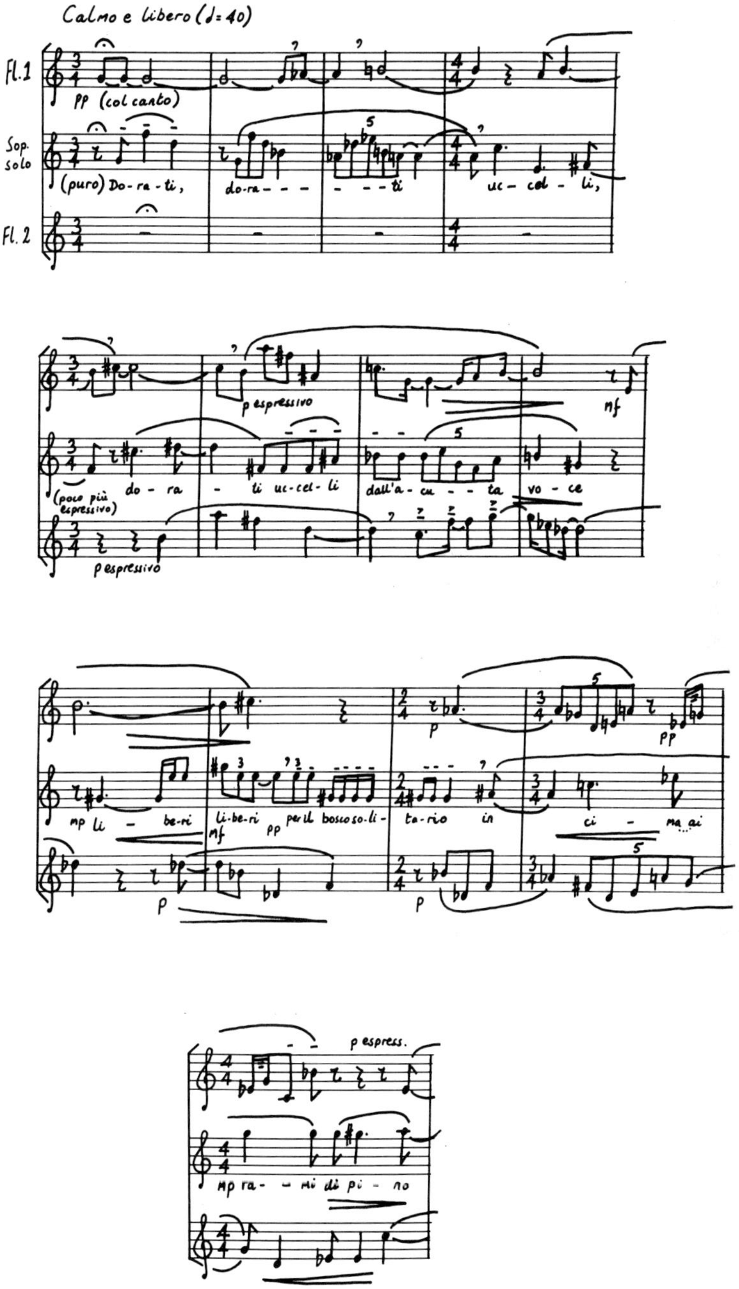

Ex. 1.14(a): Maderna: *Tre Liriche Greche I*: 1–13

Ex. 1.14(b): Maderna: *Tre Liriche Greche I*: analysis

Ex. 1.15: Maderna: *Tre Liriche Greche I*: 16–20

However, the composer does not continue with this adherence to the forms of the prime series, but in the ensuing passage ('. . . make a confused lament freely through the lonesome wood to the tops of the pines . . . ') begins to introduce figurations which include semitonal intervals. The initial 'greenness' of the opening passage now gives way to a freer, and at the same time more angular expression. [Ex. 1.15]

This freer expression, no longer bound by the initial series but incorporating an echoing of melodic phrases between the three performers, ends in vocalisations by the soprano soloist and in flute-trills ('one begins, another delays, another calls towards the mountains . . . '), and in the final bars of the piece the employment of a simple canonic device marks a return to the mellifluousness of the opening, but not to the initial series. Here, the harmony makes use of the augmented intervals which had appeared earlier, and the piece ends in an F# major triad. [Ex. 1.16]

Ex. 1.16: Maderna: *Tre Liriche Greche I*: 34–41

In the second song of the set, the text is treated in bi-partite manner, corresponding to the description of the wildness of the Danaïds' furious chariot-racing through the woods, and of their contrasting search for incenses: the longer first part of the piece, for chorus and instruments, is followed by a short, slow concluding passage for the solo soprano ('rather child-like' as Maderna describes this in the score) which is without any accompaniment. The melodic material of this piece consists of running phrases for the instruments which are underpinned by the rhythmic material provided by three groups: timpani, and two groups of unpitched percussion instruments placed one near, one more distant from, the front of the platform. [Ex. 1.17]

Ex. 1.17: Maderna: *Tre Liriche Greche II*: 1–9

The rhythmic material of the percussion is given great attention by Maderna: the four pitches of the timpani (G-Ab-Db-Cb) are organised in repeating patterns (marked A and B in the Example) in which pattern B is a reversal of A; the nearer group of unpitched percussion (placed next to the timpani) have similar patterns organised in imitation of those of the timpani; the group nearer to the front of the platform have somewhat different material, but in which repetition of rhythmic patterns also occurs: this group's pattern is based upon the rhythms of the speaking chorus. [Ex. 1.18] This 'quasi-melodic' treatment of unpitched percussion instruments also interested Luigi Nono when, in 1950–1, he composed *Polifonica-Monodia-Ritmica*, and as we saw earlier, this was one of the works which had resulted from the composer's contact, via Eunice Catunda, with the folk-rhythms of Brasil and Spain. Nono organised the 'rhythmic cells' which appear at the opening of this work in the parts for four cymbals in a manner which corresponds to the organisation of pitches in the other instruments of the ensemble, and this has been demonstrated by Gianmario Borio to have provided an important element in the development of Nono's manner of composition during that period,[21] to be given a further impulse when Nono met Edgard Varèse in Darmstadt.

Ex. 1.18: Maderna: *Tre Liriche Greche II*: percussion-groups

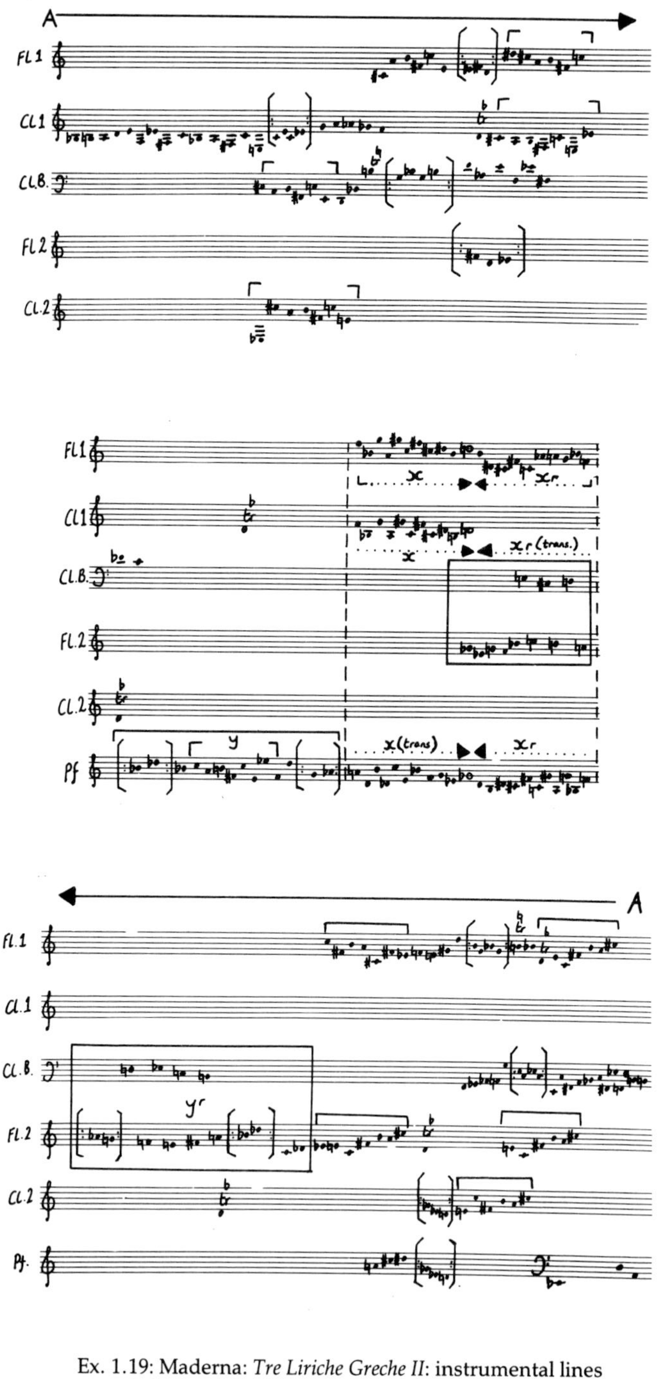

Ex. 1.19: Maderna: *Tre Liriche Greche II*: instrumental lines

Ex. 1.20: Maderna: *Tre Liriche Greche II: 32–35*

Maderna organises the pitch-element in a manner which corresponds, on a larger scale, to the organisation of the percussion's rhythmic units: the winds and piano have a variety of melodic units which are arranged in palindromic fashion and together provide a *moto perpetuo* which runs through the whole first part of the piece. [Ex. 1.19] This *moto perpetuo* intensifies as the metre changes from 4/4 to 2/2 (bar 32): here, the 'rhythmic cell' A from earlier is given to the group of percussion placed near the timpani, and the cross-rhythms created by this in combination with the timpani-*ostinato* give greater urgency to the rhythmic motion. [Ex. 1.20]

However, it is also from this point in the piece that the choral voices begin, intermittently at first, to employ some fixed pitches interspersed between the spoken intonation of the text which they had earlier been assigned. These pitches, on vowel-sounds, are combined with trills in the wind instruments and with a gradually changing pattern of running semiquaver figurations in clarinet and

Ex. 1.20: *Contd*

flute, to form a variegated texture, and the pitches encompassed by all of these elements (voices, trills and running-figures) are closely interwoven. As the climatic point in bar 46 is reached, the voices' pitches begin to outline a melodic phrase. [Ex. 1.21(a), (b)]

From here onwards, the vocalisations of the chorus-parts are organised in episodes in which the pitches employed have a certain symmetry of construction, employing the serial devices of inversion and retrogradation. Maderna seems here to be using these choral vocalisations as a means of linking the two parts of the piece, the expression of the Danaïds' furious chariot-racing and of their contrastingly passive collecting of narcotic herbs, and the gradual movement from *fortissimo* in bar 47 to the *pianissimo* ending of the episode in bar 61 aids this slow change of atmosphere. At first (up to bar 61), the instrumental accompaniment to these vocalisations follows closely the lines of the chorus-parts, but in the concluding bars (61–79), the accompaniment moves

Ex. 1.21(a): Maderna: *Tre Liriche Greche II*: 38–43

independently. The symmetry of the chorus-parts' pitches may be seen as an exploration of intervallic content. [Ex. 1.22(a), (b)]

In the final choral passage, from bar 64, the instrumental accompaniment begins, independently of the choral parts, to outline the melodic line which will form the second part of the piece, for solo soprano. This had, in fact, also been anticipated in the choral parts' hesitant introduction of pitches from bars 32–46 (bracketed figures B and C in Example 1.21(b)). There is therefore a gradual movement towards the final passage for solo soprano, which accords with a

Ex. 1.21′a): *Contd*

Ex. 1.21(b): Maderna: *Tre Liriche Greche II*: instrumental figures

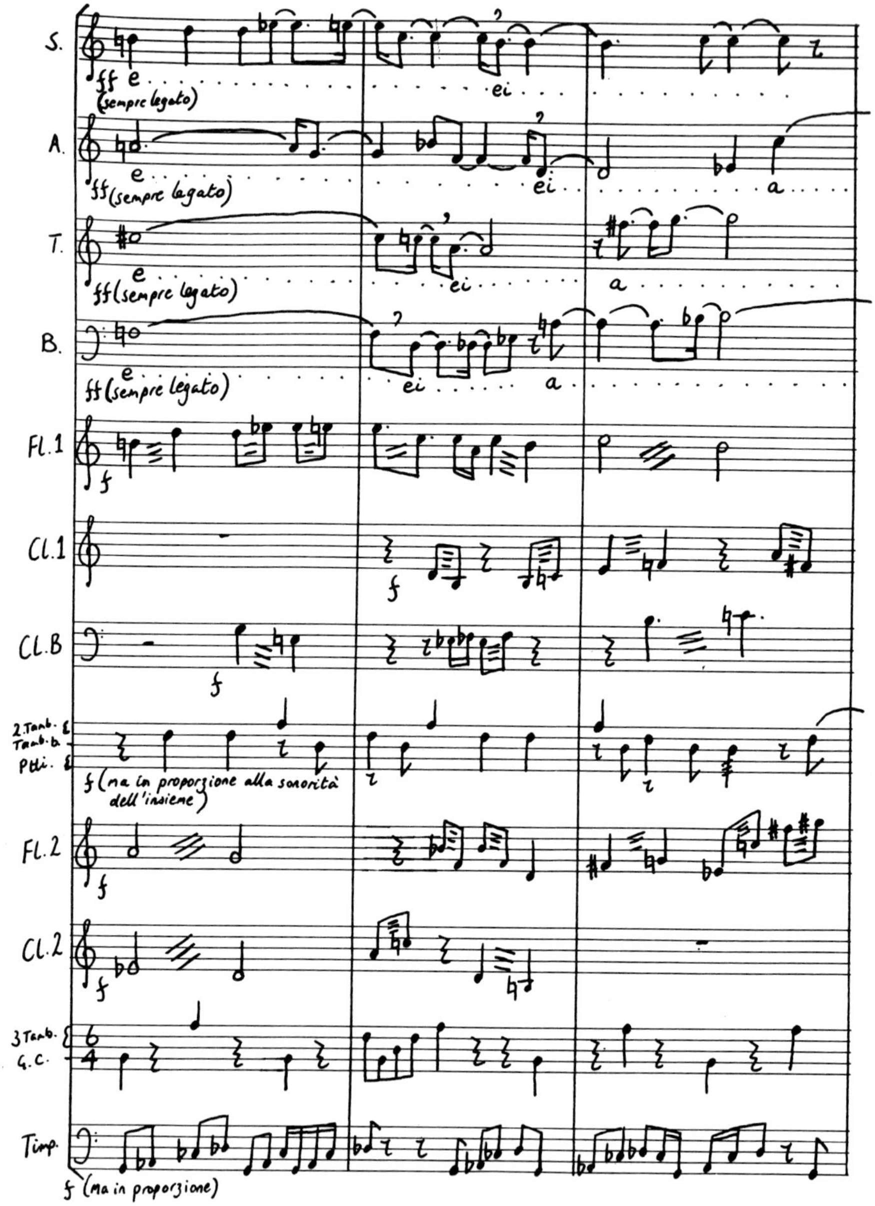

Ex. 1.22(a): Maderna: *Tre Liriche Greche II*: 47–51

Ex. 1.22(a): *Contd*

Ex. 1.22(b): Maderna: *Tre Liriche Greche II*: chorus-pitches

gradual decrease in motion and with the outlining of the final melodic line. [Ex. 1.23(a), (b), (c)]. However, the concluding soprano solo was derived from a somewhat complex 'interpretation' of a dodecaphonic phrase which appeared as one of the many running-semiquaver lines in the instrumental parts earlier in the piece (appearing first in piano, echoed by flute and clarinet, from bar 19). This dodecaphonic line is divided into several distinct 'layers', and the soprano's final melody re-orders these layers in horizontal manner one after another. This process accounts for the rather strange rhythmic setting of the text. [Ex. 1.23 (d)]

Ex. 1.23(a): Maderna: *Tre Liriche Greche II*: 64–69

Ex. 1.23(a): *Contd*

Ex. 1.23(b): Maderna: *Tre Liriche Greche II*: 80–100

In this second piece, therefore, we find the closest possible unity between rhythmic and melodic parameters, a unity which leads inevitably and conclusively to the expression of the 'incense-gathering' in the solo soprano's finale: the hypnotic *ostinati* in percussion, repeated phrases in other instrumental parts and their palindromic shape, together with the movement from spoken rhythms to pitched harmony in the choral parts, all are woven together into a tapestry of interdependence which drives onwards towards this conclusion.

In the final song of the *Tre Liriche Greche*, we find the employment, with the greatest consistency, of a series, but one through which Maderna, using a ten-note series and its immediate retrogradation and never transposing it to widen the relationship of pitch, creates a piece in which the constant rotation of this limited series of notes has a somewhat mesmeric effect, a complement to the terseness of expression in the single-line text:

Starry Night (Ibicos): They burn right through the night, the most brilliant stars.

The series itself, given out right at the opening of the piece by the first flute, passes via a *fermata* to its immediate reversal: this series contains no semitones, and its motion downward in the original version together with the ascending motion of its retrograde provides a constantly clear melodic shape which will permeate the whole piece. [Ex. 1.24]

Ex. 1.23(c): Maderna: *Tre Liriche Greche II*: pitches

As the six-part chorus enters, they gradually construct a chord from some of the notes of this series (omitting the pitches C#-G#-E-C) on the word *ardano* ('burn'): not only is the choral harmony suspended in static isolation above the constantly waving melodic line of the versions of the full series in the instrumental parts, but the harmony itself is one of great 'suspension'. [Ex. 1.25]

The soprano soloist in this piece is restricted to the function of reciter, whose phrase *attraverso la notte* ('right through the night') accompanies the choral repetition of *ardano* in fixed rhythm. At bar 17, the female voices of the chorus treat the 10-note series in a polyphonic manner, which Maderna asks should be sung 'sweetly, like children'. [Ex. 1.26] As the instruments re-enter (bar 21), still adhering to the fixed series of notes from which the whole of the piece has been constructed, the male voices of the chorus add for the first time the key-word *stelle* ('stars') on the pitches Bb and G, thus completing the full chromatic: this interval,

Ex. 1.23(d): Maderna: *Tre Liriche Greche II*: sketch

Ex. 1.24: Maderna: *Tre Liriche Greche III*: 1–3

Ex. 1.25: Maderna: *Tre Liriche Greche III*: 4–8

combining with the C#-B-A of the female voices, as the instruments fade, brings the whole work to a close. [Ex. 1.27]

Our discussion of the *Tre Liriche Greche* began with the question whether Maderna, despite his later statement that he 'never felt like . . . Dallapiccola, enclosed within his rock-crystal', had not in fact approached Dallapiccola's serial manner to some extent in this work, given the importance of the older composer's position as the first major Italian composer to adopt the dodecaphonic principle in his music some years earlier. The combination of serial and canonic procedures which had characterised Dallapiccola's early serial ccompositions (and which was to be given a further elaboration in his *Quaderno Musicale per Annalibera* a few years later) is present also in the first piece of Maderna's work, combined with a melodic and harmonic simplicity which to some extent derives also perhaps from Dalla-piccola, but is treated in a much less 'systematic' manner by Maderna. The aban-donment of the initial series after the first few bars, and the reliance of the rest of the piece upon free melodic sequence and, at the end, on a simple canonic structure, shows a desire to remain free of the series as a thoroughgoing structural principle which contrasts with Dallapiccola's practice, a move away from the 'rock-crystal'

Ex. 1.25: *Contd*

Ex. 1.26: Maderna: *Tre Liriche Greche III: 17–20*

Ex. 1.27: Maderna: *Tre Liriche Greche III*: 21–27

model towards the greater freedom, and at the same time greater complexity, of motivic working which was to become a feature of Maderna's later serial composition.

We might in fact say that the only piece of the set in which Maderna organises the pitch-material by fully serial means is the final number: here, a pitch-series is the only material of the piece, but a series consisting of only ten pitches (the final notes added only to highlight the final word of the text), and one which is never transposed, nor employed in any forms other than the prime and its immediate retrograde. This simplicity of melodic line gives to the piece an engaging directness of expression, in keeping with the directness of the text which is set. Maderna here relies upon a straightforward and obvious clarity of utterance which is immediately audible, in the constant backward and forward motion of the basic set, an approach which may well have its roots in the 'rock-crystal' serial procedures of Dallapiccola, but which becomes thoroughly personal and distinctive in Maderna's hands.

Serial procedures, then, became a part of Maderna's expressive vocabulary in

Ex. 1.27: *Contd*

the *Tre Liriche Greche*, but in a manner which owed remarkably little to the serialism of either the Viennese composers or of his illustrious Italian predecessor, and the polyphonic-canonic approaches which we saw had been in evidence in the two-piano works which immediately preceded this work are still very much in evidence in this work. Indeed, the serialism is as much a *refinement* of these canonic-polyphonic principles as it is a new element added to them at this important point in Maderna's development as a composer.

Maderna, following Scherchen's suggestion, planned to go to the Darmstadt Summer School in 1949, at which his *Fantasia* was played by Carl Seeman and Peter Stadlen, but was for some reason unable to attend the Summer School for this performance, despite the fact that his name appears on the list of participants for that year. He therefore arrived in Darmstadt in the same year that this friend Luigi Nono also went there, and at this Summer School Scherchen conducted the first performance (the only one during Maderna's lifetime) of Maderna's *Composizione No 2* for orchestra.

Maderna arrived in Darmstadt with an important advantage over many of the younger composers who went there in those years: unlike those composers from countries which had felt the oppression of totalitarian control of artistic expression more keenly than was the case in Italy, he had already had the opportunity to hear and study some music from the 'Viennese School' of Schoenberg, Berg and Webern, and Scherchen had also furthered his acquaintance with the music of the three Viennese. Amongst the other composers who were to come to Darmstadt in the next few years, only Pierre Boulez had been able by this time to absorb the influence of the Viennese composers: he had known only two of Schoenberg's works, the *Drei Klavierstücke* op. 11 and *Pierrot Lunaire*, both of them works of Schoenberg's earlier 'atonal' period, and Leibowitz had in his case been instrumental in opening up the world of serial composition for Boulez. In 1945, he had heard Schoenberg's *Wind Quintet* op. 26, and *Chamber Symphony* op. 9, but the work which made the greatest impact upon the young Frenchman was Webern's *Symphony op. 21*: it was therefore the case that for Boulez, as for many others of his generation, both the 'atonal' and 'serial' works of the Viennese composers came to his knowledge at the same time.[22]

When Maderna came finally to Darmstadt in 1950, it was only the fifth Summer School to be held in that city. It had been founded by Wolfgang Steinecke in 1946, in the first instance to aid the reconstruction of German musical life after the ravages of war and of Nazi suppression of all 'modernism' in the arts, but it very quickly gained a more international aspect, at the same time becoming a very formative influence on the younger generation of composers. In its earliest years, it did not have the specifically 'serial' aspect which it was later to assume: in 1946 Wolfgang Fortner (not yet a composer of serial music) took charge of the composition classes, and in 1947 it was Paul Hindemith who assumed this position; it was only in 1948 that René Leibowitz came, with the experience of a personal acquaintance with the Viennese composers about whom he had already published two books, and somewhat changed the emphasis of the Summer School. In the following year, it became easier for foreigners to travel to Germany, and this year therefore marked a decisive change in the nature of Darmstadt, from being a formative influence in widening the musical horizons of the students who attended towards becoming a highly important vehicle for the dissemination of the music and ideas of the younger composers themselves. Schoenberg was invited to take over the composition classes in 1949, but because of his ill-health his place was taken by Olivier Messiaen, who brought with him the *Mode de valeurs et d'intensités*, the work for solo piano which was to prove so influential in leading some of the younger composers towards the idea of serialisation of parameters other than pitch.

In this year, the 'official' teachers of the Summer School included Wolfgang Fortner, Antoine Goléa, René Leibowitz and Rolf Liebermann: also present were Ton de Leeuw from Holland, Humphrey Searle, Michael Tippett, Anthony Hopkins and Peter Racine Frickner from England, as well as Boris Blacher, Werner Egk, Hans Werner Henze and Giselher Klebe from Germany itself. In the following year, Maderna and Nono arrived (the latter going at Maderna's suggestion), and with the arrival of Stockhausen in 1951 and Boulez in 1952, the scene was set for a new phase in the history of the Summer School as well as that of contemporary music in general.

When Maderna came to Darmstadt in 1950, therefore, he was in a position to become very rapidly one of the most important and influential figures in the Darmstadt environment: he had already composed the *Fantasia, Concerto, Tre Liriche Greche* and *Composizione No 1* for orchestra (the last performed in Turin in

February 1950) and was to hear his *Composizione No 2* for orchestra performed in Darmstadt during his first visit there. However, during the next few years, when the younger generation of 'Darmstadt composers' were to take up the lead given by Messiaen's *Mode de valeurs et d'intensités* and Karel Goeyvaerts' *Sonata for Two Pianos* (1950–51) in moving towards the 'total serialism' which came to be associated with the name of Darmstadt, Maderna was to take a very independent position: this becomes evident in the group of orchestral compositions composed between 1948 and 1954.

Notes to Chapter 1

1. Maderna's mother had died when he was five years old, and when it became clear that his father, Umberto Grossato, was either unable or unwilling to take care of the child, he was at first put in the care of various foster-parents, and eventually in 1935 he became adopted by Irma Manfredi, a wealthy woman in Verona who had taken a great interest in his musical career. Cf. Mario *Baroni* and Rossana *Dalmonte* (Eds): *Bruno Maderna: Documenti*: published by Suvini Zerboni, Milan, 1985, pp. 14–15.
2. *Arrigo Pedrollo* was born in Vicenza in 1878 and died there in 1964. He achieved fame as a composer when his *Symphony* was conducted by Toscanini in 1900, and he also composed operas, symphonic poems, cantatas and chamber music. In 1920 he became Director of the 'Istituto Musicale' in Vicenza, and from 1930 to 1941 also taught at the Milan Conservatoire.
3. *Alessandro Bustini* was born in Rome in 1976 and died there in 1970. He studied at the 'Santa Cecilia' Academy and continued to teach there afterwards, becoming Director in 1947. As well as writing his book *La Sinfonia in Italia* in 1904, he composed operas, orchestral music, choral works and chamber music.
4. *Gian Francesco Malipiero* (1882–1973) was born in Venice of a musical family, and studied in Trieste, Berlin and Vienna during his earlier years. He later studied with Marco Enrico Bossi in Venice, and began to study and transcribe early Italian music (Monteverdi, Frescobaldi, Merulo etc.) in the Biblioteca Marciana from 1902. He acted as amanuensis for the blind composer Smareglia for some time, but his most formative experience came when, in 1913 in Paris, he attended the first performance of *Le Sacre du Printemps*. His composition underwent a profound change as a result of this experience (he claimed to have destroyed all his previous compositions). He settled in Asolo from about 1910, but was forced to move to Rome during the retreat from Caporetto in 1917, remaining there until 1921. From then on, Asolo became his permanent home.

    He began to edit the works of Monteverdi in 1926, a task which he completed in 1942, and in 1932 he began to teach at the Venice Conservatoire, becoming Director 1939–1952. He was President of the 'Istituto Italiano Antonio Vivaldi', directing the publication of all this composer's instrumental works, a task in which Maderna himself had some small involvement.

    His output as a composer was enormous: forty operas, six ballets, vocal, orchestral, and smaller works; and he also wrote about many aspects of music: books and articles on Monteverdi, Vivaldi, Stravinsky, and many other subjects. (Cf. *John C.G. Waterhouse*: 'Malipiero' article in *New Grove Dictionary of Music and Musicians; Macmillan (London) 1981.*)
5. *L R Lind* (Ed): *Twentieth Century Italian Poetry: a Bilingual Anthology*; Bobbs-Merrill (Indianapolis and New York) 1974; pp. 134–135.
6. *Jürg Stenzl* (ed): *Luigi Nono: Texte, Studien zu seiner Musik*; Atlantis Verlag, Zurich and Freiburg, 1975, p. 175.
7. *Camillo Togni* was born in Brescia in 1922, and studied piano with Casella in Rome and Siena, and later with Michelangeli in Brescia, in which city he also graduated in philosophy. His composition studies were also under the guidance of Casella from 1939 to 1943. He attended the 'Ferienkurse' in Darmstadt from 1951 to 1957, and has had works performed at festivals in Venice, Brussels, Cologne, Madrid, Palermo and Darmstadt.
8. *Luigi Dallapiccola: Incontro con Anton Webern (Pagine di Diario)*; published in *Il Mondo* No. 15, Florence, 3 November 1945 and in *Disclub* Year No. 1, Florence, 1963: reprinted in *Appunti, Incontri, Meditazioni*, published by Suvini Zerboni, Milan, 1970, pp. 105–109.
9. *Baroni/Dalmonte*, op. cit., pp. 89–101.
10. *Enzo Restagno* (Ed:) *Nono*: EDT (Turin) 1987, p. 4.

11. *Baroni/Dalmonte*, op. cit., p. 60.
12. *Hermann Scherchen* (born Berlin, 1891; died Florence, 1966) began his career as a viola player, and in 1911 he worked with Schoenberg in preparing *Pierrot Lunaire* for its earliest performances. He was, throughout his life, associated with new developments in music: he conducted Berg's *Three Fragments from 'Wozzeck'* in 1924 (before the opera was given on the stage) and was active as conductor of the I.S.C.M Festivals for many years. In 1933, he left Germany to settle permanently in Switzerland, editing a journal for new music (*Musica Viva*) and continuing to conduct. He taught classes in conducting in Venice (at the 'Biennale', where Maderna was amongst his pupils), and later in Darmstadt. With financial help from UNESCO, he founded in 1954 a studio for electro-acoustic research in Gravesano, the Swiss village in which he had made his home, and conducted the first performances of innumerable works (Dallapiccola's *Il Prigioniero* in 1950, Dessau's *Das Verhör des Lukullus* in 1951, Henze's *König Hirsch* in 1956, and the *Dance Around the Golden Calf* from Schoenberg's *Moses und Aron* in Darmstadt in 1951). He died from a heart attack during a performance in Florence in 1966.
13. *René Leibowitz* (born Warsaw 1913, died Paris 1972) studied with Schoenberg and Webern in Berlin and Vienna from 1930 to 1933, and also with Ravel in Paris. He was principally known as a conductor, notably of the Orchestre National of the O.R.T.F, and founded an International Chamber Music Festival, where many works of the Viennese composers were heard for the first time in Paris. His pupils included Pierre Boulez and many other composers of his generation, and his writings on serialism attracted a lot of attention, but his own compositions, close in style to Schoenberg and Berg, were not successful.
14. *Baroni/Dalmonte*; op. cit., pp. 194–195.
15. Cf. *Fearn, Raymond,: At the Doors of Kranichstein: Bruno Maderna's Fantasia per due pianoforti*; in *Tempo*, December 1987, pp. 14–20.
16. Interview with Maderna of 23.1.1970, given in Appendix.
17. Interview with Maderna by Leonardo Pinzauti in 1972, given in Appendix.
18. *Enzo Restagno* (Ed.): op. cit., pp. 22–3.
19. *Fiamma Nicolodi: Luigi Dallapiccola: saggi, testimonianze, carteggio, biografia e bibliografia*; Suvini Zerboni, Milan, 1975, p. 75.
20. Idem, p. 81.
21. *Enzo Restagno* (ed): op. cit., pp. 82–86.
22. Cf. *Antoine Goléa: Recontres avec Pierre Boulez*; first published 1958; re-issued by Slatkine, Paris, 1982; p. 20.

Chapter 2

Works for orchestra — *Composizione No 2* — meeting with Varèse
— the Milan Studio di Fonologia Musicale —
electronic, live/electronic, and instrumental works of 1950–1962.

Maderna arrived for the first time at the Darmstadt Ferienkurse in the summer of 1950, and apart from the performance of his *Fantasia on B.A.C.H.* just a year previously (which he was for some reason unable to attend), the first work of his to be played there was *Composizione No. 2* for small orchestra (sometimes called *Musica (No. 2) per orchestra*), conducted by Scherchen. In no sense can this be regarded as a 'Darmstadt work'; in fact, it might almost be thought rather anachronistic in its mixture of elements: in its 'Neo-classical' or 'Expressionistic' usage of popular dance-forms as a major part of the structure, in the employment of an Ancient Greek melody (the famous *Epitaph of Seikilos*) at the beginning and end of this one-movement piece, in the distinctly Bergian writing in the Waltzes, the Webernesque pointillism of the Rumba, and in its overall quality of lyrical expressivity as the main impetus. This 'visiting-card' of Maderna's appeared, to be sure, of somewhat dubious 'authenticity' in the Darmstadt of 1950.

The work was the second to be composed of a group of five works for orchestra during this early period: these were *Composizione No 1* (1948–9), *Composizione No 2* (1950), *Improvvisazione No 1* (1951–2), *Improvvisazione No 2* (1953) and *Composizione in tre tempi* (1954); a further work was begun during this time, but remained unfinished.[1] The first of the group, *Composizione No 1*, was written for a huge orchestra of about ninety players, whereas the rest demand more modest forces.

Maderna thus placed great emphasis on orchestral composition during this period and the group of works neatly counter-balances the group of orchestral compositions which he was to write in his last years (*Quadrivium*, *Biogramma*, *Aura*). One might conjecture that Maderna, having spent his youth as an orchestral conductor, was naturally disposed towards the 'traditional' orchestra. During his last years, he was again to approach this medium in an imaginative way, re-casting its consistituent elements and re-distributing it in a thoroughly un-traditional manner; during the earlier period, the body remains intact, but through his exploration of varieties of expression, he developed a very personal and distinctive manner of writing.

Like the orchestral works of his last years, these pieces (with the exception of the *Composizione in tre tempi*) are cast in single movements clearly articulated in distinct 'episodes'. In the first work of the series, *Composizione No 1*, whose composition overlapped with the writing of the *Fantasia*, *Concerto* and *Tre Liriche Greche*, the episodes of which the work is made up are set out in a quasi-dramatic form, delineating the developmental processes of the work itself:

1. ***Introduzione*** (*Lento, Poco meno, Allegro*) (bars 1–138)
2. ***Allegro:*** *Espozione: Tema*
       I   *Periodo: Metamorfosi*
       II *Periodo: Scomposizione*
       III *Periodo: Metamorfosi 2a*
       IV *Periodo: Integrazione*
       V   *Periodo: Sintesi*
       VI *Periodo: Distruzione*
       VII *Periodo: Disperisione* (bars 139–266)
3. ***Andante*** (bars 267–337)
4. ***Allegro Moderato e Vigoroso*** (bars 338–420)

The single-movement format was, in fact, to remain a constant characteristic of many of Maderna's subsequent instrumental compositions, ranging from small-scale chamber works such as *Honeyrêves* and *Serenata No 2* to larger soloistic works such as the *Violin Concerto, Oboe Concertos* and *Grande Aulodia*.

The episodic construction is important for the whole nature of Maderna's musical expressivity: sections are defined one from another by means of instrumental combinations of varying kinds, harmonic density, rhythmic energy and contrapuntal complexity, and this homogeneity of texture within sections of a work enabled the composer later on to move quite naturally towards that integration of 'aleatoric' or 'mobile' procedures in his instrumental works which became such a feature of his later style. The 'free flow' of mobile units, sometimes mingling, at other times strongly contrasting one with another, and dispersed in many cases over the whole orchestral body (distributed spatially, perhaps influenced by the procedures of his beloved Gabrieli in San Marco), was to become a cornerstone of Maderna's later instrumental style.

The period of composition of these orchestral works coincided with the most crucial period in Darmstadt: some composers associated with the Ferienkurse, notably Boulez and Stockhausen, having felt the influence both of Webern's later music and of Messiaen's *Mode de valeurs et d'intensités*, were led to the radical conception of 'integral serialism', a conception which aimed above all at a 'purity' of musical thought, devoid of elements of reference to the past, and equally devoid of either 'neo-classical' or 'expressionistic' formal elements. The fact that Maderna in this selfsame period was composing works imbued to a large extent with these 'impurities' is a measure of his independence of spirit and of his overriding desire for an expressivity which could involve the past as well as the present. He was, of course, not alone in composing orchestral works based on broad interpretations of the serial principle: this was also the period of Nono's *Variazioni canoniche sulla serie dell'op. 41 di A. Schoenberg* and Berio's *Nones*, but Maderna's free inclusion of referential elements was unique in the avant-garde of that time.

In *Composizione No. 2*, the episodes of which the work is comprised are delineated one from another in a particularly clear manner, as though the composer wished to emphasise the sudden changes of manner from one section to the next, changes which are sharp, almost brutal, in outline. The move from the 'Greek Melody in Phrygian Mode' of the first section, for example, with its static harmony derived from the *Epitaph of Seikilos*, to the linear-contrapuntal serialism of the ensuing 'English Waltz', appears as a sudden jolt from one mood to another in violent contrast to it; similarly, the end of the 'Viennese Waltz' which gradually evolves from the 'English' variety suddenly gives way to the almost frivolous pointillistic 'Rumba' after only the slightest break.

This incorporation of material of both ancient and popular varieties in the work is of particular interest for an understanding of Maderna's whole compositional aesthetic. For Maderna, the Darmstadt ideal of 'purity' had no great fascination: his desire was rather to involve references to past musical types in a 'modern' musical structure, and we find a Polka and a Can-Can in *Improvvisazione No 1*, three Veneto folk-melodies in *Composizione in tre tempi*, as well as the Waltzes, Rumba and Ancient Greek *Epitaph* in *Composizione No 2*. One reason for this inclusion of referential material in these works was undoubtedly Maderna's desire to give the clearest possible articulation to his thought at this earliest stage of his serialism: it is not without significance that the Waltzes and Rumba appear in the serial episodes of the work (the opening of the 'English Waltz' coincides with the first presentation of the series). However, this is not the whole picture: conscious as Maderna must have been that Schoenberg had similarly felt the need to revert to dance-forms from an earlier age in his first serial works (such as *Suite* op. 25), he was certainly equally conscious of Alban Berg's use of popular dance-forms in *Wozzeck*, in *Lulu*, and in other works. Maderna here approaches the 'Expressionistic' use of these popular types of music, that is to say, employing them in order to make references outside the 'narrow' world of classical music, and in order to summon up in the listener a certain response, a 'nostalgia' for the musical past which the composer deliberately wishes to be in a certain incongruity with the 'modernistic' musical language in which it is expressed. This deliberately 'Expressionistic' employment of popular styles was one of the reasons why the audience at its first performance in Darmstadt was puzzled: Expressionism as well as Neo-Classicism had been 'banished' from the Darmstadt ethos at that time.

The opening episode of the work, *'Calmo e libero'*, using the *Epitaph of Seikilos*, was originally quite lengthy, and in the Darmstadt performance of 1950 we hear the 38 bars which were later excised from the passage before the work's publication (he evidently forgot to re-number the bars in this second version). Maderna here treats the *Epitaph* as a generative agent for the melodic and harmonic workings of this most haunting and evocative episode: right from the start, the Greek melody is 'sung serenely' by cor anglais, accompanied by a static chord gradually derived from prominent pitches of the melody. Maderna here evokes a musical 'primal age' in his employment of one of the oldest pieces of Western music, and in giving this melody to the cor anglais, he takes a step towards the 'aulody' idea which was some years later, to appear once more in the *Grande Aulodia* for flute, oboe and orchestra. (Ex. 2.1]

In the final bars of the episode, Maderna places together in counterpoint strands of melody in different modalities, each derived from the *Epitaph*, thus creating a bi-partite texture of static harmony in strings and melodic flow in winds. [Ex. 2.2(a)]

In curtailing the first episode of the work, for reasons which are not known, Maderna might in fact have excised material which is of some importance in making the musical thought clear: in his sketches for the work, he had attempted to bring together modal and serial procedures, whereas in the published score the two procedures are clearly delineated from each other between the *Epitaph* and 'Waltz' episodes. His attempt to fuse modality and serialism becomes clear in a

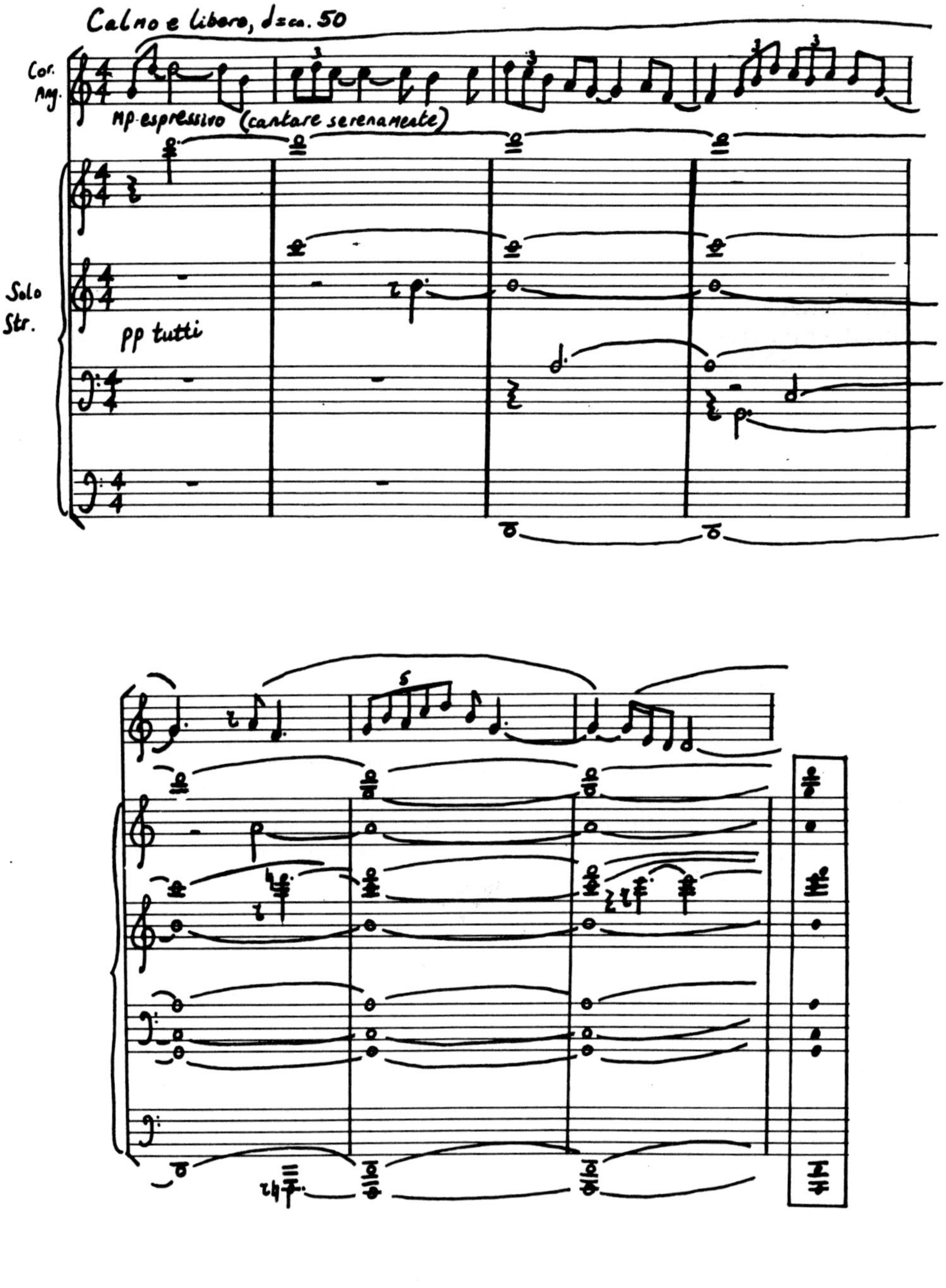

Ex. 2.1: Maderna: *Composizione No. 2*: 1–7

Ex. 2.2(a): Maderna: *Composizione No. 2*: 53–57

page of sketches marked *Proporzione Dodecafonica* ('Dodecaphonic Proportion'), in which he superimposes the *Epitaph* (*Dritto:* Basic set) in Phrygian mode, its retrograde in Lydian mode, inversion in Dorian mode and retrograde inversion in what he describes as 'dodecaphonic' mode. These strands, with the exception of the last-named, appear, in fact, in bars 53–67 of Ex. 2.2(a). [Ex. 2.2(b)] It is clear from this sketch that Maderna, treating the *Epitaph* in Phrygian mode as a 'basic set' from which other strands of the polyphony were derived, wished to bring together elements of both ancient and modern practice, as he had done in his derivation of the final soprano melody in the second of the *Tre Liriche Greche*, through techniques grounded as much in the Renaissance polyphonic procedures which he had earlier studied, as in the new-found serial technique which Scherchen had revealed to him.

As we have already noted, the transition to the second episode, that of the 'English' and 'Viennese' Waltzes, is a quite abrupt one, and the language of the work similarly shifts to serialism. The serial aspect is presented in a quite simple and straightforward manner at the opening of the episode: the prime series given

Ex. 2.2(b): Maderna: *Composizione No. 2*: sketch: 'Dodecaphonic Proportion'

Ex. 2.3(a): Maderna: *Composizione No. 2*: 68–88

Ex. 2.3(a): *Contd*

Ex. 2.3(b): Maderna: *Composizione No. 2*: series

out by 'cello solo from bar 67, consisting of 13 pitches, is treated contrapuntally in combination with its derivatives in the first *stanza* of the 'English Waltz'. The little phrase of 12 notes given to the solo flute at the conclusion of this *stanza* appears, for the moment, to be merely a cadential 'flourish'. [Ex. 2.3(a), (b)] The five episodes of this 'English Waltz' succeed each other in a progression of gradually increasing complexity, each heralded at the double-bars by a suspended cymbal clash. The contrapuntal elaboration of varieties of the prime series continues in the second episode, but at the third episode beginning in bar 98, a further element appears, a melody beginning in saxophone and continued by cor anglais, motifs

Ex. 2.4(a): Maderna: *Composizione No. 2*: 99–107

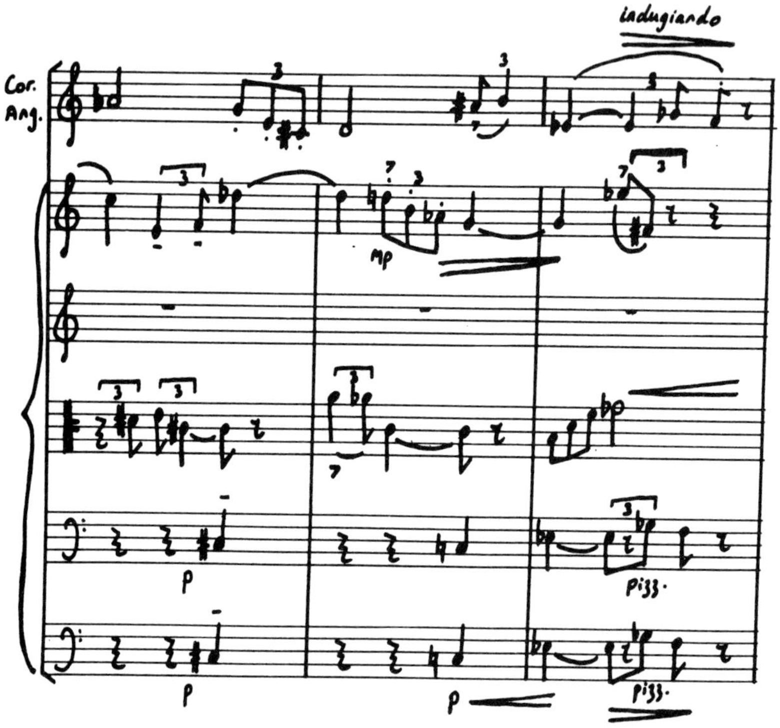

Ex. 2.4(a): *Contd*

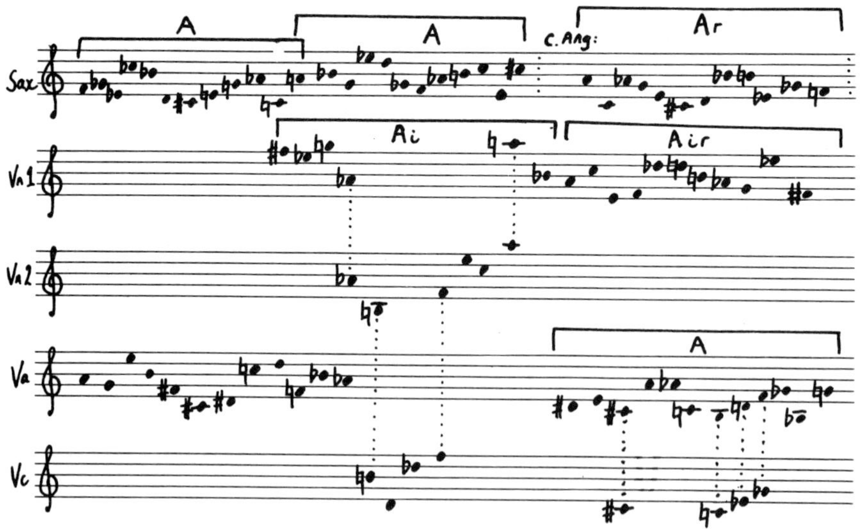

Ex. 2.4(b): Maderna: *Composizione No. 2*: analysis

from which are reflected in the accompanying string parts. This melody, free-roaming and casual in character, is in fact derived from the 12-note flute 'cadential flourish' from the end of the first episode, treated here as a new series (A), whilst the original series of the waltz (P) continues in the viola. [Ex. 2.4(a), (b)] This superimposition of two 'serial layers' one upon another continues, and in the fifth episode (bar 118), the major- and minor-3rds from which this new series is constructed are opened out in chains of parallel thirds in divided string-parts: the episode extends to much greater length, developing the elements of chains of thirds and both series until the 'Wiener Walzer' begins at bar 143. Here, the chains of thirds dominate the texture at first, the rhythmic impetus is more strongly marked in Viennese character, and the melody in upper strings which is carried through the Viennese Waltz is accompanied by the rest of the orchestra in a texture of great clarity. All of the melodic and harmonic working in this Viennese Waltz is of the simplest kind in a manner clearly influenced by Alban Berg. [Ex 2.5.]

A further abrupt change of direction appears as the 'Viennese Waltz' gives way to the 'Rumba' (bar 199), the final episode of the work. Here, once again, a 'new' series is introduced, and once more the initial serial derivations are clearly delineated. [Ex. 2.6 (a), (b)] The Rumba, like the Waltz-episodes, is articulated in distinct sections marked by double bar-lines: here, the first section of 27 bars (199–225) is succeeded by a second of 12 bars (226–237) 'poco piu mosso' and a third of 12 bars (238–249) 'ancora un poco piu', whilst the fourth, which is 'open-ended', occupies the remaining bars of the work (250–294). The elaboration of motivic working in these sections becomes increasingly more intense, but from the third section onwards a new element is added to the texture, a complex of ascending and descending melodic lines which begins to predominate over the rest of the texture. These lines, in fact, are based upon chromatic scales mixed with modes, as the composer gradually brings the work full-circle, having begun with a modal melody in the opening episode, and moved to serial writing in its central portions, and now the process is reversed, the serial elaborations gradually giving way to modality once more. [Ex. 2.7(a), (b)]

In the final section, this rich texture continues, reaching a climax in *fortissimo* as the timpani enter at bar 258: from this point onwards, the texture begins to thin out, over a repeated timpani figure, with the scale-figures gradually subsiding, and giving way (bar 263) to percussion which will be maintained through all the remaining bars of the work. Above this, the cor anglais, which had opened the work with the 'Epitafio di Sicilo' re-introduces this melody prominently above the rest of the orchestra, accompanied by further chromatic melodic figurations in the flutes. [Ex. 2.8] The work comes to an end with the horn, taking up from the cor anglais the last notes of the 'epitaph', fading away to leave only the 'old fragrance' of the percussion with its suggestion of the Rumba. [Ex. 2.9]

Composizione No 2 is a work of great originality and expressivity: as in the *Tre Liriche Greche* which preceded it, Maderna has brought together several elements and approaches to form a diversified musical language, one which does not lean on any particular model, but is thoroughly personal and distinctive. One might see in Maderna's approach to serialism a parallel with the adoption of serialism by Stravinsky shortly afterwards: with both composers, their serial manner was idiosyncratic, malleable and adaptable towards varying expressive needs, and in the case of both composers the roots of a serial approach may be traced back to procedures in previous compositions. However, whereas Stravinsky's serialism

Ex. 2.5: Maderna: *Composizione No. 2:* 143–151

Ex. 2.5: *Contd*

leans towards that of Webern in its permutational 'consistency', for Maderna the free interaction of serialism with quasi-diatonic procedures, with modalism, and with an 'Expressionistic' employment of popular dance-forms is of paramount importance in the formation of the expressive language of *Composizione No 2*. The synthesis of these diverse compositional approaches is not one of 'eclecticism': the elements of the synthesis are not distinguishable as distinct stylistic 'mannerisms' held together in tenuous unity, but flow one into another. If we observe the basic material which Maderna employs to build the variegated perspective of the work, the *Epitaph* and the series of the subsequent episodes, we can see that not only are the series of the Rumba and the 'second' series of the Waltz-episode related by a retrograde inversion, but also that the materials share a certain intervallic content (major and minor thirds and semitones). In this way, the work's variety of means and expressions is held together. [Ex. 2.10]

The 'referential' aspect of *Composizione No 2*, its incorporatioin of traditional dance-forms as an essential element in the structure, was to be continued in

Ex. 2.6(a): Maderna: *Composizione No. 2*: 199–207

Ex. 2.6(b): Maderna: *Composizione No. 2*: analysis

Improvvisazione No 1 composed in the following year, but this element became less essential as the nature of Maderna's writing became articulated in rhythmic and melodic structures of a harder, more 'pointillistic' kind, and were no longer to be present in *Improvvisazione No 2* composed in 1953. The other 'referential' element however, the employment of pre-existing melodic material, which had appeared in *Composizione No 2* in the form of the *Epitaph of Seikilos*, was to re-appear in the *Composizione in tre tempi* in 1954: where the *Epitaph* had been a dominant, and always clearly recognisable, feature of the earlier work, we find in the latter the employment of three Veneto folk-songs (*La biondina in gondoleta*, a Venetian Gondoliers' song; *Splende la luna ciara sora Castel Doblin* from Trentino; and the Friulian *L'allegrie le ven dai zoveni*) which are transformed by highly complex canonic treatment, providing the main impetus of the work. This treatment is revealed in the sketches which Maderna made for the work. [Ex. 2.11]

It was during the period of composition of these orchestral works that Maderna began to experiment with the new electronic medium, and his first work involving tape, *Musica su due dimensioni* (a further, completely revised version of which was to be made in 1958) was made in 1952, and given its first performance in the Darmstadt Ferienkurse in that same year. There might appear to have been no reason to expect Maderna, who was so intimately bound up in instrumental composition at that time, to move in this direction: however, in common with his

Ex.2.7(a): Maderna: *Composizione No. 2*: 238–246

Darmstadt colleagues Stockhausen and Boulez, he rapidly became interested in the possibilities offered by electronic composition, and one can account for Maderna's involvement in terms of the exploratory nature of his musicality. The 'prime mover' in Maderna's orientation towards the new medium was undoubtedly Edgard Varèse, whom he had met in 1950 in Darmstadt: Varèse had composed his first work involving tape, *Déserts*, in that same year, in which tape and live performance had been brought together, and Maderna was the first composer to take up this idea from the older Frenchman. Varèse, along with Webern and Messiaen, became a beacon lighting the way towards the 'New Music' of the Darmstadt composers in the early 1950s, and was an essential 'agent' in Stockhausen's collaboration with Herbert Eimert in the founding of an electronic studio in Cologne; Boulez' brief flirtation with the new medium at Pierre Schaeffer's *musique concrète* studio in Paris was not to be pursued further when he realised the inadequacy and disorganisation of Schaeffer's approach to the medium.

The 'two dimensions' to which the title of Maderna's first electronic work refers are those of live instrumental performance and music on tape which is connected to it, and the composer referred to these dimensions in a lecture he gave in Darmstadt in 1959[2]:

Ex. 2.7(a): *Contd*

Fl.
Ob.
C.Ang
Sax.
Cl.P.
Cl.
Cl.B
Bn. 1/2
Hn.
(a2)
Trpt.
Trbn.
mp
Pf.
Vn 1
Vn 2
Va
Vc
pizz.
gliss.
arco
Cb
pizz.
gliss.
arco

Ex.2.7(a): *Contd*

Ex.2.7(b): Maderna: *Composizione No. 2*: Modal lines

Ex.2.8: Maderna: *Composizione No. 2*: 267–271

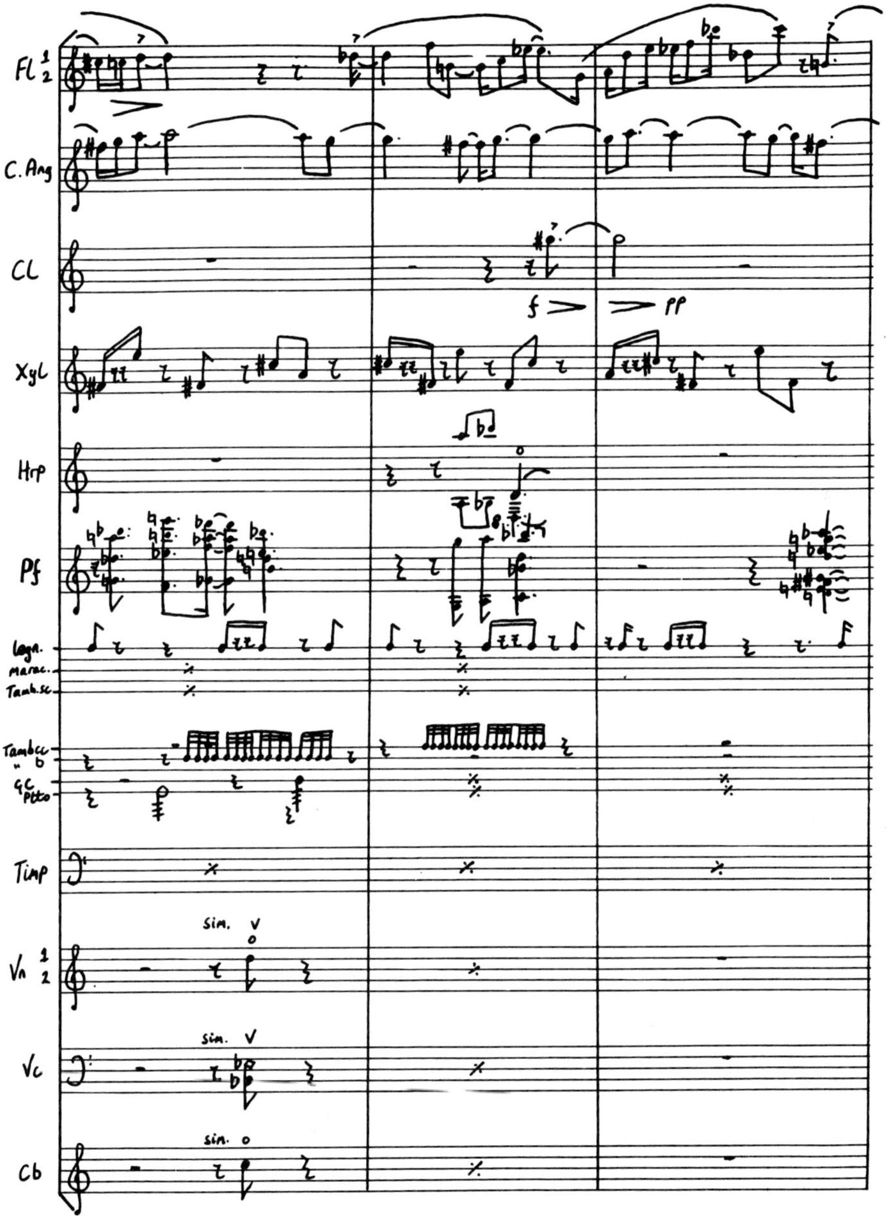

Ex.2.8: *Contd*

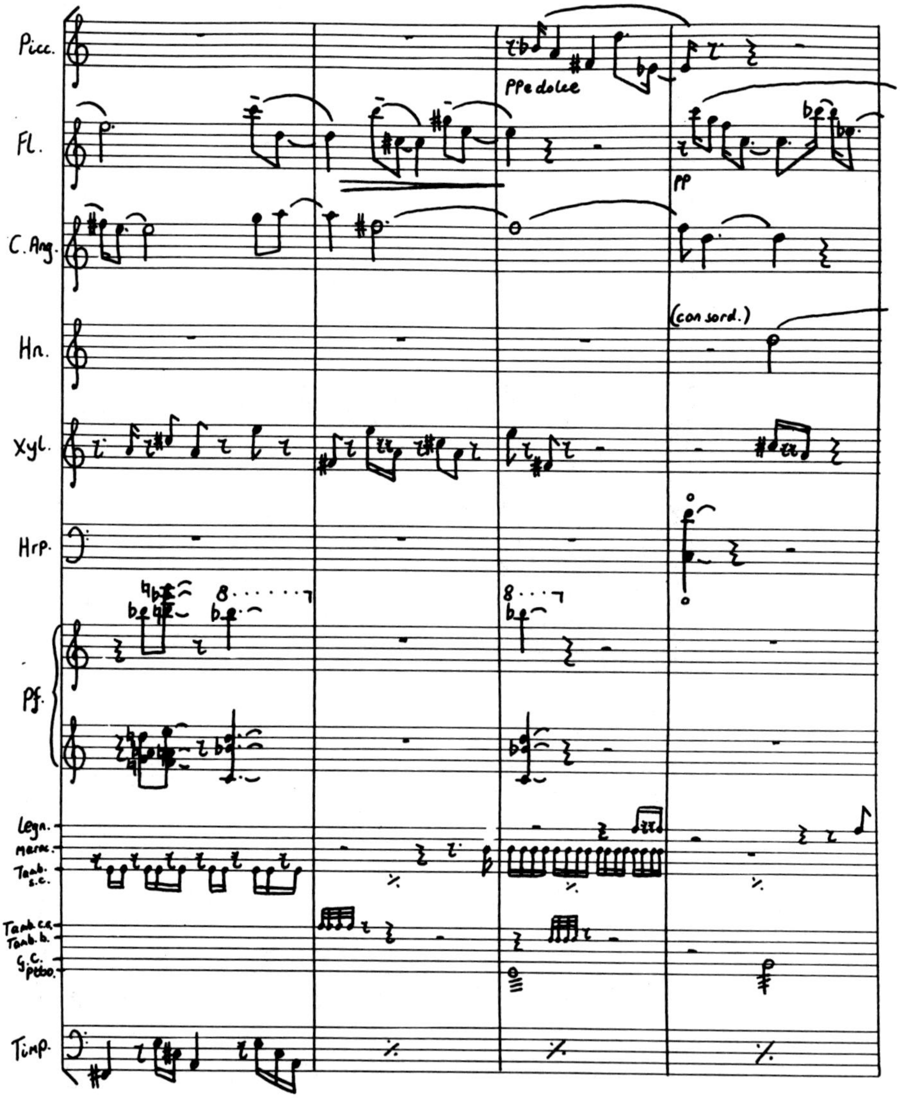

Ex.2.9: Maderna: *Composizione No. 2*: 283–294

Ex.2.9: *Contd*

Ex.2.10: Maderna: *Composizione No. 2*: basic materials

'Music in two dimensions! What does the concept of 'dimensions' mean to me? By dimensions, I mean forms of musical communication: by the traditional means, with performers playing or singing in front of an audience, and secondly by means of electro-acoustical recording and reproduction, in which purely electronic sounds, or instrumental sounds which have been recorded and sometimes transformed, or sound-materials on tape reproduced by loudspeaker, are employed. Where in the beginning one could see a clear division between electronic and instrumental music, in the last couple of years or so works have been produced in which these two dimensions have been combined.'

The instrumental 'dimension' in the earlier version of the work made in 1952 included a cymbal and possibly also a piano alongside the part for solo flute: the score of this version has unfortunately been lost, only the recording of its Darmstadt performance remaining as evidence of this tentative combination of the dimensions which were to be completely re-cast in 1958.[3] Some sketches for the 1952 version have however survived, and we might glean some idea of the composer's conception of the work, its interaction between the two dimensions, from these pages: Maderna, as was his custom in work later in the Milan Studio di Fonologia, gave descriptive titles to varieties of electronic sound (*'freddo allucinato'* :'cold hallucination'; *'suoni fissi gli altri'*: 'the rest fixed sounds'; *'suoni morbidi, ondulati'*: soft, undulated sounds'; *'Lamiera'*: 'sheet metal'). [Ex. 2.12(a), (b)]

The tape for the work was prepared by Maderna with the assistance of Werner Meyer Eppler in the Institute for Communications Research and Information Theory at the University of Bonn (it was Meyer Eppler who had first demonstrated the possibility of 'electronic music' in Darmstadt in 1951, and whose researches prompted Stockhausen and Eimert to found the Cologne Studio). There was at this time no facility in Italy for work in electro-acoustic music, but by 1955 the Milan Studio di Fonologia Musicale had been founded as

Ex. 2.11: Maderna: *Composizione in tre tempi*: sketch and score

a section of RAI (Radiotelevisione Italiana): Milan was during the 1950s the most important cultural centre in Italy, and Maderna, along with Berio, Luigi Rognoni and Piero Santi, was instrumental in the new foundation. Berio had recently returned from America, where he had been studying with Dallapiccola, and where he had heard his first examples of the new electronic medium in a concert in New York: the parallels between the musical experience of Maderna and Berio were close, both having studied initially with very strict masters of tradition (Berio with Ghedini, Maderna with Bustini), and both had been introduced to serial techniques shortly after the war (Berio by Dallapiccola, Maderna by Scherchen), and their musical relationship therefore set off immediately on this common basis. The first production in which the two composers collaborated in the Studio was a work of a rather tentative kind: *Ritratto di Città* (Portrait of a City), in which a collage of 'concrete' sounds from daily life formed the basis of the work; the title

Ex.2.11: *Contd*

bears, interestingly, a close resemblance to the *Risveglio di Città* which Russolo had produced for his Orchestra of Noise-Instruments during the 1920s.

Ritratto di Città was, in fact, prepared before the authorities of RAI had finally accepted the viability of the Studio di Fonologia project, and was made partly to exhibit some of the radiophonic possibilities of the intended Studio. It is in effect a text to which have been added concrete sounds on tape; the text is by Roberto Leydi, and describes one day in the life of Milan from dawn to dusk. The text is a colourful and evocative collage of images in precisely the same way as the tape-element of the work is a collage of sound-images:

'Dawn awakening . . . Silence. Locked-up houses . . .
the ringing of the last night-watchman's bicycle bell. The strangely deserted streets of the city.
    The ghost of a distant church-bell . . . silence, with the little steps of a cat

Ex. 2.12(a): Maderna: *Musica su due dimensioni* (1952): sketch

Ex.2.12(a): *Contd*

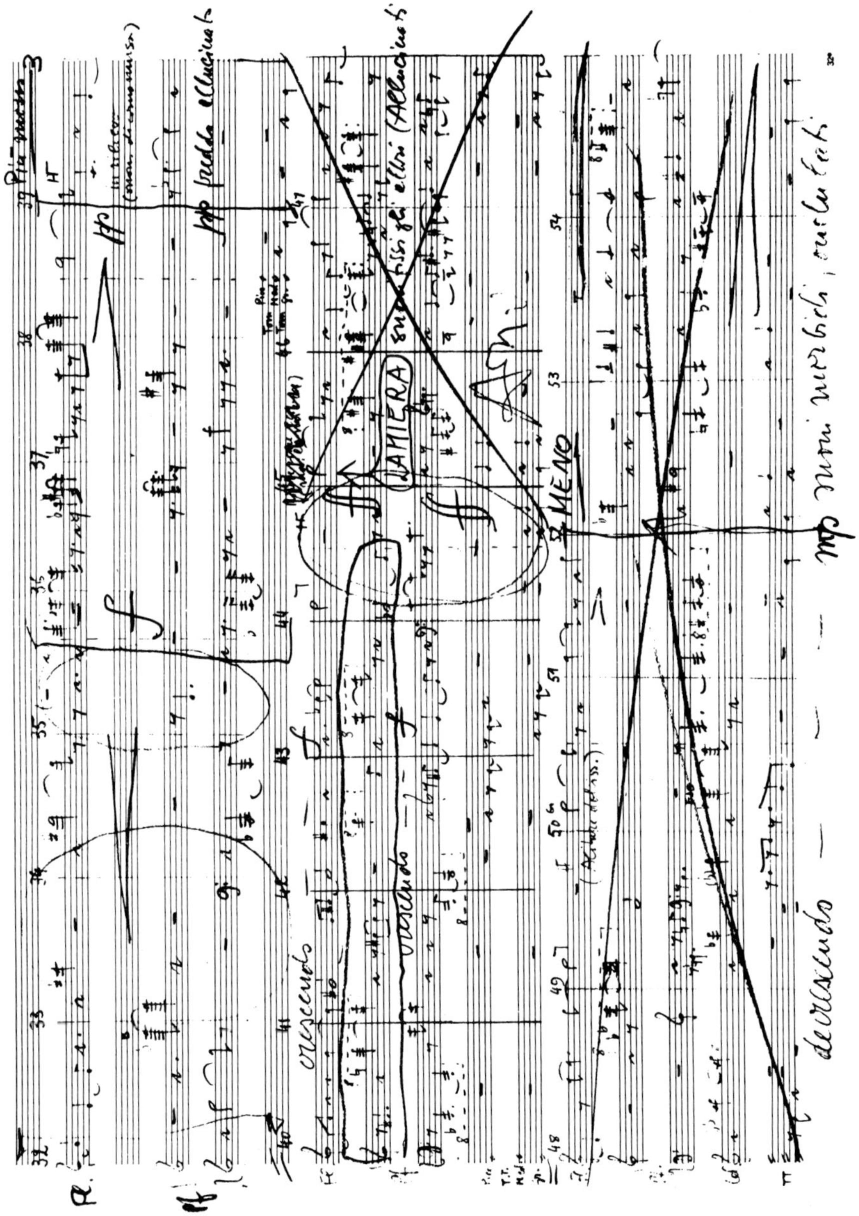

Ex. 2.12(b): Maderna: *Musica su due dimensioni* (1952): sketch

crossing Milan . . . wide streets, a bank . . . a church, the central squares. And offices . . . deserted offices. Factories, the trams in their sidings. Without any violence, silence reigns over the city, while it is unaware of it . . . the city waits'.

The 'electronic' element in the work is of two distinct kinds: simple recorded sounds and voices of the day-to-day life of Milan (trams, bells, typewriters, traffic, etc), and sounds manufactured by electronic means (which Maderna may have prepared in Cologne with the help of Meyer Eppler). However, the two kinds of sound work together harmoniously, and together with the text produce a work of an engaging simplicity and directness.

It is of considerable significance that, even in the earliest experiments conducted by Maderna in the Studio, he aimed always to present a 'human face' in his electronic works: even if we put to one side *Ritratto di Città*, which as a work of a frankly radiophonic and evocative kind was perhaps in a different category than the 'pure' electronic works, we can see in his next work *Notturno* an attempt to forge some links with 'traditional' instrumental music. This work employs sine-waves and white noise, and in it Maderna used superimposition, montage and filtering through a narrow band-filter (±2Hz), a filtering which was achieved by chance-manipulation, and involving a wide range of tone-colours which Maderna describes as 'irridescences'. In fact, during the brief space of the work (which lasts 3'23") he achieves many sounds of an 'instrumental' and especially 'flautistic' kind. *Notturno* did not derive its title from any poetic association, nor from any association with the Romantic works of this title, but simply from the fact that Maderna, who was not employed on a full-time basis by RAI at that time (only Berio and Marino Zuccheri were so employed for the first year or so of the Studio), was forced to take various odd-jobs to make a living, and consequently *Notturno* was composed mainly during the night-time. Maderna described the nature of his treatment of the electronic means in *Notturno* as creating 'the possibility of a link, almost of a continuity, between natural sound production and that produced electronically'.[4]

Notturno was composed in the spring of 1956, and his next work, also for the electronic medium, *Syntaxis*, dates from the following year, when it was given a performance at Darmstadt. It may be found puzzling that the number of works which Maderna produced at this time appears to be drastically reduced from his production of previous years (and underwent a sudden increase again after about 1962). However, this is explained simply by the needs which Maderna had during this period for making a living, and if we examine a list of some of the music for films, for radio and television in the first years of the Studio di Fonologia, this becomes clear:

Opinione Pubblica (music for film of Maurizio Corgnati: 1954)

Don Giovanni e il Commendatore
Brigada non vuole sposarsi
Macbeth (Shakespeare)
Julius Caesar (Shakespeare)   } Music for radio-plays c.1954–60
Cavallo di Troia (Morley)
Augellin belverde (Gozzi)
Medea (Anouilh)

Padri nemici }
Vizio occulto }   Music for television-plays c.1954–6

Syntaxis was, then, composed in 1957, and was one of the works which Maderna himself presented in Darmstadt in that year. In his introduction to the concert there in which tape-pieces by himself, Berio and Pousseur were presented at the Summer School, he said:

'I composed *Syntaxis* in 1957, not fixing any immutable schemes in advance, but rather, choosing the best effect produced from time to time by the sound-material in this or that point in the work. In this way, the composition became the result of my continual reactions to the suggestions of the material which had previously been produced.'[5]

Mainly sinosoidal sounds and white noise are again employed as the material at the basis of the composition. Maderna refers to a large degree of 'chance' in his selection of the sounds and techniques of elaboration which operate in his composition of the piece, and it may not be altogether fortuitous that Boulez and Stockhausen were, at this time, beginning to experiment with the introduction of the 'chance-element' into European music.

In the following year, Maderna produced *Continuo*, whose title refers with precision to the structural basis of the composition: in place of the 'chance' operations of *Syntaxis*, we have a work whose structural unity is derived from the very nature of the material, and Maderna wrote in a programme-note for one of the first performances:

'(It is constituted) from a single electronically-produced sound which undergoes 22 stages of slow and gradual transformation. The various stages follow each other without a break: in the formal course of the piece we do not encounter a dialectic of sound/silence, but one between greater or lesser density ('pregnance') of the material . . . Formally, the composition is therefore comparable with the idea of a real continuo'.[6]

The materials and techniques employed in *Continuo* are once more of the simplest kind: again, white noise and sinosoidal sounds, with tape-montage, speed-change and filtering. *Continuo* became part of the highly complex 'borrowings' which are characteristic of several Maderna's works: we find a section of this work in *Hyperion en het geweld*, the second staged version of *Hyperion* given in Brussels in May 1968; one also finds a passage in *Ages* which probably also derives from *Continuo*; and a similar passage also in the second version of *Musica su due dimensioni* (composed in the same year, 1958). What the use of this material in other works tends to show is that, for Maderna, the material of a rather 'abstract' kind which we find in the electronic works of this period such as *Continuo*, becomes employed in subsequent works as simply a part of a much richer and more variegated sound-palette, and as part of a work with a more direct and 'human' appeal, becoming, that is, linked to a poetic or dramatic scheme (as in *Hyperion* and *Ages*).

The period during which Maderna was composing what we might call 'pure' electronic works (that is to say, works which did not initially have any reference to external 'poetic' or 'dramatic' schemes, nor any reliance on instrumental or vocal performance), lasted only a remarkably short time: really, only during the years 1955 to 1958, from *Sequenze e Strutture* to *Continuo*. From this point onwards, we can see a very clear movement towards the integration of 'impure' elements into works of an electronic kind, and specifically in two pieces in which Maderna's imagination radiates outwards from the electronic medium, in the same way that his imagination had moved quickly on from a 'classical' serialism in the immediate post-war years. These two pieces 'personify', in fact, two close friends of the composer: in *Musica su due dimensioni* (1958) the flautist Severino Gazzelloni, and in *Dimensioni II/Invenzione su una voce* (1960) the voice of Berio's wife Cathy Berberian.

We have already observed earlier in this chapter how Maderna had taken up the lead given by Varèse in formulating two 'dimensions' of instrumental performance and music on tape in his *Musica su due dimensioni* in 1952, when he had first entered the field of electronic music through work he undertook in the Institute for Communications Research and Information Theory directed by Werner Meyer Eppler at the University of Bonn. However, the work which carries the same title from 1958 is a work differing completely from the earlier piece, sharing with it simply the title: Maderna had, in the intervening six years, been able to pursue his work in the electronic medium to a very much greater degree of assurance, and the 1958 version may therefore, with some confidence, be called his first fully mature work of this kind. It is as though his use of flautistic sounds (produced electronically) in *Notturno* had borne fruit in the live/tape combination we find in this new work.

Although the work is specifically designated 'for flute and stereophonic recording', this work has, curiously, been performed (during the composer's lifetime and presumably with his approval) for flute alone, without any tape-interpolations, by A. Sweekhorst, with the title *Dimensioni I*: this title may possibly be authentic, since Maderna did compose, in subsequent years, three further *Dimensioni*, beginning with *Dimensioni II/Invenzione su una voce*.

The 1958 version of *Musica su due dimensioni* is, as we have already suggested, one in which the two dimensions referred to in the title are of equal significance, whereas in the 'prototype' work from some six years earlier the composer was not at that point fully conversant with the new medium of music on tape, and this resulted in a certain imbalance between the two 'halves' of the work. It is in the *interaction* of these dimensions that Maderna's main point of interest lay, and in the later version the freedom of the two performers (flautist and tape-technician) to vary this interaction arose from the very nature of such a combination of live and pre-recorded elements. We should therefore beware of assuming too readily that the 'aleatoricism' of performer-choice which entered European music just a year earlier, in Stockhausen's *Klavierstück XI* and Boulez' *Trosième Sonate*, was of great influence upon the freedom of structure and interpretation which Maderna employed here. In both the Stockhausen and Boulez works, the freedom was one which involved only one performer faced with material of an interchangeable and interdependent character, whereas in Maderna's piece the overall form and the organisation of material were to a high degree 'fixed', only the interactions on a 'micro-level' being determinable from moment to moment. In this sense, we might describe the Stockhausen and Boulez works as 'mono-dimensional' in their overall working, whereas the freedoms in the Maderna piece operate *between* dimensions. This operation can be most clearly seen if we draw out a 'sketch-plan' of the piece:

'MUSICA SU DUE DIMENSIONI': Formal Scheme

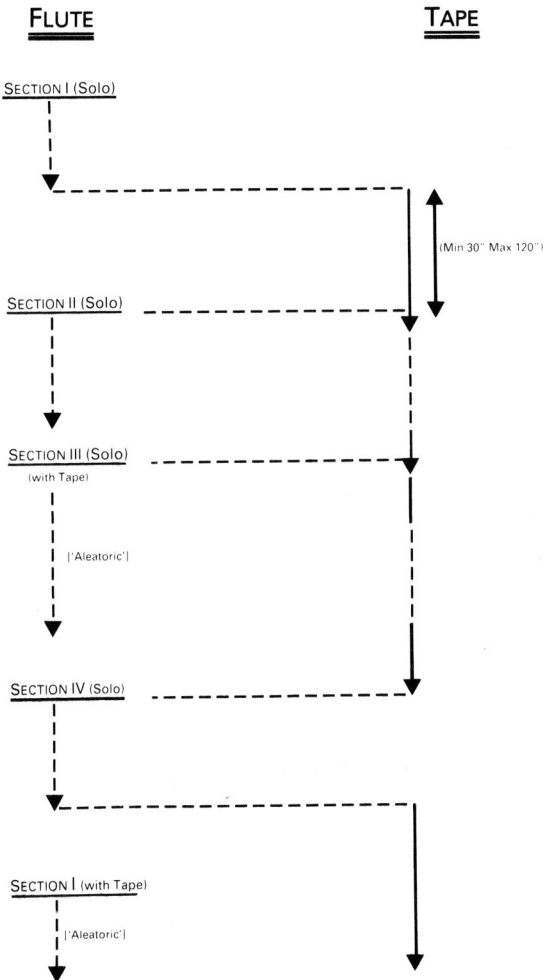

It will be seen from this sketch that the entries and timing of the tape-part in relation to that of the flautist constitute the most important element in the interaction, and the composer outlines this in the preface to the score:

'The tape-part (Section I) which begins at the end of the first part for flute, continue alone, for a minimum of 30″ up to a maximum of 2′, according to the environmental and acoustic conditions. The flute's Section II begins halfway or towards the end of the tape's Section I, continuing alone. All the remaining parts will blend *ad libitum*, according to the aforementioned environmental and acoustic conditions . . . ′

A second type of interaction arises from the the freedom with which the flute part is composed: the composer has provided for the possibility of repetition of some of the fragments of which Sections III and V are built. He describes it in this way:

'The flute's Section III can be performed interpolating and also repeating the various fragments, excluding those placed in brackets which should be played only once. The same applies to Section V (flute soloist), which has no fragments in brackets, and in this case therefore all of them may be repeated ad lib. When he arrives at Section V, the soloist can interpolate fragments from this section with those of Section III, but excluding the bracketed fragments. The repetition of these fragments can only be alternated, which means that the same fragment should not be repeated immediately, but only after a series of different fragments.'

The purpose of this freedom for repetition and interpolation of fragments is to provide the soloist with the possibility of *reacting*, on the spur of the moment, to the 'suggestions' which will come from the tape-part as it moves at its own speed through the material on it, which will obviously be gauged differently by the flautist in each performance of the work. In this way, the freedom of the technician and that of the soloist (whose part is written throughout in a very free, unmeasured manner), will create a great flexibility in the execution, and mobility, of intersecting dimensions such as, for example, is to be found in the 'Mobiles' of the sculptor Alexander Calder. Maderna ends the preface to the work with a clear explanation of this:

'The whole performance of this composition should arrive at a kind of bilateral interpretation of the soloist and the technician, an interpretation which can be 'invented' from moment to moment'.   .

The second of the works in which Maderna began to extend the range of his explorations of electro-acoustic music, *Dimensioni II/Invenzione su una voce*, takes a very different path: in this work, the extension of the medium is achieved by the inclusion of the voice of Cathy Berberian, whose vocal pyrotechnics had already formed the basis of Berio's Thema – *Omaggio a Joyce* in 1958. Berio's work had grown, as he himself said, from 'researches with Eco into poetic onomatopeia' and it was his first important work in the electronic medium.

Berio pointed to the possibility that, in those historical moments when music is 'venturing into unexplored territory', it can do so with greater confidence when it is supported by another significant dimension, namely that of language, and mentions both *Pierrot Lunaire* and Stockhausen's *Gesang der Jünglinge* as examples in which 'word and voice are the protagonists of these steps into the unknown'.[7] Stockhausen may therefore be said to have worked in the same direction in his *Gesang der Jünglinge*, about which he wrote in the first issue of the *Darmstädter Beiträge zur neuen Musik* in 1958, after analysing vocal works by Boulez and Nono.

For Berio, this relationship between poetry and music has remained a constant element in his musical thinking, as works such as *Chamber Music, Circles, Folk Songs, Laborintus II, Sequenza III* and *A-Ronne* testify.

Maderna, in *Dimensioni II . . .* removed from the text on which he based the work all possible interpretative 'meaning' by asking his friend Hans G. Helms to construct for him a sequence of 'phonemes' which would themselves be the text: in this way, it might be said, he aimed towards an uncovering of new strata of meaning. Helms said of this:

> 'This text was composed with the intention of excluding any kind of explicit sense of the word (sema); only vocal sounds (phonemes) would make up the material of the text, just as in the whole musical work. The text has only a phonetic meaning (and was written in phonetic notation in the IPA system); its communicative expression is music. One would therefore search in vain for any accidental equivalents (words) in any language, even if the text might here and there arouse a certain fantasy of association. I employed as a means 35 consonants, 1 semivowel and 15 vowels, phonemes which occur like this, or similarly, in Arabic, Danish, German, English, French, Greek, Hebrew, Italian, Japanese, Spanish, Czech and Welsh . . . The frequency of each of the phonemes runs from 1 to 18 and was established according to an almost serial plan. The ratio of consonants and vowels was chosen by me bearing in mind the eventual musical work of B. Maderna. From it there arises a scale of sounds of a greatly differentiated kind . . . '[8]

Having established the material of the work in terms of a 'text', the second stage was to ask Cathy Berberian to record a large amount of material (about an hour of this was apparently recorded), and in this she had, like Gazzelloni in *Musica su due dimensioni* a very large degree of freedom in her 'interpretation': she could read the 'text' (system of phonemes) with very varied intonation suggested by her own fantasy. The 'proto-material' of the phonemes in this way became the 'material' of the work, and the work of musical composition could then begin.

At least two versions of the resultant work exist: both are held by the International Music Institute in Darmstadt (one of 16', the other 19'), and both employ similar techniques of elaboration, superimposition, montage, acceleration and reverberation. The work, like others of the same period, was to be employed in other contexts: in the *Hyperion* performance it became associated with the 'Machine' in Scenes 5 and 6 of the staged version of the work, and parts also appear in sections of *Tempo Libero* and of *Ages*, the composer using in these works both versions of *Dimensioni II*.

We can therefore observe in *Musica su due dimensioni* of 1958 and in *Dimensioni II* two ways in which Maderna expressed a certain kind of *aleatoricism* in the fabric of his work: in the first, by the freedom given to the two performers involved (flautist and tape-technician); in the second, the total freedom given to Cathy Berberian in the preparation of the material from what we have called the 'proto-material' of the piece, and also considerable freedom for the selection, curtailment and use of the work in other pieces he wrote in later years. This 'aleatoricism' was to assume very great importance in some subsequent works of Maderna, as we shall observe later.

Maderna composed two works in 1961, *Serenata III* and *Serenata IV*, in which the relationship with instrumental composition is expressed in different ways. *Serenata III* employed the recorded sounds of two instruments, marimbaphone and flute, subjecting the initial material to manipulation such as speed-change, montage and echo-effects, but retaining a clearly instrumental form. He said of this work:

> 'It is a composition made only from the sounds of marimbaphone and flute, in which the musical form and the technical interest are based upon proceeding from a short sound of a percussive character (that of the marimba) to a long sound of an expressive and interpreted character (the sound of the flute). The form recalls that of the prelude, but it is conceived in this case as a transmutation of the sound-material'[9]

If we accept Maderna's description of the work as a kind of prelude, we might perhaps think of an analogy with the *Ricercari* of earlier Italian composers such as Frescobaldi, in which the initial musical material, in the form of melodic figures, is treated to a process of elaboration by contrapuntal and fugal means; here, Maderna seems to suggest that he was attempting to elaborate the initial recorded material in a similarly 'rhapsodic' but equally 'organised' manner by the electronic means which he employs in the Studio.

Serenata IV, on the other hand, attempted an integration of music on tape and live performance, along the lines which Maderna had already explored in the two works called *Musica su due dimensioni*: unfortunately, we no longer possess the score and instrumental parts of this work, but only the recording of the first (and presumably only) performance, given in Darmstadt during the 1961 Summer School under the composer's direction. The precise instrumental layout of the work may only be deduced from this recording, but, as in the two works already mentioned, great prominence is given to the solo flute. The tape part itself was prepared by Maderna during work in the Milan Studio in preparation for his radio opera *Don Perlimplin*, and the material for this work therefore provided the basic material also for *Serenata IV*. Francesca Magnani has deduced from listening to the recording of the work the provenance of all the material in other works of the same period. [10]

It is thus clear that in the two *Serenatas* composed by Maderna in 1961, instrumental and electronic thought are brought into a close proximity: in the first, by the basis of the material in instrumental sounds elaborated by means of tape-manipulation; in the second, by the employment of instrumental material in live performance which had its origins in other works of the period, and by the elaboration of instrumental material for *Don Perlimplin* in the tape-part of the *Serenata*.

Following the production of the two *Serenatas* in 1961, Maderna worked in the Studio on the preparation of the tape-parts for inclusion in the *Komposition* for oboe, chamber ensemble and tape (the 'original version' of the *Oboe Concerto No 1*) and for the radiophonic opera *Don Perlimplin*, both works produced in 1962: these works will be discussed later. However, one very important work on tape which was performed for the first time in Berlin in September 1964 deserves special attention: this was *Le Rire*, whose significance lies not so much in the work itself as in its importance as an integral part of the various versions of *Hyperion*.

It is possible that the original title of *Le Rire* was to have been *Ritratto di Marino Zuccheri* ('Portrait of Marino Zuccheri', the presence of whom as technical assistant in the Milan Studio was a constant source of help to Maderna), or possibly that the latter should be read as a sub-title to the work. Whatever its title, the work was given in different forms during Maderna's lifetime, sometimes as a purely electronic work, sometimes in combination with live performance (but with varying instrumental contribution), and sometimes incorporating instrumental performance on tape alongside the electronic element. In the first performance in Berlin in September 1964 (which was, unfortunately, not recorded), it was described as '*Le Rire* with flute, marimba and tape', whilst for performances given in Venice in 1966 and Rome in 1968 it became simply '*Le Rire* for tape'. Amongst Maderna's manuscripts examined by Tiziano Popoli[11] were found two sets of instrumental parts marked *Le Rire*, the first containing parts for flute and piccolo, the second parts for piccolo and xylophone. We can not now be certain whether these parts were used for any particular performances of *Le Rire*, but Maderna did integrate some of this material in the tapes which he prepared for the performance of *Hyperion en het Geweld* (the second staged version of *Hyperion* given in Brussels in 1968): here, a tape called *Le Rire* included a piccolo part corresponding to part of this manuscript material, and a further tape called *Introduzione* incorporated a flute melody also found in the manuscripts.

Luigi Rognoni states that it was he who suggested the title *Le Rire*, basing it upon the title of an essay by Bergson[12] in which the philosopher wrote of the origins of laughter. Rognoni says that:

> 'I remember how *Le Rire* was born, in 1962, the last of Bruno's compositions of that period. He had recorded the voice of Marino Zuccheri and then elaborated it with sinusoidal sounds, filtering and superimposition. When I heard it, I said to him that it seemed to me a demonstration of the definition which Bergson gave of laughter: 'Quelque chose de mecanique plaquée sur du vivant'. So, he said, we shall call it *Le Rire*'[13]

This 'superimposing something mechanical upon something living' does reflect that element in *Le Rire* in which the 'human' aspect of real sounds (everyday noises and the human voice) become subjected to interference from 'mechanistic' aspects (produced electronically), and this provides a further involvement of the work in the two dimensions already seen in earlier works.

In *Le Rire*, Maderna attempted to integrate sounds of varying kinds (vocal, concrete, instrumental and electronic in origin) into a structure: within the framework of the whole piece, which lasts 16'01", we may detect a gradual shift from the initial rather chaotic and fragmentary sounds, which are concrete or vocal in type, to the more organised sounds of the end of the work, in which instrumental sounds (of the timpani) come to dominate:

1. 0–1' circa: minute fragments, lasting less than a second, consisting of vocal sounds and concrete noises (dropping and scraping of metallic objects, with many spaces between the sounds),
2. 1'–5' circa: introduction of electronic sounds, mainly sinosoidal in origin, interspersed between the spaces of the tiny vocal fragments,
3. 5'–11' circa: some vocal 'screeches' and, particularly, water sounds (not

running water, but water being poured or waved by hand) alternating with vocal/electronic/concrete sounds; the water sounds fade as more sustained sinusoidal sounds come to the fore, often in descending/ascending pitch-shapes,

4. 11′–16′ circa: electronic sounds of a distinctly 'bell-like' kind (metallic and with a fairly definite pitch), accompanied by the sound of timpani (at least four, with some occasional chromatic sliding); no further vocal or concrete sounds appear and the work ends with the timpani alone, gradually accelerating in rhythmic excitement.

In this manner, Maderna structured what was in other respects a very free and improvisational fantasy of mixed sounds; he did this without recourse to any overt poetic or narrative framework, a framework which was to provide such an important part of the formal organisation of some later works on tape, particularly *From A to Z* and *Ages*.

Le Rire became an important element in several of Maderna's later works of various kinds: we may summarise its employment in these works in the following way:

(a) **Hyperion:** In the Venice production of this work, the second episode of *Le Rire* (which Maderna later simply called *Introduzione*) was used in Scene 3.
    In Brussels (*Hyperion en het Geweld*), this *Introduzione* was used in Scene 1 ('Ouverture'), and possibly also in Scenes 2 ('Film: Popeya') and 8 ('Scena delle sentinelle'). In Bologne (*Hyperion – Orfeo Dolente*), *Introduzione* is used similarly in Episodes I and IV.

(b) **Venetian Journal:** amongst the nine taped sections which form part of this work, fragments which are evidently from the first episode of *Le Rire*, (particularly vocal, percussion and water sounds) are used in Tapes 5–9.

(c) **Satyricon:** the fifth of the five tapes used in this work include similar fragments from *Le Rire*, on which are superimposed bird-sounds and the barking of dogs.

It is evident from this that Maderna came to employ some sections of *Le Rire* in later years in a dramatic or narrative context: it was as though the 'realism' and also the 'fantasy' which characterised the substance of the original work provided the composer with a rich fund of material from which to draw in the varied tapestry of musical styles and references which became an essential element in some of the composer's later works.

Although Maderna spent a good deal of time from 1955 onwards in the Studio di Fonologia Musicale in Milan, preparing those works through which his fame as a composer of electronic music spread throughout Europe, this by no means exhausted his compositional activity at that time. The period from 1950 to 1962 also saw the production of a number of very important works in traditional vocal and instrumental media: *Studi per 'Il Processo' di Kafka* (1950) *Quattro Lettere* (1953), *Serenata No 2* (1954/1957), *Quartetto in due tempi* (1955), and *Honeyrêves* (1962).

Maderna's day-to-day existence during the early 1950s was somewhat precarious. He had spent a couple of years teaching basic subjects at the Venice Conservatoire (having been recommended to this post by Malipiero, then its Director), and had a number of private pupils, but he also had to take on whatever musical (or indeed non-musical) jobs which presented themselves: he composed a great deal of light music for theatres, for radio and for films, and he occasionally worked as a night-porter and electrician in Milan. Berio and Maderna sometimes worked together in four-handed manner in the composition or arrangement of scores for such light music, Berio composing the string-parts while Maderna was simultaneously busy with the wind parts, with a copyist at their side awaiting the pages of score to copy.[14]

It is evident that Maderna nevertheless had ambitious plans: he had begun in 1950, during the period in which he was composing the group of orchestral compositions which we examined earlier, to make preparations for a stage-work to be based upon Franz Kafka's novel *The Trial*,[15] including the assembly of large sections of a possible libretto and some staging-indications. The plan did not prove entirely fruitless: he had to modify considerably the idea of a work for the stage, no doubt because the likelihood of a production, whether in Italy or elsewhere, was fairly remote, but no doubt also because he was not yet able to cope with the demands of such an ambitious plan. We can only conjecture about the nature of the stage-work which might have resulted, but the work which was eventually to appear, *Studi per 'Il Processo' di Kafka* ('Studies for Kafka's *The Trial*') is nevertheless of considerable interest in itself.

Dallapiccola's second opera *Il Prigioniero* ('The Prisoner') composed under very difficult circumstances during the later war-years and produced with great success in Turin in 1949, had given a considerable impetus to Italian musical drama and, although there is no evidence of common musical ground between Maderna's *Studi . . .* and Dallapiccola's work, we can see some similarities between the two works on a dramatic level. Both are based around a small group of characters in a situation of close dependence: in *Il Prigioniero*, the Prisoner himself, his Jailer, Grand Inquisitor, and his Mother, with the Prisoner offered an illusory freedom which is then shown to be another and greater torture; in *Studi . . .* , Josef K. is entrapped within a mechanistic process of the Law whose workings are hidden from him, and only his friend Leni offers, or seems to offer, an escape-route in his predicament. Both works present a dramatic scene in which the darkness in which the protagonist finds himself is penetrated by a shaft of light, and in which the threat from external forces operates, as it seems, almost independently of any human intervention.

In Maderna's work the presentation of the drama is made in a highly original manner: Josef K. does not appear, but his situation is simply described by a narrator at the opening of the work:

' . . . It was absolutely necessary for K. to intervene personally. In states of intense exhaustion, such as he experienced this winter morning, when all these thoughts kept running at random through his head, he was particularly incapable of resisting this conviction. The contempt which he had once felt for the case was no longer justified. Had he stood alone in the world he could easily have ridiculed the whole affair, though it was also certain that in that event it could never have arisen at all. But now his uncle had dragged him to this Advocate, family considerations had come in; his position was no longer quite independent of the course the case took, he was in the middle of it and must look to himself.'

This 'elliptical' manner of presenting the predicament in which Josef K. is tightly bound is, of course, in complete contrast to the 'heroic' manner in which Dallapiccola's Prisoner presents himself: Maderna clearly wished to delineate the dramatic situation of his protagonist by outlining it in terms of the forces which come to bear upon him (the intractibility of the inhuman legal process, and the consolation which appears to be offered by Leni), rather than by Josef K's own self-expression. What is presented in the dramatic framework of the *Studi . . .* is therefore a triangular interdependence of Man–Woman–Law, in which Josef K. is himself 'mute'. Leni, the 'guardian angel' in Maderna's work, is therefore in some senses an inner voice for the protagonist, and also perhaps a parallel to the Mother in *Il Prigioniero;* in the musical expression of her part, Maderna lays considerable emphasis upon a lyrical expressivity which is wordless, but which communicates its powerful emotion in a manner which is clearly indebted to Alban Berg. This can be seen in the *Tempo di Wiegenlied,* in which the figure of Marie in Berg's *Wozzeck* (a similar figure of both comfort and provocation in her relationship to the protagonist of that opera) is lightly invoked.[Ex. 2.13]

Ex. 2.13: Maderna: *Studi per 'Il Processo' di Kafka:* 'Wiegenlied'

The *Studi . . .* is therefore a work of considerable power, a 'dramatic cantata' in effect, in which important elements appear which in later years were to assume considerable significance in Maderna's work. A somewhat similar triangular relationship will appear when, some fourteen years later, he composed *Hyperion*: here, the 'mechanistic forces' become a grotesque and gigantic Machine on stage, from which electronic sounds are emitted; the 'mute protagonist' becomes the Artist struggling for self-expression through the flute of Severino Gazzelloni; the 'comforting woman' becomes a soprano *Aria*, appearing suddenly both to express the inner doubts of the Artist and at the same time to offer the consolation of lyrical expression.

The *String Quartet* which Maderna composed in 1955, and which the Drolc Quartet performed in Darmstadt in June of that year, is the work of Maderna's from that period which has received the most critical attention. It was dedicated to Berio, whose own *String Quartet* was composed at the same time with a reciprocal dedication, and formed a significant part of the discussion of Maderna's works in the article written by Giacomo Manzoni for *Die Reihe* in 1958; it has been analysed by Horst Weber, on the basis of the differences between the manuscript and the inaccurate published score, in an essay written in 1978.[16]

Berio has commented on more than one occasion about the significance of Maderna's *String Quartet*, and it is clear that it was this work more than any other of Maderna's which had an impact on the younger composer. Berio has written of the significance for Maderna of the use of strict numerical procedures which performed a generative function in his composition, and stated that:

> ' . . . The 'machine' came to the aid of the musician, and from that moment Bruno took hold of that material and transformed it. In fact, one of Bruno's works which is dear to my heart, partly because it was written more or less at my side, is the *String Quartet*, where in the first part this permutational machine, appearing as a rather rigid, sparkling and largely immobile object, is set out. In the second part this same object is transformed and re-invented. Bruno here opens up spaces, changes intensities, enlarges the proportions and reveals the melodic characters. This means that he alters things in such a way that the rigid body heard in the first part becomes something different, like a face which is immobile and stiff in one expression, finally beginning to articulate and to express different emotions. The dialectic between these two moments is very suggestive.'[17]

The *String Quartet* of Maderna is of great importance in the composer's work as a whole in revealing to us the intricacy and subtlety of Maderna's musical thought. In this work, the two elements of compositional rigour and of imaginative fantasy are held in a finely-judged balance, those elements which Berio has called the 'machine' and its 'transformation'. In no other work did Maderna adopt any comparable degree of strictness in the form-building of the whole composition (he was, much later, to express the greatest disdain for what he called 'consistency', which he saw as a dead hand in artistic creation), but this 'machine' is present as a catalyst in the development of structures whose profile is eventually free and uninhibited.

The work's primary series is one which already contains a certain degree of consistency: based on four groups of three pitches, of which the first employs

perfect fourths, the remaining three minor thirds, this series will be employed in
varying forms throughout the entire work. [Ex. 2.14] From this series, Maderna
then constructed, by free permutation of its components, a group of twelve
variants (A–N), in which vertical intervals appeared up to a maximum of three
pitches, all but two commencing with the pitch B and all ending with pitches from
the fourth 'module' of the original series. [Ex. 2.15]

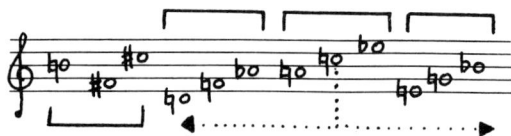

Ex. 2.14: Maderna: *String Quartet*: series

Ex. 2.15: Maderna: *String Quartet*: serial derivatives

The manner of presentation of the series may be observed in the appearance of
the prime series in the opening bars of the work: the series A is given out in a
continuous flow between all four instruments in such a way that the duration of
each pitch is determined by the intervallic progression, rhythmic values in 32 ndth
-notes equal to semitonal movement around the axis on the pitch C. [Ex. 2.16] The
composer adopts a strict ordering of presentation of the various series from A to
N, with some overlapping, whilst a parallel presentation beginning on the final
pitch Eb of N is also heard and progresses in the reverse direction. [Ex. 2.17(a), (b)]

In this manner, the formal shape of the work is determined in both pitch and
rhythmic aspects (Maderna adopts varying rhythmic values as units for
multiplication in later presentations of the series, but the underlying principle
remains unchanged), but one should also note that his adoption in the work of
principles of 'integral serialism' is circumscribed, limited to these two parameters:

tone-colour elements remain free, and the dynamic element is employed simply to give the maximum clarity to the presentation of each successive entry of the series. The canonic principles which, as we have seen, permeated Maderna's thinking in his earlier serial compositions, are here applied to the whole work, and at strategic points in the first movement the 'prime series' A re-appears as a kind of 'theme' in clear relief (bars 1, 100, 141 and 172).

Ex. 2.16: Maderna: *String Quartet*: pitch and duration series

The large-scale organisation of the work is based upon the ordering of presentations of the series A to N: in the first movement, we hear four cycles A–N, plus an incomplete cycle A–D; at the same time, there is a cycle of the reverse presentation N–A plus a similarly 'incomplete' N–E. The second movement, in which the whole of the first is retrograded in entirety, is so constructed that it completes the symmetry left open at the end of the first movement:

I: [A–N] [A–N] [A–N] [A–D]
       (R)[N–A] [N–E]

II: [E–N] [A–N] [A–N] [A–N]
       (R)[E–N] [A–N] [A–N] [A–N]

The comments which Berio made about the 'machine', the process of strict permutation and ordering, are therefore clearly seen to work with great precision and clarity in the work as a whole. His comments upon the relationship of the two movements of the work, with the second 'opening up spaces, changing intensities, enlarging the proportions and revealing the melodic characters' are of equal significance in the nature of the composition: this can be seen clearly if we place side-by-side two passages each from one of the movements, each sharing with the other the reversal of procedure which we have already observed. The passages in question are bars 100 to 130 of the first movement, bars 70 to 100 of the second: here the greater articulative expression of the second passage can clearly be observed, with each motivic element placed in greater relief and with clarity given by repetitions and by spacing-out and silences. [Ex. 2.18(a)–(d)]

Maderna was never to return to the 'consistency' of content and form which we see in the *String Quartet*. He was, as a composer, ready to investigate in a wholehearted and thorough manner all the aspects of compositional behaviour

Ex. 2.17(a): Maderna: *String Quartet*: I: 1–26

which the 'New Music' of the time gave rise to, but it is of great significance that his 'interpretation' of the principles of integral serialism which we see in his *String Quartet* moved strongly in the direction of imaginative expressivity, towards, in fact, an interpretation which revealed 'two dimensions' in instrumental composition as much as he had already revealed in his compositions on tape.

Serenata No 2 for 11 instruments is a work of quite extraordinary character, and reveals to us the way in which Maderna created a musical language of particular subtlety and expressivity during the early 1950s. It is in no way connected with the earlier 'lost' *Serenata* which had been performed in Venice in 1946: although both works were written for 11 instruments, it is clear from the programme-notes of the

Ex. 2.17(a): *Contd*

1946 performance that their constitution differed somewhat, and that in form and style the two works diverged radically. A further confusion arises from the fact that the later *Serenata* was published in two versions, the first in 1954 by Hermann Scherchen's 'Ars Viva' Edition as *Serenata – Komposition No. 3*, the second by Suvini Zerboni in 1957. The first version was given only one performance, in Darmstadt in April 1956, whilst the 'revised' version has been frequently played and recorded.

The 1954 version had been dedicated to Scherchen, but this was removed from the subsequent revision: it appears that Maderna had not been able to obtain a contract for its publication from Scherchen, as the composer mentioned in a letter to Berio.[18] The divergences between the two versions of the work are of some importance, and may be seen in the following table:

Ars Viva version	Suvini Zerboni version
Moderato (1–80)	$\mathbf{d} = 108$ ca. (*un poco liberamente*) (1–80)
Scherzando (81–168)	*Scherzando* (81–142)
Allegro (169–194)	*Allegro alla Danza* (143–158)
Allegro alla Danza (195–210)	*Allegro*) (159–182)
Maestoso (211–215)	
Allegro (216–239)	
Meno Mosso (240–264)	*Meno Mosso* (183–207
Ancor Meno Mosso (256–327)	*Ancora Meno Mosso*

Ex. 2.17(b): Maderna: *String Quartet*: I: 1–26: analysis

Ex. 2.18(a): Maderna: *String Quartet*: I: 100–130

Ex. 2.18(a): *Contd*

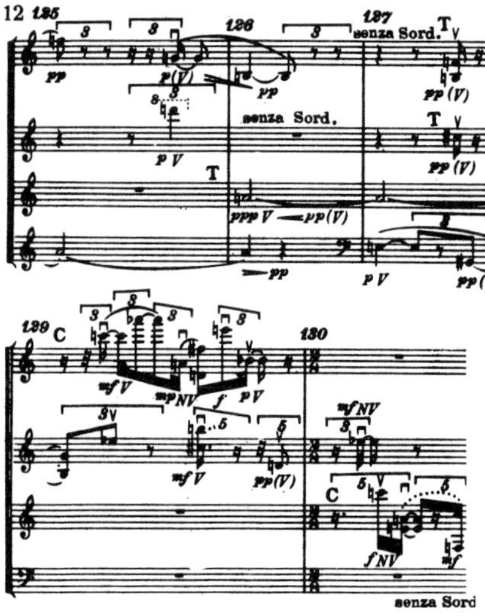

Ex. 2.18(a): *Contd*

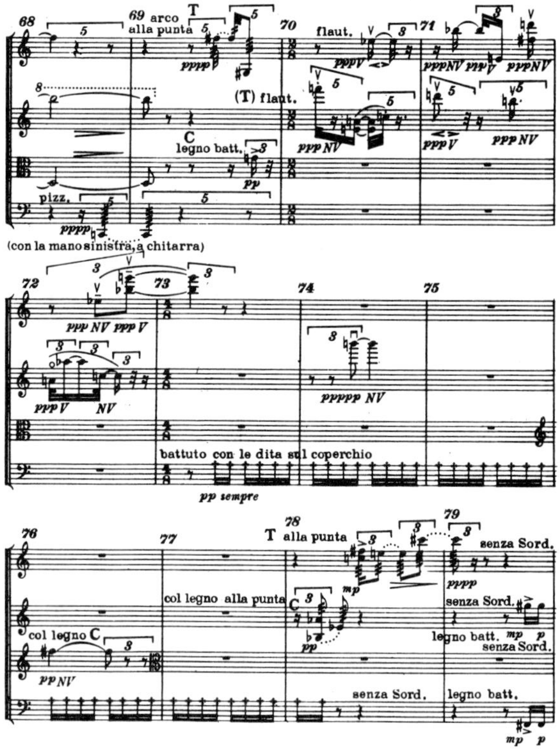

Ex. 2.18(b): Maderna: *String Quartet*: II: 70–100

Ex. 2.18(b): *Contd*

Ex. 2.18(c): Maderna: *String Quartet*: I: 100–130: analysis

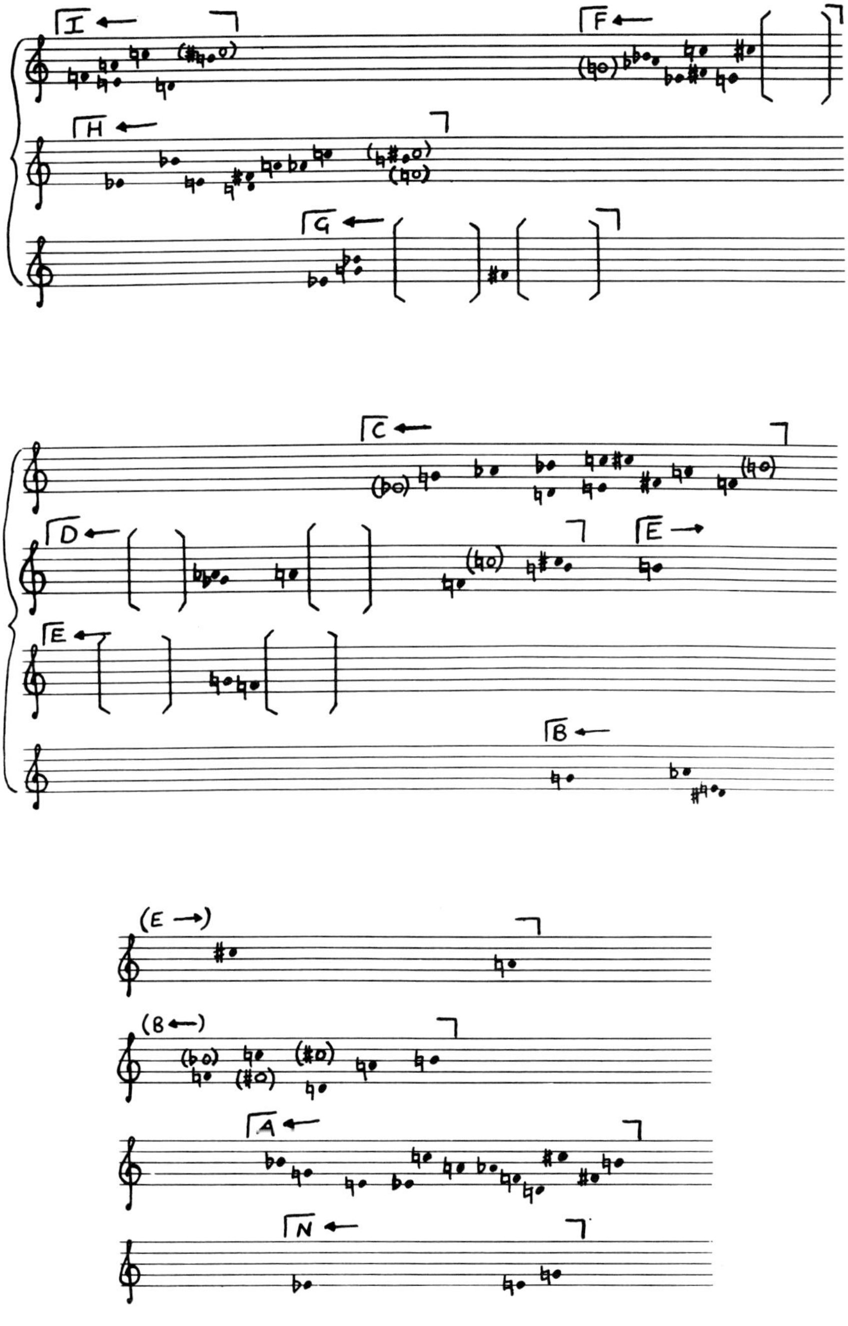

Ex. 2.18(d): Maderna: *String Quartet*: II: 70–100: analysis

In *Serenata No 2*, the element of 'neo-classical' reference which we observed in several earlier compositions becomes fully integrated with Maderna's serial thinking: the resultant work is one of great wit and charm, in keeping with the eighteenth-century models. Around this period, several Italian composers engaged in the writing of works of a *Serenata*-type, including Berio (1957), Petrassi (1958), Donatoni (1959) and Fellegara (1960): in each case, an attempt was made to bring to the fore the 'traditional Italianate lyricism' within a work cast in serial mould.

Maderna's *Serenata No. 2* is in a single continuous movement, in common with virtually all of his instrumental compositions, but it is clearly articulated in sections. The series employed is set out right at the start by the piccolo and clarinet: this 11-note series omits Bb (in the same way that the composer had omitted the 'complementary' group Bb-A-C-Bb in the opening passages of both the *Fantasia* and *Concerto* some years earlier), and the final note is reserved for an entry in the Allegro section from bar 159. The quality of the series which is most striking is the use of consonant diatonic steps and, in the last four pitches, of whole-tone progression, and in this it might be said to be similar to that employed by Alban Berg in his *Violin Concerto* [Ex. 2.19]

Ex. 2.19: Maderna: *Serenata No. 2*: 1–10

The very relaxed flow of this melody, like that of the 'Tema Greco in Modo Frigio' at the opening of *Composizione No. 2*, is maintained through the whole episode, and the unchanging series (used initially only in its prime version, and without any transposition) is treated as a '*cantus firmus*', with constantly changing instrumental sonorities. The presentation is canonic, with some occasional displacement of pitches within each appearance of the series. [Ex. 2.20(a), (b)]

Ex. 2.20(a): Maderna: *Serenata No. 2*: 1–40

This treatment of the series, with a constantly clear reference to the melodic characteristics of the opening solo and with the '*Klangfarbenmelodie*' of a sharply-defined instrumental group, appears not as one of highly-charged serial Expressionism, but rather, as a cool and graceful canon or chaconne, a reference back to the world of Baroque and Classical formality. Canonic forms had played a considerable part in Maderna's work already, in the works of the late 1940s, and there can be little doubt that Maderna's predilection for such forms arose from his studies of Renaissance and Baroque music with Malipiero. The harmony created by the superimposition of the canonic layers one above another emphasises the consonant intervals of major seconds, perfect fourths and fifths, and minor thirds: dissonance is rare, and arises quite naturally from occasional conflict between the canonic strands.

We observed earlier how Maderna, in the years during which he was composing the series of orchestral works between 1948 and 1954, had adopted the device of references to dance-forms such as the Waltz, Can-Can and Rumba, and how such explicit references gradually became less necessary as his style evolved between *Composizione No. 1* and *Improvvisazione No. 2*. In the *Serenata No. 2*, the variety of texture, rhythm and character which he is able to employ within the overall serial language is such that, without recourse to explicit reference to the various moods and dance-types which are to be found in the eighteenth-century Serenade or Divertimento, he is nevertheless able to integrate an extremely subtle variegation of musical 'characters' within this single-movement work. At bar 81,

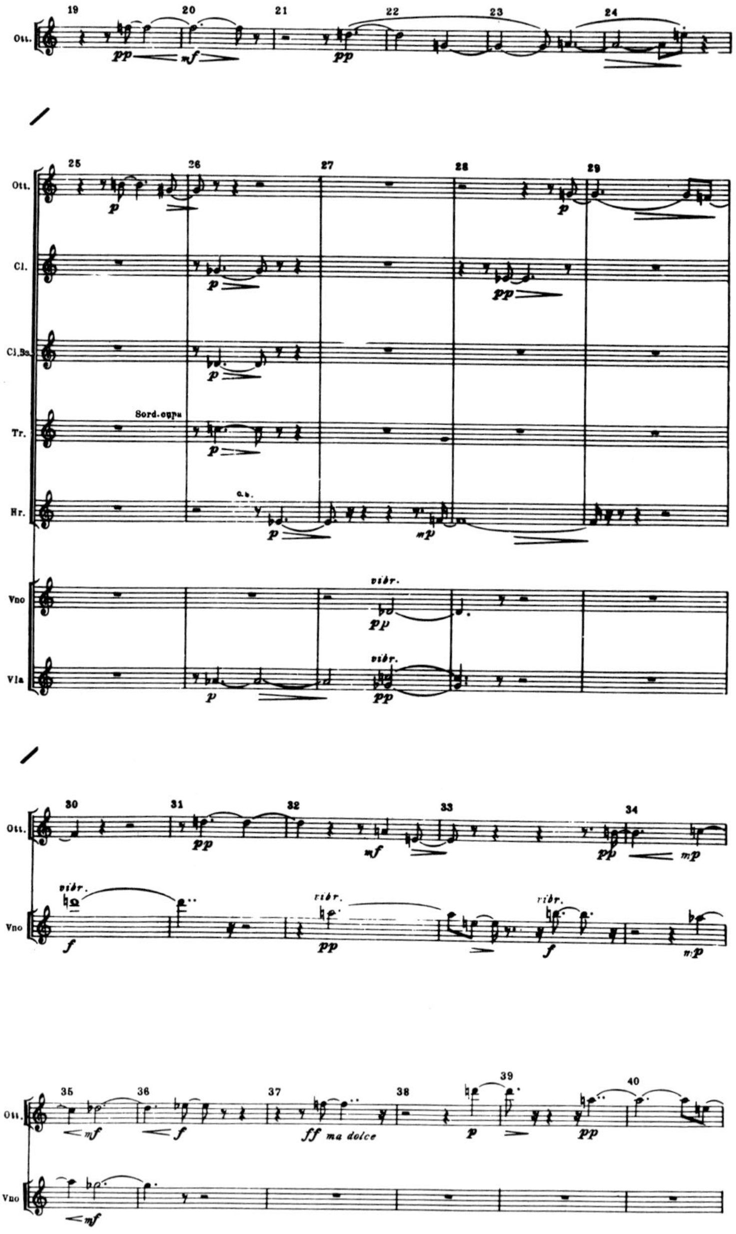

Ex. 2.20(a): *Contd*

Ex. 2.20(b): Maderna: *Serenata No. 2*: analysis

for example, a '*Scherzando*' episode whose staccato and 'pointillistic' character is derived perhaps from that of the 'Rumba' in *Composizione No. 2*, disperses the intervallic form of the initial series, whilst the '*Allegro alla Danza*' beginning in bar 143 throws into high relief groups of repeated-note figures in duplet, triplet and quadruplet form within an episode of light-hearted character. [Ex. 2.21]

One of the most important ways in which Maderna varies the character of the episodes in *Serenata No 2* is to be found in the passage from bar 159 in which the restless, nervous energy of constantly-changing perspective in the '*Allegro alla Danza*' is replaced by more slow-moving harmony, with a gradually evolving chordal movement throwing into high relief the varying colours of each instrument in tiny '*ostinati*' based upon single-note or at most two-note groups in harp, piano, vibraphone and xylophone. [Ex. 2.22]

By the time that Maderna composed *Honeyrêves* for flute and piano in 1961, a considerable broadening of what we might describe as the 'sound-spectrum' of his instrumental thinking had taken place. This work was first performed by Severino Gazzelloni and Frederic Rzewski at a concert in Venice in April 1962, and the title is a backward-reading of the flautist's name in combination with a 'descriptive' title (Severino = Honeyrêves = 'Sweet Dreams'). The dedicatee of the title had occupied a position of considerable importance in the development of the flute's possibilities in the language of the 'New Music', and Maderna had

Ex. 2.21: Maderna: *Serenata No. 2*: 143–148

already composed for him a *Flute Concerto* in 1954 as well as the *Musica su due dimensioni* in 1952 and 1958.

The enlarged sonic spectrum is applied to both instruments, and this is revealed right at the start of the work, where the flute solo is a miniature compendium of what became known as 'Gazzelloni-music', with rapid changes of dynamic and character, *glissandi*, and detailed indications of *vibrato* and non-*vibrato*; the piano, in the passage which follows, makes use of string-*glissandi*, clusters, and plucked strings. [Ex. 2.23]

The main central section of the work, occupying some 49 bars, consists of a rapid crossfire of motivic ideas between the two instruments, and here the echoing of motives between the flute and piano assumes a conversational character. Once again, plucked strings and string-harmonics, as well as flutter-tonguing in flute, form an essential part of the instrumental sound. [Ex. 2.24] The final page of the

Ex. 2.21: *Contd*

score introduces the pianist's touching of the already-vibrating string with a metal beater, and the flute's alternation of fluttering and harmonics, as the music reaches back to the 'improvisational' freedoms with which it had begun. [Ex. 2.25]

During the 1950s, Maderna became established as one of the leading figures of the generation of composers whose works had begun to appear in the post-war period, and in both instrumental and tape composition, his importance grew from a group of works whose inspiration was of the highest degree of originality. Through the orchestral compositions of 1948–1954, the works on tape beginning with *Notturno* in 1957, and the *String Quartet, Serenata* and *Honeyrêves*, Maderna's 'voice' came to be known as one capable of great variety, subtlety and expressivity in the New Music.

His involvement in parallel explorations of instrumental and of electronic compositioin was, and remained, a *unified* one, and we can in fact see some of the same concerns in both aspects of his work. We have observed a large degree of

Ex. 2.22: Maderna: *Serenata No. 2*: 159–166

interpenetration of instrumental and tape works at this time, and in works such as *Musica su due dimensioni*, *Serenata III* and *Serenata IV*, the presence of an 'instrumental' element, whether real or else implied, in the sound palette of each work was an essential element in their fabric.

We can also see, in the nature of both instrumental and electronic works of the 1950s, some common concerns in the musical thinking. In both, an *episodic* construction is very often apparent, a tendency to demarcate passages of one character from those of another contrasting one, each episode becoming an exploration of specific materials, whether of instrumental or electronic sound. *Material* and *organisation* are closely related, not in either case as pre-conceived 'methods' of working, but rather, as a tendency to formulate material of a highly-charged variety in each part of a work, and to elaborate this material fully and freely within a specific episode.

The composer might be said to have worked from 'moment to moment' within a work, and the elaboration of sound-materials or else of intervallic or other properties is pursued with the highest degree of imaginative fantasy. We can see

Ex. 2.22: *Contd*

this in operation for example in the opening episode of *Serenata No 2*, in which the 'quasi-canonic' treatment of a fixed series is pursued towards greater and greater density, giving way eventually to the quicksilver '*scherzando*' of kaleidoscopic tone-colour changes. We can observe it equally in the progression of material of greater or lesser 'density' in *Continuo*, all of which arise from a single electronically-produced sound-source.

Maderna stated that his contact with music on tape 'caused a real revolution in my relationship with the materials of music', and welcomed the possibility that the composer could work *directly* on the sound of a composition: perhaps within the context of his dual exploration of the traditional and newer media we might suggest that the enrichment of the sound-resources with which he was able to work broadened the possibilities for musical expression in the same way that his expressive vocabulary was enriched by the possibilities offered by serialism. Maderna was one of the pioneers of the new sounds and their manipulation, not least in their integration with, and placement alongside, traditional media. His

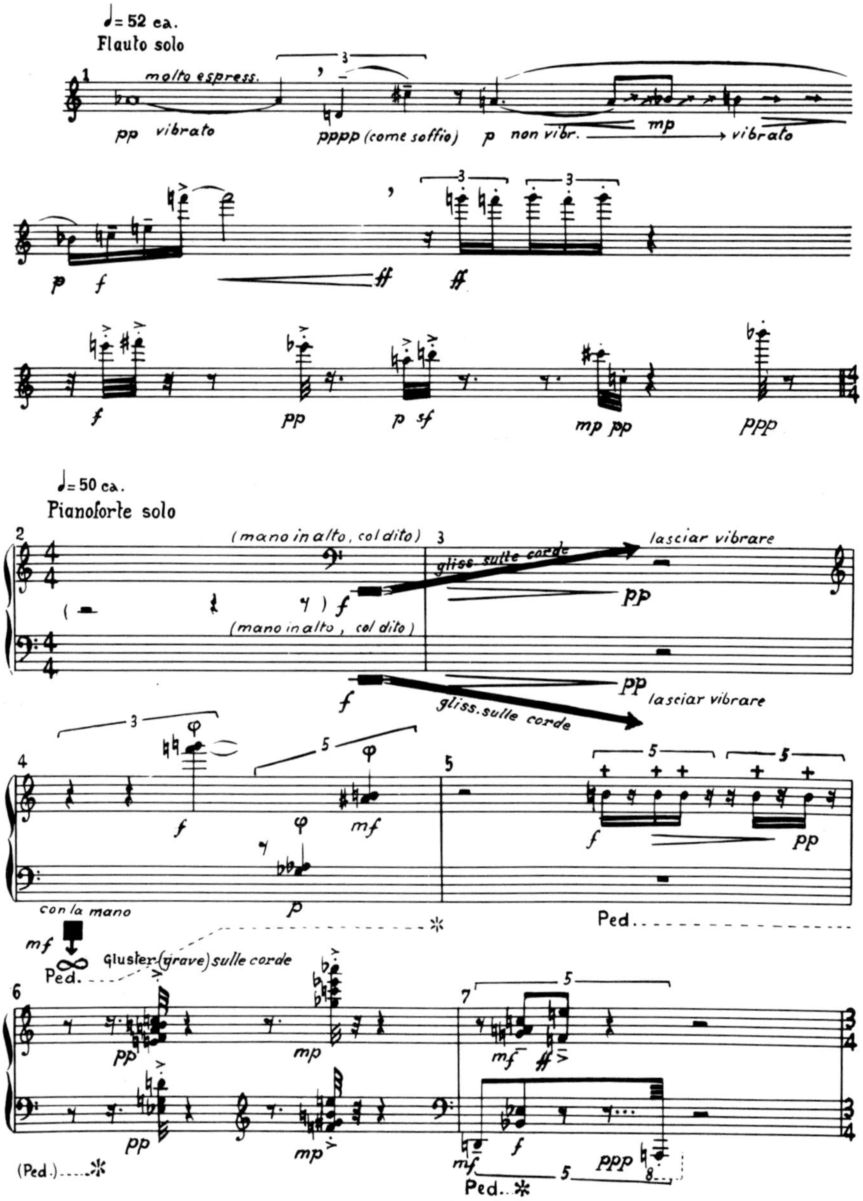

Ex. 2.23: Maderna: *Honeyrêves*: 1–7

Ex. 2.24: Maderna: *Honeyrêves*: 10–21

production of works on tape was to diminish sharply after about 1962, only to re-appear in a group of works on tape in his last years which included the 'radiophonic invention' *Ages*, a work which might with some justification be regarded as his masterpiece in this genre.

Notes to Chapter 2

1. *Baroni/Dalmonte* op. cit. p. 197.
2. idem p. 85.
3. idem p. 205.
4. idem p. 84.
5. idem p. 84.
6. idem p. 225.
7. *Berio: Two Interviews*, publ. Marion Boyars, New-York-London 1985, p. 114.
8. *Baroni/Dalmonte* op. cit., p. 229.
9. idem p. 231.
10. idem p. 232.
11. idem pp. 243–4.
12. Henri *Bergson: Le Rire*, translated as *Laughter, An Essay on the Meaning of the Comic:* Macmillan, London, 1911.
13. *Baroni/Dalmonte* op. cit., p. 150.
14. *Berio*: op. cit., p. 64.
15. *Baroni/Dalmonte*: op. cit., pp. 200–201.
16. 'Die Reihe' No. 4 'Young Composers', pp. 114–120; Horst *Weber: Form und Satztechnik in Bruno Madernas Streichquartett* in *Miscellanea del Cinquantenario*: Suvini Zerboni, Milan 1978, pp. 206–215.
17. *Baroni/Dalmonte*, op. cit., p. 128.
18. *Baroni/Dalmonte*, op. cit., p. 216.

E

Ex. 2.24: *Contd*

Ex. 2.25: Maderna: *Honeyrêves*: 60

Chapter 3

Dramatic enterprises — Maderna's conception of the
stage — *Don Perlimplin; Hyperion; Aria.*

It had perhaps been clear from the nature of Maderna's musical thinking right from the start that poetic or dramatic expression would be an essential part of his creative work. He had not produced any significant vocal works since the *Tre Liriche Greche* of 1948 with the exception of a small cantata for solo voices and ensemble, the *Quattro Lettere (Kranichsteiner Kammerkantate)* of 1953 but as we have seen works such as *Ritratto di Città, Le Rire* and *Dimensioni II/Invenzione su una voce* had incorporated poetic or quasi-verbal gestures in the fabric of their musical make-up. However, it was not to be until the creation, in 1962 and 1964 respectively, of *Don Perlimplin* and *Hyperion* that Maderna succeeded in establishing a framework for dramatic expression which enabled his very free, mobile conception of the 'musical stage' to be fully expressed. Both of these works were cast in modes which were at some distance from the traditional operatic stage: *Don Perlimplin* as a 'radiophonic opera', *Hyperion* as a Music Theatre work (which the composer described as a *'lirica in forma di spettacolo'*, 'poem in stage-form').

Don Perlimplin, ovvero Il Trionfo dell'Amore e dell'Invenzione, was prepared in the Studio di Fonologia Musicale in Milan Radio, and broadcast on 12th August 1962, winning the Italia Prize for radio-presentation for that year. This work owes its conception, and indeed its very nature, to the medium of radio, and represents a culmination of much of the work which the composer had done in the Studio during the previous eight years, beginning with a similarly radiophonic venture in *Ritratto di Città* in 1954.

Maderna employed for the text of *Don Perlimplin* a *'ballata amorosa'* ('love-ballad') by Federico Garcia Lorca in the Italian translation of Vittorio Bodini: the play had originally been written in 1928, but was not performed in Spain during the Rivera dictatorship because it was felt that the portrayal of Don Perlimplin as an Army officer who is 'cuckolded' would be subversive, and it was therefore only given in a theatrical club in Madrid in 1933. The form of the play is that of an *'entremes'* (*intermezzo*), a traditional form of short comedy given between the acts of a more serious play, a form which in the time of Cervantes had often appeared in puppet-play guise (a medium also cultivated by Lorca, who had its own puppet-theatre). *Don Perlimplin* is in fact a play with all the characteristics of the popular farce of earlier times, and the original sub-title was 'The Love of Don Perlimplin and Belisa in the Garden: an Erotic Alleluia in Four Scenes and a Prologue'.

Maderna arranged Lorca's play into four *'Quadri'*, preceded by an Introduction and a Prologue, and carefully edited the text of the play in order to maintain as far as possible the lines of its action. This action concerns the confirmed bachelor Don Perlimplin, whose housekeeper Marcolfa encourages him to take as his wife the young girl Belisa; when they are married, Belisa receives love-letters from an anonymous stranger asking her to meet him in the garden in the evening; when she meets him, it is none other than her husband Don Perlimplin, who kills himself, thus gaining the 'Triumph of Love and Imagination' of which the sub-title of the work speaks.

It was perhaps this strangely complex and rather forward-looking fusion of farce and tragedy which appealed so much to Maderna, as well perhaps as the very strong musical element which is already present in Lorca's stage-play. Lorca had in fact been more than a dilettante musician: Manuel de Falla had been amongst his music-teachers, and de Falla had provided and played the musical accompaniment for at least one of the puppet-plays produced by Lorca in 1923[1] using music by Debussy, Ravel, Albeniz and Pedrell. De Falla had regarded Lorca as his most promising pupil, and later the poet had not only arranged and composed the music for ballads in the repertoire of 'La Argentinita's' Dance Company, but also the music for songs in some of his own plays. The musicality of Lorca's poetic style has been commented on by many writers, and several of the collections of poetry which he published bear titles which indicate the reliance of his poetic style on a basis in song (*Primeras Canciones* 1922, *Canciones* 1921–4, *Cantares Populares*); the songs which he incorporated in his plays were published as a collection, edited by Gustavo Pittaluga in 1960.[2]

The most important facet of this strange and haunting work is the *radiophonic* nature of the opera. It was not simply that Maderna had received his first opportunity to compose a dramatic work through his close association with Italian Radio, and that this radiophonic aspect is therefore in any sense incidental: rather, it is an inherent element in the dramatic and musical fabric of the work, a work which it would be different to imagine presented in any other form, although this has been attempted on one occasion (in a performance conducted by Elgar Howarth in Cologne in 1975). The 'stage' on which the opera is enacted is that of the listener's aural imagination, and is therefore an eminently mobile one, and it may well be that Maderna's choice of this particular play arose to some extent from its early association with a similarly mobile stage, that of the traditional puppet-play. The composer of a radiophonic opera is offered the possibility of making transitions and superimpositions which would be very much more cumbersome on the normal operatic stage, and Maderna made here the fullest use of these enlarged possibilities.

This re-creation of Lorca's play in radiophonic terms influenced the composer in fundamental ways. It was not simply that he was, through the medium of radio, able to maintain the 'dream-like' nature of the original play (the sensuous suggestiveness, the very rhapsodic and smooth transitions from one scene to another, from one mood to another), but the medium itself offered possibilities for dramatic presentation which would not have been available in any other medium. Thus, the character of Don Perlimplin becomes a non-speaking one, expressing himself simply through Gazzelloni's flute; Belisa sings only twice (a brief '*Amore*', and a '*Canzone*' in which her voice is superimposed polyphonically upon itself); and the Mother-in-Law ('Suocera') appears as a group of saxophones. All of this 'unreal' presentation of the characters in the drama contributes to the 'dream' in which the action takes place. The 'dream' is that of Don Perlimplin himself: the play may be seen as an enactment of his psyche on the stage, and it is therefore important to understand how the composer drew together the disparate elements of the work into a whole which centres upon this main character whose voice is mute in the normally-accepted sense of a dramatic work.

Maderna's first attempt to compose a dramatic work had been the Kafka-plan which we observed in the previous chapter: this plan, eventually modified to a concert-work, contained some elements which were to be transformed and to assume considerable dramatic significance in Maderna's later dramatic works. The mute protagonist, and the lyrically-expressed female rôle both appear in the Kafka work of 1950 as well as in *Don Perlimplin*, and will later become of great importance in the version of *Hyperion* produced in Venice in 1964.

Some two years later, a further dramatic plan was conceived, one which was again not to be realised, but for which we have considerable information regarding its dramatic outlines. This was to have been a *'Ballett-Schauspiel'* (Ballet-Spectacle) called *Das Eiserne Zeitalter* ('The Iron Age'),[3] which Maderna planned with his friends Egon Vietta and Harro Dicks of the Landestheater in Darmstadt; he composed some sections of the music for this work, but did not bring it to completion. It was to be centred on a similarly triangular relationship, this time that of Theseus, Ariadne and the Minotaur, interpreted in a 'modernistic' manner. A chorus was to relate the action, and the text was assembled by Maderna from Hesiod, Sophocles, Rilke and Nietzsche; three speakers would also take part, an 'Author' (dressed as a tourist), a 'Robot' (dressed as a hockey-player, but with the mask of Homer), and 'Lukian' (in ancient costume). The action in the first part of the drama concerns the ensnaring of the Bull by Ariadne: when he is immobilised, other Ariadnes would appear by 'multiplication' (each dressed in one profile as Ariadne, in the other profile as the flowered columns of the Palace of Knossos). When he is presented to Minos for sacrifice, he breaks loose and kills the King, taking his place on the throne. In the second part of the work, Theseus would appear, and his 'multiplication' would cause the construction of a giant Machine.

In 1961, Maderna conceived a further plan for a dance-drama, this time to be based upon *Macbeth*, but this, again, was not realised: there can be little doubt that the composer had begun to see the medium of radio-presentation as that best suited to his free-roaming and essentially fantastic conception of musical drama, and in this way it was almost inevitable that he should, in this same year, turn to this medium for his first fully-realised dramatic enterprise.

Within the dramatic conception of *Don Perlimplin* one of the most important elements is that of the non-speaking protagonist, which, as we have observed, links this work with the Kafka work of some twelve years earlier. In the first dialogue of the work, for example, in which the housekeeper Marcolfa tells Don Perlimplin of the necessity for marriage, Maderna simply suprimposes the words of Marcolfa above part of *Honeyrêves* (*Honeyrêves* bars 53–59: *Don Perlimplin* bars 51–57), with the words of Don Perlimplin added in parenthesis to the score. [Ex. 3.1]

A further element in this 'non-realistic' treatment of character may be seen in the composer's portrayal of the Mother-in-Law (Suocera) in terms of a wind-group comprising flute in G, clarinet, baritone saxophone, three trumpets, electric guitar, marimba and vibraphone: in the Prologue, when Belisa has been 'informed' of the decision of Don Perlimplin regarding their marriage, the

Ex. 3.1: Maderna: *Don Perlimplin*: 51–54

Mother-in-Law waves her greetings to Belisa from a distance without any words being spoken, the music of this wind-group speaking, as it were, on her behalf, repeated similarly in the ensuing passage whenever the Mother-in-Law is referred to [Ex. 3.2]

Belisa herself has little to sing. When she first appears on the scene, and Marcolfa points her out to Don Perlimplin as his future wife, she is heard singing merely the word 'love'. [Ex. 3.3] Later, in a *'Tempo di Rag'*, her *'Amore'* is combined with the 'Suocera Sax' music of the Mother-in-Law as agreement is reached between the girl and her mother about the necessity for the marriage. [Ex. 3.4] When Belisa awaits the arrival of her unknown 'lover' in the garden, she sings 'Upon the banks of the river the passing night paused to bathe, and on the breasts of Belisa the flowers languish of their love . . . ': in this, her voice is superimposed twice upon itself, producing a folk-like or madrigalesque quality of engaging simplicity. [Ex. 3.5]

The instrumental forces employed in *Don Perlimplin*, consisting of a chamber-orchestra in which a large and varied percussion section together with mandoline, electric guitar, harp and piano and a solo string-group are set against a wind-group of somewhat unusual constitution (flute, flute in G, clarinet, five

Ex. 3.2: Maderna: *Don Perlimplin*: 'Suocera Sax'

Ex. 3.3: Maderna: *Don Perlimplin*: 'Amore'

Ex. 3.4: Maderna: *Don Perlimplin*: 'Tempo di Rag'

saxophones, bassoon, horn, three trumpets and three trombones) are used in a variety of ways in the course of the work. The flute, as protagonist of the drama, has a special role: it begins the work with a long solo in which, at first, the material consists of a re-constitution of the opening of *Musica su due dimensioni*. [Ex. 3.6(a), (b)] Later, as we have seen, material from *Honeyrêves* is also employed, forming Don Perlimplin's part of the dialogue with Marcolfa about marriage. Maderna also treats this opening material (for flute, piano and, at the opening, marimbaphone) as a source for further instrumental improvisations: a note in the second page of the score says:

'The preceding page and those which follow represent the musical material which various instruments (harp, piano, mandoline, vibraphone, two violins, viola, 'cello and two double-basses) elaborate and interpolate from time to time. Constant reference should be made to these pages whenever the various instruments play the material contained in them.'

In the 'Intermezzo' which occurs during the wedding-night of Don Perlimplin and

Ex. 3.4: *Contd*

Belisa, before the appearance of the mysterious 'Sprites', the composer gives to various instruments further improvisatory passages, indicating that these form an interval between the two halves of the work and all the other instruments are directed to add freely fragments to be taken from the opening flute-episode of the work: all this improvisatory material is to be modulated in volume as the Speaker describes the 'love which has been wounded by past love; wounded, dead, of love'. [Ex. 3.7]

The 'Blues' episodes which occur during the work are of some importance: these appear immediately after the Speaker has described the 'wounded' love of Don Perlimplin and Belisa; in the third '*Quadro*' as the Speaker and Marcolfa speak about the assignation of Belisa and her 'lover' in the garden ('*Il Blues di Don Perlimplin*'); and finally as Belisa goes to the garden for her fateful meeting ('*Blues "Dark Rapture Crawl"*'). In each of these highly atmospheric episodes, Maderna

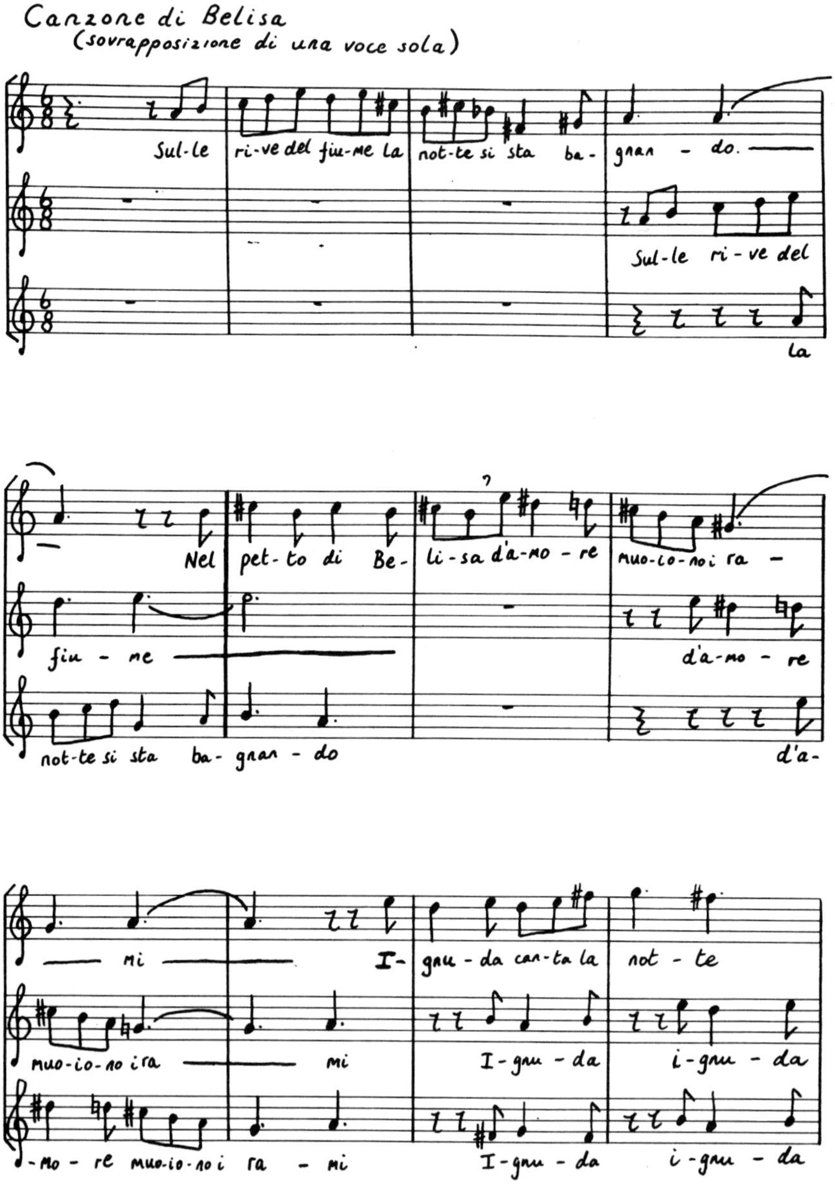

Ex. 3.5: Maderna: *Don Perlimplin*: 'Canzone di Belisa'

Ex. 3.6(a): Maderna: *Musica su due dimensioni* (1958): opening

makes use of the skills which he had developed during the previous decade as a composer of light-music scores for many radio presentations, and his experience, much earlier in life when from a tender age he had played in the light-music band run by his father Umberto Grossato in and around Venice. [Ex. 3.8]

We can therefore see in *Don Perlimplin* a clear tendency towards the technique of musical collage: the variegation of musical procedures in the work range from those episodes with a clear reference to the styles of the Rag and Blues, through the incorporation of reference to works composed earlier (*Musica su due dimensioni* and *Honeyrêves*), techniques which had their basis in work in the Studio (voice-superimposition in Belisa's '*Canzone*', dynamic manipulation in some instrumental episodes, recordings of bells with which the work is concluded), to improvisatory mobiles and the free use of material from the flute Introduction by other instruments in later parts of the work.

What, then, is the significance of this work in the output of Maderna as whole? We have already seen how the composer had been drawn towards musical dramatisation in previous years, and *Don Perlimplin* was the first such venture to be brought to full realisation; there can be little doubt that the radio-medium, with which Maderna was already very familiar indeed by this time, was the ideal medium for his quite strange, non-realistic, fanciful and dramatically fluid conception of the musical stage. In later years he was able, after the experience of this work, to bring to fruition works of a very varied kind which had either an explicit or an implicit 'dramatic' content, and these were to include the '*lirica in*

Ex. 3.6(b): Maderna: *Don Perlimplin*: opening

forma di spettacolo' Hyperion (based very freely upon the poem of Hölderlin, and also, like *Don Perlimplin*, with the beloved flute of Severino Gazzelloni as protagonist), the free-roaming fantasy of the radiophonic work *Ages*, based upon Shakespeare, the parodistic work *Venetian Journal* based upon Boswell's Travel Diary, which brought together vocal, instrumental and tape elements, and finally the opera *Satyricon*, after Petronius, in which the collage of stylistic parody and a certain aleatoric element in both the music and the scenic action were to reach their final expression.

The composition and assembly of the works which may be considered parts of what we might call the 'Hyperion Cycle' occupied Maderna for so much of the period from 1960 to 1969 that it is tempting to call this the 'Hyperion Period' of the composer's life: the various works of the 'cycle' occupy also a very important position in the composer's whole output, whether individually or in terms of the various works which bore the title of 'Hyperion'. These various works present us with considerable problems regarding the order of composition, arrangements into several larger-scale works (whether for the stage or concert-performances), and differing versions of works with the same title, so we should first of all set out the 'ground-plan' of the component parts of the cycle in terms which will clarify the sequence and ordering of the materials:

1960 (Milan):	*Dimensioni II/Invenzione su una voce* (tape).
1962 (Darmstadt):	*Le Rire* (tape).
1964 (Hannover):	*Dimensioni III* (orchestra).
1964 (Darmstadt):	*Dimensioni IV* (chamber version of *Dimensioni III*: included *Aria* played on flute).
1964 (Venice):	*Hyperion* (staged): incorporated *Dimensioni IV with Aria* now sung, *Le Rire, Dimensioni II*.
1964 (Cologne):	*Dimensioni III*: included complete *Aria*
1965 (Darmstadt):	*Hyperion II*: comprised *Dimensioni III, Entropia II*, more flute Cadenzas.
1966 (Norddeutscher Rundfunk):	*Stele per Diotima.*
1968 (Brussels):	*Hyperion en het Geweld*: second staged version: included new tapes and instrumental/vocal material, *Le Rire, Dimensioni II, Dimensioni III, Stele per Diotima* and *Aria*.
1968 (Bologna):	*Hyperion-Orfeo Dolente*: third staged version: Venice version interspersed between acts of Domenico Belli's *Orfeo Dolente* (1616)
1969 (Berlin):	*Suite aus der Oper 'Hyperion'*: material taken from *Dimensioni II, Entropia II, Stele per Diotima, Entropia III* and new solos for oboe and musette.

It would seem that the original conception of a work *for the stage* based in some way around the Hyperion poem of Friedrich Hölderlin (*'Fragment von Hyperion, oder Thalia Fragment'*)[4] occurred to Maderna *after* the composition of some of the component parts of the work: we have testimony for this from the producer of the work in its Venice performance on the stage of La Fenice in 1964, Virginio Puecher:[5]

'Bruno came to me one day and handed me some tapes, some sheets of music, a big *Aria* for soprano. With that irresistible smiling-mocking tone of his he said to me 'This could be the material for an opera, but you are the one who will have to give it a form . . . ' Anyway, even if he left it up to me to decide, he already had a clear idea of *Hyperion* in his head . . . So when he told me that he imagined the protagonist in *Hyperion* as an instrument and that the instrument would be a flute, with its player Gazzelloni, I understood that he aimed high and that, without giving it a name, it brought Poetry directly into the action . . . I must say that our first thoughts were not concerned with the drama but rather with the staging aspect . . . The first thing to be conceived was what in the stage-directions was to appear amongst the performers as the 'strumpet Machine' . . . The container, either closed or open, ended up as the central element of the performance (it was of colossal proportions) and took on various functions in the action . . . almost as a part of that mechanical theatre

Ex. 3.7: Maderna: *Don Perlimplin*: Intermezzo

Ex. 3.8: Maderna: *Don Perlimplin*: Blues 'Dark Rapture Crawl'

Ex. 3.8: *Contd*

which was placed in opposition to the human theatre represented by
Gazzelloni and his flute'.

Maderna, then, appears to have conceived the idea of the action and stage-setting
of *Hyperion*, at least in outline, before he got in touch with Puecher, and the
materials which he wished to employ in the music for the work consisted already
of the tape-works *Dimensioni II/Invenzione su una voca* and *Le Rire*, and the scores
of *Dimensioni III*, *Aria* and 'some Flute Cadenzas' (which had appeared in the
Darmstadt performance of *Dimensioni IV* in July of that year.) Since the work was
from the very beginning given the title *Hyperion*, and the *Aria* which forms such a
central role in it employs a text from the 'Hyperion Fragment' of Friedrich
Hölderlin, we must ask what importance the figure and the text of 'Hyperion'

played in the work as a whole. Hölderlin had conceived the idea of a '*Bildungsroman*', a novel tracing the creative development of the poet through his varied experiences, during his student years in Tübingen in the years 1788–90. In 1795, when he moved to Frankfurt as a private tutor in the house of a wealthy banker by the name of Jakob Friedrich Gontard, Hölderlin had fallen deeply in love with his employer's wife, Susette, who expressed for him all his ideals of physical and spiritual beauty.[6]

He gave the name 'Diotima' to this exalted being, the name of a priestess mentioned in the writings of both Plato and Socrates, and evidently identified by Hölderlin as a Greek cast up in a foreign land. In the final version of the novel '*Hyperion, oder der Eremit in Griechenland*' ('*Hyperion, or the Hermit in Greece*'), published in two volumes in 1797 and 1799, Hyperion himself is a young Greek during the struggle for independence from the Turks in 1770, and the novel is cast in the form of letters to his friend Bellarmine and to Diotima, his beloved one. When Diotima dies, he is disillusioned with the ideal of Greek Independence, and attempts to achieve happiness by a communion with Nature.

Maderna, however, employed in *Aria* parts of the text of the earlier *Fragment von Hyperion*, which Hölderlin had published in a literary journal edited by Schiller in about 1794, before his first meeting with the fateful 'Diotima': this was also cast in epistolatory form, as five letters to Bellarmine from Zante, Pyrgos, Kastri and Cithaeron (which Hölderlin never visited, remaining for virtually all his life in Germany). Passages were chosen by Maderna from this 'Thalia Fragment' which emphasised the difficulties encountered by 'the Poet' in his attempt to reconcile his poetic desires with external reality: thus, the text of *Aria* represents the aspirations and desires of the Poet, rather than those of 'the Woman' who sings them: the singer is his Muse and expresses his innermost thoughts:

'*Wie eine lange entsetzliche Wüste lag die Vergangenheit da vor mir, und mit höllischem Grimme vertilgt ich jeden Rest von dem, was einst mein Herz gelabt hatte and erhoben.*

The past lay all before me, like a long and frightful waste-land, and in furious rage I swept away all that remained of what had once refreshed and uplifted my heart.

Dann fuhr ich wieder auf mit wütendem Hohngelächter über mich und Alles, lauschte mit Lust dem grässlichen Widerhall, und das Geheul der Tschakale, das durch die Nacht her von allen Seiten gegen mich drang, tat meiner zerrütteten Seele wirklich wohl.

Then I set out once more scornfully laughing at myself and everything, listened joyfully to the horrible echoes, and the howling of the cicadas which came to me from all sides throughout the night healed my confused soul.

Eine dumpfe, fürchterliche Stille folgte diesen zernichtenden Stunden, eine eigentliche Totenstille! Ich suchte (nun) keine Rettung mehr. Ich achtete nichts. Ich war, wie ein Tier unter der Hand des Schlächters.

A dull, fearsome stillness followed these destructive hours, a stillness as of death! I no longer sought salvation. I noticed nothing. I was like a beast in the hands of the slaughterer.

Noch ahnd ich, ohne zu finden. Ich frage die Sterne, und sie verstummen, ich frage den Tag, und die Nacht: aber sie antworten nicht. Aus mir selbst, wenn ich frage, tönen mystische Sprüche, Träume ohne Deutung'.

Still I wished for revenge, without finding it. I ask the stars and they are silent, I ask the day, and the night, but they do not answer. When I ask myself, there come the sounds of mystical sayings, dreams without a meaning.

Ich weiss night, wie mir geschieht, wenn ich sie ansehe, diese unergründliche Natur.	I do not know what is happening to me when I look at this impenetrable Nature.
Und dieser himmlischen Kreatur (orig.: 'diesem himmlischen Geschöpfe') zürnt ich? Und warum zürnt ich sie (ihr)? Weil sie nicht verarmt war, wie ich, weil sie den Himmel noch im Herzen trug, und nicht sich selbst verloren hatte, wie ich, nicht eines andern Wesens, nicht fremden Reichtums bedürfte, um die verödete Stelle auszufüllen, weil sie nicht unterzugehen fürchten konnte, wie ich, und sich mit dieser Todesangst an ein Andres zu hängen (brauchte: B.M.), wie ich.	And was I angry at this heavenly creation? Why was I angry at it? Because it was not poor like me, it still carried heaven in its heart, it had not lost itself, as I had, it had no need of another being, a distant kingdom, to replenish the desolate place, it could not fear a passing away as I did, and did not (need to) hang this fear of death on another, as I did.
Das alles ging mir, wie ein Schwert, durch die Seele.	Everything penetrated my soul like a sword'
Mein ganzes Wesen verstummt und lauscht, wenn der leise geheimnisvolle Hauch des Abends mich ansieht.	My whole being was silent and listened when the gentle breath of evening, full of secrets, blew over me.
Meinem Herzen ist wohl in dieser Dämmerung. Ist sie unser Element, diese Dämmerung? Warum kann ich nicht ruhen darinnen?	My heart is well in this twilight. Is it our element, this twilight? Why can I not rest in it?

The performance of *Hyperion* given in Venice in October 1964 in La Fenice consisted of eight scenes of varying length, the whole piece taking about three-quarters of an hour to perform. These scenes ran continuously one into another, and the various musical elements which made up the score of the work were placed at appropriate points in the action on stage. At the opening, the stage was quite bare, with workmen preparing for a performance, only the noises of their activities being heard. A man in tails appeared, (the flautist Gazzelloni) accompanied by a servant carrying instrument-cases. His preparations to play were interrupted by metallic noises on tape, and by the sudden appearance of a huge metal shutter, followed by others to form a cage around him (*Le Rire*). The orchestra lights went on and they began to play (*Dimensioni IV*): the soloist tried to join in, but was prevented each time by the violent orchestral sounds. He did eventually manage to play, but as he did so mysterious laughter and absurd chatter became heard (*Dimensioni II*). The walls suddenly opened up and a gigantic Machine appeared, with flashing lights and all the appearance of a fairground show (*Dimensioni III, Dimensioni IV*): the flautist was completely dumbfounded and cowered in a corner. The orchestra continued with their bombardment of sound (*Dimensioni IV*) as a group of mimes, all in identical space-costumes, enacted various scenes of violence and mechanical repetition, struggle and humiliation. Another metal object then appeared on stage, and from it the woman emerged (the soprano soloist): she sang, and the flautist could at last take part with the flute in G as part of *Aria*. The Machine and Woman finally left: the flautist took up a piccolo and made his exit playing this (piccolo solos from *Dimensioni III*).

Maderna described this first staged version of *Hyperion* as a *'lirica in forma di spettacolo'* ('poem in staged form'), and it is clear that Hölderlin's poem occupied a central position in the framework of this piece of Music Theatre. The work was very badly received by its audience in La Fenice: whether this was in response to the strange, 'absurd' actions on stage, with the mixture of the comic, grotesque, pathetic and despairing gestures of Gazzelloni, together with the monster Machine and its pyrotechnical display, or whether to the musical language, with its combination of powerful orchestral writing, 'realistic' tape-sounds, and the highly-charged *Aria* for soprano (still clearly incomplete, with the final passage spoken), cannot now be distinguished.

A second staged version was given in the Théatre Royal de la Monnaie in Brussels in May 1968, performed in Flemish, with the title *Hyperion en het Geweld* (*'Hyperion and Power'*). The dramatic shape of this new working of the Hyperion-theme differed radically from that seen in Venice four years earlier. In place of an 'abstract' stage-setting, this was now placed in a specific location, a high-technology plastic bunker in the midst of a war. Maderna had in fact been asked to write a Music Theatre work based upon a text called *Morituri* prepared by Hugo Claus, a plan about which the composer was evidently enthusiastic, but which he wished to combine with elements taken from *Hyperion*, and so a libretto was made which placed together the two distinct schemes.

This amalgam of *Morituri* and *Hyperion* gave rise to a dramatic work of somewhat strange character, not all of which can now be either reconstructed or even described in detail, since some of the material on which it was based has now disappeared from view. As the curtain rose after an *'Ouverture'*, Popeye-films were being projected on a screen on stage, and a group of about ten soldiers in the bunker were nervously awaiting the commencement of hostilities. A Chaplain tries to calm them down, but the Captain reminds them of a truce already violated by 'The Rats'. Operation 'Prairie Dog' is put into action: the battle is controlled by a huge Machine giving orders, making calculations and emitting signals. Two Guards (Castor and Pollux) comment on the battle and the stage fills with smoke and noise. 'Recreation' then follows, in which the soldiers play slot-machines and dance. The Captain speaks about the enemy's miserable life, and announces that three days' leave in Donango will be given for every 'Rat' killed. During the night, the men are protected by the Machine: Castor and Pollux stand guard, but the 'Rats' suddenly begin to be heard over loudspeakers, at first gently, later with threats and jests: the soldiers in the bunker are referred to as 'Donald Duck' and 'Buffalo Bill'. They are terrified but powerless: once more a battle ensues, in which puppet-monsters appear dressed as Loup-Garou, Robot Robbie, Dracula, Doctor Demon and Superman. At the end of the battle, only three remain: Castor searching for Pollux, the Chaplain reading from the Bible, and the Captain who is praising the self-sacrifice of his men. It is at this point that the Woman appeared to sing the first part of the *Aria*. The ending is unclear: alternatives appear to be the reappearance of the puppet-monsters, the soldiers' resurrection as Mummies, or else a general lamentation on the destruction of Nature and Humanity.

The third staged version of *Hyperion* was given in Bologna some months after *Hyperion en het Geweld* in Brussels, in the courtyard of the Palazzo Bentivoglio on 18th and 19th July 1968 as part of the *'Feste Musicali'*. This again was an 'amalgam' work, but one of a quite different character from that witnessed in Brussels: *Hyperion* was here divided into five 'episodes' placed between the five acts of

Domenico Belli's *Orfeo Dolente*, an *'intermedio'* from 1616, and thus the two works each retained their distinct identity, but the placement side-by-side of the dramas of *Hyperion* and *Orpheus* gave rise to a work in which the two elements were interwoven. Slide- and film-projections around the courtyard formed an essential part of the stage-setting, and the realisation of the score of Belli's work was made by Maderna specially for the event.

Belli's work was set in a post-catastrophic world, after the return of Euridice to the underworld following Orpheus' breaking of the ban: he appeals to Pluto for her return, but Pluto is unmoved by the seductiveness of Orpheus' poetic plea. Calliope tries to intervene but she also is unable to overcome Pluto's intransigence. Orpheus renounces love: he is comforted by three Graces and a chorus of Nymphs, and the drama ends with the sad departure of the Graces, the heartbroken Orpheus, and a chorus of Nymphs singing of their hope for the return of joy.

In the interstices of this Orpheus drama, the action of *Hyperion* assumed a similar shape to that of the original Venice version of the work. The 'Poet-Flautist' Gazzelloni attempts to play a solo, but can only give out semi-articulate whistlings, disturbed by spotlights, sudden noises, and the appearance of weird technological gadgetry (*Le Rire* on tape, *Dimensioni III* in the orchestra). As the music begins to subside in its violence, the flautist throws himself into a long solo, part lyrical expressivity, part histrionics. But subdued laughter is heard, and a gigantic Machine with flashing lights and advertising-posters appears on stage (*Dimensioni III*, *Dimensioni II*). Mime-artists come on stage and enact contrasting scenes, and finally the woman appears and sings the *Aria*. The ending appears to have followed closely that of the Venice *Hyperion*, with the Poet-Flautist disconsolately departing from the scene.

In order to clarify the rather complex textual problem of *Hyperion*, the following table of materials may be found useful:

(1) *Hyperion* — Venice 1964:	**Live:** *Dimensioni IV* + *Aria* + flute cadenzas **Tape:** *Le Rire* + *Dimensioni II*
(2) *Hyperion en het Geweld* — Brussels 1968:	**Live:** *Messaggio (flute solo: second episode of Dimensioni III)* + *Entropia I and II* (episodes of *Dimensioni III*) + *Psalm* (chorus and orchestra) + *Aria* (as *Aria I* and *Aria II*) + *Battaglia*: part of *Dimensioni III*? + part of *Stele per Diotima*? + choruses and instruments. **Tape:** *Le Rire* + *Dimensioni II* + *Battaglia I* *Battaglia II* specially *Contrasti* composed *Intermizzi 1–4*
(3) *Hyperion–Orfeo Dolente* — Bologna 1968:	**Live:** *Dimensioni III* + *Aria* **Tape:** *Le Rire* + *Dimensioni II*

In addition to the three staged versions of *Hyperion*, Maderna also prepared a number of other works bearing the same title which incorporated elements from the dramatic enterprises, and yet again a number of problems arise which might hinder an 'authentic' realisation of some of these works. Maderna's publisher Suvini Zerboni, in fact, gives three possible 'plans' for works called *Hyperion*, *Hyperion II* and *Hyperion III*, and these plans correspond fairly closely with concert-performances conducted by the composer in 1965 and 1966, the last of which has been recorded on disc. It is apparent however that Maderna had conceived these realisations of *Hyperion* in a somewhat 'ad hoc' manner, and not all of the material is now available for the first two.

However, Maderna also conducted two works in Berlin and Vienna in 1969 each called *Suite aus der Oper 'Hyperion'*, and from the recording of the Berlin work we are able to give an accurate account of its material, which incorporated further Hölderlin texts not previously used, as well as a chorus on texts by Auden and Lorca.[7]

The importance of these concert-versions of *Hyperion* lies in the manner in which, by an imaginative investigation of all the materials now extant, it is possible to reconstruct with some confidence a valid version of *Hyperion* which can represent the essentials of Maderna's 'Hyperion-conception' in full. This attempt has been made with considerable success by the Italian conductor Marcello Panni, broadcast by Italian Radio in 1979.

In the course of our discussion of the somewhat tortuous history of *Hyperion*, one thing will have become very apparent: that the *Aria* for soprano and orchestra represents what we might call the 'essence' of the whole enterprise. It had appeared in all three stage-versions at crucial points in the dramatic action, as well as in the three concert-versions (in *Hyperion III* played on flute); in the Berlin *Suite aus der Oper 'Hyperion'* texts from Hölderlin's 'Hyperion' were recited by a speaker, using passages not used in *Aria*; and in Marcello Panni's 'composite' version of the work made after Maderna's death, he placed *Aria* right at the end of his scheme. The inclusion of *Aria* in so many of these versions, as well as its nature as a free-standing work of remarkable power of expression, warrant a closer look at this piece. As we have already seen, in the first Venice version of *Hyperion* in 1964, the work was included in its chamber-version heard some months earlier in Darmstadt, but without its final bars which had not yet been composed: there are however no substantial divergences between the chamber and full orchestral versions, and for the purposes of our discussion we shall refer to the latter.

The overall character of *Aria* is that of an inward meditation prompted by the poet's response to his observance of outward Nature. In this respect, it might be said to have an affinity with Schoenberg's *Erwartung*, in which we see similarly reflected the varying moods and anxieties of the soprano soloist as she is confronted with the terrors of the external world. In both works moreover the character of the expression moves very freely between 'recitativo' and 'arioso' sections, with important orchestral interludes. We can observe this shape in *Aria* if we sketch out the progression of the work and its relationship to the text:

Bar 1:	*Orchestral Introduction*
Bars 2–23:	accompanied recitative: *'Wie eine lange . . . und erhoben'*
Bars 24–37:	accompanied recitative (*'sprechstimne'*): *'Dann fuhr ich . . . Seele wirklich wohl'*
Bars 38–54:	*Orchestral Interlude*
Bars 55–88:	accompanied recitative, spoken at first: *'Eine dumpfe . . . ohne Deutung'*
Bars 89 bis–97:	Solo bass flute, later with soprano: *'Ich weiss nicht . . . Natur'*
Bars 97–124:	*'Arioso'*: *'Und dieser . . . verloren hatte'*
Bars 125–140:	soprano and full orchestra: *'Wie ich . . . hängen brauchte'*
Bars 140 bis:	soprano spoken *'Das Alles . . . die Seele'*
Bars 141–164:	*Orchestral Interlude* (bass flute solo gradually enters)
Bars 165–173:	soprano and orchestra: *'Mein ganzes Wesen . . . mich anweht'*
Bars 174–191:	(Bars added later): soprano and three bass flutes: *'Meinem Herzen . . . darinnen'*

There are, nevertheless, some important differences between *Erwartung* and *Aria*. Firstly, *Erwartung* was conceived by Schoenberg as a *dramatic* work (*'Monodram'*) to which he gave precise and detailed instructions for its performance on stage; *Aria*, on the other hand, despite its placement within the dramatic context of *Hyperion*, could appear in quite different dramatic contexts in each version of the larger work, or quite independently of it, and did not need to be aided by scenic representation. Secondly, *Erwartung* consists of four scenes in which the scenic settings were conceived as an essential part of the changing moods of the protagonist, whereas *Aria* does not involve such clear-cut divisions.

Many commentators upon *Erwartung* have attempted to unravel the intricacies of the work's musical expression, a work in which the 'atonal' language in which it is manifest represented without doubt one of the most complex stages in the evolution of Schoenberg's musical language from his earlier fervent and highly-charged Romanticism towards the subtle, refined and yet still 'dramatic' expression of his later series-based works. *Erwartung* was one of the pieces (along with *Pierrot Lunaire* and the *Five Orchestral Pieces op. 16*) in which the composer's Expressionism was most powerfully apparent, and all commentators on the work agree, at least, in seeing the closest possible interdependence of music and text.

We might, similarly, see the language of *Aria* as a culmination of the expressive vocabulary which Maderna's music had developed up to that point: in subsequent years, during the final decade of his life, Maderna's gradual refinement of aleatoric procedures in the formal construction of large-scale works, and the supremacy of 'primal' melodic expression which was allied with it, led to a manner of composition which was in many ways different from that which we find in *Aria*. The highly-charged Expressionism of each work is set out in a musical language which is in both cases of an extreme density and, at the same time, of a high degree of freedom.

The expressive language of *Aria* is manifest above all in a constant variegation of musical character closely mirroring the changing moods and suggestions of the text. There is, in the work as a whole, no attempt at any clear-cut repetition of musical motives or 'themes', and indeed one might search in vain for any overriding series underlying the complex fabric of the work; Maderna creates the drama of *Aria* by varying the character of expression from moment to moment ('close' or 'dispersed' in melodic flow, 'chromatic' or 'quasi-diatonic' in harmony, 'smooth' or 'abrupt' in rhythm), as well as by a skilful employment of instrumental colorations achieved by varying divisions of the orchestral body. Since the mood of each moment is determined by the text, the soprano's line, which is enormously wide in *tessitura*, reflects with great subtlety the stages through which the poet passes in his observation of Nature. In the first *stanza* of the work for example (bars 1–19), the text expresses the poet's despair in the 'frightful wasteland' of the past, and his desire to rid himself of the last vestiges of 'all that had once refreshed and uplifted my soul': the close semitonal phrases and deep, dark colours of the lower register (reflected in brief, inconsequential phrases in the orchestra) suddenly give way (bars 10–15) to a widespread, angular and rhythmically jagged expression as the poet's anger bursts forth in his rejection of the past, only to subside once more (bars 16–19) to the 'wasteland' of fragmented, isolated orchestral sounds, and to the soprano's ascent into a more 'hopeful' register as he remembers the past optimism. [Ex. 3.9]

It is in this way, by melodic, harmonic and rhythmic variety in the texture, that Maderna creates the musical expression of the work as a reflection of the text, and in this respect, again, it approaches the manner of *Erwartung*. If we ask how such a passage was arrived at in detail in the composition of the work, the sketches in the Paul Sacher Institute are intriguing, revealing a complex process of permutation and selection of material.

It is possible to glimpse to some extent Maderna's manner of working from preliminary sketches for the opening passage of the work. The first 'introductory' bar for orchestra alone had been constructed from interlocking repeated phrases for gong, harps, timpani and lower strings, which together outline a harmony (marked '1' in the Example) which, by a process of selection and addition is modified to a second chord (marked '2' in the Example). [Ex. 3.10(a)] From this resultant chord, closely related to the *ostinato* figures in bar 1, the composer then proceeded to construct a 'grid' of superimposed chromatic scales (ascending or descending at varying rates of movement), from which he selected the pitches for the soprano's melodic line, as well as for some of the other instruments, in the opening *stanza* illustrated in Example 3.9. This was done in varying colours which tend to reflect either the importance of the pitch so marked (not all of which were eventually employed), or else to indicate their instrumentation. [Ex. 3.10(b), (c)]

This process reveals the intricate, often very puzzling, manner in which Maderna derived the the pitches for some parts of *Aria*: such 'grids' were employed also in other passages of the work. What, essentially, we observe here is the composer integrating as closely as possible the vocal and instrumental elements of the work, and working in such a way that the *harmony* of such passages is a central focus of attention, providing the constant flow which is a major characteristic of the work as a whole.

In the expressive nature of the work, what we have referred to as an 'inward meditation', the solo soprano is of course the main protagonist, but she is aided from a certain point in the work by a solo bass flute (it will be remembered that Gazzelloni's flute, as the main protagonist of *Hyperion* in Venice, was comforted and encouraged in his desire for self-expression by the *Aria* itself): the bass flute acts as both an *obbligato* instrument as in a Bach aria, and also to a large extent as a further 'voice' in expressing the poet's innermost feelings. Within the context of *Hyperion*, there can be little doubt that the employment of a solo flute as a

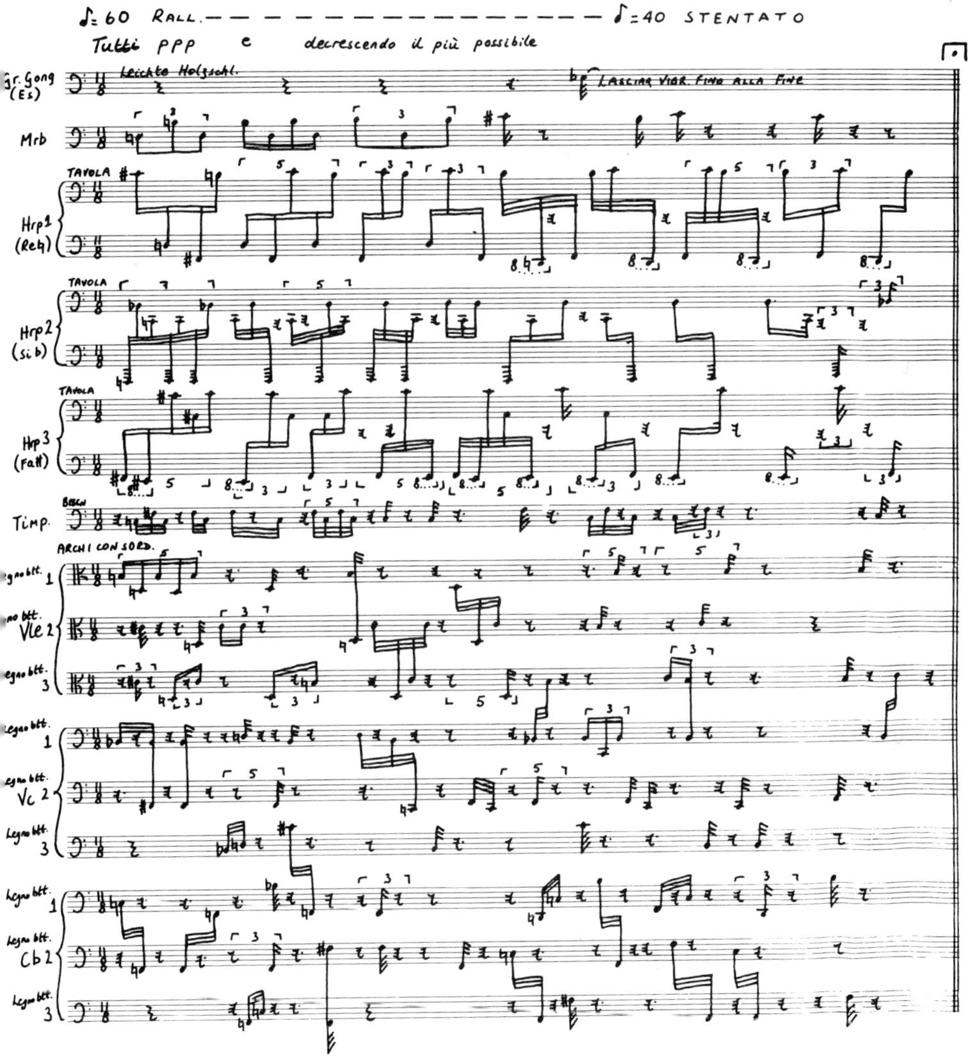

Ex. 3.9: Maderna: *Aria*: 1–19

sprachlich sehr deutlich!
Sopr.
Wie ei - ne
Plan - ge
ent-
Fl.
Alt. Fl.
(sim.)
Cl. 1
con sord. - legato
Hn 1
pp un poco espress.
Pos. 1
pp un poco vibr.
Arco
Vle
Celli
sempre ppp
Cb 1
Arco

Ex. 3.9: *Contd*

Ex. 3.9: *Contd*

Ex. 3.9: *Contd*

Sop.
und mit höl - - - - li - - - schen
Grin-
Ob 1 2
Hn 1 2 3
con sord.
Trpt 1 2
SPITZ.
pppp (non cresc.)
Pos 1 2 3
Timp
Vn 1
LEGNO BTT.
L. BTT.
Vle 1 2 3
PONTE
CORDA
AL
Vc 1 2 3
Cb 1 2

Ex. 3.9: *Contd*

Ex. 3.9: *Contd*

Sop
je – den Rest von dem Was einst
Fl.
A.Fl.
Cl. 1
BLÄSER IMMER PPP – ANFANG U. ENDE JEDES KLANGES ABTÖNEND!
Hns 1 2
Trpts 1 2 3
HARM.
CUP
Pos 1 2
CUP
HARM.
Vbr.
NON VBR. – BACCH. MORB.
sempre PPP
Mrb
TREMOLI RAPIDISS. – BACCH. MORBIDISS.
sempre PP
ARCHI SEMPRE VERSO LA PUNTA – PPP – SEMPRE SFUMANDO INIZIO E FINE DI OGNI SUONO
Vn 1 2
SEMPRE PONTE
SEMPRE PONTE
Vle 1 2
PONTE
CORDA
Vc 1 2
CORDA
PPP
VBR. SEMPRE
CORDA – VBR. SEMPRE
PPP
Cb 1
CORDA
PPP

Ex. 3.9: *Contd*

Ex. 3.9: *Contd*

Ex. 3.10(a): Maderna: *Aria*: 55–58

F

Ex. 3.10(b): Maderna; *Aria*: sketch

Ex. 3.10(b): *Contd*

Ex. 3.10(c): Maderna; *Aria*: analysis

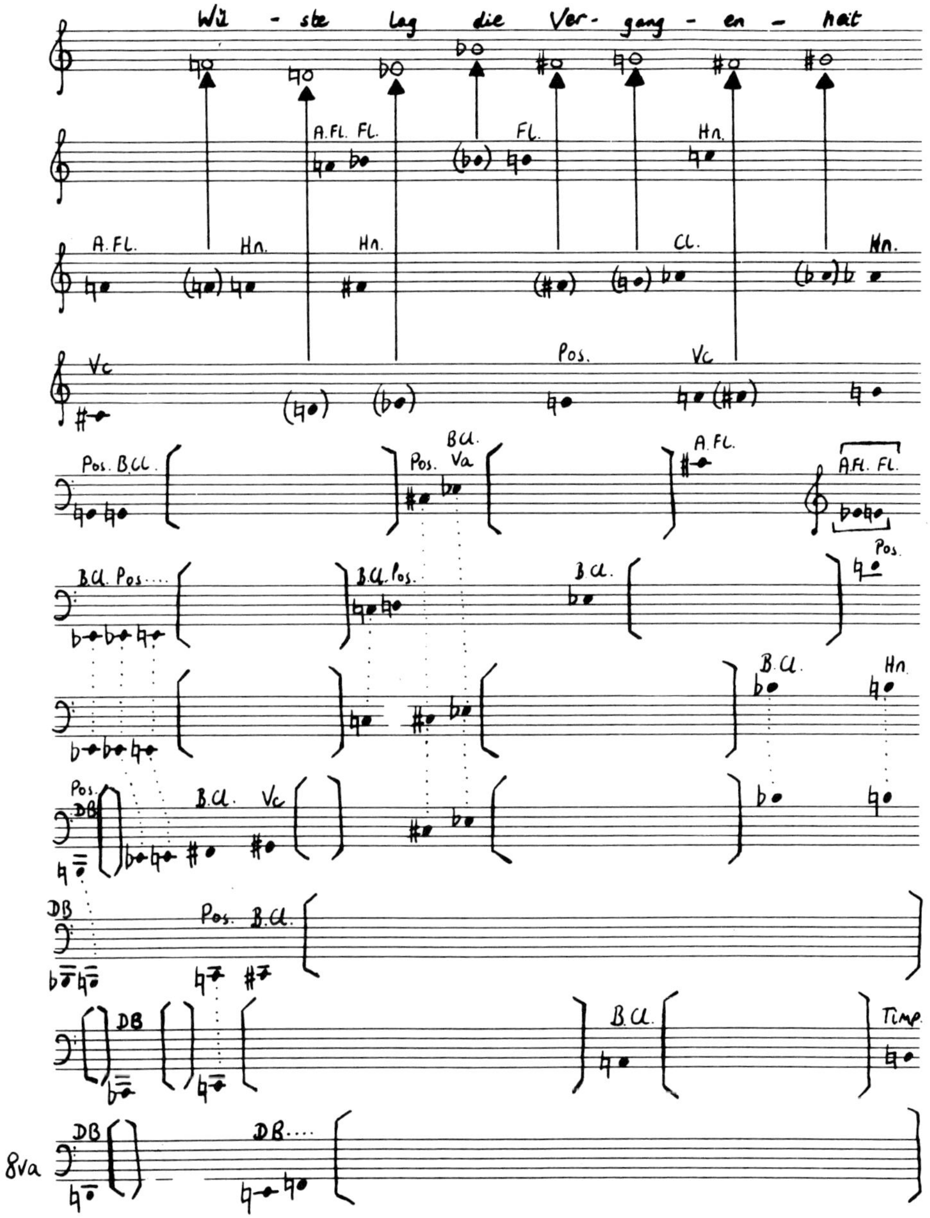

Ex. 3.10(c): *Contd*

Ex. 3.10(c): *Contd*

'character' had grown from a similar procedure in *Don Perlimplin* two years earlier: here in *Aria*, as the soprano reaches a point of total despair, losing the energy for more *cantabile* expression, she simply speaks the poet's words above a gentle instrumental accompaniment, and the bass flute enters, with a free melody of great expressivity which reverts to some of the intervallic shapes with which the work had begun. The roles of 'Poet' and 'Muse' are here exchanged, as the bass flute gives melodic 'comfort' to the soprano's inner despair. [Ex. 3.11]

Ex. 3.11: Maderna: *Aria*: 55–58

The role of the bass flute is a dual one: it at times aids the poet-soprano's quest for inner peace, acting in an *obbligato* manner, or as a complementary voice in the polyphony; at other times, it takes on a more independent role, free and uninhibited in its expression. It should be remembered that Maderna, in some

Ex. 3.11: *Contd*

early performances of *Aria,* had presented the work without the solo soprano, whose part was taken over by a solo flute. In one passage of *Aria,* between bars 88 and 97, such a possibility is indicated in the score, with the suggestion that this section should be cut in performances without the soprano: this cut is made not simply for practical reasons, but because of the intimately close nature of the vocal and instrumental soloists' lines at this point in the work. After the bass flute's solo passage, the two melodic lines intermingle and cross as the poet speaks of the unfathomable workings of Nature. [Ex. 3.12]

Ex. 3.12: Maderna: *Aria*: 90–97

We have suggested that *Aria* shares with *Erwartung* the particular importance of the orchestral interludes which are placed at various points between the *stanzas* of Hölderlin's text: these interludes serve a dramatic function, presenting to us moments in which to reflect outwards, as it were, from the situation described by the soloist, a reflection which, in the context of the expression of the text, is almost in itself a picture of the Nature which confronts the poet. We may take as an example the interlude comprising bars 38–54 (leading up to the entry of the bass flute already described): here, the poet has spoken of the howling of the cicadas in the night, which gives his soul refreshment in the wildness in which he finds himself, and Maderna writes a passage of great beauty, long-held and gradually-changing chordal sonorities dispersed over the orchestra in a quiet and gentle dynamic, nocturnal in effect. As this comes to its conclusion, *staccato* sounds in harp, vibraphone, marimba, timpani and double basses interrupt this gentle, swaying music, as the soloist will begin to speak (above the bass flute's first passage) of 'a dull, fearful stillness' which 'follows these destructive hours, a stillness as of death! I seek no more salvation, I notice nothing, I am like an animal brought under the slaughterer's hand'. [Ex. 3.13]

Ex. 3.13: Maderna: *Aria*: 37–49

Ex. 3.13: *Contd*

ARCHI SEMPRE P MA SONORO

Ex. 3.13: *Contd*

The conclusion of *Aria* is of particular importance: Hölderlin's tormented soul has found no solution to the problem of his relationship to Nature, and the soprano again reverts to a spoken recitation for the words 'Everything penetrates my soul — like a sword', spoken as the composer says in a 'dull' tone of voice. Once again, the orchestra, in this final interlude, extends and amplifies the mood of this text: the lines of the strings and solo winds are dispersed, quiet and resigned, but through the careful imitation of the various parts in the texture, Maderna creates a certain radiance, as the momentum fades away, coming to rest with a final 'cadential' fourth in the bass flute. [Ex. 3.14]

The final bars of the work, after this orchestral passage, provide an epilogue of haunting beauty of expression: Maderna had, as we said earlier, not been able to complete the final bars of the work (bars 174–191) in time for the performance of *Hyperion* in Venice, and his setting of these final words of the text simply extends the preceding bars (165–173) in a simple manner. The texture in this epilogue is of some significance: bass and alto flutes complement the soprano's melodic line by

Ex. 3.14: Maderna: *Aria*: 141–162

imitative means, aided by very quiet figures from two marimbas, and in the concluding 'added' bars, as the soprano sings of the 'twilight' existence to which the poet must become resigned, three alto flutes continue the imitative texture. The work ends with the same semitonal interval with which the soprano had begun. [Ex. 3.15] One is inevitably reminded here of the first of the *Tre Liriche Greche* composed some sixteen years earlier: the imitative-canonic texture and the employment of soprano with flutes are common to both works (see Example 1.14(a)). Maderna here employs a manner of writing which had been the starting-point for his exploration of serialism, and its employment at the conclusion of *Aria* grew naturally from the relationship of soprano and bass flute which had been established in the course of the work, as well as from the imitative writing in the orchestral interlude which preceded it. The sonority of flutes in combination is, as it were, the 'secretive breath of the evening breeze' which blows gently over the poet, a consolation without desire, and a suggestion of the surrounding twilight.

Ex. 3.14: *Contd*

We began this discussion of *Aria* by a comparison with *Erwartung*, one of the great works of Expressionism in music. The comparison was made with reference to the *structure* of each work as an 'inward meditation' prompted by 'outward Nature', to their presentation of this meditation in terms of 'arioso' or 'recitative' mingled with orchestral interludes, and to a certain common density and complexity of the musical language in which they are each expressed. However, in the final part of *Aria* now examined, we are faced with an expression which was not a part of *Erwartung*, a resigned but radiant conclusion expressed in the simplest language to be found in the whole work. Here is an example of what, in somewhat crude terms, we might call the 'Italianate lyricism' aspect of Maderna's writing, in which he reverts to a style from his own musical past which had grown partly from the style of Dallapiccola. The work reaches backwards, as it were, to find an engaging style for the work's conclusion, but at the same time forwards, towards the free melodic and lyrical manner which was to become one of the most important characteristics of his later music.

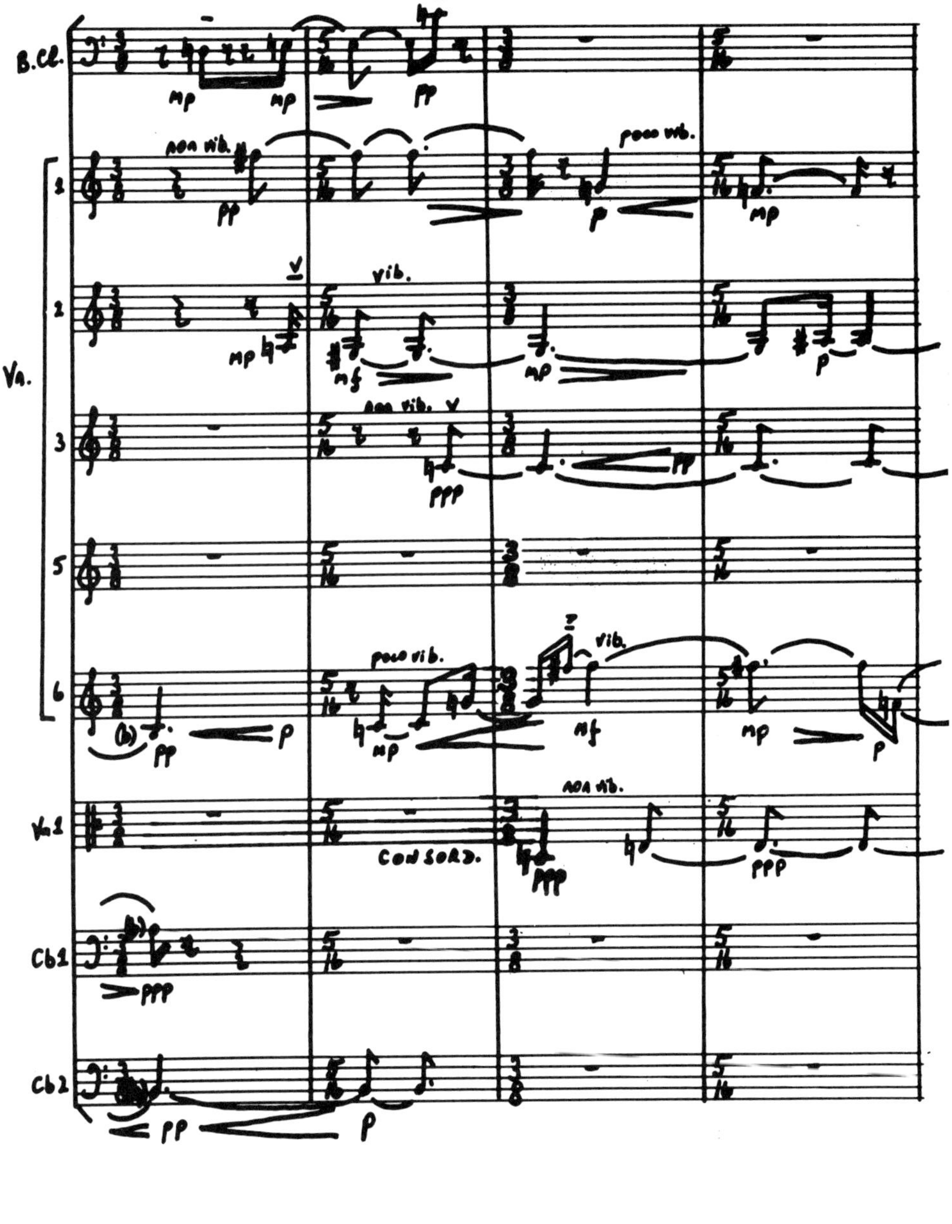

Ex. 3.14: *Contd*

Ex. 3.14: *Contd*

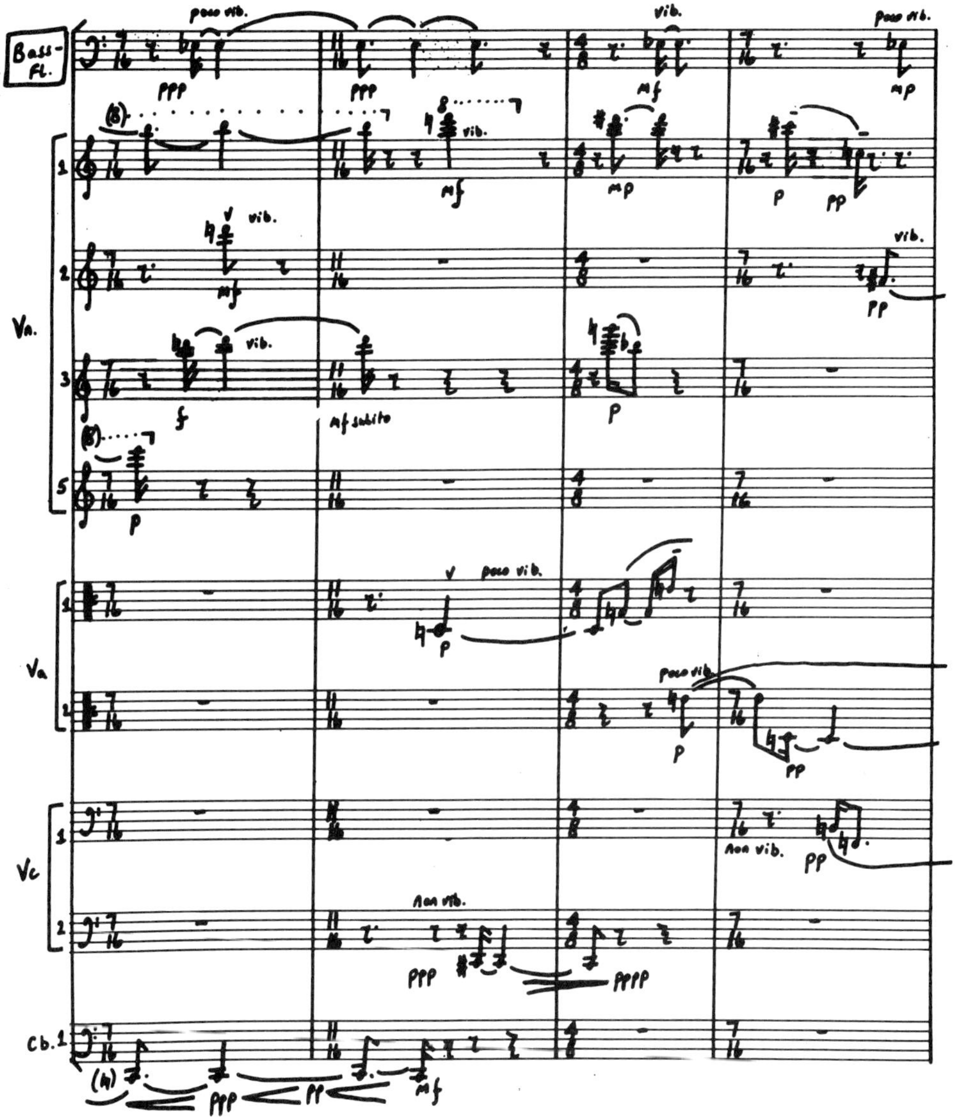

Ex. 3.14: *Contd*

164   *Bruno Maderna*

Ex. 3.14: *Contd*

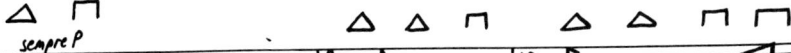

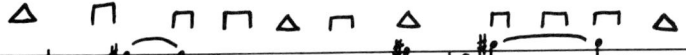

Ex. 3.15: Maderna: *Aria*: 165–191

Ex. 3.15: *Contd*

Sop.
Wohl
in die-ser
Däm - - - - - - - - - ner-ung.
Solo Alt-Fl.
Alt-Fl I
Alt-Fl II
mf
pp
ppp
mp
f, molto espr.
(cone soffio)
ff
Ist
sie
un-ser Element
die-se Däm . .
Solo A-Fl.
A-Fl I
A-Fl II
pppp

Ex. 3.15: *Contd*

Ex. 3.15: *Contd*

Note to Chapter 3

1. Edwin *Honig: Garcia Lorca*: Jonathan Cape, London, p. 10.
2. Gustavo *Pittaluga* (Ed.): *Canciones del Teatro de Federico Lorca,* Union Musical Española, Madrid, 1960.
3. *Baroni/Dalmonte,* op. cit., p. 206–7.
4. Friedrich *Hölderlin: Sämtliche Werke:* Kohlhammer Verlag, Stuttgart, 1957, pp. 163–184.
5. *Baroni/Dalmonte,* op. cit., p. 252.
6. Michael *Hamburger: Hölderlin,* Harvill Press, London, 1942.
7. *Baroni/Dalmonte* pp. 282–5.

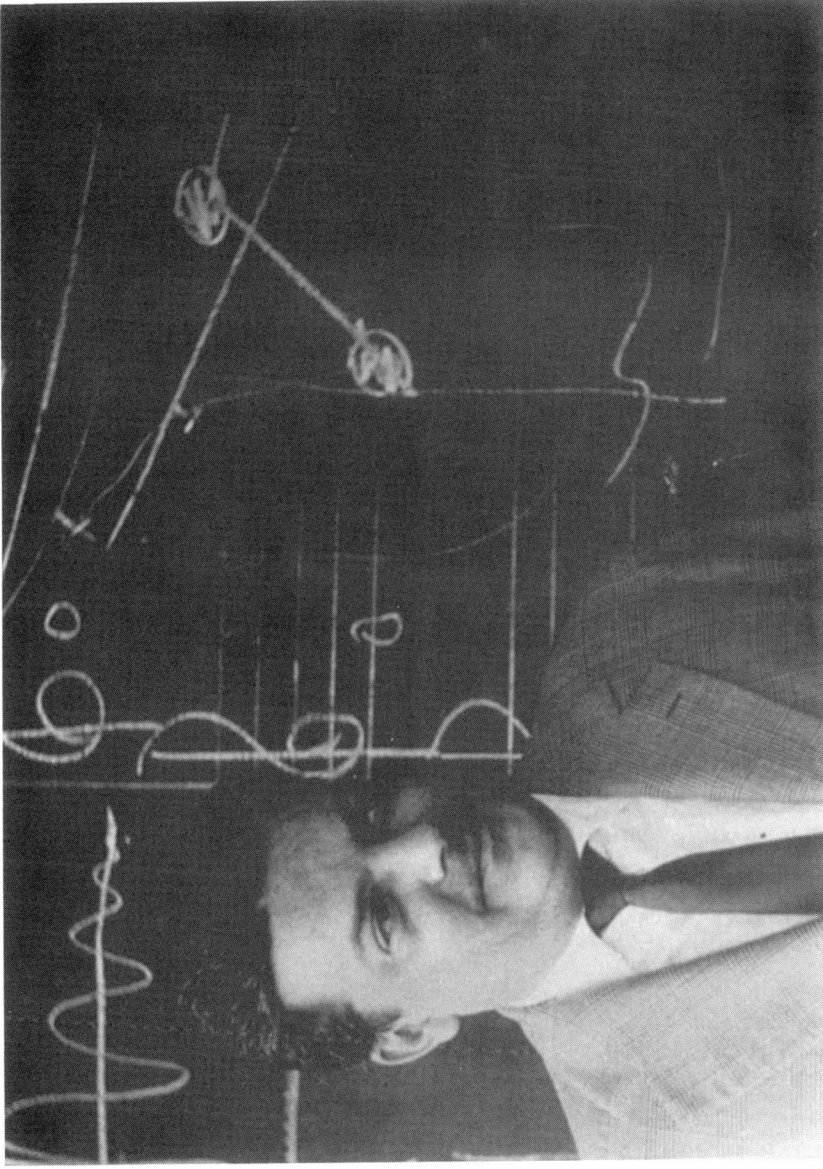

Plate 1 (Cover Photograph: Bruno Maderna, Darmstadt, 1960. (Photograph: Pit Ludwig)

Plate 2   Bruno Maderna, Darmstadt, 1952. (Photograph: Pit Ludwig)

Plate 3   International Summer School, Darmstadt, 1956: (Left to Right) Pierre Boulez, Bruno
Maderna, Karlheinz Stockhausen. (Photograph: Hans Kenner)

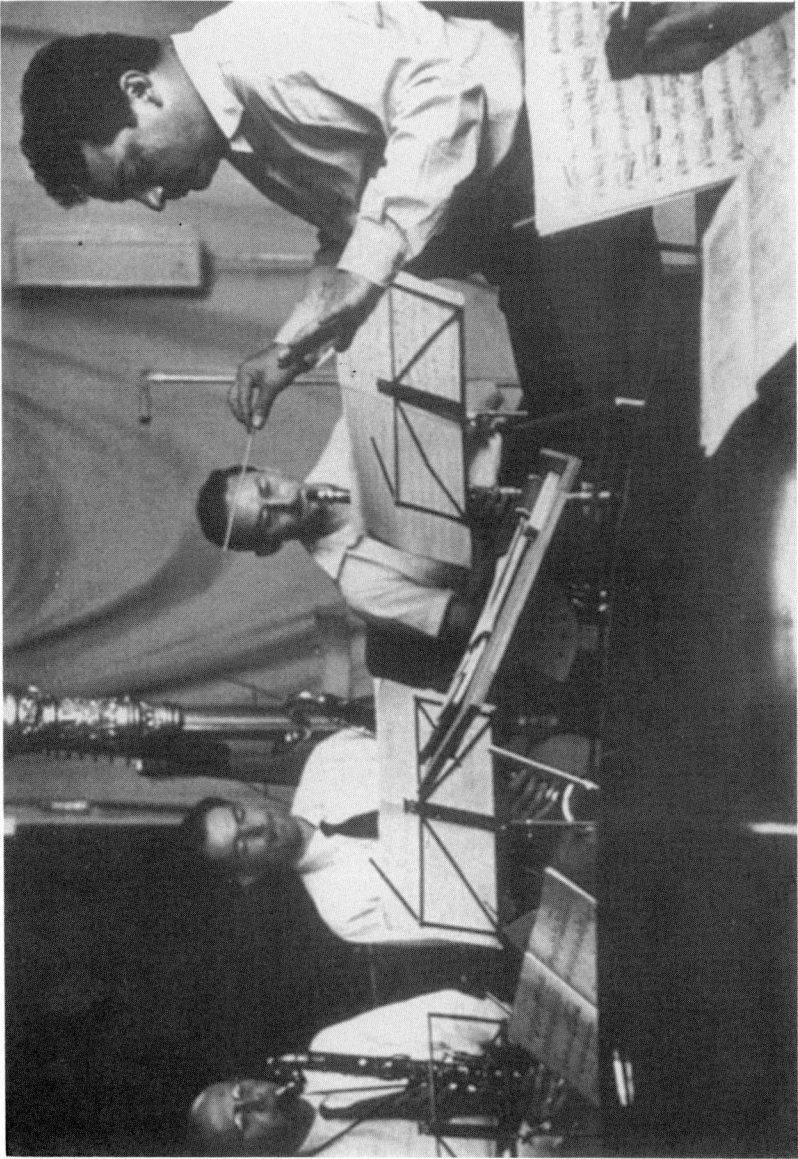

Plate 4   Bruno Maderna, Darmstadt, 1958. (Photograph: Hans Kenner)

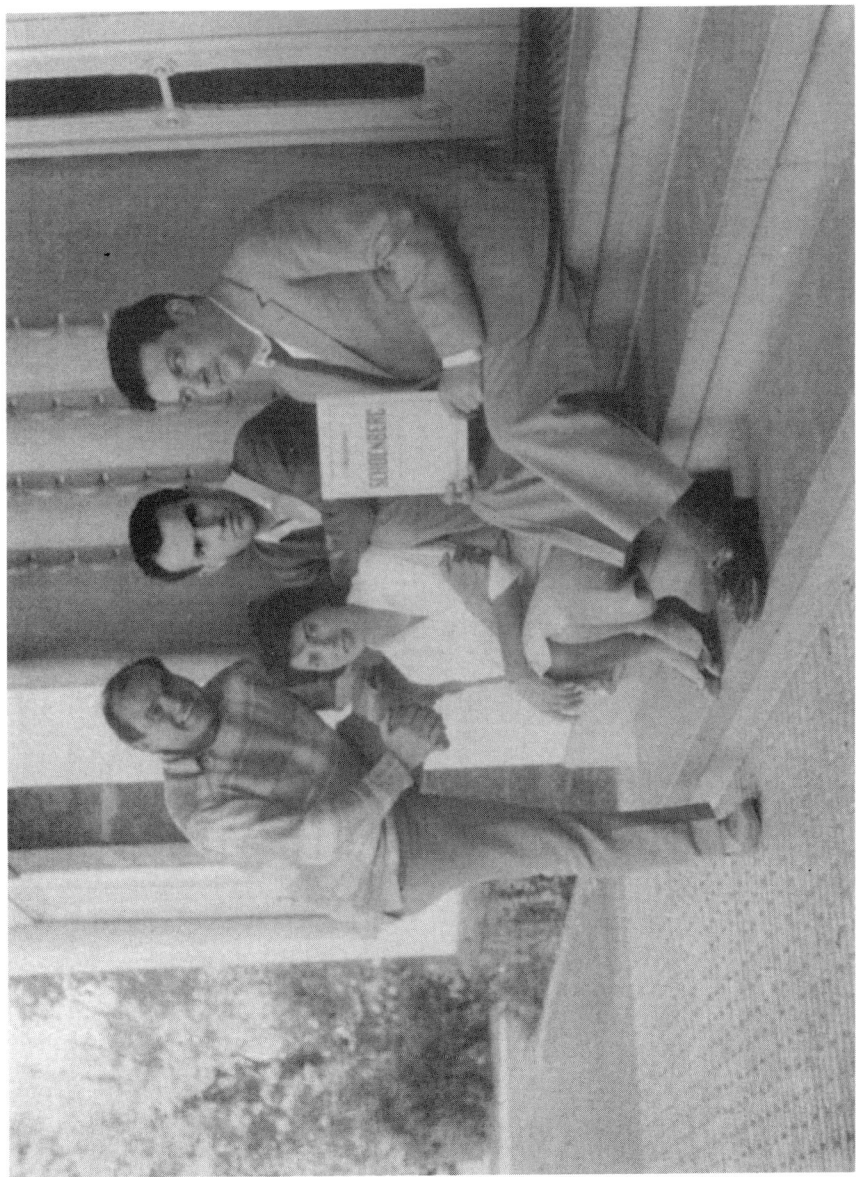

Plate 5 Darmstadt, 1959: (Left to Right) Kasimierz Serocki, Nuria Nono-Schoenberg, Luigi Nono, Bruno Maderna. (Photograph: Hella Steinecke)

Plate 6 Darmstadt, 1960: (Left to Right) Bruno Maderna, Earle Brown, Wolfgang Steinecke, Severino Gazzelloni, Pierre Boulez. (Photograph: Hella Steinecke)

Plate 7   Darmstadt, 1960: (Left to Right) Bruno Maderna, Earle Brown. (Photograph: Hella Steinecke)

Plate 8 Bruno Maderna, Darmstadt, 1961. (Photograph: Hans Kenner)

Plate 9 International Chamber Ensemble, Darmstadt, 1961: rehearsal of Earle Brown's *Available Forms 1*: conductor Bruno Maderna. (Photograph: Hans Kenner)

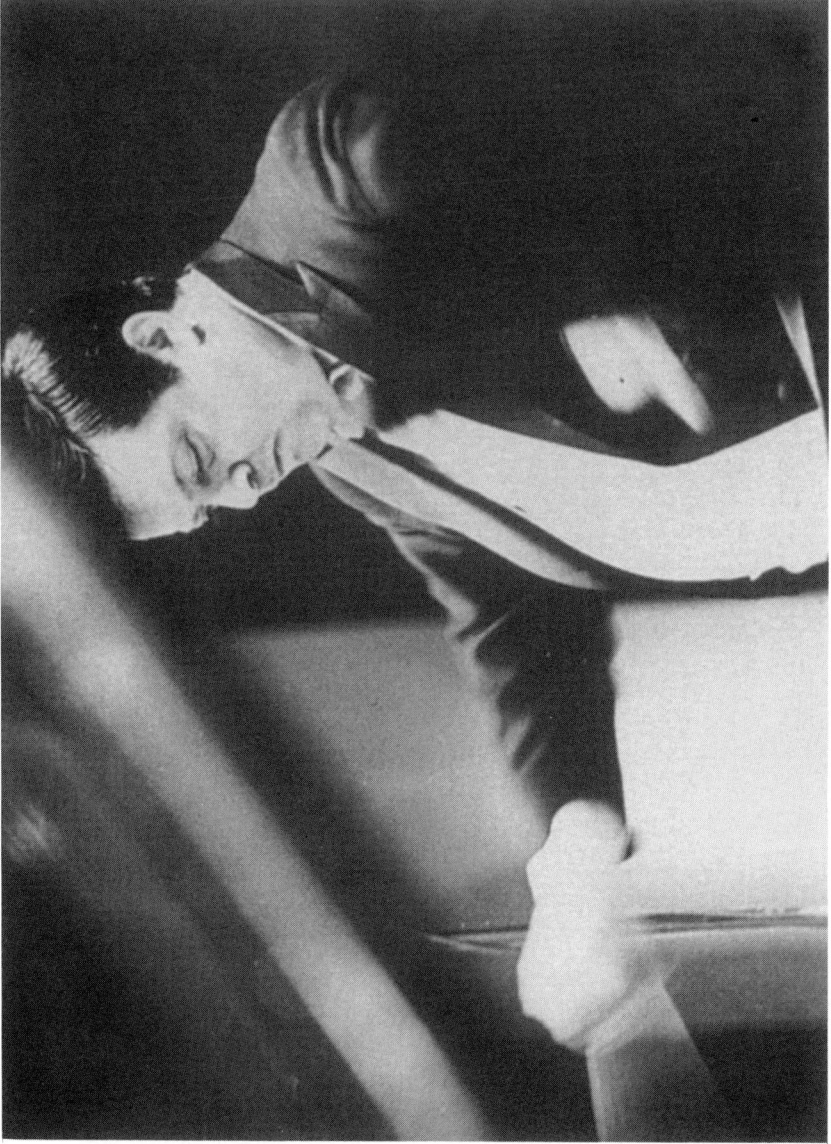

Plate 10   Bruno Maderna, Darmstadt, 1962. (Photograph: Pit Ludwig)

Plate 11 Bruno Maderna and Severino Gazzelloni (flute), Darmstadt, 1964. (Photograph: Pit Ludwig)

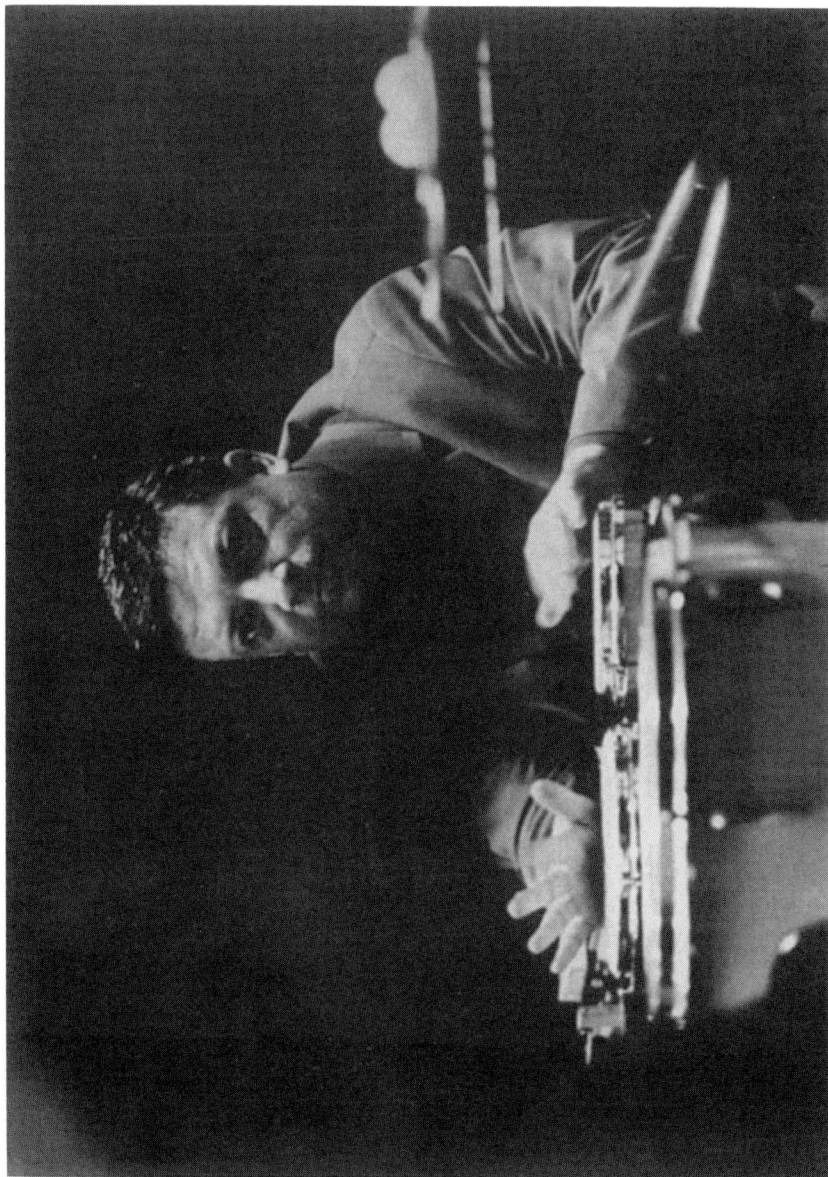

Plate 12 Bruno Maderna in performance of Varèse: *Ionisation*, Darmstadt, 1966. (Photograph: Pit Ludwig)

Chapter 4

Aleatoric principles — *Oboe Concerto No 1; Grande Aulodia; Quadrivium; Aura.*

Maderna is not a composer whose work may conveniently be divided into 'early', 'middle' and 'later' periods, as though it were capable of some clear division of stylistic tendencies or concerns. There are, as we have already seen, continuous threads running through his work, and despite the watershed which appeared with his involvement in electro-acoustic music from the early 1950s, which undoubtedly spread an influence over all his compositional activity, a certain continuum exists between one work and another in a different format which was of major importance in Maderna's thinking.

Nevertheless, it becomes clear that in his last years Maderna did adopt a manner of composition which was to a great extent imbued with the spirit of aleatoric procedures of one kind or another, and this went a long way towards determining the overall shape, as well as many of the details, of his later works. This aleatoricism had begun to appear in his work in the 1960s, and is present in one form or another in virtually all of his last compositions.

The enormous quantity of sketches and plans for his works which he left at his death in 1973, and which are now assembled in the Sacher Foundation in Basel, reveal a great intricacy in the compositional procedures of each work, but we are concerned here less with the 'minutiae' of serial and other compositional devices in each work, and much more with attempting to elucidate their overall characteristics, and with clarifying some of the problems which might stand in the way of realisation of these scores. In his later years, having experienced first the impact of serialism, and later of electronic music and of indeterminacy, Maderna believed less and less in the necessity of any overall 'consistency'. In an interview with Christoph Bitter some months before the composer's death, he expressed his loathing for artistic 'consistency', and a preference for the composer's freedom to follow his instincts in whatever direction these might lead.[1] Maderna here expressed in a cogent manner an important aspect of his artistic philosophy. His rejection of what he calls 'consistency' in artistic creation, and his desire to follow 'the different aspects of our organism, whether physical or psychological', tells us, in fact, a good deal about the reasons behind the sometimes puzzling nature of his musical works. We have already observed how, from the very beginning of his work, he had often brought together an almost bewildering diversity of procedures, styles and techniques: in *Composizione No 2*, he had combined serialism and modalism; in *Don Perlimplin*, he had brought together orchestral, soloistic, vocal and electronic elements to produce a dramatic whole; and in *Hyperion*, the solo flute, soprano and orchestra are placed alongside music on tape. The essence of Maderna's compositional procedures, in fact, lay in this very freedom to bring together disparate, and at times even incongruous, elements of expression, the freedom not only to choose one path or another, but, when occasion demanded it, to follow several paths simultaneously.

Maderna however specifically mentions *serial* 'consistency' as 'one of the worst diseases'. In this, he appears to be rejecting the idea that the principles of either 'classical' dodecaphony or indeed of the 'integral serialism' as practised by some of his Darmstadt colleagues during the early 1950s, should become an exclusive 'method' of creating a musical structure. Maderna was ever the greatest opponent of any dogmatic and rigid systems, and in fact we would search in vain for any work of his in which we might hope to find serialism of one kind or another as the sole structuring principle. Even in his earliest works after he had begun to employ serialism, such as the *Tre Liriche Greche* and *Composizione No 2*, we can see a wealth of diverse principles at work, of which serialism is only one. In the later works, Maderna was concerned far more with the integration of several disparate procedures and the structuring of the resultant material into an expressive whole, than with any 'consistent' or 'mono-dimensional' compositional principles.

Is there, in fact, any *'inconsistency'* in Maderna's work as a whole? 'Eclecticism' would be a totally wrong term to use about his work: in no work can we point to any manner which relies upon disparate styles 'borrowed' from others; rather, we can see in his work a constant desire to *explore* and to *integrate*. These explorations led him in several directions simultaneously, to a thoroughgoing investigation of the possibilities of tape-composition, of radiophonic work, of orchestral, soloistic and vocal writing, of aleatoricism, as well as, naturally, of serial techniques of composition, and all of these explorations were held together by a mind which was able to comprehend and deal with several different techniques and approaches at the same time. Maderna's later compositions in particular, those in which the different modes of working provided a dazzling variety, were the product of a kind of musical 'juggler' with objects of varying dimensions, shapes and materials, one whose brilliance of execution of the art of composition must be admired.

Above all, Maderna desired *freedom*: freedom for himself as composer to explore without prejudice, and, as a natural consequence, freedom for the performer to exhibit as close a relationship as possible with the music with whose performance he was charged. This performer-freedom led him in his last years to adopt aleatoric principles of various kinds in many works, which was achieved mainly in the field of instrumental composition, and became the most potent expression of what Berio, talking about the earlier *String Quartet*, called 'chance' and 'necessity'. Although this aleatoricism can be seen above all in instrumental works, we are faced with a particular problem with regard to the opera *Satyricon*.

Adopting a 'collage' technique of composition, Maderna created a work which, on one level at least, might be called an 'aleatoric opera', consisting as it does of a score made up of some un-numbered and un-sequenced sections which may be freely interpreted by the conductor and producer of the work, and with some sections on tape which *may* be used between some of these scored sections. It will be our task in discussing this opera to clarify to what extent the material given to us in the score and tapes for *Satyricon* may be regarded as 'authentic' material of an aleatoric kind, and to what extent the rather loose and confusing state of this material is due to the rapid decline in the composer's health during its preparation.

The principle of aleatoric composition had, in a sense, first appeared in Maderna's work in *Musica su due dimensioni* in 1958, that is, at the same time that Pierre Boulez and Karlheinz Stockhausen began to employ this principle in instrumental works. The mobility of the interaction between the electronic and live elements of this composition represented a clear step in the direction of the performer-freedoms which were to come to the fore in Maderna's work. However, it was to be only some years later that Maderna was to adopt in full measure the aleatoric principle to a significant degree, and the progression from the *Oboe Concerto No 1* composed in 1962 and *Grande Aulodia* in 1970 shows clearly how the development of Maderna's style in the intervening years began to demand such freedoms.

The three *Oboe Concertos* of Maderna represent one of the most significant contributions of any twentieth-century composer to the literature of the instrument; they were composed in 1962, 1967 and 1973. The first of these works arose from a *Komposition für Oboe, Kammerensemble und Tonband* ('Composition for Oboe, Chamber Ensemble and Tape') which Maderna wrote in 1962 and which was performed in that same year in Darmstadt, with Lothar Faber as soloist. Maderna revised the score immediately after this performance, and the work was performed during 1963 as the 'second version' of the piece, again in Darmstadt: however, it had already been given earlier in 1963 as *Concerto per Oboe* in Venice, and the score of the work retains the title of *Concerto*, with no mention of the tape part of the work, which the composer had by then withdrawn.

Francesca Magnani, writing about this work,[2] has provided a detailed account of the differences between the *Komposition* and the *Concerto*, but the important point to note is that the revision of the score went much further than simply the omission in the *Concerto* of the tape-part, and concerned the structural shape of the whole work, as well as some important details of the instrumental material. The recording of the performance of the *Komposition* at the Darmstadt Summer School in 1962 is preserved in the Darmstadt Institute, but no manuscript-materials are now to be found which would make it possible to re-construct this 'original' version of the work.

The *Concerto*, published by Bruzzichelli in Florence and recorded by both Lothar Faber and by Han de Vries, shares some of that communality of musical material which was such an important characteristic of Maderna's compositions at that time: we find part of the fifth oboe cadenza (p. 29) and of p. 26 in *Serenata IV*, and in pages 29 and 30 of the *Concerto* the piano-part from the first page of *Honeyrêves* is embedded in the orchestral material. The tape used in the performance of the *Komposition* is identical with the second part of *Le Rire*.

The instrumentation of the *Concerto* is of fundamental importance in defining the timbral characteristics which play such a decisive role in the work: a chamber ensemble is employed which consists of solo instruments in winds and strings (but with two flutes), but the percussion part makes use of no less than 50 instruments (played by four percussionists), together with celesta, two harps and two pianos; the soloist must play cor anglais and oboe d'amore in addition to the normal oboe.

The structure of the work may best be described as a 'Cadenza-Concerto': Maderna here adopts a principle which was to be of great importance in virtually all of his subsequent works in Concerto-form, with Cadenzas (most often accompanied by groupings of other instruments written freely) acting as one focus of the one-movement work, the other focus provided by orchestral 'interludes' of varying character. This structure creates a kind of free flow between 'solo' and 'tutti' which tends to obliterate any clear distinction between the two halves. A closeness between the solo instrument and various ensemble instruments treated soloistically from time to time in the course of the work also enhances the homogeneity of the total ensemble (this is apparent not only in the first section of the work, in which the figures of the oboe d'amore blend in a harmonious manner with those of the strings, but also for example in the interweaving of the oboe soloist with winds and solo strings in CADENZA 2).

The 'aleatoric' element in this structure is rather small, being limited to the placement of instrumental figurations and 'mobiles', as well as to the employment of graphic symbols for both the percussion and occasionally other instruments (as for example bassoon in CADENZA 2): larger-scale aleatoricism in the formal scheme is avoided, thus contributing to the relative tightness of the overall shape of the piece. We find some use of graphic notation, not only for percussion but for other instruments of the ensemble, which arise from a desire to stimulate the imaginative powers of the performers, not simply to provide a precise score for realisation; these examples of graphic writing make frequent use of proportional notation. Similarly, we find passages in which, combining small figurations notated 'normally' with some graphic and verbal indications, the entries of each fragment are left relatively free, but within units which have a certain homogeneity. [Ex. 4.1(a), (b)]

However, we do not, in this work, find what might be described as a 'third level' of aleatoricism: that is, the freedom given to the interpreter of the work to re-order relatively large sections of its material; this was to become of great importance in the structure of the later works of Maderna, but here in the *Concerto* the freedom of this kind given to the players is limited to one instance in which a 'mobile' for percussion may be played three times at most, each with a different dynamic level, tempo and mode of attack (by the use of varying sticks). [Ex. 4.2]

The soloist's part in the *Concerto* is characterised by a certain 'improvisatory' quality, which runs right through the work, binding together the more disparate elements of which the accompanying ensemble part is composed: this solo part includes the very occasional use of such devices at multiphonics, mouthpiece-sounds and *glissandi* (in CADENZA 2, in response to the variegated tone-colours of the accompanying ensemble), but the overall line of expressive melodic utterance is maintained throughout, as is a certain rather melancholy expression, which appears right at the start, as the solo oboe d'amore with its free-roaming melody is accompanied by harmonics and melodic fragments in the group of solo strings. [Ex. 4.3] This continuity of lyricism and expressivity in the solo-line — the 'melos' of the work — acts as a central binding-force in the work as a whole; at times the solo part is embedded in a free instrumental polyphony of sound-fragments from the ensemble-players, seeming at one and the same time to contribute to the ensemble and to exist independently of it, the other players merely 'reacting' to the solo line.

The work ends with the cor anglais, with a melodic line of a similarly melancholic character to the opening of the *Concerto*, gradually playing longer-held notes, with the percussion providing a sonorous 'aside', and showing yet

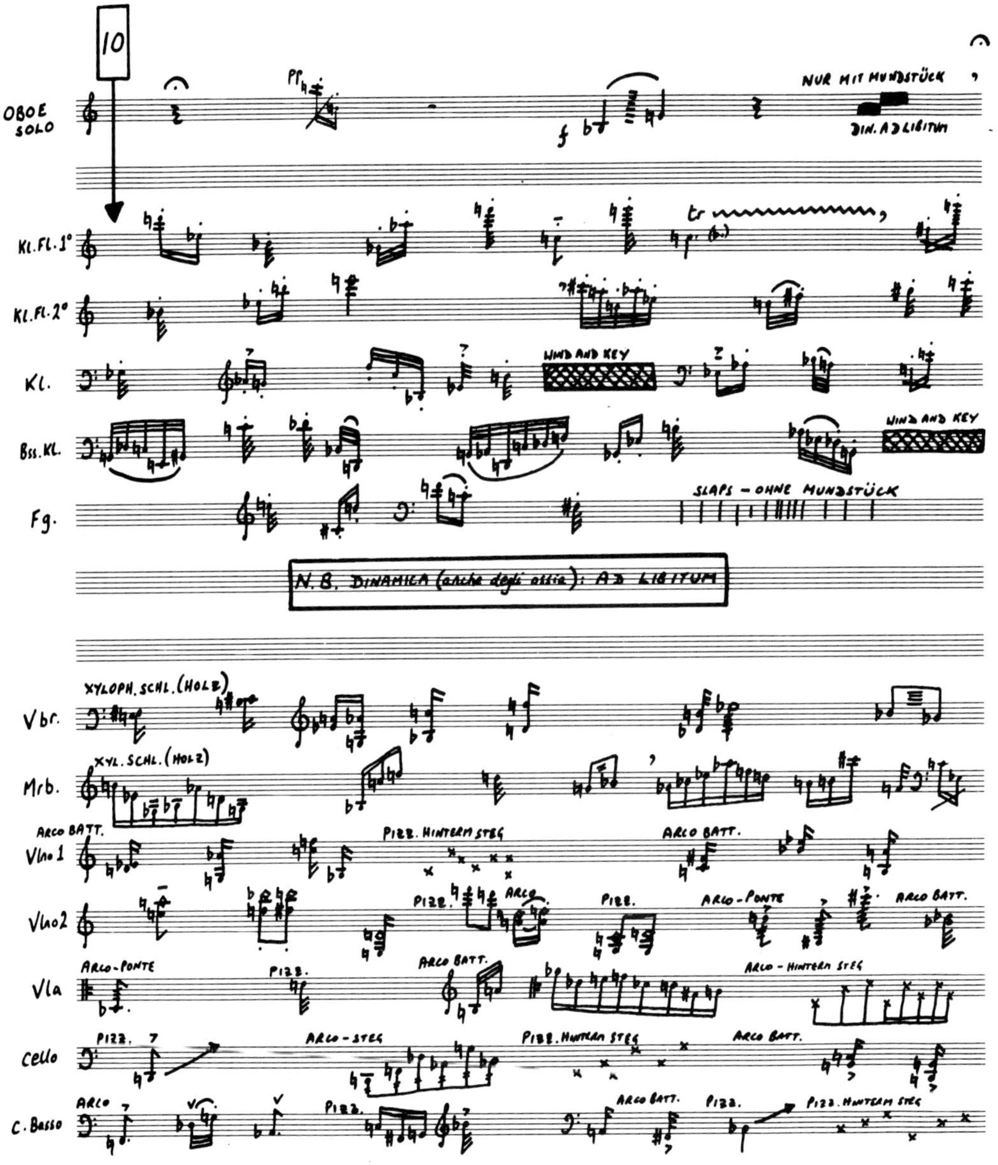

Ex. 4.1(a): Maderna: *Oboe Concerto No. 1*: page 17

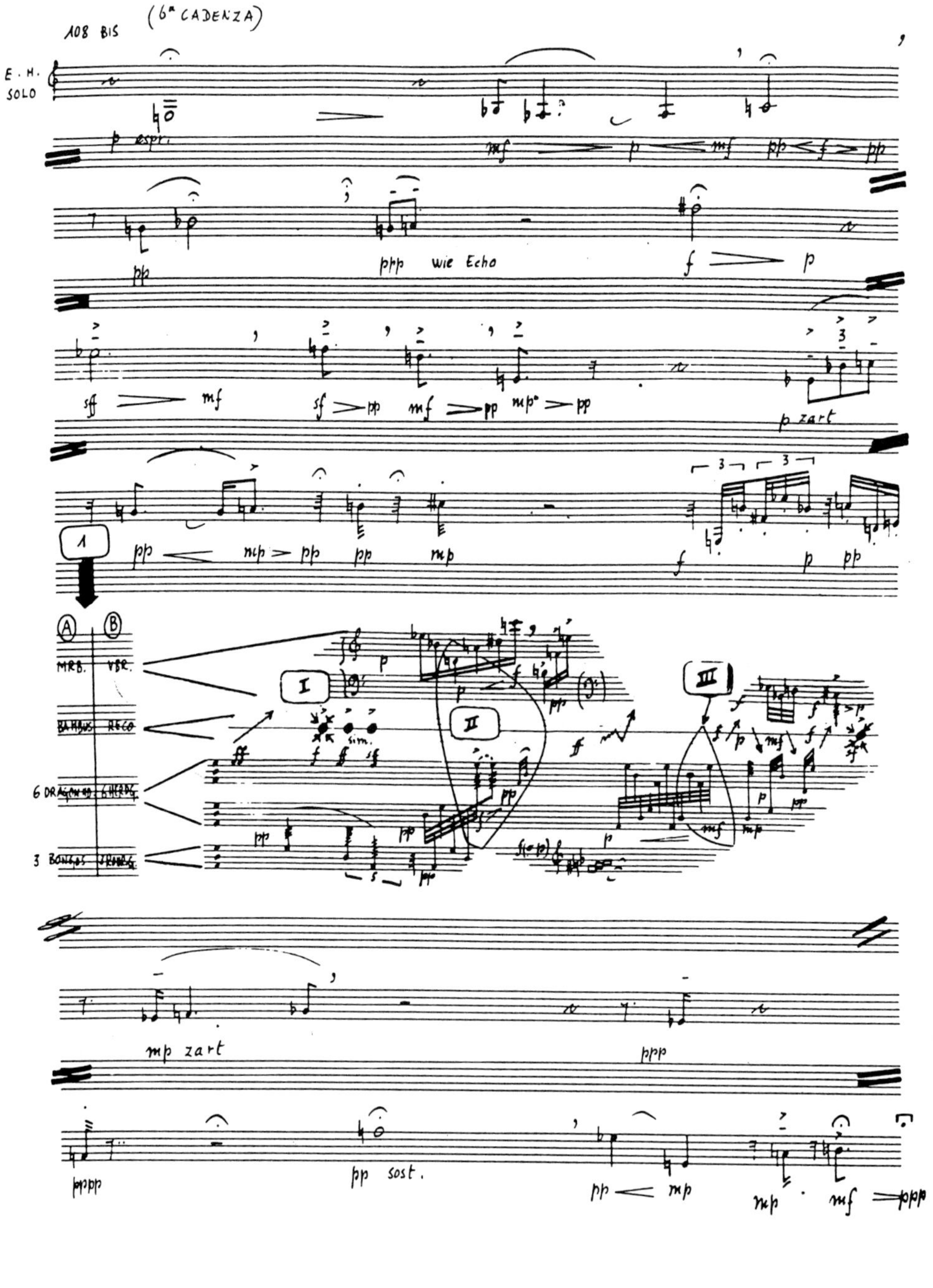

Ex. 4.1(b): Maderna: *Oboe Concerto No. 1*: 108 bis

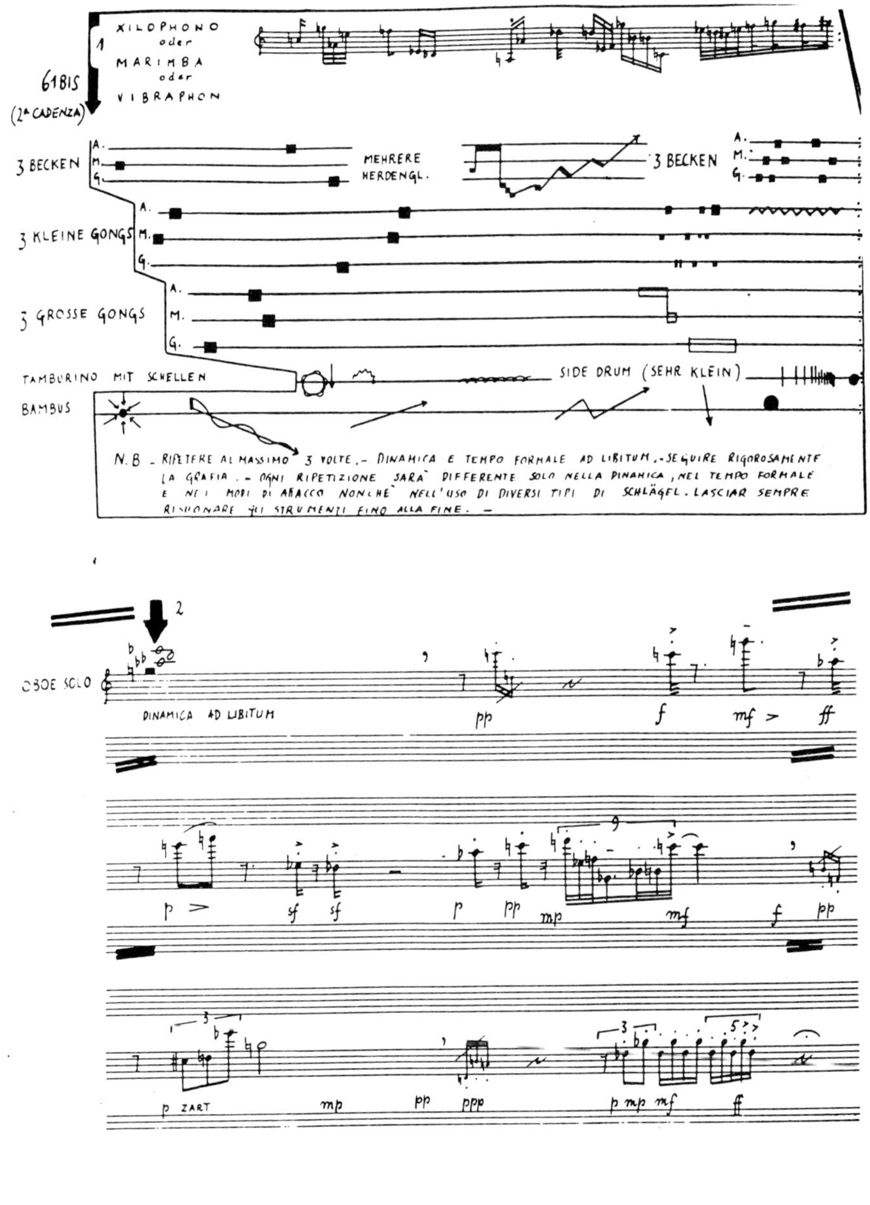

Ex. 4.2: Maderna: *Oboe Concerto No. 1*: page 13

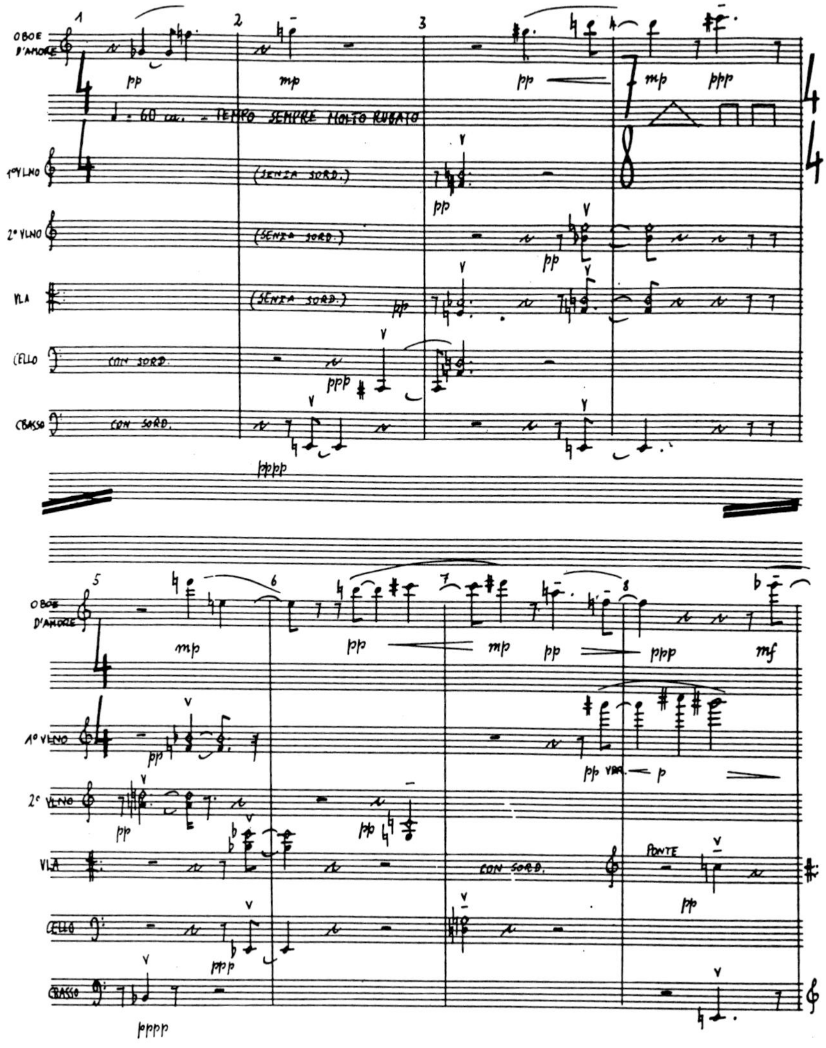

Ex. 4.3: Maderna: *Oboe Concerto No. 1*: 1–13

Ex. 4.3: *Contd*

another example of that gently-fading openness at the end of the work of which Maderna was so fond, and which had made its first appearances in his early orchestral works. [Ex. 4.4]

Grande Aulodia, which Maderna completed during 1970 and dedicated to Severino Gazzelloni and Lothar Faber, the soloists in the work's first performance in Rome in February of that year, represents a culmination of the works of a solo variety which he had composed, and one of the most important works of the composer's last years. The work is scored for two soloists (flute, piccolo, flute in Eb, alto flute; oboe, oboe d'amore, cor anglais, musette), together with a large orchestra which includes three string-groups.

The title of the work is of particular significance: in 1965, Maderna had composed, for the oboist Lothar Faber and the guitarist Alvaro Company, a work entitled *Aulodia per Lothar*, which was given at the Venice 'Biennale' in that same year, and subsequently published by Suvini Zerboni in 1977 and recorded by Lothar Faber and Vincenzo Saldarelli. The 'aulos' idea (originally a reed-instrument of Ancient Greek music, the 'aulody' being understood as music for the voice accompanied and duplicated by the aulos) incorporated, for Maderna, qualities of 'vocal' expression, but emanating from an instrument, and the *Aulodia per Lothar* embodied all the virtuosity of expressive capabilities which the composer found in the playing of his friend Faber, for whom also he composed the first two of his three *Oboe Concertos*.

Thus, the *Grande Aulodia* extended the 'aulody' idea to involve not only the melodic-vocal characteristics of the oboes of Faber, but also those qualities which Maderna found in the flutes of Severino Gazzelloni: both types of instrument are of ancient origin and, in the purity and expressivity of which they were capable, were able to summon up for the composer the 'primordial' melodic, soloistic and improvisatory qualities which had at various times during his life (notably in the

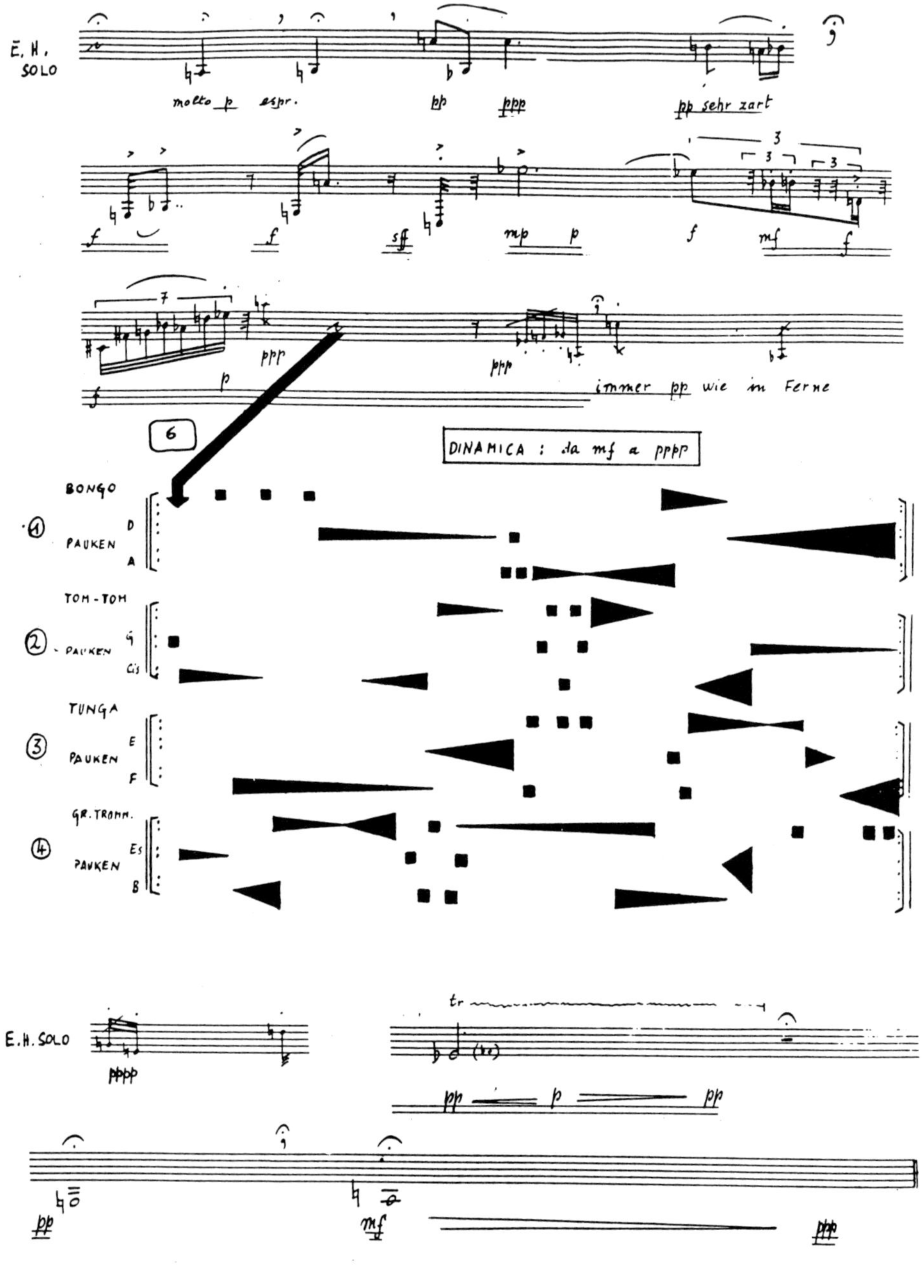

Ex. 4.4: Maderna: *Oboe Concerto No. 1*: page 40

piccolo-solo with which *Serenata No 2* begins, and the Greek melody at the opening of *Composizione No 2*) been a constant point of return in his musical expression.

The change which Maderna's musical thinking underwent during his last years, creating a manner of writing in which control and freedom, strictness and expressivity, are held in perfect balance, may be measured by the change encompassed between the *Oboe Concerto No.1* of 1962 and *Grande Aulodia* of 1970: in the former work, aleatoric freedom had been circumscribed, limited to 'internal' musical events, whereas by the time of the latter work Maderna was able to expand greatly the area encompassed by those freedoms, which inform much larger stretches of the work. This expansion of the freedoms involved in the work includes the disposition of the orchestral forces, which is designed to aid the mobility of sound-structures based on a less conventional grouping of the instruments. [Ex. 4.5]

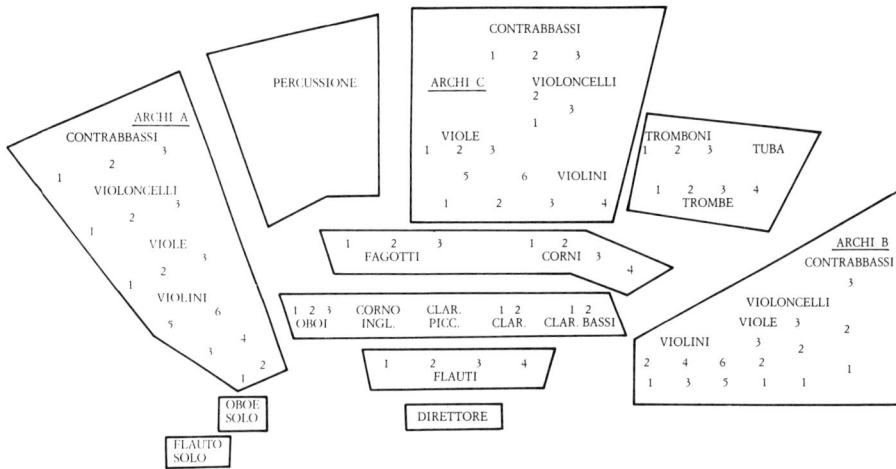

Ex. 4.5: Maderna: *Grande Aulodia*: orchestral layout

The larger-scale structure of the work may be summarised as follows:

1. *Introductory Cadenza* for flute and oboe/oboe d'amore
2. *Wienerisch*: three string orchestras (bars 1–25 repeated)
3. Flute in Eb and oboe d'amore with accompaniment of 'cellos, gradually adding other instruments (bars 26–161)
4. *Middle Section*: mobile orchestral elements against solos of piccolo, musette, flute in G, normal flute (bars 161 bis–180 tris)
5. Flute and oboe against 'normally' written background of the orchestra (bars 181–229).
6. *Final Cadenza* for flute and cor anglais, to which is added an accompaniment of quietly-sustained chords in the three string-groups (bars 230–241).

This structure, which is basically that of a 'Cadenza-Concerto' like that of *Oboe Concerto No 1*, exhibits great control of the varying characters of each episode of which it is comprised, varying in general terms in the degree of 'tension' or 'relaxation' which they each demonstrate.

Grande Aulodia begins with an atmosphere of 'improvisation': the solo instruments echo each other, only gradually becoming independent, and this cadenza evokes a feeling of the ancient origins of melody, *'aulos'* and *'melos'* held in perfect balance: the two instrumental lines flow into each other with the greatest degree of naturalness. [Ex. 4.6]

When the orchestra enters, the quality of 'improvisation' is not disturbed: in a section marked *'Wienerisch'*, the three string-groups, distributed spatially over the platform, create a flowing and multi-coloured tapestry of sound which is repeated *pianissimo* and *con sordino*. [Ex. 4.7]

In the episode which follows (from bar 26), we see a close integration of the soloists (flute in Eb, later replaced by oboe d'amore) with the ensemble in a manner which had figured only very rarely in *Oboe Concerto No. 1*: strictly-composed in a 'conventional' layout (with a steady quaver-motion), the passage begins with a filigree of brief motifs from the solo 'cellos, the flute melody flowing into the accompanying parts. [Ex. 4.8] As the episode develops, gradually incorporating other instruments of the orchestra, we hear the two soloists in an almost Bachian counterpoint of melodic lines [Ex. 4.9]

The middle section of the work, in contrast to this, is organised in a very open manner: the solo lines of piccolo, musette (which is directed to use both 'sweet' and 'hard' reeds in various parts of the episode), flute in G and normal flute are surrounded with a variable sequence of instrumental mobiles. It is at this point that the disposition of the orchestral forces indicated in the preface to the score becomes an integral part of the structure of the work: each group is directed to play, at the discretion of the conductor, a series of highly varied mobiles, set out in alphabetical order, (from A to S) in such a way that we hear a progression of instrumental sonorities beginning with those of pitched percussion. The placement of these instrumental sonorities over the platform thus makes possible a gradual shift from one space to another in the manner of Venetian 'polychoral' writing, a procedure which became of some importance in much of Maderna's later orchestral works. The mobiles range in texture from a somewhat 'Messiaenesque' wind-writing, with a mass of similar figurations held tightly together, to percussion writing of a graphic kind, relying greatly on the imaginative realisation of the score by the players. [Ex. 4.10(a), (b)] The composer envisages a gradual increase of tension and contrast through this whole episode, writing at the end that 'one should reach the greatest heterophony and, when the conductor has attained and judged this right, he should cut off the whole thing with a sudden gesture of both arms'.

It should not be thought that this episode, which extends the freedoms of the performers to their greatest degree, is conceived as a separate entity within the work as a whole: on the contrary, the freedom given here to the accompanying ensemble serves simply to provide a dramatic tension against which the solo instruments (whose parts, whilst still retaining that same degree of instrumental improvisation which we have seen in the earlier sections of the work, nevertheless do not contain such freedoms of ordering) continue on their course, either singly or in combination.

The freedom given to the two solo instrumentalities is the freedom of a cadenza, and in the final episode of the work we hear what is in effect an 'accompanied

Ex. 4.6: Maderna: *Grande Aulodia*: opening

Ex. 4.7: Maderna: *Grande Aulodia*: 1–13

Ex. 4.8: Maderna: *Grande Aulodia*: 26–43

cadenza' in which the free, expressive, and gradually lengthening, fading figurations of the alto flute and cor anglais are accompanied by (perhaps it would be better to say 'placed within') a radiant and gently moving set of chords in the three string-groups. The tempo of this string accompaniment, which enters unobtrusively during the first part of the cadenza, may vary, and Maderna gives a note to the conductor to say that 'from here to the end the conductor accompanies the soloists — who will not have any tempo, as if in an interior ecstasy — circumspectly, making sure that the string orchestra should simply be a mysterious 'alone' — one may halt at any moment, (creating ⌢'s) as if taking a suggestion from the soloists' melody. It should be so arranged that this will end shortly before the soloists, leaving the last notes to them'. [Ex. 4.11]

Ex. 4.9: Maderna: *Grande Aulodia*: 84–100

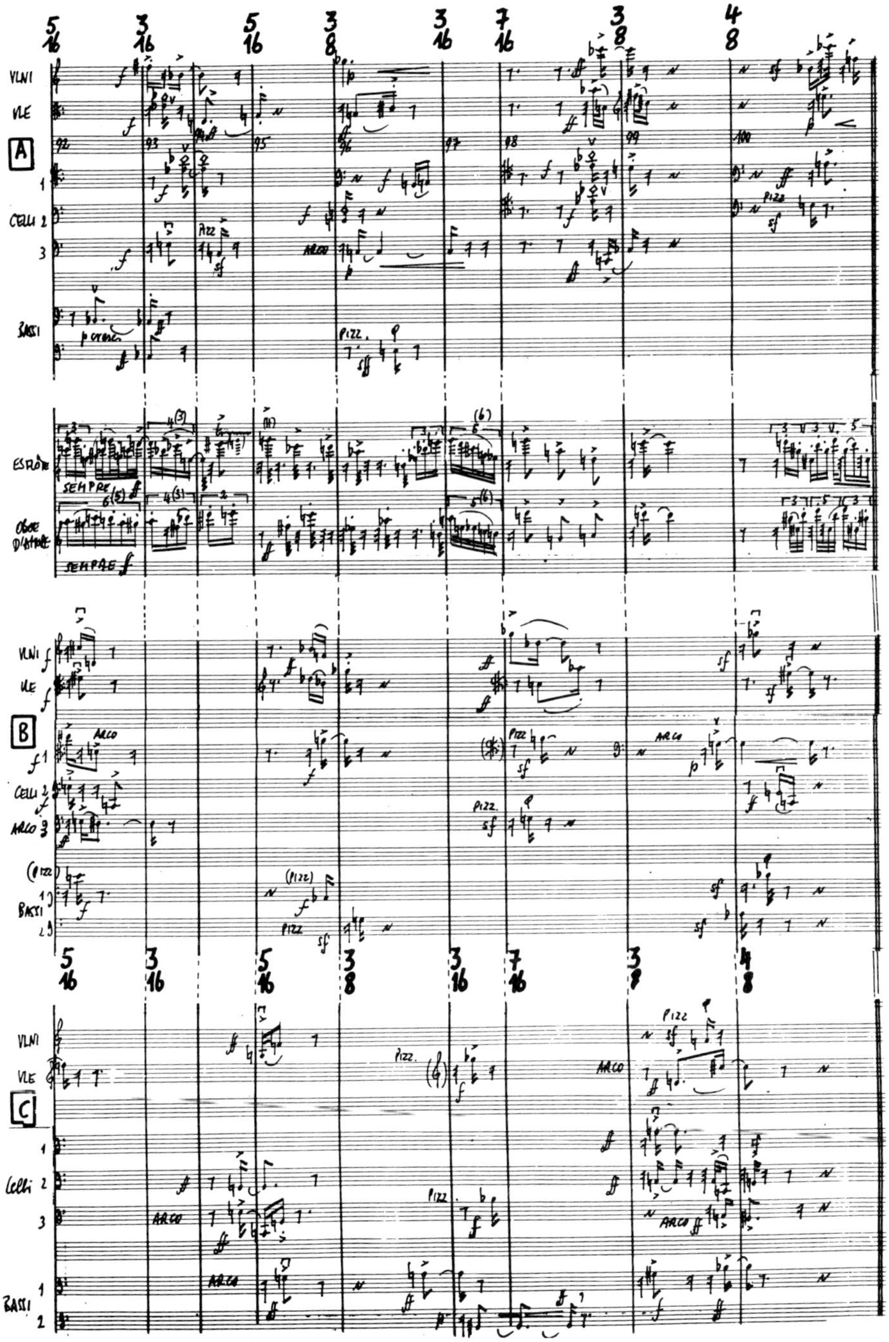

Ex. 4.9: *Contd*

Ex. 4.10(a): Maderna: *Grande Aulodia*: 163–165

Ex. 4.10(b): Maderna: *Grande Aulodia*: module

Ex. 4.11: Maderna: *Grande Aulodia*: 230–241

ALTFLÖTE SOLO
ALTFL. SOLO
ENGL. H. SOLO
ALTFL.
ENGL. H.
ARCHI A
VLE
CELLI
BASSI
234
235
236
237
ARCHI B
ARCHI C
VLN
CBSSI

Ex. 4.11: *Contd*

Ex. 4.11: *Contd*

The plaintive quality of the ending of *Grande Aulodia*, combining a rather 'vocal' lyricism with instrumental improvisatory qualities, and surrounded with a brilliant 'aura' of string-sounds, brings together those qualities associated with 'aulos' and with 'melos' which we saw as the most important characteristics of the work as a whole. This was not to be Maderna's last exploration of the Concerto idea (he was to compose *Ausstrahlung*, for female voice, flute and oboe obbligati, large orchestra and tape in 1971, and his *Oboe Concerto No. 3* in 1973), but in *Grande Aulodia* we see his ideal of expressivity, freedom and flow in the Concerto in a work which may be regarded as one of the most important masterpieces in Concerto form from the last few decades.

The series of works for large orchestra which Maderna composed during his last years (*Quadrivium* in 1969, *Aura* and *Biogramma* in 1972) represent a culmination of the composer's writing for the symphony orchestra. It is likely that these works were the product of work pursued over some considerable time, given the large-scale nature of all three of them, although they were all commissioned works (*Quadrivium* for the Royan Festival, *Aura* for the Chicago Symphony Orchestra, and *Biogramma* for the Eastman School of Music). They are amongst the most regularly played of Maderna's works, and all three are recorded on disc.

In all these later orchestral works, as also in the numerous works involving a solo instrument or instruments (the *Violin Concerto*, *Grande Aulodia*, *Ausstrahlung* and the *Oboe Concertos*), there is to be found that 'controlled aleatoricism' which we examined in *Grande Aulodia* and which became such a natural and instinctive manner of writing in all these works that one might say that it took its place equally alongside the contrapuntal, serial and neo-classical manner which we saw playing such important roles in the musical thinking of that earlier group of orchestral works composed between 1948 and 1954.

In suggesting that Maderna's involvement in procedures which may be described as aleatoric had arisen quite naturally from the interactive dimensions in *Musica su due dimensioni* in 1958 (and even in the 1952 version of this work we may find a somewhat cruder and less effective demonstration of the operation), it might seem that the introduction of aleatoricism into European music by Stockhausen and Boulez in 1956–7 (in *Klavierstück XI* and *Trosième Sonate*, respectively) had not played a crucial role in influencing Maderna's own aleatoricism during the ensuing period. There can be little doubt, however, that Maderna, who was very close to Boulez in particular during this whole period, did absorb a certain degree of influence in this direction, albeit an influence which clarified a tendency which was already to some extent present in his work. We should not ignore the fact that the two works of Stockhausen and Boulez which had been so influential in changing the course of European avant-garde music in the late 1950s were both works of a *solo* variety, whereas Maderna's later aleatoric works were almost entirely of a *concerted* kind.

Stockhausen claims that he had begun to experiment with chance-formations as early as 1953, during the period of his researches into phonetics and information theory with Werner Meyer-Eppler at the University of Bonn,[3] and like Boulez, denies that this introduction of chance-elements was influenced by the less controlled uses of chance with which John Cage had been working in America. For Stockhausen, the chance-element in instrumental performance was opposed to, and to some extent also a reaction to, that direct creation of finished and infinitely-repeatable 'acts of production' which had characterised electronic composition:[4]

'Composing electronic music involves describing sound in mechanical and electro-acoustical terms and thinking entirely in terms of machinery, apparatus, circuitry; reckoning with the single act of production and the unlimited repeatibility of the composition thus produced.

Writing instrumental music — after this — involves unleashing the performer's activities through optical signs and making a direct approach to the musician's living organism, and to his constantly varying and unpredictable capacities for response; bestowing the possibility of multiple acts of production from performance to performance, and that of unrepeatability.'

For Boulez, on the other hand, the introduction of chance-elements into performance did not arise from any such reaction to the character of an 'act of · production' and to the repeatability of electronic composition (in which he had, in fact, been only minimally involved at that time): rather, it arose from a poetic model, derived in particular from Mallarmé, involving the concept of the 'labyrinth', contrasted with the 'straight line' which had characterised traditional thought:[5]

'As against this classical procedure the idea of the maze seems to me the most important recent innovation in the creative sphere. I can already hear the malicious retort that I shall inevitably receive — that quite a number of Ariadne's clues may well be needed to make any progress in such a maze possible, and that not everyone feels the call to become a Theseus. Don't let this worry us! The modern conception of the maze in a work of art is certainly one of the most considerable advances in Western thought, and one upon which it is impossible to go back.'

Boulez had foreseen the idea of forms of aleatoricism applicable to works of a concerted kind:[6]

' . . . According to traditional principles one element, A, was immediately followed by another, B, to which a third, C, was linked directly. The distinguishing feature of the new form consists in the fact that it is in a way created from one moment to the next — in other words it is possible, under certain conditions of course, to move directly from A to C without first passing through B. Imagine a network of railway lines in a station. The disposition of the rails and the points is precisely fixed, but to change the course of any network no more is needed than to press a button or work a lever, in the same way local decisions taken by the players and the conductor enable the form of a work to be modified at any moment in performance.'

Maderna's aleatoric procedures in the concerted works of his last years may be seen as exemplifying in precise terms the idea which Boulez here sets out, and it was precisely in this area, of controlled use of chance within a concerted framework guided by the conductor's pre-arranged signalling to the players, that Maderna chose to concentrate in the series of works of an orchestral and ensemble kind which he composed between 1964 and 1973. Boulez recognised the innateness of Maderna's sense of freedom, and gave expression to this in his obituary notice for his Italian friend in 1973:[7]

'Bruno Maderna was someone who knew what it meant to be rigorous but had never decided to apply it to himself, simply because it did not appeal to him . . . His kind of rigorousness had nothing to do with numbers, it was simply the knowledge that he could express his personality only by disregarding punctilio of any kind.

The best things in his own music, the prize moments, sprang from this immediate, irrational musical sense, and for this reason his most successful works are those that leave the most initiative to the players. At the end of his last work, an oboe concerto, he wrote: 'I hope that I have provided enough material for soloist, conductor and orchestra to come to terms and enjoy playing what I have written'. In a way he gave birth to a music that he carried, like a mother, and then absolutely trusted.'

Maderna's adoption of aleatoric procedures in many of his later works, a move prompted as we have said by his innate desire for freedom, involved performers in decisions regarding the ordering and timing of elements of a composition within broad spaces of the formal structure, and the composition of such works therefore necessitated a degree of mobility in the structures themselves. We might describe the resultant works not as examples of an *'opera aperta'*, with performer-freedoms largely replacing the composer's structuring of events, but more accurately as an *'opera componibile'* in which the various elements of which the structure is built may be re-arranged at will within natural limits set by the nature of the material which the composer has given.

If the most important impetus and inspiration for Maderna in the works in Concerto-form of his last years (the three *Oboe Concertos*, *Grande Aulodia* and the *Violin Concerto*) came from the 'personality' of the solo instruments and of their players (Lothar Faber, Severino Gazzelloni, Theo Olof and Han de Vries), it was upon the personality of the orchestra itself, as a vehicle capable of the most diverse musical expression, and capable also of a high degree of mutability, re-disposition and varying division whilst still retaining its orchestral characteristics, that the expression of those orchestral compositions was based. It was this very mutability which became for Maderna, in the first of the group of late works for orchestra, *Quadrivium* (1969), for four percussionists and four orchestral groups, a cornerstone of the musical thinking in the work. The four-part division of instrumental forces, and their disposition on the platform, are at the heart of the piece, and although in *Aura* and *Biogramma* some three years later Maderna was to adopt a more conventional placement of the orchestral forces, he may well have shared to some extent the dissatisfaction with conventional placements of orchestral instruments which Boulez, in speaking about his *Figures-Doubles-Prismes*, composed in various versions in 1958, 1964 and 1968, had expressed with some force:[8]

'This orchestral structure, this succession of immovable planes, has always worried me. In 1958, when I decided to compose this work, I thought about modifying this structure by separating the individual groups while leaving them a certain autonomy, and doing so in such a way that the woodwind in particular would be split up among different groups, and the same with the brass. The advantage of such a scheme was first to split the wind instruments from their homogeneous grouping, and then to produce effects of movement and combination in different corners of the platform, the combination coming not simply from an overall perception. I shall still keep this scheme if I add to the work since it gives good results from the point of view of sonority. When you hear the work live, the sonorities are extremely homogeneous yet at the same time scattered, so that it is not a homogeneity of neighbouring groups but a homogeneity of fusion'.

The basis of the overall musical thinking in *Quadrivium*, in fact, may be said to lie in two aspects of the work which are closely interwoven: firstly, the four-part division of the orchestra (each group consisting of a different combination of woodwinds, brass and strings, and each with one of the percussionists placed in its midst, the four groups spaced over the platform in separate units), and secondly, the movement between 'fixed' and 'mobile' musical episodes from one section of the work to another. Maderna saw this four-part basis as an essentially poetic and suggestive idea:[9]

'The title is perhaps a bit literary. I was thinking of the four liberal arts: arithmetic, algebra, music and astronomy . . . In any case the number four is magic. Four elements . . . four revolutions of the earth . . . '

but there can be little doubt that the idea of the 'quadrivium' also as a 'crossroads' played a large part in the formation of the work. At two points in the course of the work, episodes designated by the composer as 'happenings', the conductor is given a complexity of choices for his progress through these episodes, choices which will influence the very nature of the episodes (these occur in the two pages marked 9A and 9B, and that marked 20).

The four percussionists, as the 'soloists' in the ensemble, begin the work with what may be regarded as a 'Cadenza for percussion' (bars 1–93), [Ex. 4.12] in which pitched material only begins to appear with the xylophone I (in Group I) at bar 30, the material of the xylophone being brought together with material of a similar rhythmic and melodic character in the three wind-instruments (placed in Group III, diagonally opposite the xylophone on the platform) which appear together with it. [Ex. 4.13]

Further similar 'links' between the pitched-percussion and elements of the set of the orchestral body appear: solo-strings at bar 33, and trombones at bar 69, but Maderna treats these 'comments' from the other instruments simply as an integral part of the overall percussion sonority in this opening episode of the work. As the incisive melodic fragments of the four trombonists increase in excitement, however, and begin to overwhelm the four percussionists' contribution (each trombonist placed with each percussionist, so that the sound appears from the four corners of the platform), we are led naturally towards the more urgent and varied sounds which will characterise the ensuing episode, [Ex. 4.14]

The new episode, which is separated from the passage quoted above by a slight break, forms the first of the passages designated by the composer as 'happenings': Maderna says, in the preface to the score, that 'in the course of rehearsals, the conductor will set out a suitable plan for the performance of the various elements contained in this unified section; the arrangement of these elements will vary each time the work is performed, in accordance with possible variations in acoustic conditions and with the standard of the players the conductor has at his disposal.

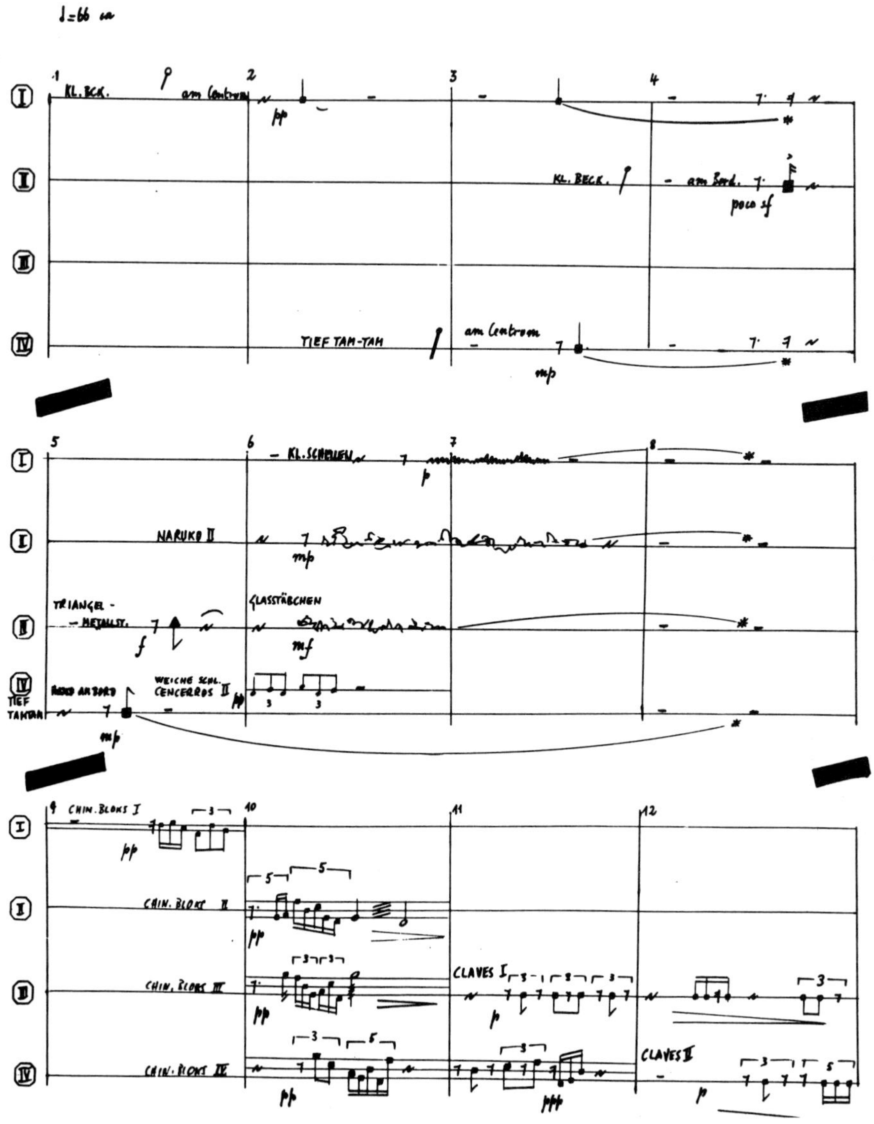

Ex. 4.12: Maderna: *Quadrivium*: 1–12

Ex. 4.13: Maderna: *Quadrivium*: 29–36

Ex. 4.14: Maderna: *Quadrivium*: 69–76

The conductor should exercise his personal taste and imagination also in consideration of the type of audience listening to the piece, bearing in mind that the composer's intention is to interest and entertain the audience and not simply to dazzle the listener'.

In this 'happening', we see the four-part division and wide placement of the orchestra as an essential part of the musical thinking: the material here is, in fact, spread cross-wise over the orchestra, in such a manner that similar instruments in each of the four groups share a similarity of material, but each type of material being quite distinct in character from that of other instruments close by on the platform. The effect of this is that several layers of material, each spread over the platform, are heard to be maintained simultaneously. However, the precise timing and placement of each layer is left to the discretion partly of the players and partly of the conductor, thus giving a considerable mobility to the episode. In each of the two pages which comprise the episode, a different section of the orchestral body is employed (winds, brass and percussion in page 9A; harps, celesta, double basses and percussion in 9B), so that the two halves of the 'happening' are heard as being quite distinct in terms of timbre. The freedoms given to the conductor and the players may be seen in the parts given to trumpets and horns in 9A: the conductor, at any point he wishes, merely indicates the start of this mobile, and the players, individually, play their indicated parts at approximately ♩ = 60, leaving pauses at the points indicated by ⱽ ; when he reaches the repeat-mark, he may begin again from the start of the mobile, or from any of the pause-indications, interpolating the fragments freely, and continuing until indicated (either individually or as a group, by pre-arrangement) by a circular motion of the conductor's hand. The material given to each play here is *staccato*, fragmentary and *pianissimo*, and bears some resemblance to the kind of material given earlier in the work to the two flutes and clarinet during the percussion episode. [Ex. 4.15]

Thus, both the major formative forces which are present in *Quadrivium*, that of *fixity* in the relatively determined shape of the opening percussion-episode, and that of *mobility* in the openness and indeterminacy of the 'happening', have now been presented to us, and the composer moves between these two limits in the ensuing episodes. The division and spacing of the orchestra remains a very important element in the composition: at the end of the 'happening', we hear first of all a passage in which *staccato* figurations in brass are dispersed over the four groups, each associated with percussion sounds (bongos, side-drums with and without snares, and congas). [Ex. 4.16] But the greatest possible contrast of sonorities is achieved as this episode gives way to an episode based upon the swaying of block-harmonies sustained by the four dispersed string-groups alone, heralded as the previous episode ends by the entry of a 12-note spread chord in the fourth string-group. Here, the harmony changes constantly but gently on each crotchet-beat, but the dispersal in space, and the density of the texture, create the effect of a harmony gradually changing in colour. [Ex. 4.17]

As happens so often in Maderna's orchestral writing, the composer, after treating this smooth and gently-moving texture as the foreground element for a while, adds a new layer above it: this string-sonority becomes, in the course of time, simply one part of a more complex texture, in this case as a 'fixed' element, beaten by the conductor, against which mobiles from other instrumental groups are placed. This creates a split texture, with on the one hand the sustained and gently-revolving string harmonies and on the other the mobility of the remaining

198   *Bruno Maderna*

Ex. 4.15: Maderna: *Quadrivium*: 9A–9B

Ex. 4.15: *Contd*

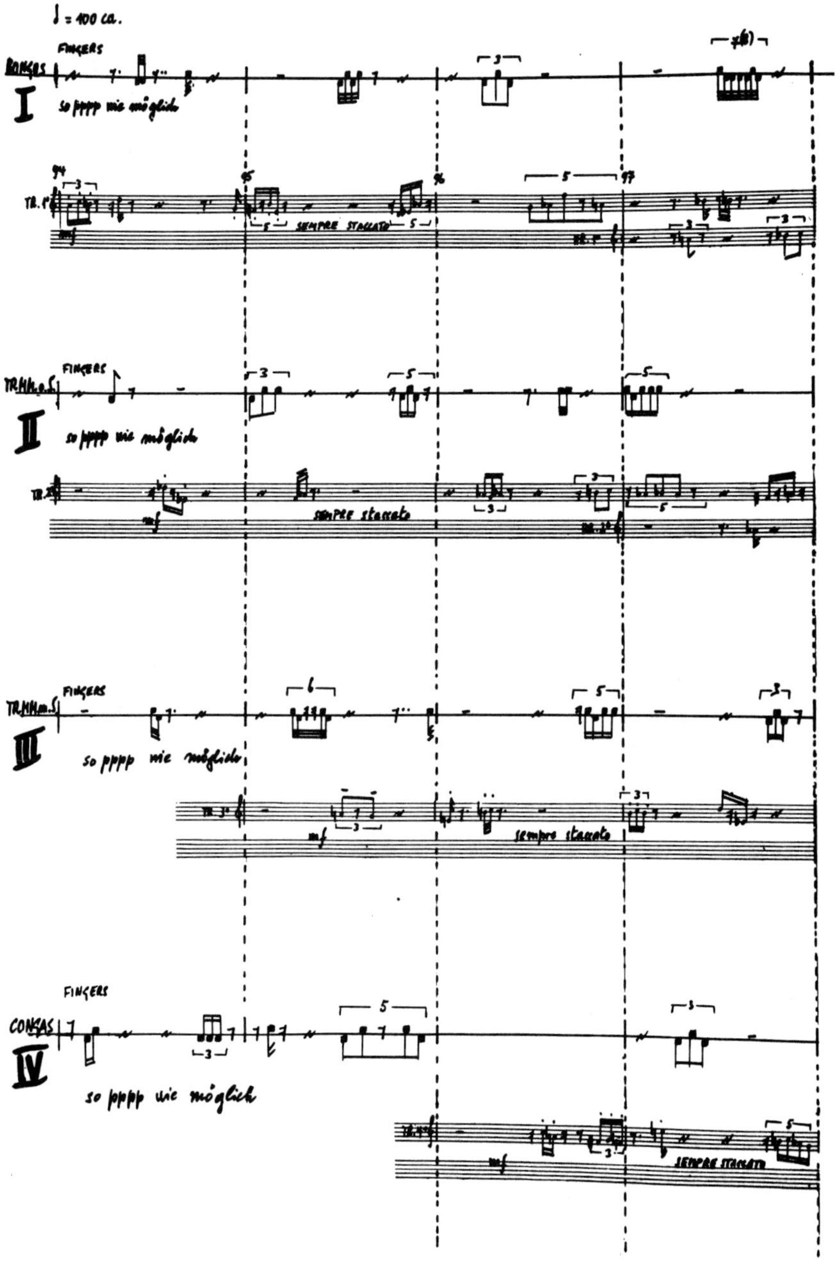

Ex. 4.16: Maderna: *Quadrivium*: 94–97

Ex. 4.17: Maderna: *Quadrivium*: 117–125

groups: with the latter, the composer asks that each 'set' should appear on a signal from the conductor, each itself split into two halves separated by varying pauses. [Ex. 4.18]

The layout of this episode prepares the ground, as it were, for the second 'happening', in which the conductor is requested to improvise with 25 string-chords (here, in contrast to the preceding episode, the string-sonority is dispersed constantly amongst the individual string-players constituting the four string-groups, and the chords are to be freely interpreted in length according to the conductor's signal). In a similar manner to the preceding episode, however, the mobiles in the other instruments which are set against this string background are each again split into two halves separated by varying pauses, and in this way each appears to have an 'echo'.

In this manner, that is to say by means of textures moving between *fixed* (bars 118–113), *fixed plus mobile* (bars 134–147) and *totally mobile* (bar 147 bis), Maderna has in effect made the distinction between fixity and mobility, which had appeared quite clear in the opening episodes of the work, considerably less clear-cut. It is as though the distinction between 'cadenzas' and 'fully composed' sections, which we saw had been a cornerstone of the structure of *Oboe Concerto No. 1* some six years earlier, had here been paralleled in Maderna's orchestral writing, only to be modified or almost completely obliterated.

By the time that, some three years later, Maderna again turned to the composition of large-scale works for symphony orchestra (having in the meanwhile composed some fourteen works for various combinations, including *Grande Aulodia* and the *Violin Concerto*), his powers in the handling of large-scale formal aspects of what may be termed 'symphonic' writing were at their highest. The two work for large orchestra composed in 1972, *Aura* and *Biogramma*, represent in some ways the culmination of his orchestral composition, and are amongst the most frequently-heard of all the composer's works. *Aura* was introduced to the audience at its first performance, with the Chicago Symphony Orchestra under the composer's direction, in a programme-note written in the composer's idiosyncratic English:[10]

> '(The title) refers to the radiations of all possible consequences which emanate from a central musical object . . . aura is the essence of things, the essence of sounds, and something like the aroma which pervades the room from the chicken cooking in the pot'.

In contrast to *Quadrivium*, we see in *Aura* no large-scale mobility or aleatoricism in the structure of the work (with the exception of the ending of the work, an ending which, as we shall observe, has been seen as problematic by some observers); here, rather, the concentration of the composer is placed upon the possibilities offered by the division of the orchestra into distinct instrumental groups, for the building of a large-scale form. The orchestra is not, as in *Quadrivium*, divided 'crosswise' into heterogeneous groupings, but the layout is the conventional one, and only the strings are divided into six groups (as, in the *Violin Concerto*, he had employed two distinct string-orchestras). The strings, in fact, may be seen as the central section of the orchestral body for *Aura*, and it is they who open the work with an episode which begins with solo melodic lines forming a simple and expressive harmony which builds gradually to a greater complexity of texture in which constantly varying melodic fragments are thrown into prominence by dynamic means. [Ex. 4.20(a), (b)]

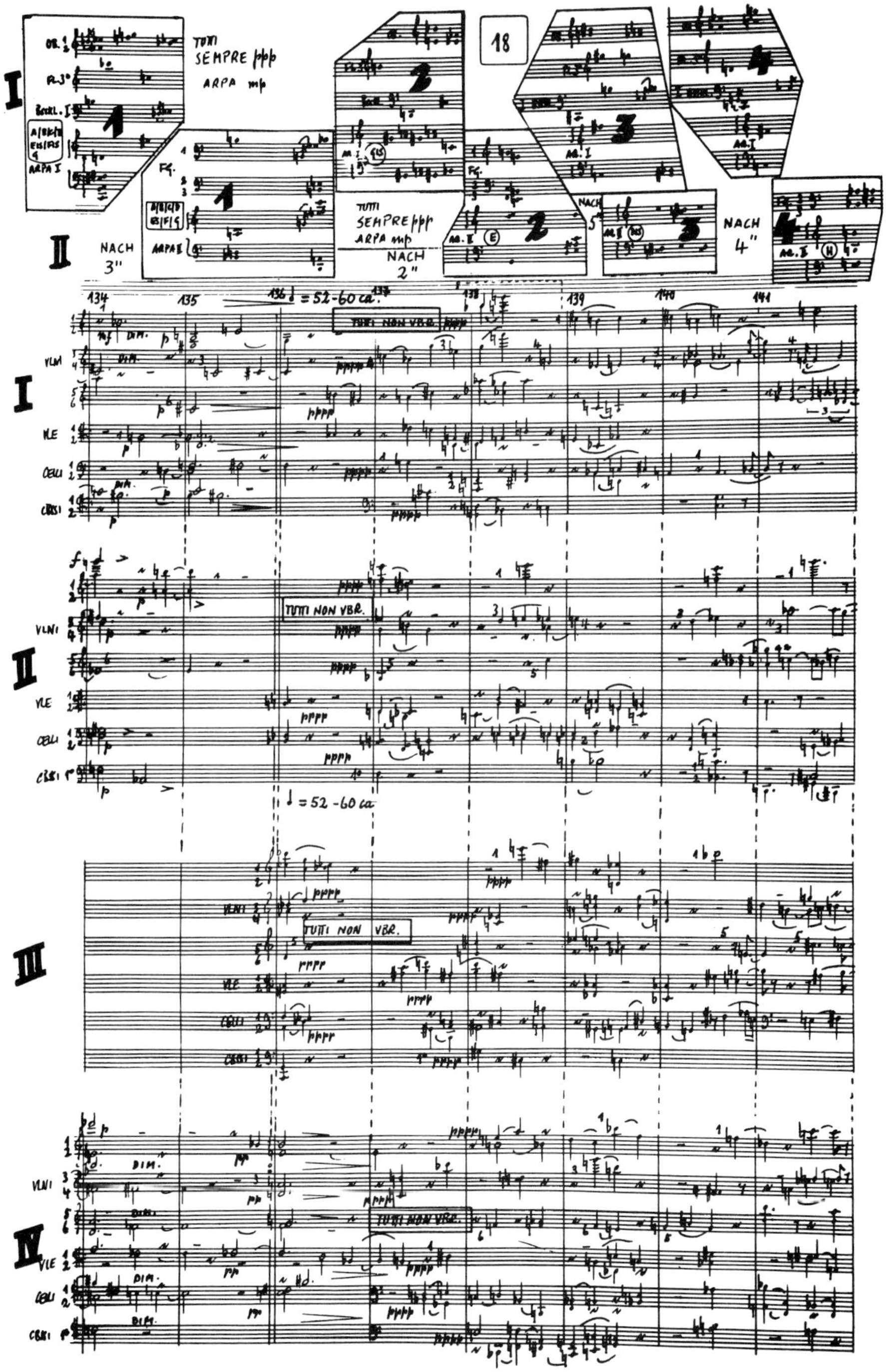

Ex. 4.18: Maderna: *Quadrivium*: page 18

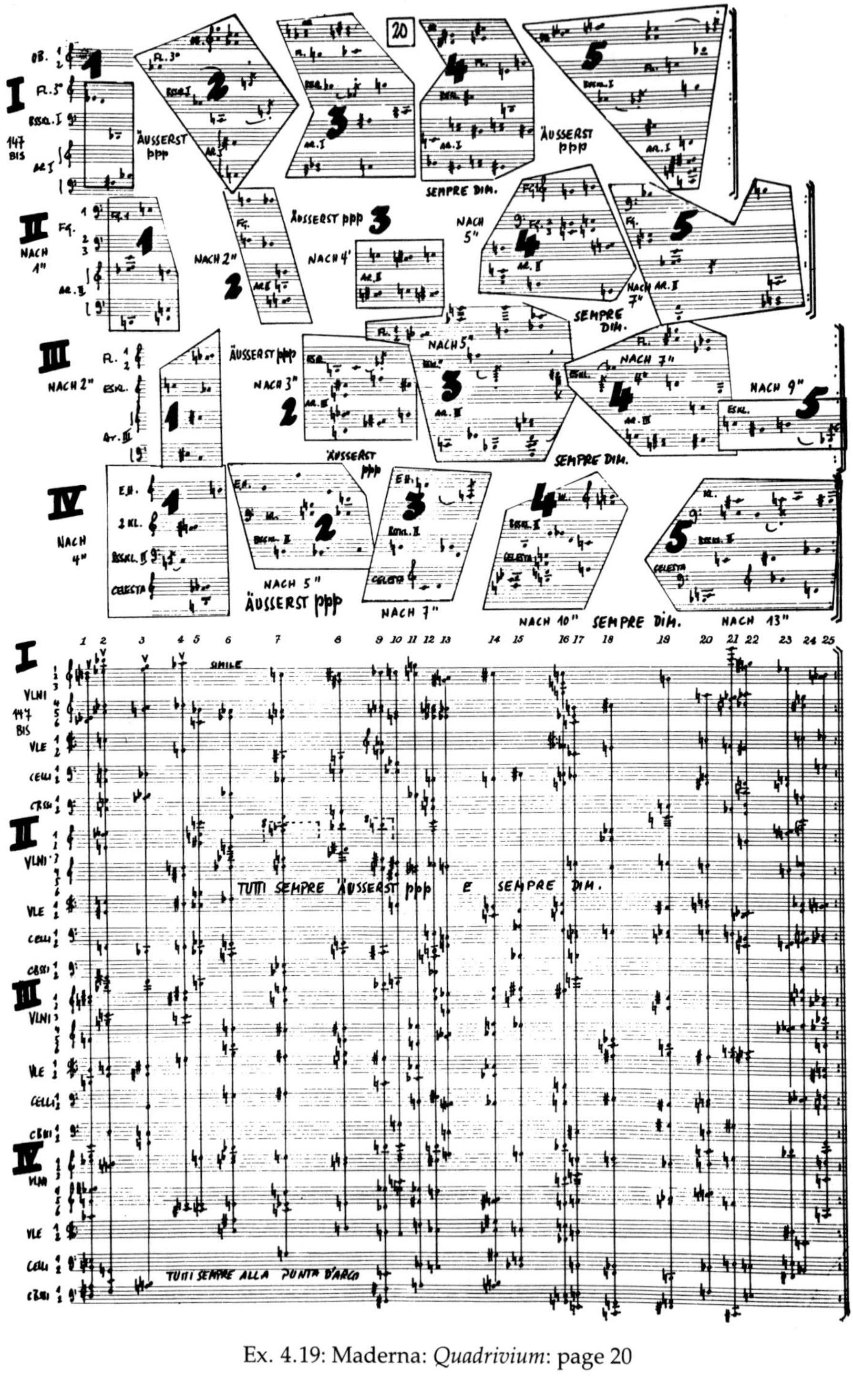

Ex. 4.19: Maderna: *Quadrivium*: page 20

Ex. 4.20(a): Maderna: *Aura*: 1–13

The constant flow of this string-polyphony becomes, as in a rather similar passage demonstrated earlier in *Quadrivium* (bars 134–147), a background to the more forceful and rhythmically jagged pitched-percussion figures which are subsequently placed above it: this disturbance of the strings' relative passivity by the percussion instruments prepares us for a fusion of the two orchestral groups which appears after a slight break, the tempo and character increasing to that of a 'scherzando'. [Ex. 4.21]

The brass instruments (4 horns, 5 trumpets and 4 trombones) and the unpitched percussion of the orchestral ensemble are reserved, in *Aura*, for a special function. Whereas, as we have seen, the strings, pitched percussion and woodwinds integrate over large sections of the music, the brass instruments, during the larger part of the work, are presented as a quite separate unit, being limited at first to modules which appear between the ensembles of strings-winds-pitched percussion: these modules are expressed in a language of close-knit semitonal figurations. [Ex. 4.22(a)–(c)]

Ex. 4.20(a): *Contd*

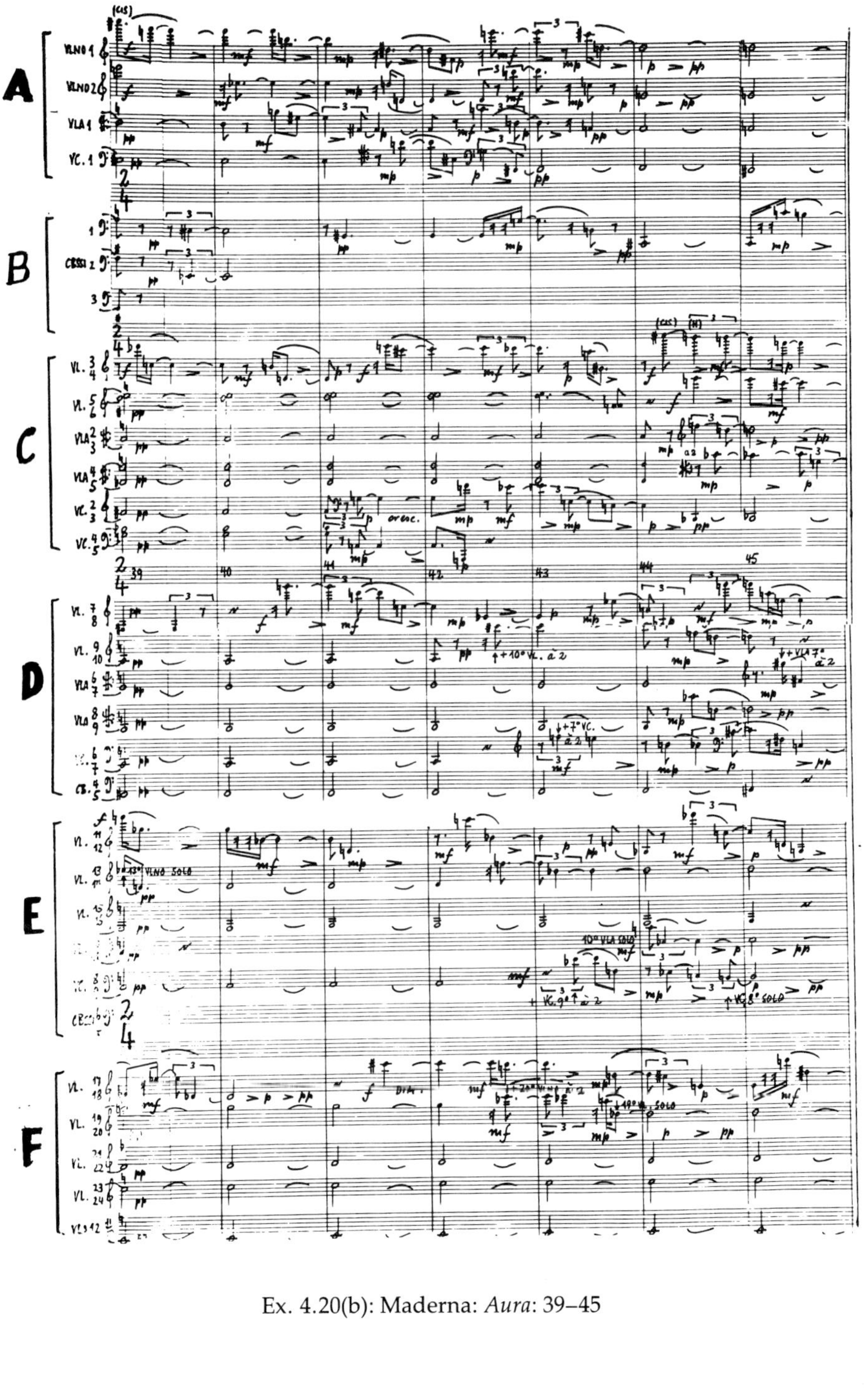

Ex. 4.20(b): Maderna: *Aura*: 39–45

Ex. 4.21: Maderna: *Aura*: 173–192

Ex. 4.21: *Contd*

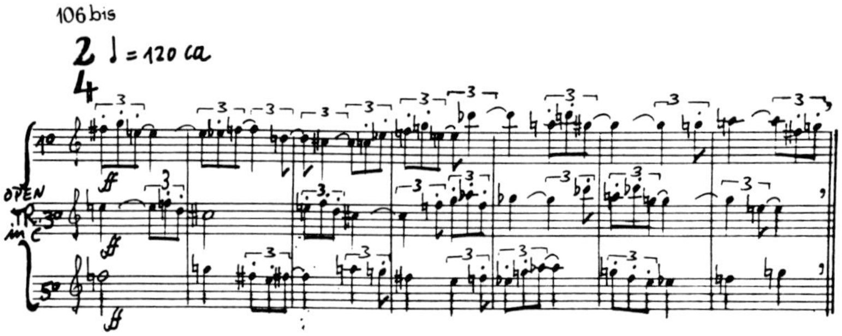

Ex. 4.22(a): Maderna: *Aura*: 106 bis

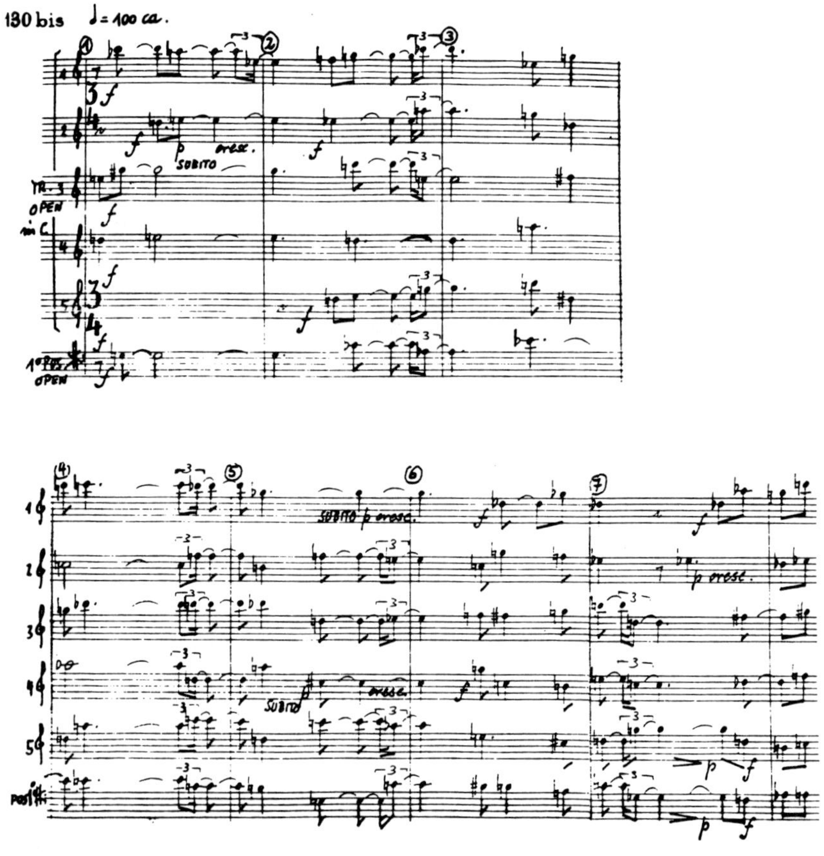

Ex. 4.22(b): Maderna: *Aura*: 130 bis

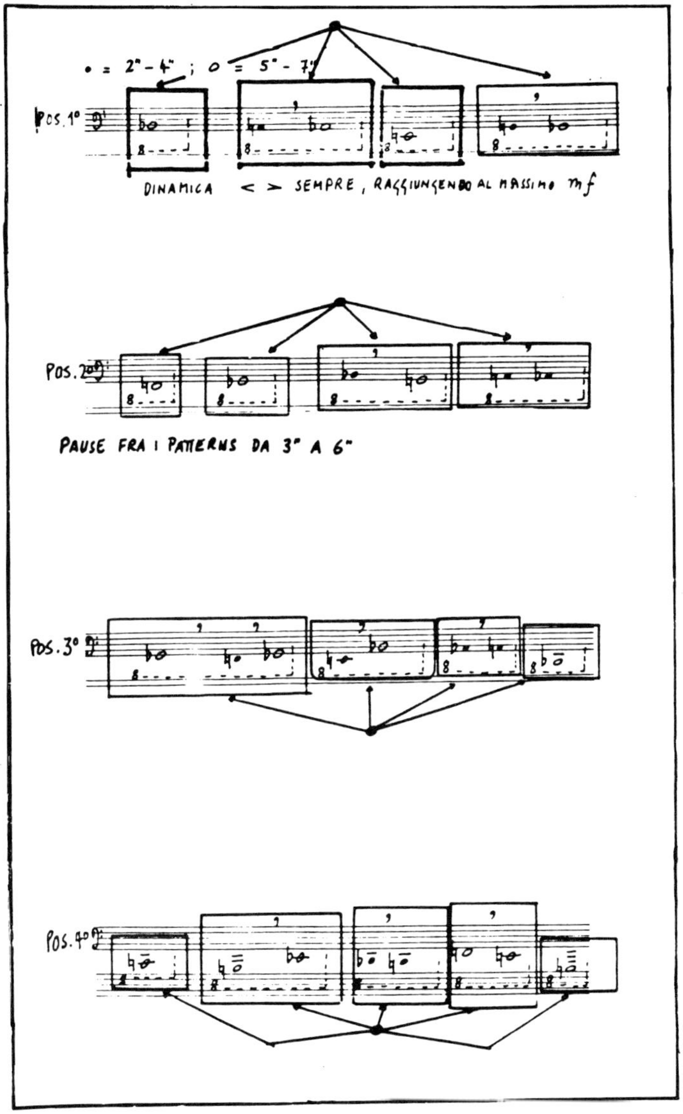

Ex. 4.22(c): Maderna: *Aura*: 164 bis

In this way, the work retains to a large extent an *identity* of material for each instrumental group of which it is comprised: *strings + pitched percussion — woodwinds — brass*, and the fusion of all these groups in the '*tutti*' episode is heard as a combination not only of sonorities, but also of types of material.

A particular problem which has been encountered with regard to *Aura* concerns the ending of the work: here, Maderna gives a quite clear indication in the score of the shape which this ending should assume:

> 'On the long *fermata*, the conductor will invite the four horns and five trumpets to begin improvisation 1 (Trumpets in C and Horns in F). This improvisation consists of the free interpretation of the notated fragments. It is recommended that these fragments should be separated by long pauses (from 3" to 9"). In the meanwhile, the strings return to the beginning of the work, one at a time, and play bars 1–68 again, as if in a 'cadenza' — pppp and *con sordino*. When the conductor wishes, he will indicate to the trumpets and horns they they should move to improvisation 2 and, later on, will invite the first flute to improvise on sections 1 and 2.
>
> From this point, the conductor will stop the horns and the trumpets one at a time, leaving the first flute alone with the strings. Then — and diminishing '*a niente*' — he will also stop the strings, group by group, leaving the solo flute which, with ever lengthening pauses between the phrases, will end in *pianissimo*'.

It is clear from this indication in the score, therefore, that Maderna conceived the ending of *Aura* as in a sense a 'concerned and improvised Cadenza' for strings, brass and solo flute, and that in this finale he had introduced into the work a measure of that mobility which, as we have seen, had characterised large sections of *Quadrivium*. However, Berio, speaking about *Aura* and some other works of Maderna in his interview with Rossana Dalmonte[11] seems not to be convinced that this ending, as it appears in the published score, may be regarded as definitive (indeed, some performances of *Aura* have ignored the prescribed '*da capo*' for the string-group, and ended simply with the 'mobiles' for brass and flute). Berio says that *Aura*, along with *Hyperion*, ought to be re-examined with a view to clarifying the score for performance. Two episodes (bar 164 bis and the ending of the work) are 'not really finished and are tacked on in a rather hurried manner': according to Berio, 'Bruno's aleatoric solutions are rarely dictated by musical necessity', but should be seen as 'sketches, annotations which were never set out in a more suitable way for lack of time'. Berio insists upon the need for a re-ordering of such passage in a more conventional manner, which would eliminate the material which might 'put off many performers of little faith'.

Berio refers here (in the original Italian verison of the Dalmonte interview, abbreviated in the English version) to an extremely important aspect of *Aura* which also has ramifications for much of the composer's later composition, and one should therefore attempt to come to terms with Berio's claims.

One may answer Berio's claims about the work by saying first of all that there is no evidence that the composer was in any particular hurry in the preparation of the score of *Aura* in 1972; despite the fact that the work had been commissioned by the Chicago Symphony Orchestra to celebrate the 80th anniversary of its foundation, there is, in fact, every reason to believe that Maderna had already begun to work on a large-scale work for orchestra *before* receiving the commission.

Secondly, we have seen already in this study that the 'aleatoric solutions' to which Berio refers were by this point in the composer's life an essential element in his musical thinking, having informed large parts of *Grande Aulodia, Violin Concerto* and numerous smaller instrumental pieces which he had composed in previous years.

Thirdly, Berio's reference to the 'materials necessary in specific and unambiguous form' at the end of *Aura* is perfectly correct in so far as the indication given in the score for this final page refers in some detail to the use of the *'da capo'* return of the strings to the opening of the work, and to the use of the mobiles for trumpets and flute which form the last page of the score. It would appear therefore to be absurd to imply that these materials need to be re-ordered or re-notated in any other form.

Fourthly, the composer's handing over of the responsibility for certain musical matters to the performers reflects a very deep-seated faith on his part in the responsibility of the performer, which, as we have seen frequently in this study, had been an essential part of Maderna's make-up as a composer.

The finale of *Aura* is, in fact, set out in such a way that the musical substance will be clearly presented. It is therefore somewhat puzzling that Berio here seems to assume that a clearer presentation could be made: there is no evidence, in the manuscripts of Maderna, of any alternative version of this ending, and we can in fact see this finale as completely in keeping with Maderna's thinking during these later years. When we observed the problems of performance of the various versions of *Hyperion* we could see that, in order to restore the work to its composer's original conception a considerable degree of imagination and flexibility is required in ordering the various materials available, (a task which has been undertaken with great success by Marcello Panni), and the case of the opera *Satyricon* presents, as we shall see, very considerable problems both to its producer and its conductor, but *Aura* is, in its published form, complete and unequivocal. [Ex. 4.23]

Sulla lunga corona, il direttore inviterà i 4 corni e le 5 trombe a iniziare l'improvvisazione ①.
Le trombe rimangono in do, i corni in fa.
L'improvvisazione consiste nella libera interpolazione dei frammenti notati. Si raccomanda di separare essi frammenti con lunghe pause (da 3" a 9").
Nel frattempo gli archi ritornano da capo, uno alla volta, e risuonano liberamente, come in una "cadenza", le battute 1-68 - *pppp* e con sordina.
Quando il direttore lo crederà opportuno, indicherà alle trombe e ai corni di passare alla improvvisazione ② e, più tardi, inviterà il flauto 1° Solo a improvvisare sulle sezioni ① e ②.
Da questo momento il direttore comincerà a far tacere, uno alla volta, i corni e le trombe, lasciando suonare il flauto 1° Solo con gli archi. Indi - e con diminuendo "a niente"- farà cessare anche gli archi, gruppo per gruppo, lasciando il solo flauto che, con pause sempre più lunghe fra le interpolazioni, terminerà in *pp*.

Ex. 4.23: Maderna: *Aura*: 258–259

Ex. 4.23: *Contd*

Ex. 4.23: *Contd*

Notes to Chapter 4

1. Interview with Christoph Bitter on 7.5. 1973: in Appendix.
2. *Baroni/Dalmonte* pp. 236–238.
3. *Karl H. Wörner: Stockhausen: Life and Works*: German version 1963, revised version in English, Faber and Faber, London, 1973, p. 237.
4. idem p. 39.
5. *Pierre Boulez: Sonate, que me veux-tu?*, first published in *Méditations* No. 7 Spring 1964; English version in *Orientations*, Faber and Faber, London and Boston, 1986, pp. 143–154.
6. *Pierre Boulez: Orientations* p. 156: essay first published in 1961.
7. *Pierre Boulez: Orientations*, p.524.
8. *Pierre Boulez: Conversations with Célestin Deliège*: published in French as *Par Volonté et par Hasard*, Éditions du Seuil, Paris 1975; English translation by Eulenburg, London 1976, p. 100.
9. *Baroni/Dalmonte*: op. cit., p. 286.
10. idem, p. 307.
11. *Luciano Berio: Intervista sulla musica*, Laterza, Rome–Bari 1981; in English as *Two Interviews*, Marion Boyars, New York–London, 1985, p. 52.

Chapter 5

Last works — *From A to Z; Tempo Libero/Juilliard
Serenade; Ages; Venetian Journal; Satyricon; Oboe Concerto
No. 3* — Maderna's importance and influence.

During the course of the earlier discussion of Maderna's activities in the Studio di Fonologia Musicale in Milan, we saw how he tended towards works with a reference to the human voice or to other instruments in the works composed for tape, and the two works *Dimensioni II/Invenzione su una voce*, in which the vocal 'characters' of Cathy Berberian became the basis of electronic manipulation, and *Le Rire*, whose college of concrete and electronic sounds provided a rich pool of resources into which he was to dip for the various versions of *Hyperion*, may be regarded as the most important compositions in this field from that earlier period.

In his last years, his work in the Studio was to undergo a further transformation: in *Ausstrahlung* for female voice, flute and oboe obbligati, orchestra and tape in 1971, which was given its first performance in Persepolis under the composer's direction, he compiled a tape in which purely vocal sounds are employed, mainly based upon readings of poetry from Ancient Persia, and including the voice of his wife Cristina as well as that of his son Andrea. This last period also saw the composition of three works, each in a quite different format, in which we can see the virtuosity of his electronic composition displayed in a final tour-de-force of imagination and diversity. These are *From A to Z*, composed originally for a play by Rebecca Rass in Holland in 1969; *Tempo Libero*, composed for the 'Biennale Internazionale di Metodologia Globale della Progettazione* ('International Biennale of Global Design Methodology') held in Rimini-San Marino in 1970; and *Ages*, composed for Italian Radio in 1972.

From A to Z very quickly became a part of the theatrical oeuvre of Maderna: after having been presented as 'incidental music' for Rebecca Rass' play broadcast in Holland (in English) in 1969, it was presented as a stage-work at the Orangerie, a small theatre in the suburbs of Darmstadt run by the Landestheater of that city on 22nd February 1970, in a production by Harro Dicks, with whom Maderna had collaborated in the preparation of the abortive stage-work *Das Eiserne Zeitalter* in 1952–3. *From A to Z* was presented in a double-bill with György Ligeti's *Aventures et Nouvelles Aventures*.

Maderna had become acquainted with Ligeti's *Aventures et Nouvelles Aventures* in a performance at the Summer School in Darmstadt in 1966, and it was also to be this work which was produced in a double-bill with his own opera *Satyricon* at the 1973 Holland Festival. It had been put on the stage for the first time in Stuttgart in October 1966, when the pantomime-artist Rolf Scharre had made a production from which Ligeti himself appears to have kept some distance; in the Darmstadt production, on the other hand, the composer collaborated with Harro Dicks in the production, and the work was one which appealed greatly to Maderna. There is, however, a clear distinction between Ligeti's piece, in which there is no verbal utterance of any comprehensible kind, (only vocal noises of a non-verbal kind are employed), and Maderna's, in which verbal and narrative expression is paramount in the presentation of the 'opera'. In Ligeti's work, the set represented a museum-room, in which a modern tourist-group observe a group of wax models in a cabinet, a Queen, Princess and an Admiral, while a Music Professor is busy at work at a desk in a corner of the room. When the tourist-group has left, the Music Professor brings the three wax models to life, and they perform actions mimicking the tourist-group and expressing the dream-images of the Professor. Whereas in the Stuttgart production Rolf Scharre had aimed towards the maximum surreal fantasy, Harro Dicks in Darmstadt produced the work by means of gesture and emotional ambiguity. Maderna conducted the seven-piece instrumental ensemble for its accompaniment.

The action of Rebecca Rass' *From A to Z* is concerned with a mythical primordial age, before speech entered the world, an age in which only Punctuation existed: 'the whole world was of one language and one word'. The many elements of Punctuation decide, as a group, to travel in search of their homeland — Punctuland — and the narrative tells of their journey there, beset with difficulties, and of the coming of Words, at first coupled together in happy antonymic pairs, but later gaining independence. The text itself, as it appears in Maderna's tape, is a collage: straightforward narration alternates with passages of poetic onomatopeia, with a great use of assonance, and although mainly in English, includes wide use of other languages, in which Dutch and French predominate.

The work makes great use of Maderna's own collage techniques, developed in such earlier tape-works as *Ritratto di Città*, *Dimensioni II* and *Le Rire*: here, instrumental passages are incorporated (the work begins with a gentle and tonal episode for guitar, harp and percussion, and later the peaceful rule of Punctuation over their new-found Punctuland gives rise to a similarly gentle oboe solo), as well as vocal and electronic passages, the latter sometimes including naturalistic sounds.

The production of the work on stage in Darmstadt, which was received with booing from the audience and highly critical press-reviews, employed theatrical techniques which had their origin in the Circus works of Frank Wedekind, Böll and Kohout, or even, at a greater remove, in the '*Commedia dell'Arte*' tradition (our source of knowledge of the production lies in newspaper-reviews of the performance). The designs were made by Ekkehard Grübler, and Harro Dicks' production involved scene-shifters, artists, children, two clowns (one a drummer, the other a piper), dancers, and a stage-manager. Huge placards appeared from time to time on stage, on which were written 'Peace', 'War', 'Heaven', 'Love', 'God', 'Earth', 'Atom', 'Angst', 'Sex', and 'Burlesque', and above the whole stage was seen the word 'Circus'. The action began with a 'Spring-Pause' in a circus, and children with hobby-horses expressed the playfulness of the pre-verbal world. The whole production had more than a little of the 'Happening' about it, and ended with the two clowns throwing flowers on to the stage.

It seems that the performance on stage of *From A to Z* in Darmstadt, whilst not without its charms as a vehicle for the endeavours of its producer, apparently lacked any overall theatrical unity, and one is left with the conclusion that the radio-version of *From A to Z* preserved on tape was not successfully transferred to the theatrical medium. It is, however, of some significance that Maderna, at this point, wished to create a theatrical work, and this was eventually to lead to the production of *Satyricon* in the composer's last year of life.

Tempo Libero was first presented as 'atmospheric music' at the International Biennale of Global Design Methodology in Rimini-San Marino in the 20th–30th September 1970. Maderna, in the course of the interview he gave about this work on Saarländischer Rundfunk in 1973 explained the thoughts which had led him to this work:[1]

> 'I thought that the attitude of someone who uses his free time should, at least in principle, be different from the attitude he has in normal life. For example, one might walk in the fields, look at flowers and trees, smell the flowers, listen to the birds, and take notice of the little things one would not notice in normal life, since one is always doing things in a hurry, going to work, performing one's duties. Then I thought what would happen if someone enjoyed listening to noises, voices in the distance, the wind, memories of music heard the evening before, or music one would like to hear, and then wished to amuse oneself by composing with all these experiences and making a collage out of them'.

The material which Maderna put on tape in *Tempo Libero* is from the most diverse possible sources: recorded fragments of orchestral rehearsals, mainly consisting of verbal indications to the players; some occasional single words and phrases in the voices of Marino Zuccheri and the composer himself; vocal fragments from some pre-existing works, notably from *Don Perlimplin* and *Dimensioni II*; concrete sounds, including falling objects, water, applause, paper-folding and the like; some instrumental sounds, again mainly taken from *Don Perlimplin*; only occasionally, electronically-produced sounds. The manipulation of these sounds, and their placement on the tape, closely resemble the procedures adopted in *Dimensioni II* and *Le Rire*, with which it may be said that *Tempo Libero* has a certain family-resemblance.

The composer described the work as in 'open form', and his attitude to the work was summed up clearly in the interview with Christoph Bitter:[2]

> ' . . . It is a collage, but not in the sense of surrealism. Rather, we are dealing with that experience of musical composition known as open form, comparable in practice to Calder's 'Mobiles', whose proportions are maintained unaltered through different moments of time and points in space . . . While I was working on this tape, I each time added a new element, a new contrast, but not such as would disturb the harmonic balance of the whole. So in this way it grew by itself until I felt, I would not say the need for a limit, but at least the possibility of bringing it to an end. So one could say that the piece is complete, even if by its nature it could go on for ever; in fact it is conceived for a space where people can work on the music directly, like with a cassette. The piece is in four channels and one can choose different proportions, by which means — in different combinations — it can even last many millions of years . . . What I wanted was to offer listeners the possibility of beginning when they wished and stopping when they were tired of listening . . . this piece is a stimulus to relaxation; not intellectualism, it is to be hoped, but simply relaxation'.

It is clear from these remarks of the composer that the work was conceived in a rather different spirit from that of Maderna's other works for the tape-medium (Christoph Bitter, in the conversation, makes an interesting comparison with Stockhausen's *Aus den sieben Tagen*, and the spirit of Zen is invoked by the composer himself). It might also be said that *Tempo Libero* represents in the tape-experience of Maderna what was represented in the instrumental field by his *Serenata per un satellite*, written with considerable freedom of instrumentation and duration for the launching of the satellite ESRO I B 'Boreas', and given its first performance in the European Space Operations Centre in Darmstadt in 1969.

Maderna made three different versions of *Tempo Libero*, each employing similar material with the exception of the third version, which employs only those sounds recorded in the Maderna family house in Darmstadt, and apart from its use as a 'pure' tape-piece (as on the occasion of the interview with Christoph Bitter), and its use as 'background music' in the Rimini exhibition, it may be combined with the instrumental piece *Juilliard Serenade*, composed in 1970 to produce the work known as *Tempo Libero II*, whose score mentions the possibility of using 'one or two tapes'. It is not at all clear from this what is meant by the second tape, but Maderna does give an indication of the combination of tape and instrumental matrial:

> 'The conductor will thus have at his disposal an enormous quantity of phonic and heterophonic situations which can be organised in divertimenti, contrasts, integrations, imitations, etc. With the help of the technicians, he will be able to introduce the tape at the desired moments and with the intensity he wants. The composer recommends that the volume of sound of the instrumental group and that of the tape should be exactly controlled. It is better to have a pre-eminence of the instrumental group which should always be there to carry out the interplay in this *Tempo Libero II*. With or without the tape, the Serenade can be played, singly or in different combinations, by the following instruments: flute, violin, harp, pianos I and II, with the addition of xylophone and marimba ad. lib.'

It is perhaps significant that Maderna, in his last years, had gained such a mastery of the possibilities offered by electro-acoustic medium that he was able to move with ease from the openness of form and content represented by *Tempo Libero* to the tightness of control which he exhibited in his final work for the medium of Tape: *Ages. Ages,* an '*invenzione radiofonica*' composed during 1972, which won the Italia Prize for radio-presentation in the same year, may be considered Maderna's masterpiece of the genre, combining voices, chorus and orchestra in a manner of which only the radio medium was capable, just as, earlier, he had combined vocal, instrumental and tape elements in his opera for radio *Don Perlimplin*. The work is based upon the famous speech of Jacques in *As You Like It*, Act 2, Scene 7:

> 'All the world's a stage,
> And all the men and women merely players;
> They have their exits and their entrances;
> And one man in his time plays many parts,
> His acts being seven ages . . . '

Ages is without doubt a work conceived in full recognition of the *radiophonic* medium, but its conception is also that of a *musical* work: if we observe the overall shape of the piece, taking into consideration the comments about the episodes of the work made by Maderna, as it was set out by the composer in a programme-note for its first presentation,[3] we can see that the various parts of which it is composed exhibit a clearly-structured musical form, incorporating not only a kind of *'Scherzo'* (Part 3) and an *'Adagio'* (Part 2), but a Prologue in the shape of a *'ductus'*, as the composer describes it:

(i)   *Prologue:* the composer said of this section that 'the vocal procedure adopted has the appearance of a *'ductus'*: voices of children speak fragments of the text, highlighting especially the word 'stage', appearing in small 'groupings'.

(ii) *Part 1:* the composer spoke of this as conceived like an adagio: preceded by a 'montage' of orchestral passages, the children's voices from the Prologue, and a solo for flute, it incorporates also the radio title and credits: Maderna spoke of the voices here employed in 'a series of pulsating structural games'. The 'games' are those of children at play, and the composer also spoke of 'various procedures of filtering and echo which constitute almost a closed form of a responsorial variety'.

(iii) *Part 2:* the composer says that 'the third part is more or less symmetrical to the first and is conceived as a contrast to the second': this encloses a recitation of Shakespeare's text in full, accompanied by a slow, gentle and delicate texture of flute-sounds in superimposition.

(iv) *Part 3:* this comprises, like the first part, fragments of the text in vocal counterpoint one with another, but now in the voices of men, as if shouting from one market stall to another; orchestral sounds are heard throughout, but in the background.

(v)   *Part 4:* in the final section, female voices of a highly seductive quality sing, whisper and giggle; the composer spoke of this as 'a kind of *chaconne d'amour'*; gradually, as the composer says, 'old, tired voices enter, which sadly repeat long fragments of the text'; this final episode also incorporates parts of the choral-piece *All the World's a Stage*.

The composer's references here, in his comments on the formal aspects of each episode of the work, provide perhaps some clues to the ways in which he went about the structuring of the work from what is in fact to a large extent basic material of two kinds: voices and instruments. Maderna's references to the *'ductus'* (a thirteenth-century dance-form consisting of short sections, each repeated), and to the *'chaconne d'amour'*, suggest that, in putting together the elements of vocal material on tape in these opening and closing episodes (children's voices at the opening, older voices at the end, but both repeating fragments of the Shakespeare text over and over again), he made use of repetitive forms from earlier musical styles as a basis for his thinking. The intervening episodes provide, in their turn, contrasts of a quite dramatic kind, and the work as a whole therefore exhibits a quite remarkable degree of structural unity through its employment of a narrative structure based upon the Shakespeare text itself.

In the final section of *Ages*, Maderna employs a female chorus, singing the first part of Shakespeare's text: 'All the world's a stage, and all the men and women merely players; They have their exits and their entrances; And one man in his time plays many parts, His acts being seven ages'. In only three previous works (in the unpublished *Requiem* of 1945–6, of which only some fragments are still in existence; in the *Psalm,* a setting of words by Auden and Lorca which was included in the *Suite aus der Oper Hyperion;* and in the *Tre Liriche Greche* of 1948) had Maderna composed any choral music.

The placement of *All the World's a Stage* in the final episode of *Ages,* coming as it does at the point at which the voices fade, becoming older and more tired, and before the final fragments of text are spoken (by Maderna himself), gives to the chorus a disctinctly elegaic tone: the female voices appear only in the distance, and only sections of the soprano and alto parts of the choral piece are employed in *Ages:* it might perhaps be that the composer decided only *after* the tape-piece had been composed that he would make a full choral setting of the text, including also the tenor and baritone parts. The score of *All the World's a Stage* was in any case published separately, in the format of two separate choral scores marked 'A' and 'B'. In this score, we find some rather quaint word-settings, indicating that the composer (whose knowledge of English, as is clear from his interviews in that language, was rather limited) had misjudged some matters of accentuation and pronunciation: for example, the setting of the word 'entrances' as thought it were 'en*tran*ces' and that of the final word 'ages' as a monosyllable. However, the work has some interest for us, not simply as the only published example, after the early *Tre Liriche Greche* of a considerable polyphonic ability: the writing for double-choir shows skill in the handling of the antiphony between the two choirs, and gives us, perhaps, a taste of what the composer might have achieved in this field had he been granted the time to do so.[Ex. 5.1]

When Maderna's opera *Satyricon* was given its first performances, at the 1973 Holland Festival, the 'sensational' nature of the production was clearly seen as an essential element in the overall impact of the work. Grotesque, exaggerated, erotic and parodistic by turns, the work appeared to combine a vast array of stylistic references and quotations in the music with theatrical (and often melodramatic) gestures on stage, all gathered together in a work which seemed to hover between a 'number-opera' and a work of Music Theatre.

The performance, which linked *Satyricon* with Ligeti's *Aventures et nouvelles Aventures* in a double-bill, was an immediate success. It was becoming all too apparent by this time that Maderna was suffering from a disease which gave him little time to live, and it was only through the assistance of others, notably the producer Ian Strasfogel, the Dutch conductor Lucas Vis (who took over from Maderna at the podium) and Hans de Roo, Director of the Netherlands Opera, that the work was brought to fruition. Those who, knowing of Maderna's previous stage-work *Hyperion,* might have expected a similarly 'symbolic' or 'poetic' work, must have been taken somewhat aback by the colourful theatrical spectacle on stage during *Satyricon.*

When, a year later, after Maderna's death, the score of the work was published, it became clear that enormous problems would attend any future attempt at a production: this score, set out in quite separate units without any indication of their sequence, together with a number of tapes, and no stage-directions whatsoever, seemed to indicate that the opera was perhaps simply a work written in a hurry. One might feel that the work was intended for only the one performance (as had already evidently been the case with the stage-version of

Ex. 5.1: Maderna: *All the world's a stage*: 18–32

Ex. 5.1: *Contd*

From A to Z) and that any further attempts at a production, without the guiding hand of Maderna himself, were inappropriate.

Further performances were, however, given in other cities, and we are left with the tantalising situation of a work whose very form and staging appear to be left entirely in the hands of the producer and conductor of the work on each occasion on which it is tackled. There are therefore questions which we should attempt to answer about the work: how was the work conceived by the composer? In what manner, and to what purpose, did he arrange the text for the work? What actions, and sequence of events on stage, did he envisage? How should the various tapes be employed in performance of the work? What is the nature of each individual number of which the score is composed, and in what order should they be used? Of what significance is the work in Maderna's output as a whole?

On 8th August 1971, during the Tanglewood Festival in Massachusetts, a work described as a 'little musical drama', the product of work undertaken by students of the Berkshire Music Center's 'Music Theater Project', was performed, under the musical guidance of Maderna and the dramatic guidance of the American opera-producer Ian Strasfogel. This little work, which lasted just over twenty minutes, was based on the 'Satyricon', that classic of Roman satyrical literature by Petronius Arbiter: whether the choice of this text arose from preliminary discussion amongst the participants or whether Maderna himself, who had a lifelong interest in Classical literature, had the idea already in his mind, is unclear. What is certain, however, is that this idea of a musico-dramatic work based upon the text of 'Satyricon' provoked in the composer, whose intensity of work never diminished even after the diagnosis of his fatal illness was given early in 1973, a great flood of preliminary ideas and sketches towards an opera which was eventually to be given its first performance at the Holland Festival in March 1973.

What drew Maderna towards the composition of an opera, and what in particular drew him to the subject of 'Satyricon'? He had earlier completed, as we have already seen, two works of a musico-dramatic kind, the 'radiophonic opera' *Don Perlimplin* and *Hyperion*, and we have also examined some of the reasons why the staged version of *From A to Z* performed in Darmstadt had not managed fully to convert the work from a radiophonic piece to the demands of the stage. Maderna had meanwhile been very active as an opera conductor: the number of operas which he conducted in the last decades of his life is very large, and we should in particular mention the first performance of *Intolleranza* by his friend and former pupil Luigi Nono in 'La Fenice' in Venice in 1964, where Nono's political opponents had caused a riot in the theatre.

It was clear from *Don Perlimplin* and *Hyperion* that Maderna's conception of the stage was one characterised by great flexibility in terms both of dramatic action and of musical structure: in both these works, we find a certain 'looseness' in the dramatic events portrayed (in *Don Perlimplin* arising from the 'dream-like' nature of the Lorca play, in *Hyperion* from the essentially 'non-dramatic' character of Hölderlin's original poem). It was therefore natural that the openness which Maderna desired within a musico-dramatic work would draw him to the framework of a work of 'Music Theatre', with its more casual, less tradition-bound possibilities.

As for the composer's choice of the 'Satyricon' text, his own explanation for this was as follows:[4]

'I chose the *'Satyricon'* text some time ago. In it a society is portrayed which, in many ways, is neither better nor worse than ours. Whoever belongs seriously to a political party, whether to Right or to Left, has a precise idea of the society in which we live, and I believe it would be difficult to find an image as close to our own reality as that given by Petronius in his description of Roman decadence. I don't wish to sing morality or politics, my aim is to make for the theatre a political act, and it was for this reason that I was drawn to this text . . .'

Maderna therefore saw in the *'Satyricon'* an image of present-day society, for which the Roman society portrayed in Petronius was a metaphor. The opera is therefore in some senses to be understood as a work of 'social comment' in the same way as Nono's *Intolleranza* and Brecht-Weill's *Dreigroschenoper*, both works which he had been involved in performing. However, there is in *Satyricon*, as Maderna warns us, no suggestion of moral or political 'preaching': we see in the opera an image of society, with masters and slaves, and the possibility of gaining power and influence over others by ruthless means, whether, political, financial or frankly sexual. We can thus view *Satyricon* as in some sense a part of the Italian 'tradition' of committed music which has been noted as characteristic of some Italian music of the present century, to which Dallapiccola's *Il Prigioniero*, Manzoni's *Atomhood*, Nono's *Intolleranza* and Berio's *La Vera Storia* also being.

The *image* of society which *Satyricon* presents to us is, then, one which becomes a *metaphor* for modern European society. We should therefore ask what musical means Maderna uses to present this image and to search for some connecting-points between the image and its musical portrayal. The society which Petronius allows us to see is one which is essentially *decadent*: a society whose very heart was being eaten away by disturbances of a political, economic, social and moral kind, whose pride in its glorious past was still there to be invoked, but whose paranoia was fed by the corruption, greed and exploitation which it had itself engendered. In this situation, it fed on itself, it parodied itself, while gorging itself on its own achievements, and often, while glorifying itself, gave way to sentimentality. The 'lingua franca' of the Empire, with its common language, social and political institutions and cultural heritage, was being eroded by a growing individualism in its constituents.

Maderna's image-making procedure in this work provides parallels to all these qualities. We hear the decadence of musical reminiscence, parodies of former musical styles, bombastic pride and also, on occasion, the sheer sentimentality of musical 'tear-jerkers' from our cultural past. The work displays no 'lingua franca', no obvious consistency of musical procedure either within or between its musical numbers, no logicality of musical development which had been of such importance in the operas of a previous age; instead, we find an almost uncontrolled individualism, each character in the opera having his or her own moments, in which pride, jealousy, fear or simple crudity is allowed, for the moment, its time to hold the stage. The 'patchwork' nature of the musical fabric of *Satyricon* is therefore parallel to the similar quality in the dramatic action (if that is indeed what we might call this series of 'Music Hall Sketches'), and the composer's description of the collage of styles and materials in the music of the work should in fact be examined bearing in mind the aims of the composer as we have now attempted to elucidate them.

It is therefore for this reason above all others that Maderna felt it necessary *not* to provide any tight musical, or even dramatic, structuring in *Satyricon*: the looseness of its structure paralleled the looseness of structure in the late Roman society which it portrayed. It was not simply that the free, often improvisatory character of Music Theatre, as distinct from the imposition of a musical upon a dramatic structure which had characterised traditional operatic procedures, gave the work a certain openness; more cogently, the demands of the image-making element in the work's fundamental metaphor had to be transmitted through a series of snapshot-images, each largely distinct one from another, and each relying upon its own particular focus, angle and viewpoint. For this reason also, the work brought together an enormous diversity of musical frameworks, of techniques for elaboration, of styles and references, as well as languages, both musical and linguistic, in order to build an overall image by a technique which the composer described as 'collage'.

The technique of collage, the placing together of diverse elements taken from a variety of sources and having a variety of individual 'resonances', all bound together by an overall image, was a technique which was by no means new to Maderna: he had employed a similar technique in several works, notably in *Hyperion, Don Perlimplin* and *Venetian Journal*, all works with an inherent dramatic or narrative basis. All of these works had relied upon the interaction of all of the elements of which they were comprised, in each case of (a) material on tape, itself of a 'collage' kind, consisting of vocal, orchestral, electronic and environmental sounds, (b) instrumental material played live, in some cases taken from pre-existing works, and (c) vocal (sung or spoken) material. In the case of *Hyperion*, this vocal material consisted of *Aria* (and in some versions also of choral sections), in *Don Perlimplin* of spoken dialogue and the 'Canzone' of Belisa, and in *Venetian Journal* of tenor-solo parts which exhibited a great variety of manner.

It was from this last work, *Venetian Journal*, that Maderna derived a 'model' for the specific varieties of collage to be found in *Satyricon*. *Venetian Journal* was composed for the American tenor Paul Sperry (who was to take the part of Habinnas in the Holland performances of *Satyricon*); the points of contact between the two works may be summarised as:

(a) vocal parts which range over passages of 'recitative', 'arioso' and 'aria', in several parts of which we find reference to earlier vocal styles, and in which the portrayal of individual personality is made as much by musical as by textual means,

(b) instrumental contributions which involve free accompaniment, some aleatoric or mobile procedures, and a great many references to generalised historical styles or specific quotations,

(c) an important usage of tapes, in the case of *Venetian Journal* of a group of tapes for use at specific points in the progression of the work, and in *Satyricon* some tapes used to facilitate dramatic action of a mimic kind between the various 'numbers',

(d) an overall character of parody: in *Venetian Journal* the setting of passages taken from the Travel Diaries of the eighteenth-century Scottish writer James Boswell concerning his visit to Venice, and in *Satyricon* a similarly 'decadent' image of its late Roman society.

The free-roaming interplay of all these elements in the collage is, in *Venetian Journal*, centred around specifically *Venetian* or eighteenth-century contributions: a popular Gondoliers' song ('*La biondina in gondoleta*') whose melody runs through many parts of the work (including the sections on tape), an 'Aria' in Venetian operatic style for the portrayal of Boswell's visit to the opera, and a Fugue which, interspersed with tape-interludes, brings the work to a close.[Ex. 5.2(a)–(c)]

It is clear from these examples that Maderna aimed to use these evocative style-quotations as a means of capturing a certain very specific resonance, that of Venice in the eighteenth century. In *Satyricon*, the employment of specific 'objects' from a variety of sources and with a variety of resonances seems to have appeared to Maderna as analogous to the procedures of 'Pop Art', and to have been particularly well-suited to the subject of the work:[5]

> 'Yes, there is a collage, there are naturalistic effects, or rather, 'exaggerated' naturalistic effects; there is in it something of the Musical, and so on. In short, I tried to make in music what nowadays we think of as 'Pop Art'. But as I said, I don't think for one moment that this way of composing would be valid for other pieces: it's fine for me, because it goes particularly well for Petronius'.

As in *Venetian Journal*, in which the tenor's attempts at Venetian dialect in his renderings of the popular and operatic music are placed within a context of mainly English parlance, the variety of languages employed in *Satyricon* (again mainly English, but with smatterings of French, German and Latin) are part of the collage. The language to be used at various points in *Satyricon* had been indicated in Maderna's sketch-plans for the work at specific places in the text, along with some 'aides-memoire' for the use of specific musical quotations: in this, we can see that both the linguistic and musical references were part-and-parcel of the overall image, an image of a kind of 'Tower of Babel', and one which also provided a means of moving between layers of comic, serious, pompous and banal utterance in several parts of the work: musical and textual aspects thus moved in some senses in parallel.

We know that during his preparatory work on the text, Maderna had to hand French and Italian translations of Petronius, as well as an English translation of the poems of Propertius and an Italian translation of Catullus, but the translation he employed for the largest proportion of the text for his opera was the English version of Petronius made by William Arrowsmith.

On what basis did Maderna make his choice of the particular passages of the Petronius text for inclusion in the opera? The passages he chose are centred around the scene he was to depict, the '*Cena Trimalchionis*' (Chapter 5 of the original), but he enclosed within this framework passages which were taken from other chapters of the original text. He also introduced into the action of the work characters whose contribution to the '*Cena Trimalchionis*' of Petronius is minimal, or who in fact do not appear in this chapter at all. His aim was to provide for the opera a small group of strongly-delineated characters of markedly different personality, and to choose for the text those passages which were capable of most emphatically expressing, in as few words as possible, their outlook and personality. For Trimalchio, the host of the dinner, he chose four passages: in '*Trimalchio e le Flatulenze*', he apologies for the poor state of his stomach, which causes him to have to make an exit from the scene for the relief of his bowels; in

Ex. 5.2(a): Maderna: *Venetian Journal*: 1B

Ex. 5.2(b): Maderna: *Venetian Journal*: 41A

Ex. 5.2(c): Maderna: *Venetian Journal*: 10 I–II

'*Carriera di Trimalchio*', he tells of his varying fortunes in life; in '*Trimalchio contro Fortunata*' he reacts to Fortunata, his wife, in a violent manner, reminding her of her 'former station in life'; whilst in '*Trimalchio e il Monumento*', he gives instructions regarding his tombstone. Fortunata herself expresses a mixture of her pride at the power she can exercise over her husband and pride in his wealth in '*Fortunata*', whilst in '*Fortunata e Eumolpus*', she attempts to exercise her own power of seduction over Eumolpus, but unsuccessfully. Habinnas is given two solo numbers: '*The Money*', in which a poem from a later chapter of Petronius' original is transferred to the mouth of Habinnas expressing the power of money, and '*La Matrona di Efeso*', a 'moral tale', of rather cynical sexual overtones. The other characters of the opera, Eumolpus, Quartilla, Criside, Niceros and Scintilla, have more limited roles to play in the dramatic fabric.

The scene is laid for the lavish banquet which Trimalchio has arranged for his friends, with many slaves in attendance to their every desire. The framework of the opera is therefore that of the 'party', an already improvisatory and free-wheeling event, and there is little doubt that it was this framework which appealed to Maderna's imagination in the first place. He began by sketching out a possible plan for the action, making mention, even at this early stage, of some aspects of the music. This plan, however, does not concur precisely with the order of events given in Petronius: Maderna reversed or interchanged events freely, and it is clear that even at this stage he wished to use passages of Petronius' text which were not included in the '*Cena Trimalchionis*' chapter.

It would seem, therefore, that at this stage we are dealing simply with a re-ordering of events, a displacement of sections and the composer wishing for dramatic reasons to edit the original material in a way which would facilitate the maximum dramatic coherence. This plan, which we shall refer to as Plan I, was followed by a second, more detailed one (Plan II), in which further sections of the eventual score are specifically mentioned.

The two 'sketches' for the dramatic action and sequence of the opera provide us with some indication of the ways in which Maderna's thoughts on the opera developed from the first rather generalised outline (in which may still lie embedded some of the semi-improvisatory Tanglewood experience) to the second more fully worked idea. If we place together the sequence of 'numbers' which is implied in these two plans, we arrive at the following schemes:

Plan I	*Plan II*
CARRIERA DI TRIMALCHIO	CRISIDE
CRISIDE	('LE RIRE')
'MILIONI'	CARRIERA DI TRIMALCHIO
LOVE'S ECSTASY	LOVE'S ECSTASY (on tape)
'MILIONI'	'MILIONI'
TANGO AND FUGUE (FORTUNATA E EUMOLPUS and EUMOLPUS FUGA)	TANGO AND FUGUE (FORTUNATA E EUMOLPUS and EUMOLPUS FUGA)
THE MONEY	THE MONEY
TRIMALCHIO CONTRO FORTUNATA	TRIMALCHIO CONTRA FORTUNATA
TRIMALCHIO E IL MONUMENTO	(Tape: BIRDS' — LE RIRE')
	(TRIMALCHIO E IL MONUMENTO)

It will be noticed that in Plan I, no mention is made of the use of tape-sections for the work, which suggests either that this plan was made before the composer saw any necessity for their use, or that he wished at this stage merely to sketch out a preliminary idea for the action and sequence of the other numbers of the opera. In Plan II, on the other hand, the tape-piece known as *Le Rire* is specifically mentioned as an integral part of the dramatic plan, as also are the tapes of '*Turkeys*' and of '*Birds*' during the reconciliation of Trimalchio with Fortunata.

In Plan II, Criside is given both a solo number at the opening of the work and also takes part in the LOVE'S ECSTASY later in the action with Niceros: in the score published by Salabert, CRISIDE I and II are for Criside accompanied by a solo flute, and cor anglais respectively with the only words 'Love's Ecstasy', and 'LOVE'S ECSTASY' (a vocal quartet with instruments for Criside, Scintilla, Niceros and Eumolpus) is based musically on a polyphonic re-working of CRISIDE I and II with the same two-word text. It would seem that Maderna eventually abandoned the idea of a piece for Criside alone which would mix together texts from Petronius and Propertius, as his Plan II had envisaged.

Neither of these plans, in fact, contain reference to all the sixteen 'numbers' of which the Salabert score is compiled: LADY LUCK (sung by Quartilla), LA MATRONA DI EFESO (sung by Habinnas), FORTUNATA (sung by herself) and TRIMALCHIO E LE FLATULENZE (sung by Trimalchio, with a second purely instrumental version in a separate score), as well as the instrumental-mobile numbers FOOD MACHINE and SCINTILLA I do not appear in either scheme.

What reliance may we therefore place upon these two Plans as far as the dramatic and musical ordering of *Satyricon* is concerned? Whilst it is clear that they both represent 'work in progress' and not in any sense recipes for performance, at least Plan II comes close enough to the work as it was eventually performed in Holland for us to assume that the material which is not mentioned in this plan was conceived after the dramatic outline had been laid down. It may even be the case that LADY LUCK and LA MATRONA DI EFESO were added in order that Quartilla and Habinnas might be given solo-numbers, in the tradition of eighteenth-century opera!

We must now turn to the matter of the performances of the opera which were given in Holland in 1973, a matter of the greatest importance for our consideration of how it is in fact possible to perform *Satyricon*. We should take into account all the documentation available to us regarding the various performances, of which there were no fewer than four different versions presented during that year: firstly, the performance given on stage in Scheveningen and Amsterdam as part of the Holland Festival, where the opera was given in a double-bill together with Ligeti's *Nouvelles Aventures*; secondly, a performance broadcast by Dutch Radio at about the same time which Maderna conducted; thirdly, a television-version also made for Dutch Television, conducted by Maderna's pupil Lucas Vis with the same singers; and fourthly, the American première, staged at Tanglewood in August, with the same producer as in Holland, Ian Strasfogel, and conducted by Gunther Schuller.

Both the NOS Radio and NOS Television versions of the opera arose from the stage performance of the work in Holland, but were each adapted to the special needs of the media through which they were presented, and consequently they each assumed a different shape from the stage-version. In the radio-version, none of the pre-recorded tape material which was used in the stage-version was employed (material which evidently served the needs of this original presentation for music to accompany stage-actions), but in the television version some use was made of tapes. In both radio and television, the sequence of musical numbers differed both from the stage-version and from the plans we have already observed. Where in the case of the radio version of the opera we are confronted simply with a version which attempted to present the main musical sections of the work without any scenic action, and therefore without the need for any linking of the numbers of tapes, the case of the television version is of considerably greater interest for us in studying the ordering of the musical and dramatic material in *Satyricon*. This latter version was adapted for its television production by Wilhelimina Holdeman, and made considerable use of televisual techniques such as fading from one action or number to another, and splitting numbers into separate units.

The original version on stage in the Holland Festival took a form and sequence which differs from any of the schemes we have observed so far, and may be summarised as follows.

The guests at Trimalchio's dinner amuse and gorge themselves and one couple are engaged in love-making: CRISIDE II — LOVE'S ECSTASY — (Criside and Niceros, with three wind instruments: fading at end) — TAPE (1). Fortunata enters and sings her 'Aria': FORTUNATA. Trimalchio apologises for the poor state of his stomach: TRIMALCHIO E LE FLATULENZE. He has to leave the stage for while: FOOD MACHINE. Habinnas sings the praises of money: THE MONEY. The love-making continues: TAPE (2). Bass drum and Cymbal lead in Quartilla, who sings of the vagaries of fortune: LADY LUCK (second verse without voice, but with Tuba *obligato*, omitting final note). Trimalchio again has to retire: TRIMALCHIO E LE FLATULENZE. TAPE (3) Habinnas tells the fable of the woman of the woman who saves her lover by placing the body of her dead husband on a cross: LA MATRONA DI EFESO. TAPE (4). Trimalchio tells his life-story: CARRIERA DI TRIMALCHIO. The love-making continues: CRISIDE I. 'Milioni' ending from CARRIERA DI TRIMALCHIO taken up by everyone, with underpinning of Bass Drum and Cymbal. LOVE'S ECSTASY: Criside, Scintilla,

Niceros and Eumolpus. 'Milioni' as before. Fortunata attempts to seduce Eumolpus with a sexy Tango: FORTUNATA E EUMOLPUS. Eumolpus' 'learning' prevents him from responding: EUMOLPUS FUGA. Percussion 'break'. SCINTILLA I Fortunata discovers her husband kissing one of the slaves, but he reacts violently, threatening to remove her statue from his tomb: TRIMALCHIO CONTRO FORTUNATA. There is general lamentation at their disagreement, but eventually peace is restored: TRIMALCHIO E LE FLATULENZE (instrumental version). Trimalchio gives instructions for his tombstone: TRIMALCHIO E IL MONUMENTO. Bass Drum and Tuba: fading. TAPE (5)

   This version does, finally, make use of all the material which is presented to us in the Salabert score, but the question still remains whether we can in fact regard this as the 'definitive' version, and as a model for any future performances of the opera. Even if we regard the two preliminary outlines which we called Plans I and II as no more than ideas for a 'work in progress', as attempts by the composer to sketch possibilities for shaping the dramatic action, nevertheless the very different forms taken by the NOS Television version and the stage-version of the opera would suggest that the producer and conductor have considerable freedom at their disposal in ordering, omitting and linking the numbers of which the score is composed, and this is particularly so in the matter of the tapes used in any performance.

   Maderna seems, doubtless because of his deteriorating health, to have put together the tape-material for *Satyricon* in a rather hurried and haphazard manner: he listed a collection of 18 tapes, containing the most varied sound material (vocal sounds made by himself and Marino Zuccheri, instrumental sounds from specified sources, and a large body of animal and bird sounds), but the specific placing of these in the opera was indicated for only four of these, in episodes which would highlight Eumeros and Criside, which were eventually deleted from the work. We have already seen how some of this large body of material was employed in the stage version of *Satyricon* in Holland: to Salabert, on the other hand, he sent a different group of tapes for inclusion in the score of the work when published. His 'index' of these tapes also differs from the tape which Salabert now possesses!

   It is clear from this examination of the stage-performance in Holland that the material on tape used here differed from the tape-material sent to Salabert, with the exception of the second tape *EROTICA*. All the other material was therefore used solely in these performances, and we may therefore conclude that the conductor or producer of the opera has, on each occasion that the work is produced, to make a choice of the material on tape which he will employ, and might not even be restricted to that material held by the publisher.

   In order to clarify all the issues regarding the sequence and nature of the material used in each of the versions of the work which we have now investigated, it is perhaps useful to draw up a general scheme which will show the material in each case: in Plans I and II, the NOS Radio and Television versions, and the stage-presentation [SATYRICON-PLAN].

   From our investigation of all the sources of information regarding the ordering and connection of the material of which the opera is made up, it now becomes clear that there is no fixed sequence for the numbers of the opera, nor any fixed scheme for the dramatic action. What this investigation does *not* however suggest

Carriera di Trimalchio Criside Love's Ecstasy Fortunata e Eumolpus	Love's Ecstasy Fortunata e Eumolpus	Eumolpus Fuga The Money	Lady Luck Trimalchio e il Monumento Love's Ecstasy Scintilla	Trimalchio le Flatulenze Tape: voices and pigs Fortunata Tape: pigs and instruments	Criside II Love's Ecstasy Tape Fortunata
Eumolpus Fuga The Money			Fortunata Carriera di Trimalchio	La Matrona di Efeso (i) Tape: instruments and birds	Trimalchio e le Flatulenze Food Machine
Trimalchio contro Fortunata Trimalchio e il Monumento		Trimalchio contro Fortunata Tirmalchio e il Monumento	The Money	Trimalchio e le Flatulenze	The Money
			Fortunata e Eumolpus	Carriera di Trimalchio (broken off)	Tape
			Eumolpus Fuga Trimalchio e le Flatulenze Trimalchio contro Fortunata La Matrona di Efeso Lady Luck	Love's Ecstasy 'Milioni' Scintilla I	Lady Luck Trimalchio e le Flatulenze Tape
				La Matrona di Efeso Tape: voices and cats Fortunata e Eumolpus Eumolpus Fuga Trimalchio contro Fortunata	La Matrona di Efeso Tape Carriera di Trimalchio Criside I 'Millioni'
				Tape: 'Erotica' Trimalchio e le Flatulenze (insts.)	Love's Ecstasy 'Milioni'
				La Matrona di Efeso (iii) Tape: dogs barking Lady Luck (insts., then Quartilla)	Fortunata e Eumolpus Eumolpus Fuga Scintilla I
				Trimalchio e il Monumento Tape: pigs	Trimalchio contro Fortunata Trimalchio e le Flatulenze (insts.)
SATYRICON-PLAN				Lady Luck (with Tuba)	Trimalchio e il Monumento Tape

is that *Satyricon* is an 'aleatoric opera': rather, that the dramatic action and sequence are open to considerable freedom on the part of the producer and conductor, but always within the limits of plausibility suggested by Petronius' text and by the necessity for the whole work to possess some dramatic unity and purpose. It is not necessary that all the numbers should be included in every performance, and the inclusion or omission of the tapes is also a matter for discretion. The conception of aleatoricism which is to be found in the later scores of Maderna (such as *Hyperion, Quadrivium, Violin Concerto, Serenata per un Satellite* or *Venetian Journal*) is thus naturally extended to encompass the dramatic as well as the musical aspects of *Satyricon*.

Of particular relevance here is perhaps the manner in which Maderna had conceived the various arrangements of musical material in the versions of *Hyperion*: we saw how pre-existing works, or parts of pre-existing works, had contributed to the formation of all the different manifestations of this work, both as a stage- and as a concert-work, and this model may be thought comparable to the choices available to the conductor and producer of *Satyricon*. One might argue that the various versions of *Hyperion* had been the responsibility of the composer himself, and that it would be impertinent for anyone to assume a posthumous responsibility for Maderna's opera, but given the paucity of indications given by the composer for the realisation of *Satyricon*, this is a responsibility which must nevertheless be assumed if we are to be able to perform the work at all: in any case, this has been done on several occasions after the composer's death.

As we have already noted, Maderna prepared the score of *Satyricon* by a collage – technique which, whilst it undoubtedly owed something to the 'Pop Art' of the 1960s, also had its roots in the compositional procedures with which he had experimented in works on tape, from *Ritratto di Città* to *Tempo Libero* and *Ages*, procedures of placing together diverse elements and creating thereby a variegated image in sound. This process of composition of the work was undertaken in a hurry: Maderna knew that the disease which had taken hold of him gave him little time to live, and so the arrangement of all the elements of the work continued even into the final rehearsals in Holland. We shall be concerned in this study with the Holland performance which is recorded on tape, and with the score published later by Salabert, but we shall also take into account some of the sketches and preliminary workings which are available, in so far these cast light on the composition and nature of the work.

The questions which we shall attempt to answer with regard to *Satyricon* are:

- By what means did Maderna diversify the *vocal* element in the work, creating various types of vocal expression appropriate to the text?
- What *styles* of vocal or instrumental music are to be found in the work?
- At what points did Maderna employ specific musical *references* in the work?
- To what extent are 'mobile' and 'aleatory' procedures a part of the expression of the work?
- Is there any large-scale *organisation* discernible through the work as a whole?
- What can we learn from the available sketches for the work about the composer's approach to its composition?
- What is the importance of *Satyricon* within Maderna's work as a whole?

One thing which becomes very clear from an examination of the available sketches for *Satyricon* is that Maderna approached the composition of the work largely from the perspective of the vocal element, composing a great deal of this before the instrumental material was planned, and most often, in fact, sketching out the vocal line in the form of a rhythmic skeleton before adding pitches to it. Thus, the treatment of the *text* on which the work was based was of paramount importance; he also had a good idea at a fairly early stage of the singers who would be taking particular roles in the first performance, and could therefore to some extent base his writing of individual parts on a specific singer's vocal qualities.

We find a great variety of vocal utterance in the work, both between and within the various numbers and characters, and an essential quality of the work is to be found in the way the composer moves between these different types of expression. As Alban Berg had done in *Wozzeck*, Maderna here employs vocal means which move freely through the various stages between spoken recitation on the one hand and full-blown 'Aria'-singing on the other, in order to establish from moment to moment the most appropriate declamation of the text in its dramatic context. This variety of manner and its basis in the dramatic context may be observed in the following examples. [Ex. 5.3(a), (b)]

In the first example, the opening of '*La Matrona di Efeso*', the narrator of the tale, Habinnas, singing of the 'eternal fidelity' of the Woman from Ephesus to her husband, employs a *cantabile 'arioso'* manner, smooth and diatonic, yet somewhat casual in expression, in keeping with the easy homeliness of his description of marital bliss. All of a sudden, this manner becomes broken off, with a change to spoken recitation: this highlights both the sudden death of her husband and a change to greater irony through the matter-of-factness of the string *pizzicati*, relieved only by the mock-sombre quality of the winds' and marimba's mobile. We are to be treated to a tale of *infidelity*, as the woman will make love to the soldier guarding her husband's tomb, and so the romantic 'idyll' of the opening here gives way to the 'reality' which will come to the fore in the subsequent tale.

In the second example, which comprises the whole of Quartilla's '*Lady Luck*' the tone is philosophical: Quartilla expresses the vagaries of Dame Fortune and the impossibility of any attitude other than resignation. The number is also a kind of 'Drinking Song' in the midst of the orgiastic scene at Trimalchio's feast, and Maderna sets the text in a straightforward 'Aria' manner with a suggestion of the style of the *Beggar's Opera* in the simplicity of the vocal line and its accompaniment. The whole number is repeated with the *obbligato* Tuba as soloist in the reprise, and a final touch of humour is added as the 'inevitable' resolution into the final chord is simply omitted.

Alongside the diversity of the vocal expression in *Satyricon*, we also find a diversity in the styles or manners to which the composer makes reference, whether directly or else more obliquely, in the course of the work. The purpose of this diversification is again to underline the dramatic aspect of the work in terms of delineation of mood or character, but an important part of the composer's purpose in the reference to various styles is ironic: the character on many occasions says one thing, whilst the style in which it is couched says something quite different. The following examples will again make this clear. [Ex. 5.4(a)–(c)]

In the first example, which is the whole of Trimalchio's number '*Trimalchio e le Flautulenze*', the host of the evening is troubled by the flatulence which has bedevilled him for several days: 'You'll excuse me, friends, but I've been

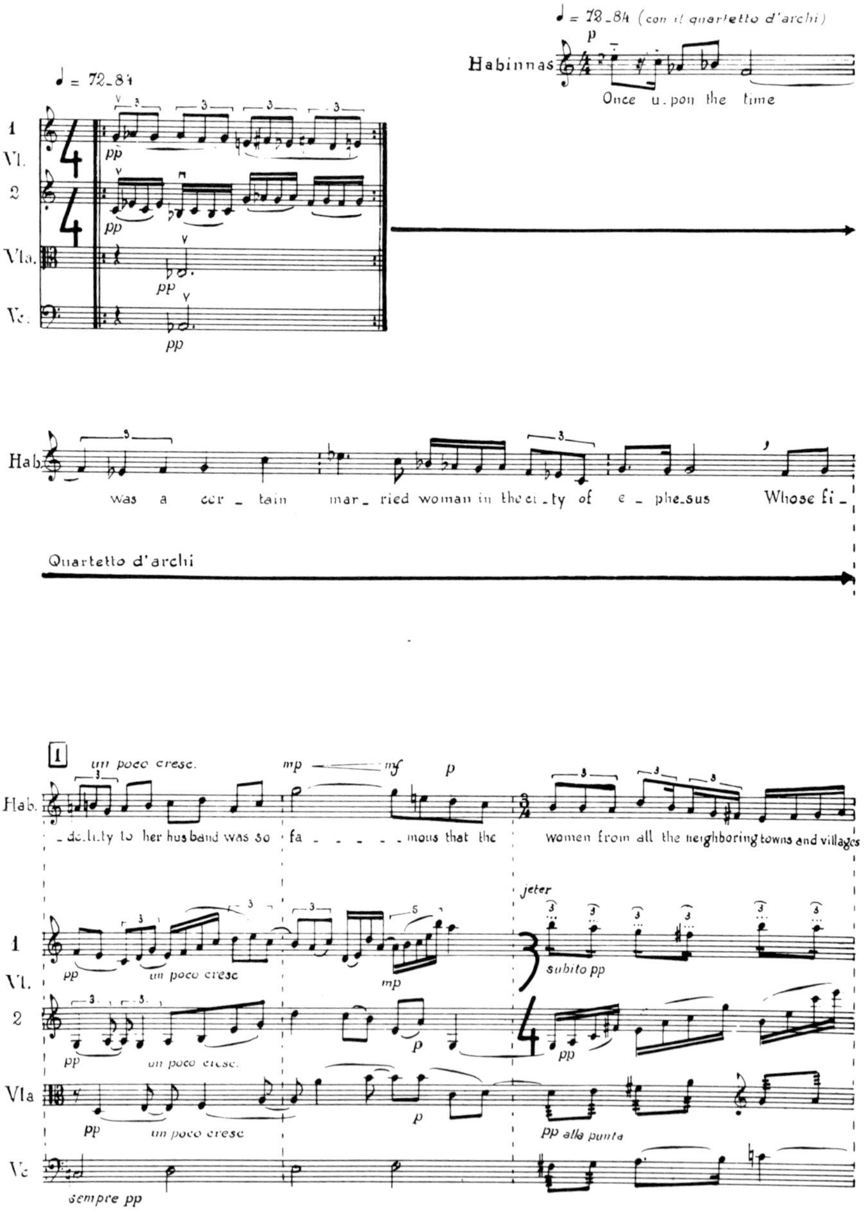

Ex. 5.3(a): Maderna: *Satyricon*: 'La Matrona di Efeso' 1–5 bis

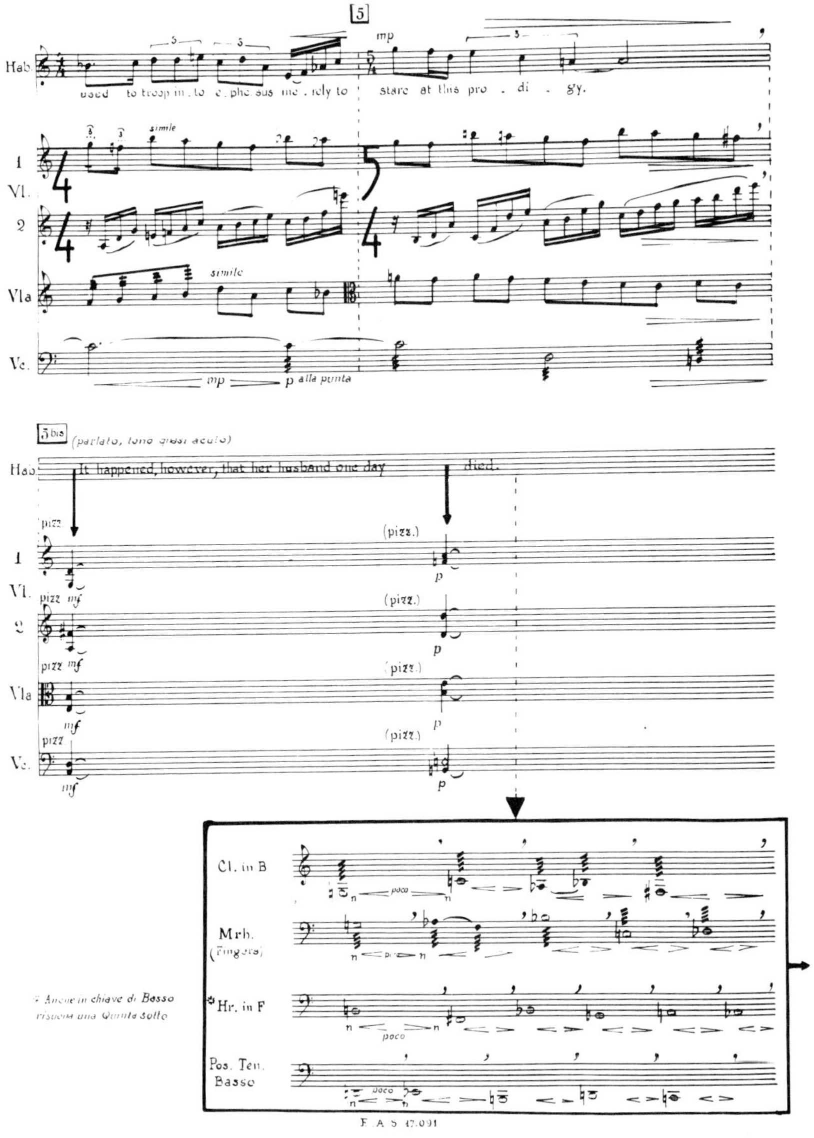
5
Hab
used to troop in to e phe sus me rely to
stare at this pro di gy.
simile
Vl.
Vla
Vc.
mp
p alla punta
5 bis
(parlato, tono quasi acuto)
It happened, however, that her husband one day
died.
pizz
(pizz.)
mf
p
Cl. in B
Mrb. (Fingers)
Hr. in F
Pos. Ten. Basso
poco
* Anche in chiave di Basso risuona una Quinta sotto
E. A. S. 17.091

Ex. 5.3(a): *Contd*

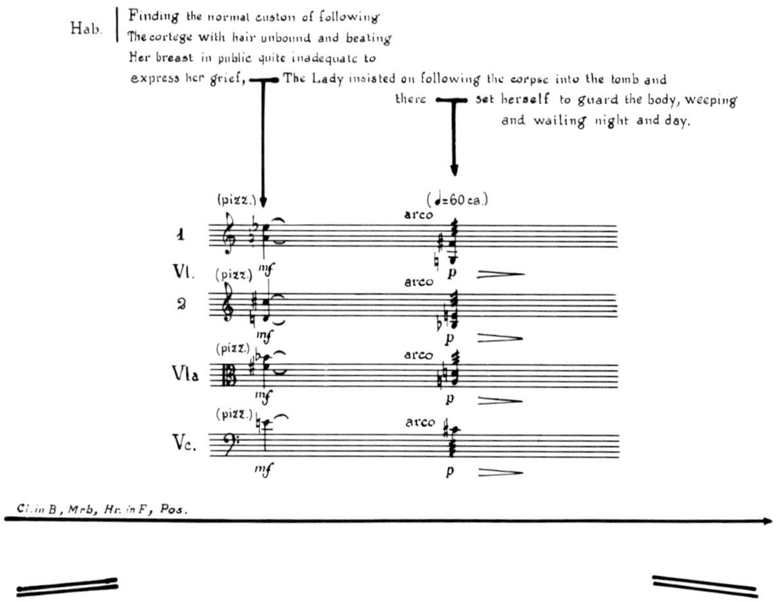
Hab.
Finding the normal custom of following
The cortege with hair unbound and beating
Her breast in public quite inadequate to
express her grief,
The Lady insisted on following the corpse into the tomb and
there
set herself to guard the body, weeping
and wailing night and day.
(pizz.)
(♩=60 ca.)
arco
1
Vl.
2
Vla
Vc.
mf
p
Cl. in B, Mrb, Hr. in F, Pos.

Hab.
Although in her extremes of grief she was clearly courting death from starvation, her parents
were utterly unable to persuade her to leave.
♩ = 52 ca
(on conductors cue)
Oboe
pp
Cl. in B, Mrb., Hr. in F, Pos. (Pause sempre più lunghe . . . . . fino . . a . . sparire)

Ex. 5.3(a): *Contd*

Ex. 5.5(d): Maderna: *Satyricon*: 'Trimalchio e il Monumento' 36–58

40bis
♩=84 ca. Ma liberamente
rall. . . . . .
Tuba
f
p
f
cresc.
Tuba
(So lang wie möglich)
ff
p
p
ff
Trim. – Well, old friend Niceros, will you make me my tomb exactly as I order it ?
41
♩= 52
Trim. - First, of course, I want a statue of myself;
p
I want a statue of my -
Open
Hr. in F
legato
♩= 72 ca.
45
Trim.
mp (appassionato)
- self. But carve my dog at my feet, and give me gar - lands of flow - ers,
Hr.
Vla
mp
p
Vc.
mp
p
CB.
mp
p

Ex. 5.5(d): *Contd*

Ex. 5.5(d): *Contd*

Ex. 5.5(e): Maderna: *Satyricon*: 'Trimalchio e il Monumento' 66 bis–78

Ex. 5.5(e): *Contd*

Ex. 5.5(f): Maderna: *Satyricon*: 'Trimalchio e il Monumento' 99–100

Ex. 5.5(f): *Contd*

100
Trim.
tied to her girdle. And don't for. get my pet slave.
Ott.
Ob.
1
Cl.
2
Fg.
Cel.
Hr.
Tr.
Pos.
Tuba
Ptti
Cassa
f secco

Ex. 5.5(f): *Contd*

Ex. 5.5(g): Maderna: *Satyricon*: 'Trimalchio e il Monumento' 104–1112 bis

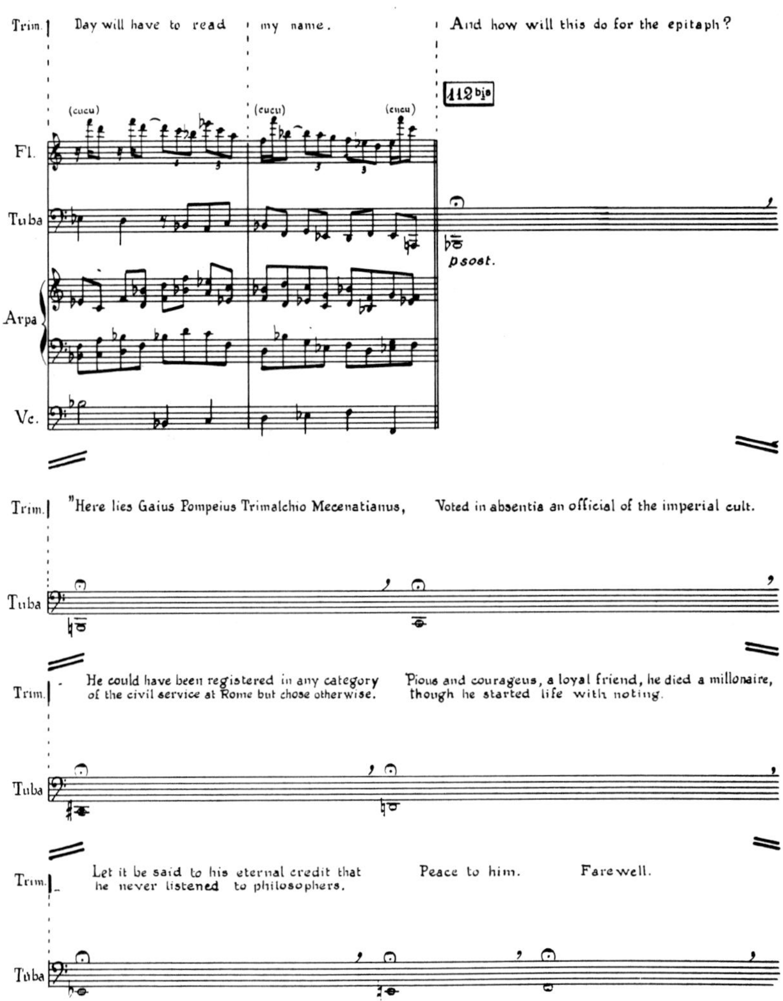
Trim.
Day will have to read
my name.
And how will this do for the epitaph?
112 bis
(cucu)
(cucu)
(cucu)
Fl.
Tuba
p sost.
Arpa
Vc.
Trim.
"Here lies Gaius Pompeius Trimalchio Mecenatianus,
Voted in absentia an official of the imperial cult.
Tuba
Trim.
He could have been registered in any category of the civil service at Rome but chose otherwise.
Pious and courageus, a loyal friend, he died a millonaire, though he started life with noting.
Tuba
Trim.
Let it be said to his eternal credit that he never listened to philosophers.
Peace to him.
Farewell.
Tuba

Ex. 5.5(g): *Contd*

jars of perfume and every fight of Hercules' career.' This sentimentality is exactly reflected in the quotation from *La Bohème* in which it is cast: a suggestion of mortality evoked by the *Till Eulenspiegel* horn-theme is added in half-mocking counterpoint to the bathos of the Puccini-quotation.

The fifth, sixth and seventh examples continue the wholesale use of musical references, which come to dominate the latter part of '*Trimalchio e il Monumento*'. Trimalchio becomes more and more specific in his instructions regarding the monument to be erected in his honour. In the '*Hesitation Waltz*', in which he asks for his memorial to be protected from vandalism, the 'valedictory' music of *La Bohème* is invoked in an attempt to arouse his listeners' sympathy for his cause. His wife is also to be honoured, sculpted with a dove in her hand and her pet dog at her side, and the theatricality of Trimalchio's magnanimous gesture towards his spouse is emphasised by the *Circus March*, his heroic stature simultaneously by *Tipperary*. Sentimentality of the most liquid kind dominates the conclusion of the number, a request for a sobbing boy beside a broken vase to be added to the frieze, and Gluck's '*Che farò senza Euridice*' from *Orfeo* adds a particular irony at this point: Trimalchio's relationship with Fortunata is the very opposite of either a heroic or tragic one except in the most banal senses of both these epithets.

The parodistic element in the employment of musical reference from the 'popular classics' and 'tear-jerkers' in *Satyricon* is of considerable importance in the atmosphere of the work as a whole: however, its use is restricted either to the numbers assigned to Trimalchio or Fortunata, or else to the equally parodistic number '*La Matrona di Efeso*'. The mocking or else self-mocking tone in these 'cameo portraits' is consistently maintained throughout the work, comedy of a broad, low variety at which Maderna seems particularly adept, implicit in which is also perhaps a suggestion of the comic types of '*opera buffa*', even of the 'Commedia dell'Arte from which it grew, a type of theatrical presentation with which *Satyricon* might be said to have a more than casual relationship in terms of manner, as well as of the semi-improvisational nature of the work.

The 'mobile' nature of *Satyricon* is, as we have already suggested, an integral element embedded in the very philosophy of the work, part and parcel of its presentation of an image of decadence, and the large-scale malleability with which the sequence of numbers and actions can be treated in performance grew, in all probability, from the 'Music Theatre Exercise' which the composer directed, together with Ian Strasfogel, in Tanglewood in 1972. At the same time, the individual numbers of the score have a large degree of self-containment, and the composer has provided for some flexibility in the performance within particular passages of them: we should therefore ask what this flexibility consists of, where it is used, and why at these particular points in the score. At no point in the work does Maderna offer the possibility of re-arrangement of the sequence *within* a number, but there are nevertheless a number of points at which 'mobile' or 'aleatory' procedures, of the kind that we discovered in operation in some other later instrumental works, assume great importance.

We might summarise the use of such procedures as:

(i) passages in which a particular instrumental 'texture' is given to be repeated *ad libitum* as an accompaniment to some stage-action: this occurs most clearly in the first entry of Fortunata at the opening of her first number '*Fortunata*',

    (ii)   passages in which instrumental 'mobiles' are used in the accompaniment of recitation (either spoken or else sung *recitation):* this occurs in 'Fortunato', 'The Money', 'La Matrona di Efeso', 'Carriera di Trimalchio' and 'Trimalchio contro Fortunata',

   (iii)   two numbers in which free instrumental 'mobiles' make up the whole substance of the piece: in 'Food Machine', this is constructed from material taken from other sections of the work: in 'Scintilla I' of a free pitch-sequence to be interpreted *ad libitum* by a small group of instrumentalists.

The following examples demonstrate these procedures. [Ex. 5.6(a)–(d)]

In the first example, from 'Carriera di Trimalchio', we see an example of the many occasions on which the use of mobiles becomes part of a recitative – manner in the work: here, the three wind instruments and piano have rapid, busy figurations which they continue throughout Trimalchio's account of his capitalistic enterprises. This gives an impression of great activity to this passage, and once more is continued until brusquely cut off by the conductor.

The second example is similar to the first except that here, as Habinnas is enraptured by the phrase 'Jupiter is money in the bank' at the end of his number, both voice and strings choose freely between various given phrases, varying the dynamic level and character on each repetition: this is, in comparison with the previous example, of a more relaxed and casual manner, and provides an open ending to the whole number.

The third and fourth examples, each a complete number of the work, are the only occasions when freely-written mobiles are the sole material: both are to be used as an accompaniment to stage action. In 'Food Machine', the material given to the various instrumental groups is taken from other parts of the work: that for piano from 'Fortunata' (bars 34–37) and 'Carriera di Trimalchio' (bar 83 ter), that for winds and strings from 'Trimalchio contro Fortunata' (bar 36 bis), with the addition of parts for marimba and flexation added freely. Maderna here brings together material of a broadly similar nature, all busy and somewhat disjoined, in order to form an instrumental 'entr' acte', as it were. In 'Scintilla I', again to be used to accompany action, Maderna has simply made a series of pitches which, improvised upon by flute, oboe and clarinet, will have a certain degree of homogeneity, but whose character will be determined in each performance by the conductor in response to the kind of action on stage which it will accompany: this is the point of greatest freedom in the whole score, a 'recipe' for instrumental improvisation of a similar kind to that which Maderna had given in the *Serenata per un satellite* a few years earlier.

We have referred to the 'collage' nature of the score of *Satyricon* as an essential element in the work's 'image-making' technique, and the examples given of the various musical procedures will have demonstrated that this collage, consisting of style-quotation, specific quotation and some simple aleatoric elements, as well as the nature of *Satyricon* as a work conceived in largely self-contained numbers, would tend to preclude any possibility of larger-scale musical organisation. We would search in vain for any overriding serial or other organisation of the material of the work: there is certainly no evidence, from the large body of materials in manuscript form which are available to us, that Maderna had attempted to impose any organisation of a thoroughgoing kind upon the highly contrasted elements of which the collage is made up.

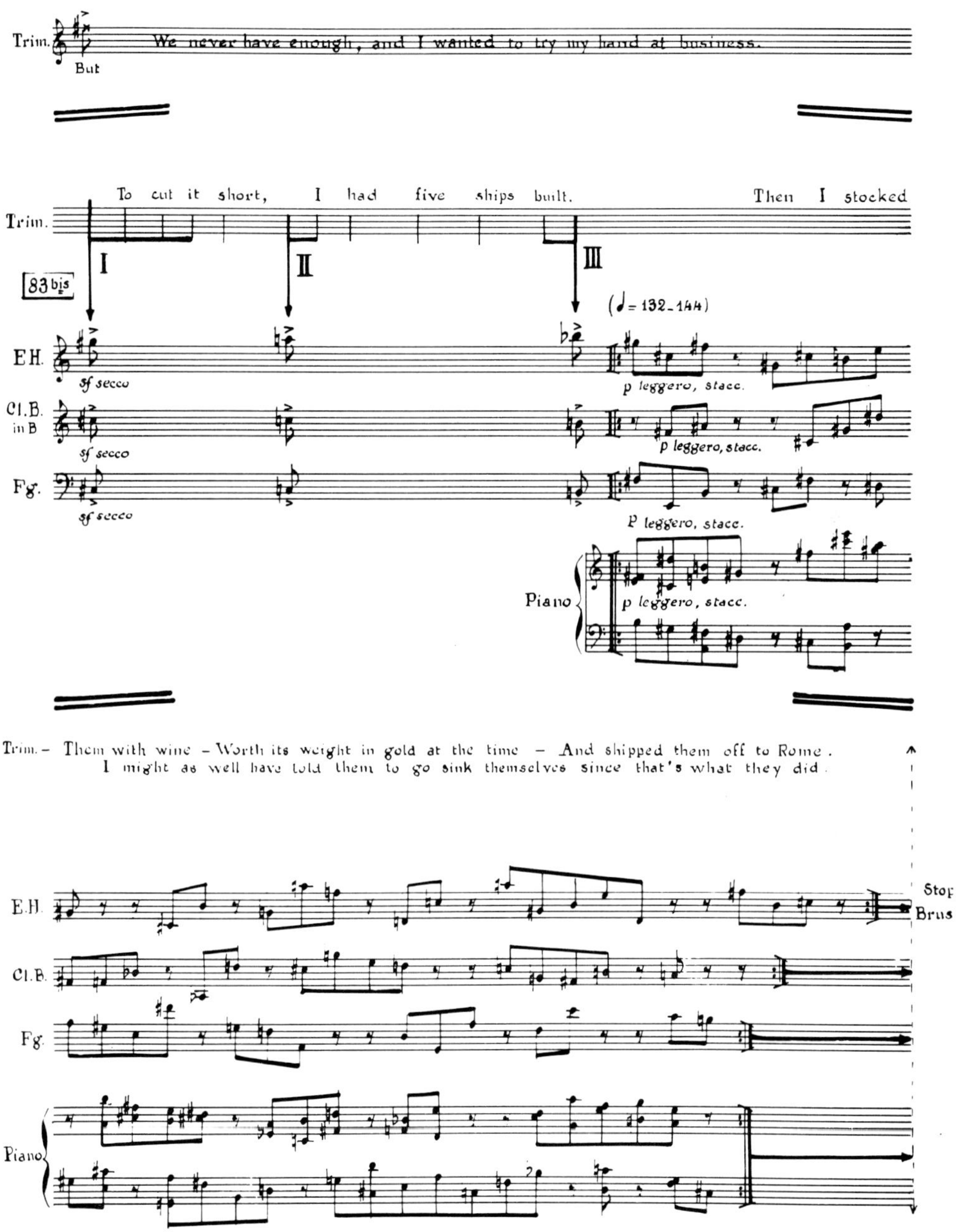

Ex. 5.6(a): Maderna: *Satyricon*: 'Carriera di Trimalchio' 83 bis

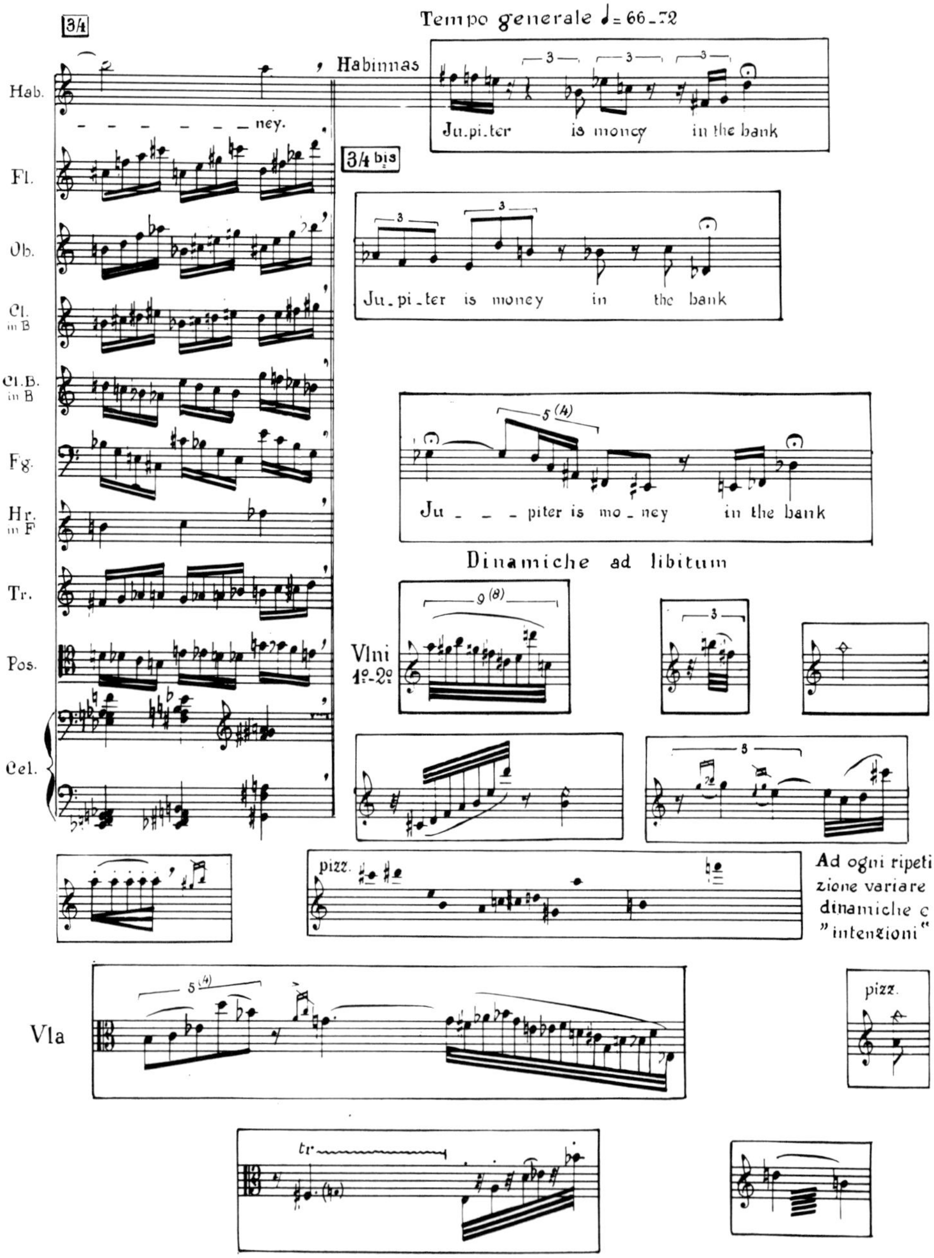

Ex. 5.6(b): Maderna: *Satyricon*: 'The Money' 34 bis

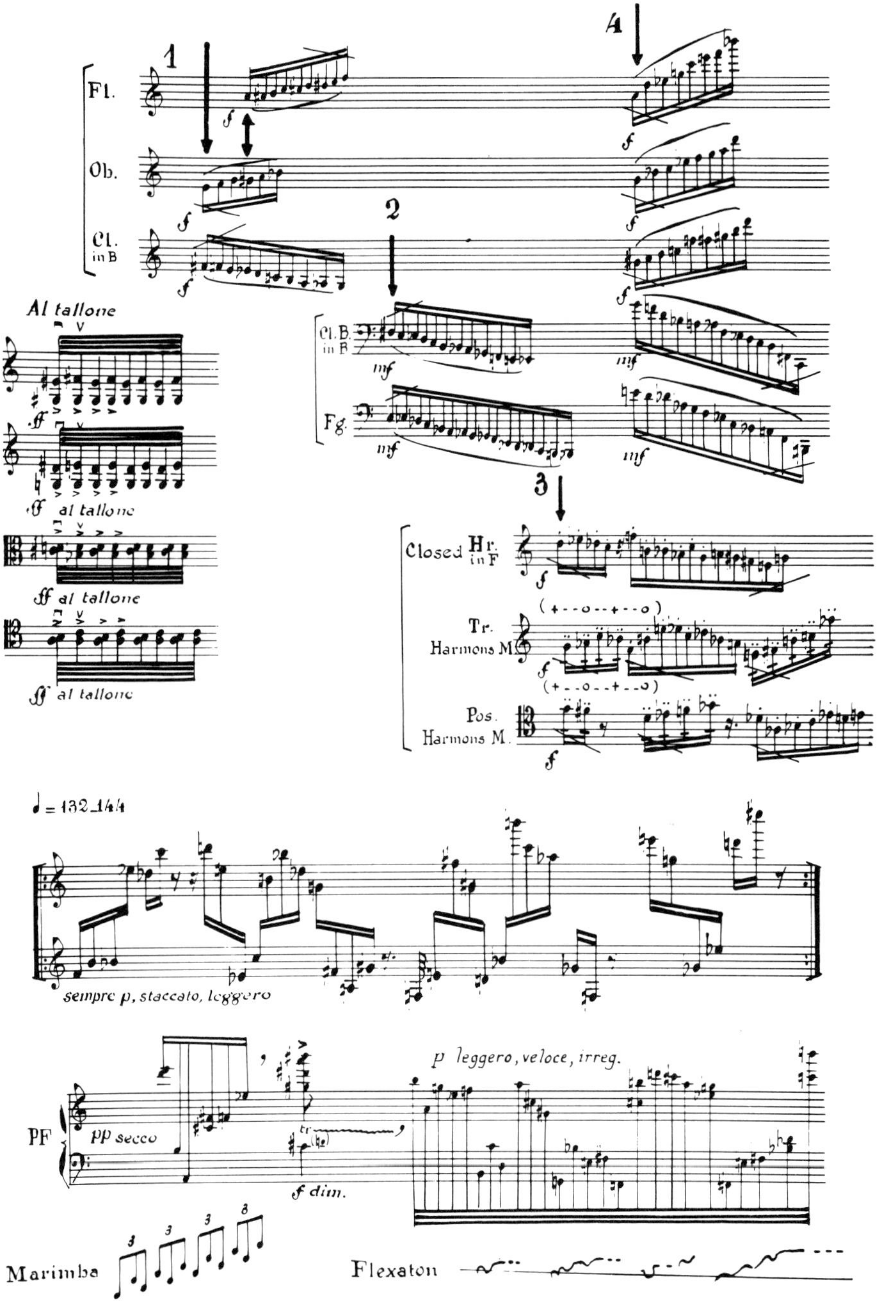

Ex. 5.6(c): Maderna: *Satyricon*: 'Food Machine'

Ad libitum mit Flöte, Oboe, Clarinetten in B

Ex. 5.6(d): Maderna: *Satyricon*: 'Scintilla I'

any organisation of a thoroughgoing kind upon the highly contrasted elements of which the college is made up.

Maderna, in fact, appears to have worked in a largely *ad hoc* manner in the rapid preparation of the score: his procedure here had a great deal in common with his manner of working in the field of tape-music, when he had accumulated an often vast amount of material by more or less random experimentation, shaping the work as he went along, and allowing the material, in effect, to determine the form. We might say that *Satyricon* is closer to *Tempo Libero*, in which the material may be used in a variety of ways in performance in differing circumstances, than to that of *Ages*, in which the form of the piece was shaped by the Shakespeare text on which it was based. *Satyricon* is a work in 'open form', 'aleatoric' in the sense that its shape is determinable by dramatic and musical circumstances.

There are only the very slightest examples of any 'connections' betweeen the various numbers of the work: a certain communality of procedure between 'Criside I' and 'Criside II' which, together with 'Love's Ecstasy' (all three sharing the same text: 'Love's Ecstasy'), are all linear and chromatic in style; and the use of mobiles from two other numbers in 'Food Machine' as we have already noted. Beyond this, there is no evidence of any thematic relationships from one number to another, nor any evidence from the sketches that Maderna had planned any such relationships in the preparation of the work.

What, then, is the connecting thread which binds the work together? We might say that such a thread exists only in the sense of a certain consistency in the *techniques* employed throughout the work: in, for example, the use of 'mobiles' within passages of a 'recitative' kind, in the constant reference to 'received' styles and to the music of the past in certain passages, but above all, in the 'ethos' of the work. *Satyricon* is a work whose collage brings together 'past' and 'present', 'popular' and 'avant-garde', 'satire' and 'expressivity'. The multi-faceted image of society which it presents to us is one without the necessity of a strong structuring thread, but one which, nevertheless, is bound together by the overall conception which Maderna had derived from Petronius' image of Later Roman Society. We find here no sense of a 'valedictory' work: Maderna did not wish to present to us any such swan-song, despite the finality which hung over his work in these last months of his life. Instead, we have a work almost overflowing with life, with humour, with the most positive expression of continuity.

Maderna composed *Satyricon* in a hurry, during the busiest period of his life, when his conducting career was at its most intense, and while he was also at work on several other large-scale works including *Ages, Juilliard Serenade* and *Oboe Concerto No 3*. There is considerable evidence that some of the process of composition was continued right into the period of rehearsals: 'composition' in this sense implying the ordering of existing material on tape, as well as the arrangement of passages to be used in particular ways in the Holland performances in response to the needs of the stage-action (an instance of this, the percussion 'break' at the opening of 'Fortunata' added in all likelihood at this stage, has already been mentioned; another is the use of the 'Milioni' ending to 'Carriera di Trimalchio' as a 'burlesque' in other parts of the performance).

The body of material for *Satyricon* which is available to us is very probably the complete material for the piece: there is virtually no material of a 'preparatory' kind (harmonic, contrapuntal or serial schemes and the like) which might have suggested a lengthy composition-process, since it is evident that Maderna's ideas for the work were already clearly established in his mind, or else, more likely, that such preliminary 'workings' were not necessary in such a work as *Satyricon*, in which the composer did not wish to impose a high degree of organisational 'cohesion' upon this free-roaming work.

Several points of interest regarding Maderna's compositional approach in *Satyricon* are, however, revealed by a study of the 'sketches'. Firstly, his initial approach to the vocal treatment of the text was almost invariably from the *rhythmic* perspective: he set out a rhythmic scheme for the text-setting on many occasions before adding pitches to this scheme. This rhythmic 'skeleton', in fact, was placed above the sketch for its instrumental accompaniment, and only later does he appear to have added pitches to the vocal line. [Ex. 5.7(a)–(b)]

Ex. 5.7(a): Maderna: *Satyricon*: sketch

Ex. 5.7(b): Maderna: *Satyricon*: 'Fortunata' 28–37

It will be observed from this example from 'Fortunata' that Maderna had conceived the setting of the words in an integral manner with the instrumental accompaniment: that is to say, he had a clear idea, set out early on, of the rhythmic shape of the vocal line, which he placed with the text, and derived pitches for this line from the harmony of the instrumental accompaniment in a simple manner. The harmonic framework is of considerable importance in several of the numbers: Maderna spent some time in the detailed working-out of the harmony for these passages, beginning with a rough harmonic sketch (often simply with the vocal line and a figured-bass at this first stage), before gradually adding further refinements to this until the final result was achieved with all the necessary details of the instrumental parts. We can observe this process in the following sketches for a passage in 'La Matrona di Efeso' (bars 40–46), where the first sketch began with the rhythmic scheme of the text-setting together with the harmony to be based upon a descending chromatic line, the second adds details to this, the third is the section in the published score. [Ex. 5.8(a)–(c)]

Such straightforward processes of composition were adopted for many sections of the work, but in sections in which 'mobiles' were employed, Maderna approached the composition in a rather different manner. One such case is to be found in 'Fortunata' (bar 8 bis), in which a repeated vocal pattern is accompanied by a group of mobiles in the five strings: here, Maderna had composed the five

Fort.
Your ordinary rich man
one in ten has e - ver seen his Ma - ster
Fl.
sempre p
Ob.
sempre p
1
Cl. in B
2
sempre p
Fort: is just peanuts compared to him; He could knock them all under a cabbage and you'd never know they were gone.
35
Fl.
Ob.
1
Cl. in B
2
veloce ma irregolare
PF
pp secco
tr
f dim.
p leggero

Ex. 5.7(b): *Contd*

Ex. 5.8(a): Maderna: *Satyricon*: sketch

quite disparate string parts in 'consequent' manner, and had then divided each part (with the exception of the bass-part, which is simply to be repeated) into a series of phrases contained within blocks. The instruction here is that the string-phrases should 'imitate and complement the soprano'. A similar process of composition is to be found in some other mobile parts of the score. [Ex. 5.9(a)–(b)]

There are remarkably few cases in the sketches for *Satyricon* where we find indications of a change of mind on the part of the composer: he had evidently had a clear idea of the musical shape from the start. However, in one instance, '*Lady Luck*', an early sketch for this contains, underneath the vocal line, a counter-melody in duple time whose words are not part of the 'original' text (its provenance is in fact unclear). Perhaps Maderna had thought of a combination of the two as a duet, or else that it represents a second 'verse' for the same number; in any case, it was not adopted in any later versions of the number (the number as published was shown earlier in Example 5.3(c). [Ex. 5.10]

We began our investigation of *Satyricon* by attempting to pinpoint what is the essential 'philosophy' of the work: its presentation of an image of society as reflected in Petronius' classic, for which Maderna attempted to provide a complementary image in the very nature of the music. This, as we have now seen,

Ex. 5.8(b): Maderna: *Satyricon*: sketch

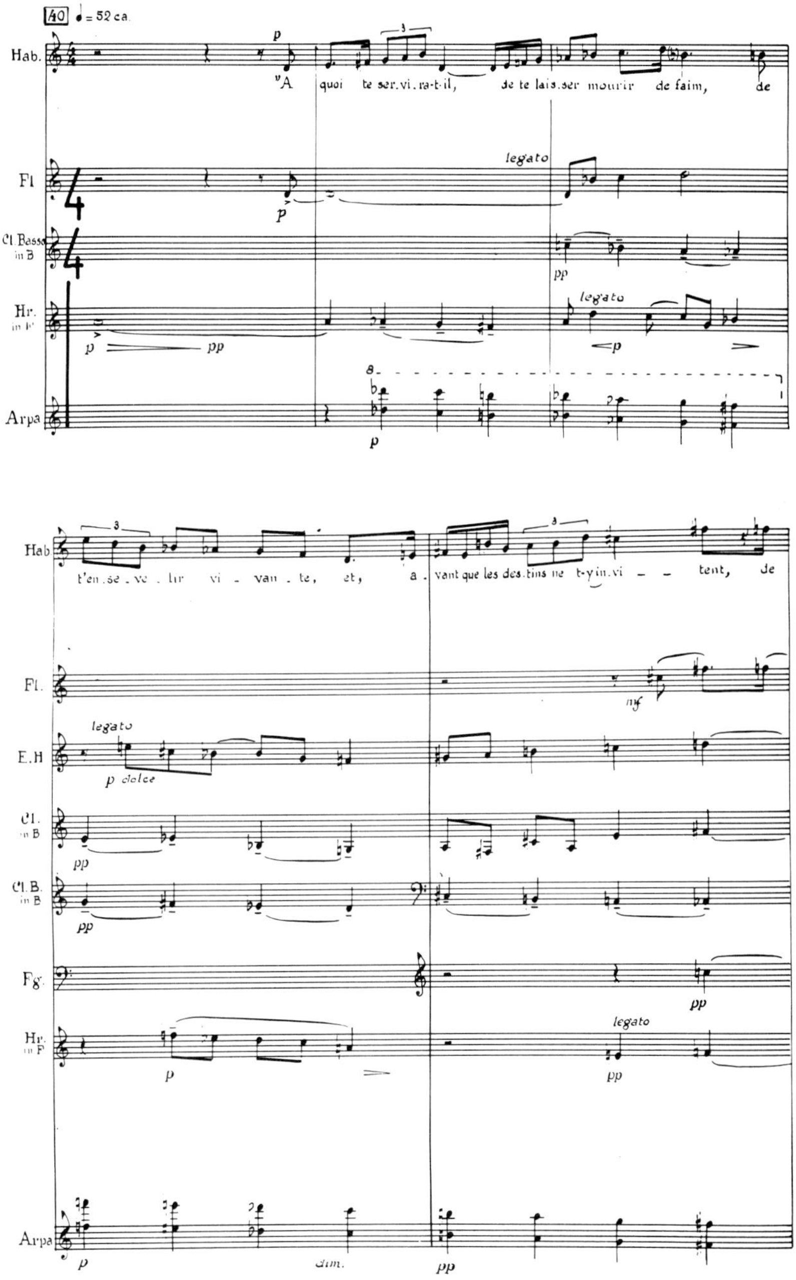

Ex. 5.8(c): Maderna: *Satyricon*: 'La Matrona di Efeso' 40–46

45
Hab.
rendre un souffle in - no - cent ?
Id
ci - ne - rem aut manes credis sen - ti - re se - pul - tos ?
Fl.
E.H.
mf espr.
Cl.
(legato)
pp
Cl.B.
p
Fg.
pp
Hr.
(legato)
pp
Tr.
legato
pp
Pos
pp
Arpa

Ex. 5.8(c): *Contd*

Ex. 5.9(a): Maderna: *Satyricon*: sketch

had important consequences for the process of composition of the work, in which Maderna highlighted the 'collage' of very disparate elements taken from an enormous range of sources, at the expense of any thoroughgoing musical structuration. In both dramatic and musical parameters, *Satyricon* is a work which leaves a very high degree of important decision-making to the performers: just as, on stage, the actions and sequence of the work is left largely to the producer and singers, so also in the musical aspects the conductor has a wide spectrum of possibilities for the use (or omission) of the 'numbers' and their ordering.

We spoke earlier of Maderna's conception of an *'opera componibile'*, in which given elements could be used with great freedom by performers, and this conception lies at the heart of *Satyricon*. The success or failure of the work in performance will depend entirely upon the degree to which the participants are able to exercise this function. The work leaves far behind any traditional 'operatic' ideals of unity, preferring to work from the conception of 'Music Theatre' of which this is a particularly pregnant example.

The very 'open' conception of the musical stage which Maderna had put forward in his earlier dramatic works *Don Perlimplin* and *Hyperion*, as well as the earlier abortive dramatic enterprises *Studi per 'Il Processo' di Kafka* and *Das eiserne Zeitalter* had led him towards the freedoms, both musical and dramatic, which we have now observed in *Satyricon*. In place of the solitary flautist surrounded by a technological cage which we found in *Hyperion*, we now have a stage full to the

Ex. 5.9(b): Maderna: *Satyricon*: 'Fortunata' 8 bis

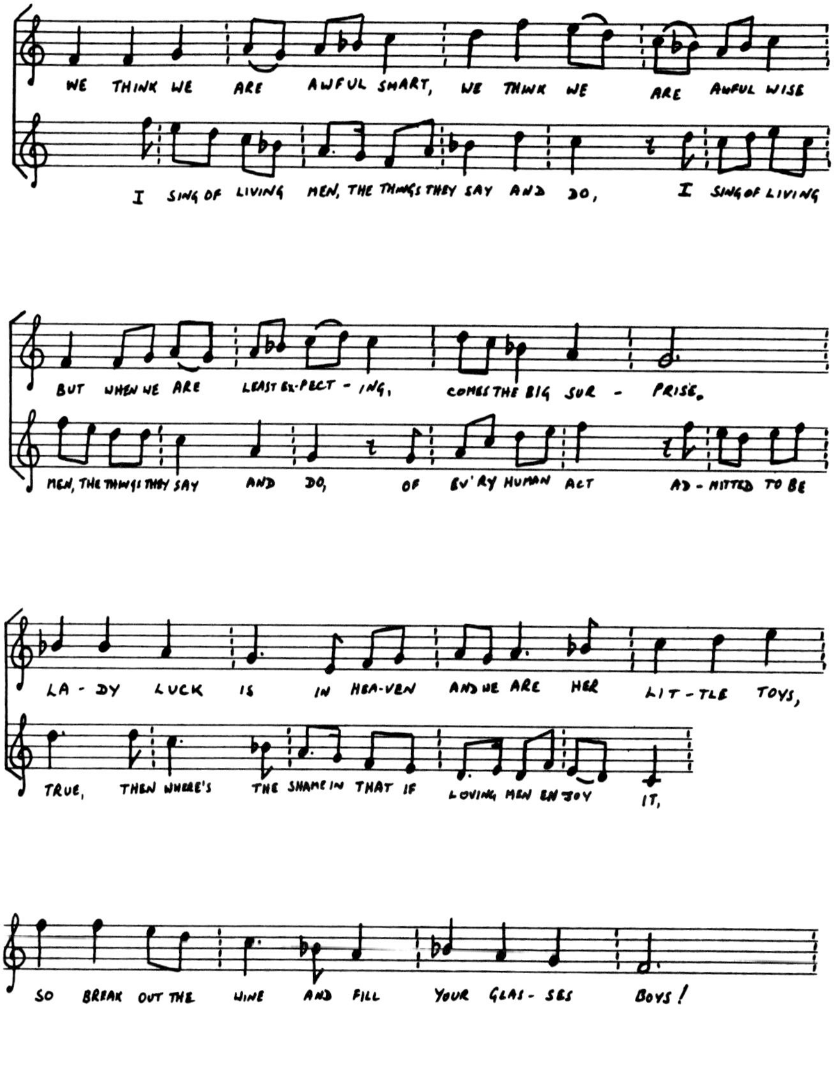

Ex. 5.10: Maderna: *Satyricon*: sketch

brim with the greatest possible diversity of character; in place of the dream-like fluidity of *Don Perlimplin*, we now have the reality of money-grubbing, sentimental slobbering and lasciviousness.

In its musical aspects, *Satyricon* brings us face-to-face, not with the 'Existential Angst' of the *Aria* in *Hyperion*, but on the contrary with parody of the musical past: with, in fact, a musical past whose most banal corners Maderna often explores in order to heighten the ironic aspect of the characters' gesturing. Maderna was a composer with, as we have seen, a keen sense of the musical past, in both the 'popular' and 'cultured' sides of which he had a remarkable knowledge and facility. In *Satyricon*, there is no 'homage to the past', however, simply a desire to plunder some moments from the instantly-recognisable in the building-up of a musical image.

Satyricon is, then, a work which combines Music Theatre with Burlesque, Musical with Music Hall, and its significance lies in the mixture of low, instant comedy with social satire which it contains. Maderna, who had already become a master of electronic and instrumental composition, here suggests that Music Theatre might well also have become of considerable importance in his hands, had he lived to pursue this path.

Maderna's last completed work was *Oboe Concerto No 3*, commissioned by the Netherlands Opera, which was first performed by Han de Vries with the Netherlands Radio Philharmonic Orchestra, conducted by the composer in the Amsterdam Concertgebouw in July 1973, just four months before Maderna's death. The score of this work represents a culmination of the freedoms which had permeated all of the composer's last works, freedom for the performers in the realisation of the composition, and freedom of expressive utterance in the elegiac, *'melos'*-imbued clarity which had appeared in *Grande Aulodia* some three years earlier. The soloist is here no longer asked to play musette and cor anglais, but performs throughout on the normal oboe, and the solo-part is conceived as a free cadenza which the player may begin and end at any point, a circularity of progression which contains within itself the most enormous possibilities for contrast of expression, from the *aggressivo* of rapid, angular figurations to the plaintive melancholy of sustained, gentle phrases.

Maderna, in this his swan-song work, fully reveals his nature as the inspired 'improviser' of contemporary music, one for whom the aleatoric conception begun by Boulez and Stockhausen in the late 1950s had become the most natural mode of expression, and one who was able with the greatest ease to create powerfully expressive musical forms through a large degree of informality. There can be little doubt that we see in *Oboe Concerto No. 3* Maderna's highest achievement in the field of instrumental composition. The composer once described himself, with grotesquely exaggerated modesty, as simply a composer of 'Kapellmeister-music'; or perhaps this self-description may be justified in ways which he did not intend. The 'Kapellmeister'-figure may well at lowest be one who treads paths already well-charted by more innovative musicians (and in this sense Maderna's modest epithet could hardly be less true), but at the highest levels the 'Kapellmeister' is one whose intimate day-to-day contact with the practicalities of music-making, and sense of inspired craftsmanship with the materials of music, could create some of the highest forms of the art. The note added to the final page of *Oboe Concerto No. 3* presents possibilities for the performers with which they are to work freely, to create what cannot fail to be a plaintive, elegiac ending to the work, in which the two 'personae' of oboe and cor anglais in gently-flowing fragments of melodic lines are placed as it were above the fading horizon of the strings' passive polyphony:

'The oboe soloist should interpolate and repeat the boxed fragments at will. In accordance with the conductor, the soloist's insertions should occur between pauses (the conductor either gently or more abruptly interrupting the orchestra), or else during the unfolding of the elements given to the various instrumental groups. The cor anglais should come in only 'on the conductor's cue' — his part is *ad libitum* and could even be omitted. In the repetitions, the oboe soloist should try to vary as much as possible the character of each individual fragment, using phrasing, tempi, dynamics and accents which are completely different from those indicated. Between orchestra and soloist, numerous expressive relationships should be established: contrasts, protests, acquiescences, agreements, integrations, affections. In this atmosphere the composer provides and hopes for the soloist and conductor 'finding' a suitable way for the piece to come to an end'. [Ex. 5.11]

What, then, is the importance of Bruno Maderna's work as a composer? It is clear that for the generation of composers whose work began to appear in the years after the Second World War, as well as for many younger composers who came into contact with him in Darmstadt or elsewhere, the whole musical personality of Maderna was of great significance. As a teacher and conductor as well as a composer, Maderna engendered in those with whom he worked a respect, admiration and love which was almost without parallel amongst contemporary musicians. As a teacher, he may well be comparable only with such figures as Schoenberg and Messiaen in the breadth, perception and imagination with which he approached the art of composition; as a conductor, his untiring efforts on behalf of an enormous range of contemporary music would, if fully documented, read like a history of contemporary music itself.

And what of Maderna the composer? Maderna's greatest and most significant legacy, the aspect of his teaching, conducting, editing and composition which his contemporaries and successors are united in defining was undoubtedly the element of *exploration*: an exploration unfettered by any too dogmatic, partisan or preconceived considerations, but a constant desire for viewing past procedures and manners of working in the light of new techniques, new modes of thinking, new materials and media. In his exploration of modality, of serialism, of electronics and live/electronics, of Music Theatre and of aleatoricism, Maderna was not only one who trod new paths, but was also one who wished to see the new in relation to the old, the progressive in terms of the traditional, the minutely-structured in relation to the informal. Such a figure as Maderna fits uneasily into the conventional view of the contemporary musician, and the works which remain to us from this enormously gifted and multi-faceted composer must stand as testimony of a unique personality.

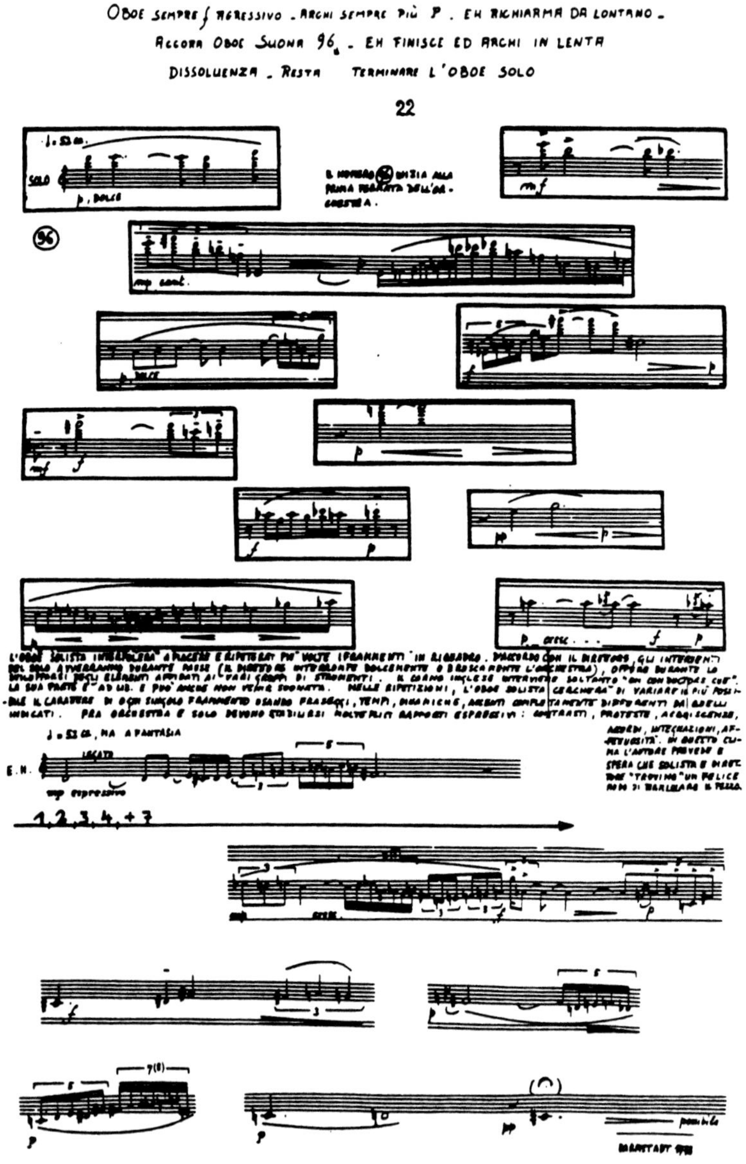

Ex. 5.11: Maderna: *Oboe Concerto No. 3*: 96

Notes to Chapter 5

1. Interview with Christoph Bitter on 7.5. 1973: in Appendix.
2. idem.
3. *Baroni/Dalmonte* p. 310.
4. Interview with Christoph Bitter in March 1974: in Appendix.
5. idem.
6. *Berio: Two Interviews*, Marion Boyars, London-New York, 1985, p. 107.

Appendix I

Interviews and Lectures of Maderna

Maderna was in no sense a writer about music: he lacked both the time and the inclination, as well perhaps as the facility with words, to devote himself to this activity. However, in order to give as full a picture as possible of the composer's activities, attitudes and personality, the material presented here, which I have assembled and translated from a number of sources, is appended. These articles, lectures and conversations range from the occasion of his first post-war appearance as a composer at the Venice 'Bienniale' Festival of Contemporary Music in 1946 to interviews he gave in the last year of his life, and cover his general approach to music, as well as his aims in some specific works.

The sources for this material are:

1. The programme of the Venice 'Bienniale' Festival of Contemporary Music, 1946: reprinted in Massimo *Mila: Maderna: Musicista Europeo* (Einaudi, Turin, 1976) pp. 125–126.
2. Lecture given in Darmstadt in 1957: in Mario *Baroni* and Rosanna *Dalmonte: Bruno Maderna: Documenti* (Suvini Zerboni, Milan, 1985), pp. 83–85.
3. Lecture given in Darmstadt in 1959: in *Baroni/Dalmonte* pp. 85–86.
4. Lecture given in Dartington in 1960: in *Baroni/Dalmonte* pp. 86–88.
5. Conversation in Chicago in 1970: in *Baroni/Dalmonte* pp. 89–101.
6. Conversation in Saarbrücken in 1970: in *Baroni/Dalmonte* pp. 102–105.
7. Conversation in Saarbruc̆ ken in 1971: in *Baroni/Dalmonte* pp. 106–110
8. Conversation with Leonardo Pinzauti, 1972, first published in the *Nuova Rivista Musicale Italiana*, October/December, 1972, later reprinted in Leonardo *Pinzauti: Musicisti d'oggi: venti colloqui* (ERI: RAI publishers), 1978, pp. 205–212.
9. Conversation in Saarbrücken, 1973: in *Baroni/Dalmonte* pp. 115–118.
10. Conversation in Holland, 1973: in *Baroni/Dalmonte* pp. 111–114.

1. From the 'Confessions' of five composers of the Giovane Scuola Italiana (IX International Festival of Contemporary Music, Venice 'Biennale' 1946)

There has been, and there continues to be, a lot of talk about 'research' (sometimes 'tormented research'), about the personalities engaged in the research, about sensitivities, moralities. It is strange that, in an age of such serious social and economic upheavals, in an age in which, precisely because it witnessed such catalysms, one might assume to be full of vitality, the practice of art has not yet been able to free itself from the consequences of that analytical but destructive dogmatism of decadence which brought forth tonal pictures and vertical conceptions of music. There is a need for enquiry as well as for construction, rather than for inventories and statistics.

We are told that scientific activity is directed towards discovering, by more or less rational means, Nature and God, and that Art is only the lyrical intuition of the Absolute. I have no scientific convictions, but as far as music is concerned, I do not believe it is about discovering but about creating. Picasso's well-known dictum 'I don't seek, I find' is incomplete in so far as it does not invest 'I find' with the meaning of 'I create'. And in any case, one has only to think of the artist's voluntary submission to aesthetic and formal canons in the most fruitful periods of the history of art to realise that in his artistic production the artist, just like the scientist, follows a process which one could legitimately call rationally constructive.

Nowadays, when we have neither schools, convictions nor poetics in common, and in which the artist no longer has an external control operating upon the quality of his work, we often submit ourselves to a subjective criticism, to a subjective idea of the 'beautiful'.

We continue even now to see the results of both the disorientated and the eclectic taste of the public, and also of the jealous isolation of musicians: '*membra disjecta*', a loss of the unity of intention and force which through successive generations animated great musicians towards the realisation of an ideal of ordered beauty.

At one time, for instance, we had great faith in the rightness of imitation, whereas nowadays each jealously guards his own pet sensibility, guarding him from influences. One can no longer deeply love the completed work, we are no longer capable of seeing behind it the person who created it, we can no longer learn from him; an almost biological incapacity to grasp what stands beyond the craftsmanship and the surface is becoming ever more common.

The philosopher Montaigne, on the other hand, confessed to feeling 'like the bees which, by plundering here and there amongst the flowers, then make a honey which is solely theirs'.

Certainly we cannot speak of a return '*ab imis*' as a palliative to that excessive particularism of the individualist stance so fashionable amongst the majority of contemporary musicians and musicologists, but there is no doubt that a serious obstacle will be removed when we approach music with the same modesty and the same desire for simplicity, communality, even anonymity, which gave rise to the 'tropes' and 'antiphons' of those monks who completely disdained fame, and who wrote their music for the greater glory of God.'

2. 'Compositional Experiences in Electronic Music': Lecture given on 26.7.1957 in the Internationales Musikinstitut Darmstadt

We shall do this: first I shall speak briefly, then my friend Pousseur, then you will hear *Scambi I* by Pousseur, my *Notturno* and *Perspectives* by Luciano Berio; after a ten-minute break we shall hear *Mutazioni* by Berio, *Scambi II*, the second version of the work you heard before, then my *Syntaxis*. At the end you will be able to ask Pousseur or myself — or Stockhausen, who is also here — all that you wish, you can argue with us all, but don't beat us up, OK? Now I shall read you what I have written. It is a pity that Luciano Berio, who meant to be here, is not: so I shall say one or two words about his pieces.

My encounter with electronic means caused a real revolution in my relationship with the materials of music. I had to completely reorganise my intellectual metabolism as a composer. Whereas instrumental composition is in most cases preceded by a development of thought which is of a linear kind — just because it is a development of thought which is not in direct contact with the material — the fact that in the studio one can try out different possibilities for the working out of structures of sound, that by constant manipulation one can renew and change the sound-images thus produced almost indefinitely, and finally the fact that it is possible to leave on one side an enormous heap of partial materials, brings the musician face to face with a completely new situation.

Time now presents us with a field full of an enormous number of possibilities for the ordering and permutation of the material just produced. We are now trying out major tendencies in this type of thought and extending it also into instrumental music. It is not necessary to ask whether it was the electronic experience which provoked such a renewal or whether this experience is itself the result of a development in this direction which was already present in recent music. But it is without doubt that electronic music made it possible to show the validity of such a way of conceiving composition. The main point is that a structure is not a thing in itself, but can take into itself a large number of functions according to its position overall. The very act of listening to electronic pieces or instrumental music deriving from the same compositional thought is characterised by this reality: we no longer listen in linear time, but there arise in the mind numerous temporal projections which can no longer be represented by a one-dimensional logic.

Perhaps in this there is much more than a renewal of the sound-image; it is this 'strange' element which often disturbs the inexpert listener.

When I began to compose with electronic means, I was above all afraid of using this instrument in an inadequate manner, and in order to overcome this fear I decided to give myself up to my musical intuition rather than let myself be guided by rational considerations.

Notturno was realised in the spring of 1956 in the Studio di Fonologia Musicale of Milan Radio. In it is employed white noise filtered in different amplitudes and in different medium band-widths. The smallest amplitude, around 2 Hz, gives the impression of an almost instrumental kind, and in fact rather resembles the flute, and this fact gave me the possibility of a link, almost of a continuity, between natural sound-production and that which is produced electronically.

I composed *Syntaxis* in 1957, not fixing any immutable schemes in advance, but rather, choosing the best effect produced from time to time by the sound-material in this or that point of the work. In this way, the composition became the result of my continual reactions to the suggestions of the material which had previously been produced.

Now I shall give some information about Berio's works. *Mutazioni* was realised in the spring of 1956 in the Milan studio. The formal process is conditioned by the continuous evolution of material which is very simple at the outset: a short structure of sinusoidal sounds of equal duration and intensity. Variations in the register, type of attack and dynamics cause a different perception of the durations; permutations, echo-effects and slow thickening of the material lead to the spontaneous construction of new sound-elements, from which there emerges a vocal timbre and, towards the end, an impulse.

Perspectives, composed in 1956, has not yet been realised in its definitive form; you will hear, so to speak, a studio-copy of the piece. Four sound-families set out

L

at the beginning in a very characteristic and very animated temporal order are placed several times, during a development lasting eight minutes in different ways and in opposition to one another. The perspective-game of the four families is not only given by sound-colours but also by shapes of movement. For every combinatory structure — for every 'family' — at least eight centimetres of tape at a speed of 38cm per second are used.

I shall now hand over to my friend Pousseur who will tell us about his experience in the Milan Studio.

3. *Lecture at Darmstadt, 4.9.1959*

Music in two dimensions! What does the concept of 'dimensions' mean to me? By dimensions I mean forms of musical communication: firstly, with traditional means, performers who play instruments or sing in front of an audience, and secondly by means of electro-acoustical recording and reproduction, in which there are employed, or processed, electronic or instrumental sounds which have been recorded (and sometimes transformed), or else electronic and instrumental sound-material on tape which is reproduced through a loudspeaker. Whilst at first one could see a clear division between electronic and instrumental music, in the last two years or thereabouts works have been produced in which the reproduction of recorded music via loudspeaker and music performed live have been combined.

In my own work I had the following important experiences: everything I composed for tape had to be realised by myself: in practical performances I was always led to perform my own work and to resolve the problems which arise from the difference between the graphic material (what I had written) and that which had to be realised in sound. In fact, the links between musical ideas reduced to figures, to graphic symbols and to technical indications are by no means the same thing with respect to the resulting sound. The immediate contact with sound-material during work in the studio always has consequences which one cannot fix for all time on paper. Even electronic machines are instruments, at least as they are as at present constituted.

Precisely through this I learned that music is a temporal art, because up to the moment of performance one has to create form, and order the unpredictable, and because I find myself as a composer confronted with myself as a performer. In the field of instrumental music these two functions were always more separated: I write a score, then hand it over to a performer. So I always have to take account of the fact that the responsibility for its realisation in sound is in the hands of someone else with his own ideas, ways of thinking, and abilities. A synthesis of both these possibilities which I call 'dimensions' seems to me to be particularly fruitful since the performer — faced with the realisations of sound which are fixed on tape, made by the composer and controlled by him — achieves a much closer contact with the composer (in fact he not only reads the score but feels at the same time what the composer wants). But on the other hand the composer must achieve this synthesis in himself, if he wishes to create a musical form which is so complex, in which the immediate performance and what he himself has made are to come together.

I felt the necessity for this synthesis for the first time in 1952, and was very happy about it, since I have always wanted to bring composition and performance as closely as possible together.

As far as the form of the particular works you will hear performed is concerned, I do not think it is necessary to analyse again the relationships between the sounds on loudspeakers and the instrumental playing. Kagel's work was discussed in detail last week in Stockhausen's seminar *'Musik und Graphik'*. Berio's *Omaggio a Joyce* was analysed by him in the *'Darmstädter Beiträge'*.

4. *Dartington Summer School, 31.7.1960*

I think that all those for whom music produces something more than a simple pleasure for the ear wish to have a general idea of this art, a concept which is valid in some way even if not necessarily with the rigour of a mathematical formula.

What music consists of is a very controversial problem and a very complex one, which has never been resolved in any definitive way. The incomplete solutions and responses given by philosophers and musicologists entice the intellect like every exercise in the ordering of thought. I would like to give my own interpretation of the problem and, with a view to a possible solution, to give some suggestions which have occurred to me in the course of my work and my thinking.

Unless we want to deny to music significance beyond that of a titillation of the ear, we have to put forward some provisional hypothesis about what it might mean. When we listen to music we understand that it has two meanings: one which is objective, in some way inherent in its very structure (since, as we shall see later, objective structures are involved), and the other subjective, external to it, but which belongs to the personality of the composer as a human being, an artisan, an interpreter.

In our search for a valid hypothesis for the aesthetic meaning of music, the greatest difficulty we have to overcome is that schemes do not, at first sight, appear as the organisation of any pre-existing material, so that music seems closer to mathematics than to any other art. Clearly music does not solve any problems: it does not 'speak' (like literature) nor 'represent' anything (like painting or sculpture); it does not put forward harmonic solutions of physical problems, as does architecture. One might be tempted to say that, unlike the other arts, music is pure art.

Psychoanalysis has tried to see in aesthetic creation a symbolic satisfaction of tendencies which are repressed from the sexual instinct and from the desire for power which, in the artist as in everyone, exist in varying degrees and which have not been able to be exercised because of particular events or taboos of an individual or social kind. If it is true that some of the elements which make up art are a symbolic expression of unconscious psychic energy, one can easily understand why artistic 'creations' can unleash such strong reactions.

That the psychoanalytical hypothesis of aesthetic creation has such a serious basis is proved in a thousand ways. However, I do not believe that this theory can provide us with any real instruments for our understanding of the problem of art in so far as its realisations are 'humanly felt'. As for the Freudian interpretation, however far it is able to probe, it cannot give us even the most elementary criteria for real aesthetic value. It can only tell us the reason for the success of a work or the type of human personality which emerges from the fantasy of the creator. This theory, in short, does not face up to the problem of the way in which the artist organises his material in order to give it that form which is the only one capable of transmitting or hinting at its more than elementary meanings.

But we should take account of perception which, at heart, is the condition for any communication by sound-objects. Without doubt a large part of the effect of music and of its content comes from its physical action, as pure sound, on the ear and on the brain. We might deduce from this that perception can tell us nothing that is really interesting about the aesthetic meaning of music, which is made up of a variety of relationships which are acted out in the sound-world. But we should take note of the fact that a large part of the influence attributed to music is in reality only the influence of sound as such (signal/perception of signal): the basic material of the art.

But before considering sound and sound-objects, the basic material of music, we must remember that this cannot be considered only as 'desire' or as 'material', but rather as a symbiosis of one and another. In short, in order to attempt a definition, even if it appears crude, one can say that music consists of the excitement of desires (in ideal conditions powerful and meaningful ones) and of their complete satisfaction (satisfaction–realisation).

Distinguishing between good music and mediocre is not the task of a psychoanalyst or anyone else who like him is interested solely in the motivations of a work and the causes which determined the choice of subject. This is rather the task of whoever is able to judge the 'power' put into practice by the artist to organise the material which his preferences caused him to employ. We should take account of the processes of connection, organisation and disposition, whether of the emotive energy or of the evocative meanings, of these processes.

5. A Conversation with Bruno Maderna *by George Stone and Alan Stout: WEFM, Chicago, 23.1.1970*

WEFM of Chicago presents: A Conversation with Bruno Maderna. This is the 45th in a series which has given listeners the rare opportunity of hearing each time the voice of an important musician. In previous broadcasts we have touched on many themes regarding music; this evening Alan Stout and George Stone have the pleasure of presenting to you the Italian composer and conductor Bruno Maderna.

It is the first time this conversation has been broadcast and it will be inserted in our weekly series. Maestro Maderna speaks in a way which is a little difficult to understand, so you should pay careful attention in order to understand fully the meaning of what he has to say. His position in the world of contemporary music is of such eminence that a lot of people will be very interested in what he will have to say: so we shall go straight over to the conversation. So that we shall not be disturbed we have asked that the commercials should be omitted during the programme. Now George Stone will ask Signor Maderna some questions.

Q: Signor Maderna, we are in agreement that there is a great gap in musical dictionaries regarding contemporary composers. For example, in a recent text I read this about you: Bruno Maderna, born in Venice in 1920, studied conducting with H. Scherchen and has conducted concerts throughout Europe. Then it goes on to point to your composition studies with Malipiero, etc. . . . Reading this, it seems as though you arrived in the world and began by studying conducting with Scherchen. Well, we know what this is not true, so can we fill out some of the gaps in this information?

A: Yes, your dictionary is rather too concise! So: I took the normal course of studies at the Santa Cecilia Conservatory in Rome, then took the advanced courses at the Accademia Chigiana in Siena; I finished my studies in 1940. Then I took part in the war — like everyone — partly on this side, partly on the other — again like everyone else — and at the end I was a nothing, a zero, like all the Italians at that time. I began to compose and I have to say that I owe my first launching as a composer, as it happens, to an American, the critic Virgil Thomson.

Thomson had made a trip to Europe to see what was left, to visit the ruins of the old continent. We met in Venice where at that time I had a little teaching post at the Conservatoire while I was taking the International Advanced Composition Course held by G.F. Malipiero, a course in which many American composers also took part. Malipiero spoke so well of me that Virgil Thomson wished to come to my house to see my scores; he then wrote a splendid article in the *New York Herald Tribune* in its Paris edition, in which he announced the birth of a great composer. This article was very useful to me; in fact, straight afterwards, I was asked to present a small composition of mine in the first post-war Venice Biennale. And this was how I began.

I then began to conduct, and this was also by accident. At that time, there were only Rosbaud and Scherchen who conducted modern music; all the others said that the music was 'impossible', that the players could not play it, etc. The conductor had also to be a composer, and, knowing the problems of modern composition, had to explain them to the orchestra. So I began to receive many invitations from Italy and from Germany, even if the music did not please many people. It is still the same today really; there are specialist conductors for contemporary music. For example, when Boulez or Maderna are invited to the United States it is above all for this. I think it is important that to conduct one should be an active composer; the very act of conducting began with composers like Mozart, Wagner, etc.

Q: Certainly. But we shall talk about this later on. For now I would like to know more about the beginning of your musical activity. You were introduced to music by your family?

A: Yes, and I began very early because my grandfather earned his living by it. He always said that when a man can play the violin he can do anything he wants and will certainly end up in heaven even if he is a thief.

Q: I also heard about you for the first time in Virgil Thomson's article, and I remember that he mentioned a *Requiem* . . .

A: Ah, yes, a large *Requiem* which I wrote just after the war. I've lost it however. It was a big composition with double orchestra and two choirs; Thomson wanted to have it performed in America, but could not get the necessary forces: if the two orchestras were there, the second choir was missing, and if there were the two choirs there was no double orchestra; so it was difficult even in America to get so many performers available. That work was a kind of visiting-card for me; nowadays it would seem a totally naive work; in any case at that time the only thing to do was to write a *Requiem* and then die.

Q: Had you already begun to write serial music at that time?

A: Yes, but the *Requiem* was a work of transition. You see, before the war, we Italians didn't know the music of the Vienna school very well, but we still knew it better than the Germans did. In fact Mussolini had a great friend, the Futurist Marinetti; Mussolini himself was not every intelligent, but he listened enough to Marinetti, who drew him towards modernity and progress in all the arts. By this means we were not completely separated from the rest of Europe; composers such as Dallapiccola and Petrassi, the generation before ours, could keep in touch with the music of Bartok, Stravinsky, and the Viennese, certainly more than was possible for German composers. It is strange: a pianist who does not love the music of the Vienna school — Benedetti Michelangeli — was the first to perform in Italy, at the beginning of the 1960's, all the works for piano of Schoenberg and Webern. Now all the musicologists talk about it, but then it was only he who occupied himself with it.

Q: The first work of yours which I have heard is the *Liriche Greche* for female voice, from 1948 I think.

A: Yes, yes: it was a great surprise to me. I had written these short pieces for Scherchen; he had a small publishing-house, he liked to do some publishing. I didn't think any more about it, then one day Berio, on his return from the United States, brought me in Milan a record of Louis Phil conducting these pieces with chorus and orchestra. It was only on this occasion that I heard the *Liriche Greche* on record.

Q: It would interest me to know when and how you began to take an interest in serial technique; when did you get to know the works of the Viennese?

A: In my case — as for all the young Italian composers — it was a logical thing; it is impossible to compose without coming across this way of thinking. One begins by studying polyphony, then the polyrhythms of Stravinsky and Bartok, then, as one looks with curiosity, one finds the Viennese way of thinking. I don't think that Schoenberg's idea is so important; or rather, it was important for him, and even more for Berg and for Webern. Just before he died, after the war, he was surprised by the success which serial technique had had. He wrote a beautiful letter which was read at a congress organised by the younger Malipiero in Milan; in this letter he said that he was not sure that it was appropriate to hold a congress on serial technique and warned about being fanatical, but rather to try to develop his idea, since any theory which does not grow is dead: one must always modify and adapt it to one's own needs. For example: an Italian and an American have had different experiences, different intellectual experiences, they do not have the same ethical and aesthetic points of view as those from which Expressionism arose.

It is said that serialism is the fruit of Expresionism, but this is not true. If one looks at Renaissance music, one finds the same mentality; in Mannerist painting one finds similar tendencies; at that point in history they were very different currents and Philippe de Vitry was moving in the same direction. And one can even leave the artistic field and think of ecology, at ways of adapting to one's environment: basically serialism does nothing more than follow the principle of development, of not remaining still. There are many composers in America who refuse to adopt Schoenberg's techniques, and why not? They are right. It is just that they refuse this system because they think that there are better ones. The right way on the other hand, is to remain oneself, perhaps without being conscious of it; and this is the way which Schoenberg pointed out.

Q: During your period of study with Malipiero, did your teacher interest himself in the new techniques?

A: Certainly, Malipiero was a personal friend of the Viennese; he used to say that they were too complicated, but he would also say how much he respected them. It's strange, however much Malipiero is nowadays capable of writing works like patch-work, he can also use the most varying languages for himself with the greatest sensitivity.

Q: Tell us something about your work with the serial technique. Did Malipiero encourage you in this, even if he himself did not like to employ it?

A: Certainly, he was a truly open person and did not pay a lot of attention to one's personality. He always said to me 'I don't like this system *for me,* but I have a great respect for the Viennese group and it would please me if *you* worked in this direction'.

Q: Was it Malipiero who awoke in you a taste for Renaissance music?

A: Undoubtedly. I had liked this music since I was a child, but I became even more persuaded by it through my study with Malipiero. We were really good friends at that time. He came to me one day — it was in 1948 — and brought me the *Odhekaton A* to transcribe, the first part, before the University of Pennsylvania became interested in it. He had found a copy of it in Treviso. Each day I transcribed a page or so, then we would study it together. He was really enthusiastic about this music and even tried to get it played by small student instrumental groups.

Q: Did you also study Nicola Vicentino?

A: Certainly, Malipiero was at home amongst these composers: so he himself appeared to me like a Renaissance man in his tastes and in his manner. His most recent music is for me the most beautiful he was written; he is an incredible person: he is always full of ideas despite his age. He is old in the same way as Stravinsky is old, isn't he?

Q: The beginning of your career as a conductor coincided with that of your activity as a composer. Is it true to say that you began to conduct so that your music could become known? Someone has to conduct it, and it was logical that it should be you. Was it this that led you to Scherchen, or had you already begun to study with him earlier?

A: Well, let's talk about Scherchen, whom you know better than I do, as he has been in America. For us Europeans, Scherchen was the living monument of contemporary music. When I met him he was in a 'good' phase. You must understand that he was rather a difficult person to deal with: in the morning everything would seem to go well, and in the afternoon he could put you in the deepest despair. He knew everyone in Europe, and was in the midst of every argument. He came to Venice in 1949 to hold a conductors' course which I attended. He asked: 'You are a composer, so why do you do this course with me?' I replied that I attended his lessons to get to know him, to have some contact with him and so that I could discuss music and get to know his opinions about many problems. Scherchen was important to me for two or three years; then, perhaps, he became too old, and in any case there occurred to him the ridiculous idea that music had died with Wagner. Another fixation of his was not to be able to compose: he always said that he would have liked to be able to do so and not just to perform other people's music, and that the only way for him to compose was to 'modify' the music he was conducting. He became very difficult in his last years.

Q: He must have been a very strange person and something of this shows in his performances; one feels it in his recordings even when he conducts the traditional repertoire: perhaps he was born under the sign of Mercury!

A: He had a strong sexuality and was terribly egocentric. It was difficult for him to live amongst others: he was a dictator. Theoretically he was against Nazism, but he was a Nazi himself deep down, in his fanaticism and lack of patience for others' opinions. He was also a racist in a typically German manner. He could say 'You have written a beautiful piece of music, so you are a superman and can do what you like. Normal life such as others lead will not do for you, because you are a superman.' And he really believed what he was saying. This is a form of intellectualism which, when taken to its conclusion, becomes racism, racism pure and simple.

Q: He used to describe Webern as a small person. . .

A: Yes, according to him even Schoenberg was small, only Berg was important! He would then add 'Even Verdi was small, Wagner scarcely reached moderate proportions, only Handel was great and beautiful.'

Q: One certainly can't comment on such points of view . . . there is one other name amongst your teachers of conducting, Antonio Guarnieri, which I don't know, I don't know whether my colleague . . .

No, I haven't heard of him either.

Can you say anything about him?

A: Antonio Guarnieri was really a fantastic conductor, but so crazy that he could never build a career for himself. He was perhaps rather limited — like Toscanini also — and like him began as a cellist; but he had gifts which Toscanini did not possess, for example the quality of the sound which he could produce from an orchestra. He did not have a career because he was not interested in it, he did not want to leave Italy; the very idea of going to Germany, of hearing another language, filled him with terror. He was certainly a provincial, but he was a very great conductor; one could not possibly imagine him living nowadays.

Q: Did you study with him before you went to Scherchen?

A: Yes, in Siena, together with Giulini, who had also been a fellow composition student in Rome. Giulini was older than I was, or rather, I was very young for the composition course; he played the viola magnificently and took part in the famous Quartetto Italiano. We then went together to Guarnieri in Siena and it was very good because the orchestra was first rate. Count Chigi did not count the cost in order to have an exceptional orchestra; so one could work well, every day, rehearsing, trying out pieces . . .

Q: If I can jump forward in time I would like to ask you something. When you are invited to the United States, as happens often, and you are asked to do programmes which are new to the orchestra as well as to the audience, do you think that the time which is normally allowed for rehearsals in our country is sufficient, or are there problems with contemporary music?

A: Not in Chicago; for every concert we have had three rehearsals plus a dress-rehearsal, which is the minimum for any kind of concert. But there are not many places in the world where one can find an orchestra like Chicago's: not only are they all excellent instrumentalists, but they are also mentally lively, very open and friendly. Even if they don't know the piece, they are not against you, indeed they try to help you. They also have an incredible capacity for reading, so that they can readily solve a lot, even the problem of contemporary music. With other orchestras on the ohter hand, there are difficulties.

I have written four difficult pieces, but there are other pieces which are even more difficult, for instance certain works by Boulez. As a composer I am against writing in too complex a manner: music should not be too cheap, but not too dear either, it should remain a social thing. If one has a good orchestra at one's disposal, like here in Chicago, one can easily do a complex piece like Schoenberg's *Variations for Orchestra*, in two or three rehearsals; I don't ask for more. But nowadays I think there is only this orchestra which is capable of so much, or perhaps also those in New York and Boston — they are also very good — or else the London Symphony Orchestra. I don't like classifying like in the Olympic Games, but those are really great orchestras. But they are great thanks to the work done by conductors like Reiner earlier on and Solti and Giulini nowadays, who are good musicians first and conductors second, not the other way round as happens often. The result is an orchestra which for a city like Chicago is a true instrument of culture.

Q: Many composers have said the same thing.

A: I have conducted many orchestras whose permanent conductors are real 'stars': in those cases the orchestra is capable only of putting on a show, it is difficult to get them to reach the heart of the music because they are not used to doing this. Orchestras, like horses, take on the character of their permanent conductors.

Q: There is a problem which is general, that of getting subscribers willingly to accept programmes containing avant-garde music. What do you think about this?

A: I think that this particular moment in history plays an important part. Just think that for the past thirty years, or perhaps less, since the end of the Second World War, audiences have begun to be a bit eclectic, and we musicians have also. I remember when I was a small child: there were concerts of old, modern, classical music, but above all one heard music by the contemporaries of Verdi; it was very selective, certainly not vast like one's experience of painting stretching back two thousands years or so. For me, it is as important to know the music of the Middle Ages as to know the music of Earle Brown. We need a wider musical horizon before we can approach today's music. Nowadays we walk on the moon, but we can't ignore Plato, so why not study old music? Music is of great importance: with music we dance, we pray, we die, we sit at table, we go to a concert, we are happy and we are sad. It is a limitless means of communication. When there are no more words to express what we feel, that is where music begins; and there are many occasions in which our vocabulary is not sufficient.

To get back to your question: I believe that it is necessary to listen to a lot of 'unusual' music so that we become independent in our judgement not only of contemporary music but also of the classics (Beethoven, Mendelssohn, and the like). You see, for many people Beethoven is like Mount Everest; bu for those who know the period in which he lived, who know for example the little dances of Schubert, Beethoven is no longer an isolated peak. Sometimes he arrives at incredible heights, and then he expresses in music the great problems of his time, revolutionary ideals — liberté, egalité, fraternité — his hope in Napoleon; only by bringing together all these things can one understand Beethoven and the culture of his time.

In each of my concerts, I try to put at least one piece of modern music, but one must be confident that one can perform it well, otherwise the public does not understand it and immediately judges it negatively; one bad performance of contemporary music leaves behind a deeper trace than four good performances. One must also be very harsh, almost cruel: not all those who write music — even if I know them personally — can be considered 'composers'. There are too many composers nowadays; in each country one can read lists of two or three hundred names: Costa Rican composers, Norwegians, from all parts of the world, it's impossible. If you were to tell me of a Norwegian or Patagonian composer living in Paris, I could believe you, but it is difficult to compose if one has always lived in Barbados. There can be pheonomena in folk music, but that is not what we mean by contemporary music. We have known the Galapogos Islands for twenty years, so it becomes necessary to play a piece from there, even if there is nothing in it; these are the jokes of many Societies for Contemporary Music; pieces are played which are really worth nothing, and in this way not only do we spend a lot of money for nothing, we also spend it against real culture. It may be that Earle Brown or Bruno Maderna write good pieces, but it is not a rule. I would be quite happy if an institution were to offer me money to write a piece, and then when they had seen it, were to say 'I don't like it, so I shan't get it played.' We all know that it isn't so easy to write a good piece! There are thousands of composers in America today; perhaps I am exaggerating but there are really a lot of people who write music; the same in France, but of real composers there is only Boulez and perhaps Gilbert Amy. It is the same in Germany: truly worthwhile pieces are a rarity. So we must be careful: for a good audience, an audience which is inclined positively, we must have only worthwhile music played.

Q: Many composers from other countries have found a welcome in Germany.

A: Germany is a special case: here music has always been at home, as in Italy in the Renaissance or England in the nineteenth century. At the beginning of this century all the great composers were Germans, think of Hindemith and Schoenberg: before Hitler, Berlin and Vienna were the capitals of music. Everything was played, often quality was sacrificed to quantity. And this was a mistake.

Q: Even the State Radio in Germany broadcasts a lot of contemporary music.

A: Certainly, and also in Italy; radio is an extraordinary means for letting recent productions get known; it is a great organisation and can allow itself three orchestras with the money from its subscribers. In Germany there are five radio stations in competition with each other.

Q: A lot is done in Sweden in this regard.

A: Yes, but perhaps your organisation is the best; here one begins to make music in the Universities, then the organisation takes the musicians and brings them into contact with the public.

Q: I don't think I've quite understood: do you think that in the United States things work better thanks to the spontaneous contribution of private people? Do you know that we have serious tax problems!

A: Taxes are a great problem everywhere. Allow me to tell you a curious tale. I live in Germany and know that country quite well. In 1952 the German orchestras were badly paid, like everyone else at that time. People went about on bicycle or at best in a Volkswagen, and saved cigarettes. Now orchestras are paid very well, composers are subsidised by the radio or by commercial organisations; people complain about only owning one Mercedes and smoke enormous cigars. But the situation of music was much better in 1952 and I ask myself why. One gets the impression that we cannot live in comfort, that we give of our best when in difficulty, and that we cannot free ourselves from restrictions without losing our humanity.

Q: To return to your question, I think that — although it can become dangerous — it is better to have subsidies from private people. Radio is a terrible medium: one can make Earle Brown heard from Miami to Chicago, and in two days everyone knows his music. One holds a conversation, as we are doing now, and a composer is made. It's a very good thing in the case of Brown, who really is a great composer; but suppose that because of political pressures or something the same medium gets used in an improper way . . .

Q: I understand what you mean. I think Boulez would say that the best system is the English one, based in part on public subsidy and in part on the receipts from performances.

A: The point that you mention, and which is often debated, is how one can obtain State subsidies without getting politically involved. The question which arises when this problem is discussed is that subsidies presuppose control, which can become worrying. To turn back to the overall climate in Germany after the war, I suppose that people of culture felt the need to fill a gap and were keen on everything. Schmidt-Isserstedt, for example, tells how when he conducted *Le Sacre* in Hamburg just after the war, no-one in the audience knew it, it was an absolutely new piece to everyone. It is difficult for us to imagine this situation. Unless there exists amongst the American public a conservative attitude which does not exist in Europe.

Q: This is a very subjective judgement; I would not be so categorical. Mr Maderna and Mr Boulez have shown that in America contemporary music has a broad following amongst younger people; the fact is that all distinguish between the Museum and the Gallery: works of the standard repertory are commodities for the Museum and those who might wish to hear them over and over again simply have to go there to hear them. But there should also be another series, that of the Gallery, to make available the newer things to those who wish to get to know them.

A: This is right, but there is another great battle to be fought: we have to fight the 'traditional' interpretations of great works. Poor old Beethoven, for instance, becomes ridiculous because of all the emphases and false magniloquence of those who take him on; many famous conductors attributed to Beethoven intentions which he never had. We in Italy are not able to perform Verdi well: too many pauses, too many fermatas and exaggerations of every kind which the composer certainly never wanted. In France they are terrible with Debussy; no French conductor is capable of conducting his works, they just make everything *pianissimo*. Even *Mother Goose* is distorted by this mania for *pianissimo*. Wagner in Germany is even worse: tempos become infinite, in order to seem more Wagnerian. In the end, one gets the same idea of these great works as one might have of the painting of Raphael or Giorgione if one had only seen posters of their work at the hairdresser's. Leonardo is only the Mona Lisa, and so on. Great music has to be discussed. I am not talking about Paisiello or Schütz, which don't interest the public at large, but Mozart, Schubert, Verdi, Wagner, Beethoven, Schumann . . . they have to be proved deeply because they are a part of our culture even today. Look at the theatre of Shakespeare: producers continue to search for new solutions, new interpretations, based on the same text; why can't we do the same with music? Of course, not in the manner of Karajan: he conducts the Seventh in a different way each time because he wants to surprise us. You know that more than twenty different interpretations of the Seventh are unthinkable: it is possible to increase the metronome a bit, but one can't transform an Andante into an Allegro! There are those who conduct the Jupiter at a crazy tempo just to do something unusual. It really is madness.

Performing Mozart is always risky; it would almost be better to leave it alone, but when one decides to do it, one has to study a great deal and pay careful attention to what he has written. One must know the period in which the work was written, the conditions in which it was born. Nowadays, of course, there is the new Critical Edition, published by Bärenreiter, which collates all the materials, and this is indispensable for a good performance; for example, one finds in it a great many embellishments which were taken out in later 'revisions'. Well, when one tries to play Mozart in this way, one meets the fiercest criticisms, because one is destroying a reality, destroying what each person thinks about Mozart; it is as though one were to try to change what someone thought about Kant or about Leibniz.

Q: For which we can hold responsible that 'tradition', by which we mean the sum of all the ugliest performances which have taken place over the years.

A: There is only one thing to do, and we can see it if we look at the Chicago orchestra: if this orchestra finds itself today at a certain level it is because it has been led by personalities like Reiner and Solti, men of culture and not merely practitioners. I have, for instance, heard a *Rigoletto* of Solti better than one can hear in Italy, and a Mozart more beautiful than one hears in Germany. If a conductor is capable of conducting well, that is to say in a manner which is historically correct, Verdi, Mozart, *Moses und Aron* and contemporary music, it means that he has a wide culture, and this is of fundamental importance. One can say the same of Giulini, but in the majority of cases the great stars of the podium are ignoramuses. A bit of music and a few languages: this is the whole of their intellectual baggage. With those one cannot talk about philosophy or mathematics because they know nothing about it; even about music they know very little. They only have physical qualities. Toscanini is the archetype of this terrible kind of conductor; it is a pity, because the 'detachment' in the Ninth has stayed in tradition and all the Herr Mullers in the world are fascinated with the thought of making so much music in ten seconds!

Q: There is a review which collects together all the wrong, incoherent and absurd things which have been said about music: paltry ideas, errors of interpretation, mistakes of perspective, all mixed up together in a horrible harmony. For example, in 1806 August von Kotzebue reviewed the overture to *Fidelio*, I think it was *Leonora II* or *Leonora III*, and wrote some incredible things about it! I would like to turn back to your interpretation of Schoenberg, the *Variations for Orchestra*, and in particular the fourth variation, which you play in a slower tempo than is indicated, bringing it into relationship with the *Serenata*.

A: It's like this: variations of a chamber-type, and in particular those by Schoenberg, are so complicated (especially in their contrapuntal workings) that we need a bit more time at our disposal to be able to appreciate their qualities, their tenderness. Perhaps it is a mistake on my part, but in all my experience I have always had problems with Schoenberg. He is without doubt the greatest of the three, but it is a lot of trouble to present him to the public, just precisely because he is so complicated: there is too much vitality, too much music in his works. If you have an idea like this (*sings*) then it is all right to play it as fast as possible; but if there are a lot of melodic lines woven together finely, then metronome 88 seems to me to be too much. And then it also depends on the acoustics of the hall: here you have a nice round acoustic, whereas in the studio the sound is drier and one automatically takes a faster tempo. Another variable is provided by the players: if they are good, they get greedy, they take pleasure in the sound and in this case they let you go along in the tempo of a Viennese serenade, which at times almost seems like an operation.

Q: What do you think about Schoenberg's rigour, his strict calculations, which means that the beginning of the finale — in the basses — becomes very difficult to play with good intonation?

A: It's for this reaon that I take it as slowly as possible; I usually get them to play it in separate parts, but not with your orchestra, because they are too good: one can't ask the Chicago orchestra to play '*divisi*', it's better to take risks. The whole finale is very difficult; I don't say that it's impossible; but it is easier said than done! Anyway, if one doesn't take a more *sostenuto* tempo one loses the tragic, dramatic, almost fanatical character of the piece. Schoenberg wanted great music, not pleasant music, and his music is often like this: this finale is a typical case.

Q: Signor Maderna, this conversation has been most interesting; we are happy to have met you and we are sure that our listeners are grateful for the opportunity to hear your voice.

A: Thank you for your patience with my bad English; next time I come I shall speak it better.

Q: Of course we understand.

A: I have been very happy these last few days; it doesn't often happen that one can do concerts with a good orchestra and with good programmes.

Q: Many thanks. You have been listening to *A Conversation with Bruno Maderna*, Italian avant-garde composer and conductor. Taking part were Alan Stout, American composer, and George Stone of WEFM.

6. Conversation between Bruno Maderna, Theo Olof and Christoph Bitter. 28 May 1970, Saarländischer Rundfunk, Saarbrücken

Q: Signor Maderna, you came to music very early; you are Venetian but you have lived for many years in Germany. When did your musical studies begin?

A: When I was five.

Q: What did you study first, piano?

A: No, violin.

Q: Did you continue with violin, or . . .

A: Yes, I continued with it, then I began to study composition.

Q: You have become very famous as a conductor of contemporary music, but I know that you conduct classical music often — even if not in Germany. Tell me, isn't it difficult for a composer-conductor to avoid the works he conducts influencing those he composes?

A: Perhaps, but not for me. For me, these two activities go very well together; at times it is very tiring because it requires two different attachments: one's own composition has to be kept inside one, whereas the works one conducts take a lot of external energy. All the same, I believe that this direct and continuous contact with music, not only as abstract thought, as theoretical formulation, but also as performing practice, as live sound material, is very important.

Q: You have spent a lot of time at the 'Ferienkurse für neue Musik' in Darmstadt, and still do; do you think that the relationships set up there between composers and performers have borne good fruit? There have been great performers like the Kontarskys and Gazzelloni, and often compositions have been written expressly for them. Do you think that this is the right way to work together?

A: Undoubtedly. As you yourself said, many compositions have been written for particular performers, but these themselves have developed their interpretative powers through the technical and expressive needs of those compositions. So the work in Darmstadt in the good years has been beneficial not only for composers but for performers as well.

Q: We have just heard, in fact, a piece which you wrote for a particular player: the *Violin Concerto* composed for Mr Olof. Mr Olof, you are Dutch?

A: I am German by birth, I was born in Bonn, but I have lived many years in Holland and I am a Dutch citizen.

Q: When did you begin to study music?

A: At the same age as Maderna, and straightaway with violin also. Since my mother was aslo a violinist, it was very natural to begin with this instrument.

Q: And you remained faithful to it?

A: Completely faithful.

Q: This concerto which Maderna was written for you and which you have just played has some particular technical difficulties, and necessitates some new ways of playing?

A: Yes, in this concerto there are a number of things which I have never seen or heard before. The fascinating thing about this work is that everything Maderna writes or asks for is absolutely 'possible'; whoever has the techniques for today's music finds plenty of work to do here!

Q: Signor Maderna, this work has a particular structure: it is not a concerto in the classical sense; here there is not a dialectical opposition between the soloist and the orchestra, but the solo violin and the other instruments have a very particular relationship. In doing this, what did you have in mind?

A: I think this also derives from *Hyperion*, from the idea of a work which I am not sure is yet finished. It is something which has occupied me more and more in recent years, and is the representation of the poet, the artist, a man who is alone and tries to persuade others, to bring them to his ideas, his ideals. But his ideals are so high, so good and so tolerant that people are not yet able to understand them, and so they try to destroy the prophet.
    As for Olof, I am happy that he has said some very important things about my work, and so I thank him for this; however, as far as the violin solo-part is concerned, I don't think it is so 'possible', inasmuch as I doubt that another violinist would have been able to understand what it is about. Great violinists, the virtuosos, would not have been so inclined to play a piece which is made up so much of ungrateful noises, almost imperceptible sounds, etc., whereas Olof, who is first a musician and secondly a virtuoso, has understood the sense of the whole, and there is no doubt that only a true musician can understand this concerto.

Q: You just spoke about artistic ideals; if I have understood you right (and I make this connection very cautiously) could we say that the violin corresponds to what you have called the prophet, and the orchestra to the masses who oppose him?

A: Yes, they oppose him, but they are also sometimes fascinated by him, at times they go with him, they are convinced by him; but then all of a sudden there is resistance. It is the problem of the man who always seeks to lose himself in collectivity without taking account of the fact that there cannot be a collectivity without the model of individuality.

Q: Mr Olof, did you contribute to the drafting of this concerto since it was conceived; I mean, did you give advice and suggestions of a practical kind to the composer like Hans Joachim did to Brahms, to give a famous classical example?

A: No, things didn't happen quite like that. Maderna, while he was writing the concerto, showed me how it was going and I tried it out, but it was quite unnecessary for me to tell him what could or could not be done with the violin; Maderna knows very well for himself the qualities of the instrument. It was rather I myself who every so often asked him what exactly he wanted me to do or whether I was managing to obtain the effect he had in mind.

Q: Signor Maderna, for me it is a very unusual thing that a composer of today, in one of his works — I am speaking of *Hyperion* — embodies an ideal which I would call very 'humanistic': the individual faced with a mass which wishes to suppress him, since he puts forward ideals which for them are as yet incomprehensible. Out of this idea, that is, around *Hyperion*, a whole series of works has been born. Do you agree in defining this project as 'humanistic'?

A: Yes, I think so, as long as by humanistic we mean the same thing. I am convinced that the only value in the present world is that of being able to think. Electronic brains are now so well-developed already — even if they are still at the first stage of their development — that they can produce an enormous amount of information. In order not to fall into a form of technocracy in the future, the only possibility remaining to us is to make the most of the man, the person, the individual; not only man as quantity, as a mass — since the mass is also made up of individuals — but man who surpasses it, who leads it. This man must also be tolerated; there should exist a country — an ideal country — where even poets can live, even if they are anarchic.

Q: Mr Olof, when you played this concerto, were you aware of the ideals which Maderna wanted to express, and did you try to bring them out in your interpretation?

A: I was very well aware of them, right from the start. To tell the truth, I have never analysed the music scientifically, since I lack the ability to do this, especially for a work like this. But here the music speaks to me directly, and this is wonderful; there is so much music in this work that anyone can understand it, even if it is modern in form. Maderna gives the violin soloist so many possibilities in this work: he makes him express his ideals, ideals of beauty of song, of expressivity. Through this work, one can understand not only that Maderna is a great composer, but also that he is a profoundly good human being.

Q: Signor Maderna, in the second part of the concert, you will now conduct the *7th Symphony* of Mahler. Mahler is also a composer who is often misunderstood, he also has in a certain sense the character of *Hyperion*, or am I mistaken?

A: No, certainly not. I am happy to have had the chance in recent years to get to know Mahler. In his symphonies — and particularly in the 7th — I think there is a man in all his complexity, with all his mistakes and his darker sides, also, but illuminated by an inner tension which is always of the greatest, like a bow stretched towards the Whole and towards the Absolute. I now feel Mahler as though he is present, I feel that he is just the poet, the ideal as I imagine it.

Q: Good luck with the rest of the concert and thank you for this conversation.'

7. *Conversation with Christoph Bitter, Saarländischer Rundfunk, Saarbrücken, 31.10.1971*

Q: Signor Maderna, there is no need for me to introduce you to the audience, since we have often had the pleasure of hearing you speak here; but today you are here not only as a conductor, in fact the first two pieces in the concert which we have just heard — those by Giovanni Gabrieli and Josquin des Prez — were arranged by you. What led you to become involved with these pieces?

A: First of all my love for this marvellous old music and a desire to hear it more often in our concerts.

Q: Of course; but wouldn't it have been possible to present it in its original form? The work by Gabrieli was originally written for two soloists, two choirs and orchestra.

A: I respect the principle of reproducing as far as possible the original, but when one thinks that three or four centuries have gone by, or two and a half up to Bach and that musical taste is very mobile and changeable, one cannot leave things exactly as they are. In any case we have to play this music with today's instruments, and just for this reason we need to make a critical revision which takes into account the historical conditions of those earlier times.

Q: There are in fact some enormous differences between Gabrieli and Josquin; almost a hundred years divide the two composers, and if we look back one hundred years from now — that is, we think of 1870, the time of Wagner, mature Verdi and early Brahms — we can see how far the history of music has travelled in this time. I think you have taken account of these differences in the instrumentation of the two pieces: for Gabrieli you used an orchestra about the same as that of today, whereas for Josquin you used guitars, harps, mandolines and bells. The bells seem to me the strangest thing in this instrumentation, or were they already in existence in those days?

A: There have always been small or large bells and the like, at least up to the time of Bach and perhaps even up to that of Mozart: we must not forget how Mozart loved the Glockenspiel. We have only to look at the paintings, miniatures and illustrations: from the Middle Ages up to the Rococo Age all the figurative evidence is full of angels playing Glockenspiels, sistra and other small percussion instruments.
    As far as differences in instrumentation of the two pieces are concerned, suffice it to say that the Josquin is more what in Jazz is called an 'arrangement' for the modern orchestra rather than a transcription. The original motets, in fact, are made in such a way that it would have been necessary to put together a special ensemble in order to perform them, and they are pieces which last 10–15 minutes in all. I have however really tried to identify myself with the times of Josquin, I tried to use instruments as I thought, (and not myself alone, but all the musicologists, from Leibowitz to Apel and Wolf, etc.) that one would have used at that time, that is, mixed together with voices or doubling them, to sustain the *cantus firmus* or other parts of the counterpoint. One might say therefore that the Josquin piece is an ideal reconstruction, but understood in a critical sense on the basis of the performing practice of those days.

Q: In your Josquin reconstruction, you have retained the separation of the different groups of performers: you have put one orchestra to the left and one to the right on stage and the chorus, organ and strings in the middle. Did this also form part of the old performing practice? Perhaps you were inspired by the way of playing which was typical of the concerts in San Marco, but which was known also in Notre Dame and San Pietro, the church for which this *Magnificat* was composed?

A: Yes, you are right, this is what I based it upon. I have also tried to act in such a way that the audience in the concert hall might have something which in a certain sense would take the place of the missing liturgical rite; for us nowadays, in fact, the function of this music is quite different.

Q: Of course; we should not forget that this music was performed during the ritual and in the responses there were the replies of the community of the faithful and of the priests, and the alternation of these with the choir and with the celebrant. I believe that if we wish to reproduce in some way the original atmosphere, one could find a justification in the fact that even in olden times music in the Church was performed by separated groups. Indeed, I think that in San Marco there are four different platforms for the musicians.

Regarding the *Motet XVI* by Gabrieli — which was written for San Marco — I would like to remind you of a testimony from his pupil Heinrich Schütz which affirms that his teacher preferred to write instrumental music and composed only a few things for chorus, thinking of them as 'exercises', so that his singers should not forget how to sing the '*a cappella*' pieces with good intonation. I think this testimony of Schütz might be considered supporting evidence of his instrumentation.

After the interval we shall hear another very important re-elaboration, the *Chorale Variations* by Stravinksy on the Christmas Hymn '*Vom Himmel hoch, da komm'ich her*' by J S Bach. Stravinksy once said that he had a strange form of kleptomania which led him to recompose the music he loved in his own manner. Can one say that even in this piece it has been 'recomposed' in this manner?

A: Undoubtedly. The fascination of the piece rests precisely in the particular very happy and loving way in which Stravinsky enjoyed doing these things.

Q: What forms does Stravinsky use here? Are they his own forms or are the original forms used?

A: Stravinsky sticks mainly to the original forms. The length of the variations is based on that of the Chorale with Introduction, and, from time to time, a short Coda. What might appear paradoxical is the use of different canonic forms; for example, in the third and fourth variations he arrives at a real absurdity in the diminution of the different canons; and here it is an amusement, a desire to make fun of the whole system.

Q: So it is really an ironic appropriation of the old ways of composing. At the end of this concert you will conduct Bach's *Magnificat*, and even in this you have not followed routine but prefer to present the first version of the work, composed by Bach in 1723 during his stay in Leipzig. What led you, in this case also, to take the less-trodden path? Is it a desire to go back to origins, or are there in this version any formal details which interest you and which are not there in the second version?

A: To tell you the truth, it was your idea, my dear Doctor Bitter! I think it was a splendid idea to let people hear the first version once: I congratulate you.

Q: Thank you. The fact is that in this first version there is the Chorale 'Vom Himmel Hoch' so there is right away a relationship with the Stravinsky. And it is also interesting to have two versions of the *Magnificat*, Josquin's from 1492 and Bach's from 1723. How would you summarise the differences between the two pieces? The first — Josquin's — seems to me to be closely linked to the liturgy, whereas Bach's is already outside the church; it is happy, clear music, almost like a secular Cantata; I think one could almost sing it to a secular text. What do you think?

A: I think so; it seems to me that in Bach there is the joy of being with God, living with God. One feels in Bach a certain familiarity with God; but a God of the world, a God of Leibniz and of the Enlightenment, whereas Josquin — musically and theologically — is more linked to the liturgical text. All the same, even in his music there are reflected various questions about the Renaissance, about Mannerism, about the Later Gothic. I would like to say that, although it is so much older, Josquin is closer to our own existence, to our problems, to the doubts felt nowadays, than is Bach. In Bach we reach the culmination of religious music, the most complete and a-problematical expression of love.

Q: This confidence, this faith in God, is not only in Bach, I think it is a characteristic of all Baroque art. It is a confidence which is rooted in the real world and does not have any doubt about God; so the *Magnificat* of Bach can ring out so clearly. The God of Josquin, on the other hand, is hidden, and is reflected through music. And the God of Giovanni Gabrieli is different again, as it appears in his motet *In Ecclesiis*, meaning 'in the church', that of San Marco. And when one enters this church, one immediately gets an impression of darkness, so much stronger from its contrast with the blinding luminosity of the Piazza and of the sea. Gabrieli's music, I think, is not dark like the church, but rather is golden and resplendent like the open air.

A: You are quite right, but don't let us forget the paintings of the Venetian School. Everything we can still see in Piazza San Marco, the monuments, pigeons, crowds, all that feast of colours, is to be found in Venetian painting. And above all the Venetian sky, an unusual and, I would say, particularly majestic sky, perhaps because the line of the horizon often blends with the sea, so that it seems there is no horizon. I think that Gabrieli wanted to bring this sky and the colours of the Piazza into the dark, mysterious, Byzantine church. There is in Gabrieli, in fact, a real voluptuousness, almost a libido of sound, as there is of colour in Venetian painting.

Q: We have spoken about churches — San Marco, San Pietro — then you recalled the painting of the Venetian School. One can also make a comparison between Josquin and a great painter who was working at that time at the Papal court, Raphael. But this relationship seems to me to show a certain lateness of music in comparison with painting.

A: It is true, but one shouldn't forget that Josquin came from the north and that his encounter with Italian culture left few traces in him: Josquin always stayed himself. He was a great composer, whereas the Italian musicians of that time were much less progressive; it was not by chance that he was called 'Princeps Musicae', an expression coined by Pope Julius II when he was still Bishop of Savona. Even some twenty or thirty years after his death it was a badge of honour for better Italian musicians to write like Josquin. He had great success in Italy, but he retained the late-Gothic characteristics of the Flemish School.

Q: Whereas Raphael brought to his painting the characteristics of the Italian Renaissance.

A: Not only this: Raphael had his roots in Phidias and Praxiteles, therefore in Ancient Greece.

Q: So one can say that Josquin carried with him the heritage of the Notre Dame School and of Guillaume de Machaut into an Italy which had not yet expressed itself in musical forms, whereas it had a great flowering in pictorial art. The influence of Josquin lasted a long time and left traces up to Gabrieli and Monteverdi, that is to say in the great Venetian School, and naturally also in Palestrina and the Roman School.

A: Exactly: Josquin is the basis of Palestrina and also of Lassus.

Q: And this is where the links with Germany start all over again: Lassus was at the Munich court, Schütz and Praetorius were pupils of Gabrieli, and Bach studied in Schütz and Praetorius certain orchestral techniques. So if we look carefully, it is possible to find in this *Magnificat* connections with the music of Vivaldi, which Bach had often transcribed with great care for organ or other instruments. Even the *Concerto for Four Harpsichords*, for instance, is only a re-structuring of a work by Vivaldi. Do you feel this influence in the *Magnificat*?

A: Yes and no. The earthly joy which one feels in Bach's *Magnificat*, the joy of praising God with song, this there certainly is without doubt in Gabrieli right from the start, but in Bach there is also a more intimate devotion.

Q: And so we can say that we have joined up the circle indicated by this evening's programme. Signor Maderna, I would like to thank you and wish you all success in the second part of the programme.

8. *Conversation with Bruno Maderna: Interview with Leonardo Pinzauti: this was first published in* Rivista Musicale Italiana *in October/December issue in 1972, and reprinted in his* Musicisti d'oggi: venti colloqui *published by ERI (RAI publishers), 1978, pp. 205–212*

'Look, I'm not a great talker', Bruno Maderna told met at the beginning of our conversation, in a hotel-room in Milan; but for me this was one of the easiest and most interesting of the conversations I have had with musicians, and I can scarcely believe that he could have told me so many things in little over an hour, in that rough voice of his with just a trace of a Venetian inflexion. And it rather surprised me, when I listened through the recording of our conversation, that serene wisdom of this incredible personality. Composer, conductor, one-time teacher in Venice, Milan, Darmstadt and Dartington, in Rotterdam and Tanglewood, there is still something of an 'infernal' atmosphere hanging about him, from his having been a founder, with Luciano Berio, of the 'Studio di Fonologia' in RAI Milan, the teacher of Luigi Nono, and one of the most active performers in the avant-garde field. And yet, when I explained to him the reason why I had interviewed the most celebrated musicians, and how several of them were bound up in plots and counter-plots one against another, he replied frankly: 'Listen, what with all my travelling, I haven't read them all, but in any case I have no intention, when talking about music, of saying yea or nay to one or another, because even when I was a member of the earliest dodecaphonic groups (in 1957 I held an open course at the Milan Conservatory), and there was, as you know, a feeling of something new beginning at that time, I never believed that serialism was the only road open. Personally, I thought that serialism offered musicians more possibilities than the, let's say, 'traditional' technique. But I never really felt like poor old Leibowitz (a very kind, civilised person, to be sure, well in touch with the world), nor yet like Dallapiccola, enclosed within his rock-crystal. There was, for instance, the business of those octaves: Leibowitz insisted that Schoenberg had never used them, and was therefore against them, but it was more or less a question of 'Talmudism . . . '

'So for you', I asked, 'is there anything in this recent idea of a 'zero year' of twentieth-century music? Do you think that it is a conviction held by every avant-garde, every 25 years or so? At one time, for instance, the 'zero year' was *Le Sacre du Printemps*, for others *Pierrot Lunaire*, and so on, right up to *Le Marteau sans Maître*, or the first important work by Stockhausen?'

Maderna lit his nth cigarette, 'to ease the stomach', as he says of his 'Celtiques', and moved continually in his armchair, as if to avoid getting stuck in it with his enormous bulk, the very opposite of one's normal image of a musician. He might almost be a seaman, or maybe a boxing-manager if it were not for his beautiful hands, mobile and expressive, which suggest the pianist and the intellectual. And when he replies to my questions, I don't seem to be hearing a man who belongs to the musical avant-garde of the last twenty years, but rather a scholar, remote from any conflicts, one who is fully at home in the past.

'There never has been any zero-year in music', he said, 'just as there never can be any zero-year of culture. It would be as though someone reaching the age of thirty were to say 'my life is now beginning'! That sounds all very well, but the preceding thirty years still happened, he still lived them, with all the experiences and errors. Certainly he could say 'today at last I have understood something I had not understood before', and he could say that just because he had gone wrong before! However, this idea of the 'zero-year', which is placed around the year 1950, did not arise from thin air: in fact, there was a more radical change than those we can see every 25 or 50 years, when the illusion of a 'zero-year', at a profound level and especially for the young, is necessary for re-ordering one's ideas before going forward. In my opinion, if we think that 1950 was somehow different from the points of reference such as take place from time to time, as for instance *Le Sacre* of Stravinsky or *Pierrot Lunaire*, this comes firstly from the very different character of the Second World War compared with the First, and secondly from new sorts of relationship between nations and civilisations. Today, compositions by Germans arrive here in Italy and vice-versa: to you it will seem the most obvious thing, but believe me, when I was 18 years old, on the eve of the War, I was already busy studying Schoenberg's *Pierrot Lunaire*, because certain problems, and certain solutions, were of interest to me; but, like others of my generation, I thought that a work like *Pierrot Lunaire*, however important it might be, was something different from our own things: it was 'German', just as we were 'Italian'. Nowadays, we no longer have this feeling, neither in Germany towards the Italians nor vice-versa.

So, if nowadays we speak about a 'zero-year', I don't believe that we should think of one of the many, more or less illusory, points of reference which the avant-garde of all times have had every 25 or 50 years. Our zero-year is one of those which happen every 200 or 300 years, or so it seems to me, like the turn of the 16th and 17th centuries, when civilisation passed from the polyphony of the Renaissance to Monteverdi's *Orfeo*. With *Orfeo*, a new world opened up, even if the old one was not put in the junk-room, and thus the old and new continued to live side-by-side for a while, innovators and traditionalists, Monteverdi and Banchieri, Monteverdi and Orazio Vecchi . . .

Well, you know why we talk about this 'zero-year'? Out of a need for an inventory, I would say: one world is ending while a new one is being born, and there is a need to start again from the beginning, looking at sounds from behind, to see how sinusoidal waves work, to study the formants, etc. But in the end — and I say this candidly, as I myself took part in this movement — I remember that at that time they were already saying 'a day will come when we shall make something more than a long sound or a short sound; there will come a time when we stop talking about structures and sequences . . . ' all very good things, I admit, but in the end it's rather as if someone were content to say only 'I'm happy' or 'I'm thirsty', and could not articulate a sentence, could not manage to say, for instance, 'if I didn't loathe you, I could even love you, but because you could not . . . ' etc.

Maderna began to laugh, and seemed to have to take account of the cigarette-smoke, which was not helping his breathing; he coughed, lit up again, moved back and forth in his armchair, adjusted his sweater over his stomach. I made use of the interruption to remind him of my interview with Stockhausen in Rome in 1968, when he told me that music should be considered a 'new science' and not as a means of expressing oneself.

'You see', he said after a moment's reflection, 'without wanting to get into any polemics with our 'great' Karlheinz Stockhausen, we have to take into account that he says certain things because he is a 'self-made' man: he's picked things up here and there with enthusiasm, but he is not a man like Boulez, who has done his Latin, been to the Conservatoire, etc. So, in good faith, Stockhausen believes in certain things because he is a 'self-made' man: he's picked things up here and there with enthusiasm, but he is not a man like Boulez, who has done his Latin, been to the Conservatoire, etc. So, in good faith, Stockhausen believes in certain things and says them, but he is like someone who does not want to cross to the other side of a hill simply because he doesn't know what's on the other side of it . . . I am sorry for him, but music cannot be anything other than an expressive thing: a sound evinces a response, and sounds are only a means. It is as if one were to say that painting is an objective fact: but even placing two colours together produces a reaction in the beholder! It is like talking about mathematics in the practice of musical composition! The mathematics which are employed in music, as compared with the true science of mathematics, are of very small account: we are always in the theory of large numbers, and even if we use square roots and logarithms, it is still a small part, it is simple arithmetic . . . so, either we know mathematics (and the same goes for aesthetics as well) or else we leave it alone . . . '

I asked Maderna whether I could report his remarks to Stockhausen. 'But damn it all!' he said, 'Stockhausen is still a great personality, full of talent . . . it is just that he hasn't got the necessary background to set himself up as a judge in these matters.

. . . However, I would like to continue our discussion of the 'zero-year'. We speak about a new world of music because, in effect, an eclecticism has come about which was never here before; and even in America, where they always lag behind in some ways. A concert-programme with *Marteau sans Maître*, Brahms' *Double Concerto* and Nono's *España en el Corazon* works well nowadays, whereas when I was young it would have been unthinkable . . . another sign, in fact of the 'zero year' we talk about so much . . . and then there is Darmstadt, a unique phenomenon: for 10, 15 years it was an ideal meeting-point for the most diverse musicians. Then, you understand, the power-struggle began: when Stockhausen, for instance, says that music is not an expressive fact, this is not an aesthetic declaration, but a manifestation of power. Because in a world which considers music 'non-expressive', the God . . . is Stockhausen!'

Maderna sniggers a bit, puts an nth cigarette out in the ashtray, and in a modest tone says: Well, life is like that . . . perhaps it is because of this power that Stockhausen is now thinking about the magic of the Word: and then we mustn't forget that this brilliant man is also and simply a German, and he certainly can't plug up a hole with an intuition: he always has to think of a machine and a system . . .

'But tell me something about your greatest loves as a musician. You know that there are those who can continually read the same book all their life, and who have one musician who is dear to their hearts. How about you?'

'I haven't got one single great love, but many. For me, however, the great ones have been Debussy, Stravinsky and Schoenberg; not Webern and Berg, who are great musicians all the same. But in recent years I have fallen in love with Mahler, and this is now an even more important thing for me than my admiration for Debussy and Schoenberg: it is the choice of a whole culture, and I could take this with me 'as a banner for storming the ramparts'. What do I mean? Just the opposite of Stockhausen: that is, music is all romantic! As for the others, even Webern, poor chap, with his minute indications, (*dolce, dolcissimo, sparire*, etc), with his notes which are each filled with a whole wealth of meaning, how can we call him 'abstract'? Take *Opus* 27: if we perform it with the greatest sensibility, it is a marvellous work, but if we realise it according to the so-called objectivity, it is an idiotic machine, with its series which go forwards, then backwards . . . '

'But amongst contemporary composers, who are you particularly interested in?'

'There are some composers from whom we can expect a lot: Boulez and Stockhausen I have already mentioned: but here in Italy there is Donatoni for example, who is really worth noting. And then there's Bussotti, completely different from Donatoni, but from whom we can expect a lot: he has great talent and a fabulous intelligence, and so he is always on the move. And then there are Berio and Nono, even with the latter's confusion in his application of political ideas in music . . . '

I reminded Maderna of some pronouncements which Nono had made about music and society, revolution and social necessity. He is far from convinced by certain affirmations of his Venetian friend, for whom he says that he nevertheless has a great love. 'You see', he continues, 'Nono's fanaticism, and that of his followers, seems to hark back to the time of the struggle between the Reformation and the Counter-Reformation. They are 'committed', and I think that Gigi is, at heart, really a romantic, and I am convinced that if he had continued on the road of his *Canto Sospeso*, he would have been just as capable of affirming those things he believes in, but as a musician . . . In short, I am firmly of the opinion that musicians should do rather than say: Stockhausen should avoid discourses on Aesthetics, and Nono those on Sociology, which is a highly complex subject, and act as a musician: because we can't believe those who say that his imagination is played out. It is certain that he fanatically refuses to do certain things which he should do, from a desire to act in a way which is not fundamentally concerned with music. Personally, I am just waiting for the day when Nono does not get so angry . . . I don't think I am opposed to him ideologically, deep down: I also believe that Socialism is the future for the world, but I can't say which will be the Socialism of future society, whether Castro's, or Stalin's, or Mao's . . . '

'You are considered as one of Nono's teachers . . .

'But how come! I have been his friend. Nono has always been radical in his choices: he realised that he had studied music badly, and started all over again, right back with common chords. But he applied himself to it with such violence (I knew him at that time, in 1946), that in a few years he had done the whole of counterpoint with me, and he is the possessor of a fabulous technique, a technique he uses how and when he wishes: it is not all true, as some have said, that Gigi doesn't know music. Look at the first things he wrote, for instance the *Variazioni* on a theme of Schoenberg: they are of a terrifying brilliance, so precise, so clear . . . '

'And in recent years, which other musicians have interested you?'

'This is complicated: for me, there has been the rediscovery of musicians who were already there to be discovered, Mahler and Varèse, and then also Ives. But I should also add Pierre Boulez: there are some works of his of real genius, even if in practice they are unplayable, and terrifying in their complexity, their extreme strictness . . . this, in any case, is at the limits of this enormous talent . . . just think that in *Doubles* there is a passage marked 'MM134', but which is also marked '*modéré*!'

Maderna began to laugh, continuing to move about and to put out more cigarettes. I asked him if he was working, and he told me about his composition for the Holland Opera House, *Satyricon*, which will be performed in 1973; he told me about the difficulty he found, with all his travelling as a conductor, the impossibility he sometimes found of finding the right atmosphere for carrying out work on his compositions ('In New York, for instance, it is impossible to write a line of music; there it is nowadays a world which, as Nono says, will come to an end'), and he spoke for a moment about orchestras, in response to my questions.

'Is it true that, in general, theatres outside Italy work better than they do here?'

'All the theatres in the world are in a state of crisis. Perhaps those in Germany are better controlled, and it is difficult to shuffle the cards . . . the Germans, anyway, don't do little shuffles, if they shuffle they do it on a large scale . . . but everywhere there is the same crisis: working with the least possible means, (except when it is a 'première', when everyone gets involved), enormous costs, enormous disparities between production-costs and deficit. But there has to be a system to overcome this situation, even if theatres can only manage with a subsidy: managements could, I think, be less hypertrophied; we have to acustom people to making less of the big 'stars', to not going all out for sensation, to not forgetting the real essentials of the scores . . . As for symphony orchestras, certainly, it is a different matter: in the USA, there are at least twenty good orchestras, and those which reach a European standard are really three: Chicago, Cleveland and Philadelphia. But we mustn't forget the English orchestras: the London Symphony and the BBC Orchestra are formidable. And then there are four or five European orchestras . . . but what is good about the American orchestras is their structure: it is true that the USA today is not as rich as it used to be, and it becomes ever more rare to find someone dying and leaving two million dollars to his favourite orchestra. Yet even the more modest orchestras are organised stupendously: with three rehearsals you can give an excellent performance, with four you can give two first performances and perhaps Schoenberg's *Variations* and Debussy's *La Mer* as well. And there isn't any need for a military kind of discipline about it all, the players are in the hall before the rehearsal, the trombones warm up, the violinists practise passages; when you arrive, it all depends on you . . . '

About Italian orchestras, with the exception of the RAI orchestras, Maderna can only lament, as everyone does now. While we were getting up at the end of the interview, I asked him if he believes in 'regional differences', he who was born a Venetian and is now a naturalised German. He looked at me and smiled: 'Well, think of Florence, where you come from: Florentines have always travelled, and this is something which made them Florentines. The great Venetian music does exist, but the greatest composers were all 'foreigners' . . . Venice is Monteverdi, but Monteverdi was from Cremona . . . how can we speak of 'regional differences': the music of Bergamo, or of 'Peretola' does not exist . . . !'

'And about Cage, what do you think? Nono was scandalised by what he did and said last year.'

'But Cage is there precisely to make fun of chaps like Nono! Believe me, Cage is an extraordinary man, a man of many aspects, some of which, those perhaps less 'scandalous' and obvious, are the most subtle. Anyway, they do the same with Cage that they do with Adorno: the 'Adornians' say the most incredible things about their Master . . . as for Adorno, believe me, he is an adorable person, fine, kind, important in what he has done for contemporary music . . . but his compositions were . . . nothing! And reading his books (I'll scandalise the Adornians by saying this), I enjoy them, but it's stale stuff.'

Maderna laughed, accompanying me to the door. And he really does not have the air of an 'avant-gardist', still less of a revolutionary. He seems to me more than ever like a kind of sailor, much-travelled and in the stormiest seas. And now he is enjoying the atmosphere of Milan at Christmas-time, with the wisdom of someone who has many tales to tell, and perhaps does not any longer believe the stories we read in books when we were children.

9. *Conversation about* Tempo Libero. *Bruno Maderna and Christoph Bitter, Saarländischer Rundfunk, 7.5.1973*

Q: Signor Maderna, it seems to me that this composition *Tempo Libero* cannot be called a work, in so far as it is rather a collection of noises, speech, instrumental sounds and electronic montages. How did you arrive at the title *Tempo Libero*?

A: I thought that the attitude of someone who uses his free time should, at least in principle, be different from the attitude he has in normal life. For example, one might walk in the fields, look at flowers and trees, smell the flowers, listen to the birds, and take notice of the little things one would not notice in normal life, since one is always doing things in a hurry, going to work, performing one's duties. Then I thought what would happen if someone enjoyed listening to noises, voices in the distance, the wind, memories of music heard the evening before, or music one would like to hear, and then wished to amuse himself by composing with all these experiences and making a collage out of them.

Q: Is this work a collage in the true sense of the word? Did you expressly look for materials already there which could be of use to you, or had you already arranged something when you set out to prepare the various pieces of the tape: speech in Italian, then in German, then music, etc? Did you yourself prepare the tapes? Did you proceed according to the old painting technique of collage, that is to say, using materials like something already made, as *objets trouvés*?

A: It is true, it is a collage, but not in the sense of surrealism. Rather, we are dealing with that experience of musical composition known as open form, comparable in practice to Calder's 'Mobiles', whose proportions are maintained unaltered through different moments of time and points in space.

I set out from various elements and different possibilities of interpolation; elements contrasting with each other, planned as psychologically opposed. For example, voices heard before a performance, or conversations between people speaking into a microphone, as we are now. I took from all this only words which had a certain 'Klangfarbe' or a certain literary relevance. Also passages of organised music, treated as *objets trouvés*, then fragments of atmospheric sounds which have been filtered and elaborated. While I worked on this tape, I each time added a new element, a new contrast, but not such as would disturb the harmonic balance of the whole. So in this way it grew by itself until I felt, I would not say the need for a limit, but at least the possibility of bringing it to an end. So one could say that the piece is complete, even if by its nature it could go on for ever; in fact it is conceived for a space where people can work on the music directly, like with a cassette. The piece is in four channels and one can choose different proportions, by which means — in different combinations — it can even last many millions of years.

Q: So this piece is not clearly delimited, it does not have a precise beginning or end; so in practice we shall hear a fragment of the many possibilities?

A: Exactly. What I wanted was to offer the listeners the possibility of beginning when they wished and stopping when they were tired of listening.

Q: On this occasion, though, it will be we ourselves who will put the listeners in the situation of 'free time' which we have chosen. You said just now that you had composed the piece for a space in which the listener — that is, the person has at his disposal an infinite tape which he can start or stop when he wishes. Would it be possible also to set up contacts and couplings through which, if I sit in an easy chair, the tape begins at that point?

A: Just so, in fact the piece was prepared for an exhibition in Rimini at a Congress on architecture, ecology and environmental problems. In the hall in which I had to put the music there was a group of architects from Stuttgart (I remember the architect Ohl) and also some strange seats, comic furniture and weird things by trendy designers, thought up for one's free time, to sit on and fantasise outside the dimension of day-to-day life. In this large space the music, given over large loudspeakers, mixed with people's chattering. People could either listen to the music or take no notice of it.

Q: So it is music thought of not for a primary function but a secondary one, like entertainment music.

A: This music has the function of stimulating and complementing conversation, or else disturbing it. People can even go away when they have had enough of it.

Q: In other words, one can break the connection. It is not like in classical music, or even in many compositions of the '50s and '60s: here, the very concept of a work as an immutable whole is modified.

A: Certainly, because each person would compose differently when they had a desire for free time, each person would use the materials he himself had experienced or which he had in his head at that time.

Q: You mean that we could each compose with what we had in our memory, whether conversations or music or whatever comes into our mind when our brain is free of everything connected with our work and with our everday life. Music then enters our memory . . .

A: Not only music, ordinary sounds and sensations. For instance, I remember that my friend Berio had an unpleasant reaction when I was also in the Studio, as if he had seen an insect in the bathtub. These things also come into our free time.

Q: But here we have a problem, because we cannot make it last infinitely, having 24 hours at our disposal. I think you are suggesting that the listener should not concentrate on listening, but should give his thoughts free rein, should find his 'free time', producing free mental associations throughout the whole duration of the piece.

A: Right: this piece is a stimulus to relaxation; not intellectualism, it is to be hoped, but simply relaxation.

Q: How does this type of piece, this free collage of ready-made objects which you have composed by association fit in with the other compositions of yours which are purely musical? Is it also for you a sort of 'composition of free time', a 'different' possibility, quite outside the strict rules of purely mental composition?

A: Yes. I become ever more conscious that in life it is not necessary to be consistent, especially if one is a composer, an artist. I believe that one should loathe consistency. Instead one should try to be so natural and alive that one can follow and express the different aspects of our organism, whether physical or psychological. I believe that famous serial consistency has been one of the worst diseases.

Q: This is strange coming from you who in the early '50s in Darmstadt took part in that group of composers — amongst whom there were Boulez, Nono and Stockhausen — for whom serial technique became a Gospel which had its prophet and apostle in Anton Webern. You however, I think, never used it in a strict manner, you always took liberties with it.

A: It's true, but then it was necessary to be unilateral, even fanatical, because we had to create a new stock of possibilities to have at our disposal. But you know that after the most rigorous period we each chose our own path freely and in very different ways. Even Stockhausen, after *Kontrapunkte*, trod many paths in music and today he writes compositions like *Mantra, Hymnen* . . .

Q: Or we can think for example of *Aus den sieben Tagen*, another work which, like *Tempo Libero*, can go on into infinity. And we can find other points of contact. You just said about *Tempo Libero* that is is a piece to listen to making mental associations and making oneself 'free'; in Stockhausen's piece, it isn't really like that, but it seems to me that it is the other side of the same coin. He, in fact, arrived at it through meditation; in reality, Stockhausen feels order in a narrower way, but even this is a way of freeing oneself from the preoccupations of work and of activities which are directed towards a practical goal.

A: Certainly: Stockhausen gives himself an order through metaphysics, that is to say in a disordered order.

Q: And does the problem of order exist for you?

A: I am not a metaphysician. Besides, as you know, Stockhausen rather tends towards an ethical philosophy: there is a great school of ethical philosophy in Japan, the Zen, which reasons more or less only through paradoxes and non-truths; thus the art of naturalness, of lack of artifice.

Q: And this would work well for you?

A: For God's sake, such a lofty, spiritual principle! In truth I am in love with music.

Q: But in this sense even *Tempo Libero* can be understood as naturalness becoming art.

A: Exactly.

Q: Many thanks, Signor Maderna.

10. *Interview on Dutch Radio after* Satyricon, *March 1973*

Q: After this *Satyricon*, are you thinking of producing any similar works, I mean any theatrical works?

A: Yes, if I get the chance. You know that there always has to be an opportunity, and this has to come by itself. The important thing is that this type of composition is not something one can generalise about. One piece is like this, another is quite different, the fruit of another way of working. What I mean is, if I were to compose another humoristic piece, it would not be written like this.

Q: Can you explain to me in brief what *Satyricon* is based on, whether on the text or the music? And more precisely, what are the main carrying vehicles of the music in the work as a whole?

A: Allow me to reply from a different angle. There isn't one overriding musical situation above all others. For me, a 'structural' situation is that which best adapts itself to the text. So for me the starting-point was the text, and I chose the 'Satyricon' some time ago. In it a society is portrayed which, in many ways, is neither better nor worse than our own. Whoever is a serious member of a political party, whether of the Right or the Left, has a precise idea of the society in which we live, and I believe it would be difficult to find an image which is as close to our own reality as that given by Petronius' description of Roman decadence. I don't want to sing morality or politics, my aim is to make the theatre a political act, and it was for this reason that I was so drawn to this text. As far as the music is concerned . . .

Q: It has been said that at times it shows a tonal framework, in other places it is polytonal, there is a collage technique . . .

A: Yes, yes, there is a collage, there are naturalistic effects, or rather, 'exaggerated' naturalistic effects; there is in it something of the 'Musical', and so on, in short, I tried to make in music what nowadays we think of as 'Pop Art'. But as I said, I don't think for one moment that this way of composing would be valid for other pieces: it's fine for me, because it goes particularly well for Petronius. There are often cheap effects, almost give-away, but even that society was worth little and was treated to techniques of alienation.

Q: I think you have only used the original texts in a small part of the work.

A: No, on the contrary. For example, Eumolpus, when he tries to resist Fortunata, quotes a poem which Petronius took from Juvenal on the decadence of Rome; I give this in the original language to that Platonic, and possibly homosexual, philosopher. The other parts are English, German and French translations.

Q: So the main part of the story is related in English, German and French so that the audience will understand it better.

A: Yes, what is said in Latin is just rhetoric, hollow words which needn't even be understood. In any case, we don't really know how Latin was pronounced, everyone speaks it after his own manner: A Frenchman differently from a German, and so on. One might say that it is a 'homely' Latin but also a very corrupt one.

Q: So like the life of those days . . . Another question: do you know Fellini's film of '*Satyricon?*'

A: Yes, certainly.

Q: And is there any relationship between your work and the film apart from the fact that they derive from the same text?

A: No. As you know, when Fellini has made a film of something it is impossible to go back to it; by chance in this case I worked above all in fantasy; he was more interested in giving a fantastic, almost mythological, interpretation of Rome in decay than in showing the banquet of Trimalchio, so one can't say the he took my idea away from me. I was afraid that he would make a kind of '*Dolce Vita*' out of it; certainly the film is marvellous and it was better for me that Fellini was drawn towards this highly-coloured sensual and erotic fantasy.

Q: You said that the method of composing which you used in *Satyricon* is not repeatable in the sense that it was conceived expressly for this idea; at the same time, you are thinking of working again in the theatre?

A: Certainly, if I get the chance, willingly.

Q: How do you mean: if you get a commission?

A: Simply: if I can in a practical sense.

Q: Anyway you had the 'Satyricon' in mind well before you were asked to write the opera.

A: Certainly, and it has been a lovely thing to be able to realise this idea.

Q: Will you come back often to Holland to conduct symphony concerts?

A: Yes, quite often.

Q: All the same, we have heard you very little in the last two years.

A: Just so, in the last three or four years; before that, I was here very often.

Q: I remember that on the occasion when *From A to Z* was given, you spoke right here. Another question: I know that you have often spoken about the music of Wagner and you certainly will know that Pierre Boulez has conducted *Parsifal* in Bayreuth. What do you think of operas on film, a very important phenomenon for all those who love opera?

A: I don't want to take too clear-cut a position, seeing that I have already cited *Parsifal* so often. I am convinced that not until we have made a clean sweep of the old, rusty and intolerable legend of Wagner's genius will we finally discover the true Wagner. Wagner is indeed a very great composer, but we must first clear away all the rhetoric around him. Wagner is a true pillar of the musical theatre, together with Verdi and Mozart.

Q: Is it in your plans to conduct a work of Wagner's?

A: These are things one does not plan but always has in mind. I have waited all my life to conduct *Tristan*, but it is very difficult. Once, here in Holland, I conducted *Tannhäuser* and many years ago *Lohengrin* in Italy, but *Tristan* is perhaps the opera I know better.

Q: Another question about the production of Ligeti's opera: has anything been changed from the original? And if that is so, are you in agreement with the composer about these changes?

A: He himself changed something in *Nouvelles Aventures*, to be precise the soprano part, in order to have the possibility of describing an internal emotional and erotic conflict. The action stayed the same, an action of estrangement.

Q: Is it the first time in Europe that there has been a stage-performance of *Nouvelles Aventures*, as there was in Tanglewood?

A: No, I did it myself in Darmstadt in a production by Harro Dicks and in the presence of Ligeti himself. It was a stage-performance which I wouldn't call abstract, but made of signs: there was the doubt of jealousy, or egoism, but nothing tragic, just the sign and what's more a slightly ironic one.

Q: I would like to ask one more question, since this is being broadcast also in Belgium. After the performance on 7 April, will you conduct again in Belgium?

A: No, I don't think so; perhaps a young friend of mine will conduct.

Q: Lucas Vis?

A: Yes.

Q: Many thanks, and I wish you success.

Towards a Biography

Bruno Maderna was born on 21st April 1920 in Venice. His mother, Carolina Maderna, whose surname he was to adopt some years later, was not a native of that city, but came from a family whose roots lay in a rural community near Rognano, in the region of Pavia. Carolina was 23 years old when he was born, and had met the composer's father, Umberto Grossato, some five years previously; he was already married with a young son, and lived in S. Anna di Chioggia near Venice, earning a living as a musician in cafés, and when he met Carolina was on military service in Stradella, whence Carolina had gone with her sisters after their father's death. Umberto was 32 years old; his father kept a tavern in Venice, and several members of the Grossato family learned muiscal instruments which they played to entertain customers there (Umberto himself played accordion, as well as double bass and piano). He was a man of considerable charm and persuasiveness, and convinced Carolina that he was employed as a journalist on a Venice newspaper; when Carolina became pregnant, he arranged that she should move into his family home alongside his 'legitimate' family. She died when Bruno was four years old.

There then began a period of great insecurity in the child's life. It very soon became evident that the child was musically gifted, and his father therefore wished to retain control of his education in order to profit by this talent, resisting the claims of the Maderna family for guardianship. The child was given instruction in violin (initially by his grandfather Francesco) and from a very early age played in the tavern which right up to the 1940s had a room called the 'Sala Brunetto Grossato'. It appears to have been assumed by all the members of the Grossato family, in fact, that he would naturally take up a musical career, and the other aspects of his education were largely neglected during this period. His father wished to exhibit Bruno's talents before an ever wider audience, and thus in 1930 he formed the 'Happy Grossato Company', a group of some half-a-dozen musicians with the ten-year-old given pride of place, to perform in cafés and restaurants in the Venice area, and even travelling to other parts of Italy. It is possible that Bruno himself made some of the musical arrangements for this band. His general education suffered somewhat from the vagabond nature of the life he led at this time.

The transformation of Maderna the café-musician into the *bambino prodigo* who conducted the most illustrious orchestras in Italy was said by Maderna himself in later life, speaking to Massimo Mila, to have come about through the intervention of the artistic patroness Princess de Polignac, who paid for the orchestra of La Scala to give concerts as early as 1927 under Maderna's direction. However, Umberto Grossato's version of this incident is different, stating that it had been through the arrival in Venice of 'a great conductor from Milan' who took an interest in the precocious child, or else that this event took place in Diano Marina when Bruno asked to take over the spa-orchestra from its resident conductor. In any case, the first concerts which can with certainty be ascribed to Maderna's direction took place in 1932, in Diano Marina, Imperia, Milan, Venice, Trieste and Padova, with programmes of the 'standard classics' of Verdi, Wagner, Rossini, Mascagni and Mendelssohn. This conducting activity continued quite intensively until 1935, when some slackening of pace became evident, no doubt due to the inappropriateness of a billing as a *'bambino prodigo'* by the age of fifteen.

By 1932 it had become evident that Umberto Grossato, with his itinerant café-musician's life, was not really in a position to provide a stable environment in which his son's musical talents and general education could adequately develop. Umberto continued for some years to direct his band, and he later opened a small music shop in Venice: he died at the age of 86 in 1974, just a year after his son.

Maderna was removed from his father's care at the end of 1932 and, under the auspices of the Fascist authorities who gave him a 'study grant' of 12,000 lire per year, was placed for a time in the care of the family of Francesco Miotto, a clarinettist in the orchestra of 'La Fenice'. It was during this period that Maderna became acquainted with Padre Policarpo Crosara, a Franciscan priest who attempted to guide the child's religious and moral education. This influence was felt by the Fascist authorities to be subversive, and Padre Policarpo was duly removed to a more distant location; however, he and Maderna were to exchange many letters over the years, and remained close friends throughout the composer's lifetime.

His concerts as the *'bambino prodigio'* were used more and more as propaganda material for the régime; he was always presented in clothing which aimed to make him look much younger than his actual age, and many newspaper articles and reviews spoke of him as a 'nine-year-old'. The concert which attracted the greatest attention was given in the Arena in Verona in April 1933 in front of an audience of 12000 people, with 'Brunetto' conducting works by Rossini, Mendelssohn, Beethoven, Cimarosa, Spontini and Mozart; photographs of the occasion display Fascist symbols placed alongside the young prodigy. It was perhaps natural that doubts about the rightness of this use of the child's talents should begin to emerge amidst all of this, doubts which were particularly expressed by Padre Policarpo, and a struggle ensued for the child's guardianship and tutelage which, in effect, was a struggle between no less authorities than Church and State. There thus entered on the scene the woman who was to become of the greatest importance in the early life of Maderna, Irma Manfredi. She was the owner of a very important dress shop in Verona who also had interests in furnishings, antiques and paintings, a woman in her late thirties at that time. Her business was a very thriving one, and she lived alone amidst some considerable wealth, donating regular sums to the Church. She had attended the concert in the Arena in Verona, and had apparently decided there and then that she was the person who should take charge of the child's upbringing. Her ambitions in this direction had some support from both ecclesiastical and civil authorities and, after a period of the most turbulent litigation, she eventually got her way, and Bruno was placed in her care from 1934. The arguments about this did not however die away immediately, and as late as 1937 we find the youth brought to court in Venice to answer charges that he had attacked one of the 'opposing party' to Manfredi for having published a poem of some 1200 verses in which he had slandered her about the matter (the case was dismissed). No less a person than Monsignor Giovanni Montini, later to become Pope Paul VI, had intervened on Manfredi's behalf, having long taken an interest in 'Brunetto', and the whole affair of the guardianship had provoked a great deal of attention in both the local and the national press.

Irma Manfredi saw the need for Maderna's education to be taken in hand with the greatest seriousness and care. Her first plan was that he should study with Ildebrando Pizzetti in Milan, but she was unhappy that she should have to see him separated even temporarily from her, and she eventually decided on a more convenient plan, that he should instead study with Arrigo Pedrollo, a composer of some distinction from Vicenza who travelled to and from Milan each week to teach at the Conservatoire, and was thus able to give the young musician lessons twice weekly *'en route'*. Other parts of his education were also taken care of by Manfredi, who decided that this would be best undertaken not by attendance at a normal school, but by the provision of a number of private tutors. He was given a good deal of instruction in German, for example, in order that he might eventually be able to study music in a German-speaking country. Manfredi, in fact, was very afraid that the turbulent earlier years of the child's life had left their mark on him in a certain waywardness and an openness to temptations of every kind, and she therefore wished to provide an antidote to these traits in his character. She took him on several visits abroad (to Salzburg, Innsbruck, Czechoslovakia, Grenoble and London). The growing sexual awareness of the youth was seen by his 'Mamma Irma' as a weakness deriving largely from the years spent in the 'Bohemian' environment of his father's home.

His studies with Pedrollo, which began in the last months of 1934, were pursued with great vigour by the young musician, and he was able to pass the examination for the 'fourth year of composition' which he entered as a private student at the Milan Conservatoire in the summer of 1935; he had already passed the preliminary part of the Corso Inferiore di Composizione at the Venice Conservatoire in the previous year. Pedrollo was a composer of some distinction at that time, but his fame rested largely on a work composed in 1900, his *Symphony in D Minor* which had been championed by Toscanini. He was also a pianist and conductor, and had been chief conductor of the Milan Radio Orchestra for some years. His musical outlook was firmly grounded in the world of Verdi and Puccini, but he was at the same time open to more 'advanced' influences, from Richard Strauss and Debussy; he was a very able and imaginative teacher, who brought to even the simplest exercises in composition a strong sense of musicianship.

It is with some surprise, therefore, that we find Maderna, at the end of his first period of study with Pedrollo, obtaining only a rather mediocre result in the final examination of the Corso Inferiore di Composizione in Milan. It gradually became evident that Pedrollo, although well able to impart the elementary training necessary for a composer, was less adequate in the more advanced levels of instruction. The exercises and small compositions which Maderna completed or attempted during this period of study with Pedrollo however, still extant amongst the vast body of material now housed in Basel, give evidence of an assiduous study of harmony and of elementary counterpoint, and the teacher seems to have had greatest strength in 'free composition', giving his pupil many themes and ideas for his personal treatment, words to set, and small 'sonatinas' to compose. Maderna's musical imagination was greatly stimulated by these exercises, and the results show a capacity for invention in all aspects of composition. The young musician had, meanwhile, continued to conduct some concerts, somewhat less intensively than before, and his programmes do show a tendency towards somewhat more 'advanced' music, including works by his fellow-composers from Verona, Pino Donati and Franco Faccio.

Maderna pursued his studies with Pedrollo for two further years after his poor result in the 1935 examination, with the aim of taking (in two years instead of the more normal three) the final examination of the Corso Medio di Composizione in 1937. He began a more serious study of counterpoint, but again the final result was rather disappointing, and it was clear that this was the point at which he should go to study under a more 'severe' teacher. Irma Manfredi was advised that the most suitable person would be Alessandro Bustini, then Vice President of the Santa Cecilia Academy in Rome. Bustini accepted Maderna for the course in Fugue from the autumn of 1937, but would not as yet admit him to the Corso Superiore di Composizione. Maderna found a lodging in Rome and his studies with Bustini began immediately.

Bustini had originally been a pupil of Giovanni Sgambati, and followed Sgambati in attempting to revive orchestral and chamber music in Italy, but perhaps his greatest fame rested on a book *The Symphony in Italy* which he had written in 1904. His interest in more 'modern' musical trends was, somewhat less strong than Pedrollo's had been; however, his gifts as a teacher were considerable, and he could number Goffredo Petrassi, Guido Turchi and Carlo Maria Giulini amongst his pupils. He was able to enrich the musical vocabulary of Maderna's composition to a large degree: the pupil composed an immense amount during his period of study with Bustini, including suites, sonatas, trios, quartets and orchestral compositions. The most profound effect of his apprenticeship with Bustini, which lasted from 1937 to 1940 and which was concluded with a brilliant result in the final examinations at the Santa Cecilia Academy, was a deepening of Maderna's sense of musical form. Whether or not this most rigorous training reflected the student's intimate and personal musical feelings, it was an indispensable basis for his later technical facility.

On his return to Verona in 1940, Maderna faced the necessity of finding a direction for the future. His days as a *bambino prodigio* were clearly over (indeed, he seems not to have undertaken any conducting engagements during his studies in Rome), but he was to conduct a number of concerts, in Turin, Verona, Venice and Milan, before he was called up into the Army in 1942. The repertoire of these concerts again showed a shift towards more 'advanced' music, works by Donati, Pizzetti, Pilati and Respighi. But at some stage in 1940, the event occurred which was to be of decisive importance for Maderna's whole future direction: his first encounter with Gian Francesco Malipiero. By the time of Maderna's concert in Venice in May 1941, in fact, the presence of Malipiero has already become influential: the programme of this concert consisted entirely of Italian works of the seventeenth and eighteenth centuries, in keeping with Malipiero's position at the forefront of the revival of this earlier music, a revival in which Maderna himself was also to play a significant part.

There can be little doubt that Maderna, even before his first meeting with Malipiero in 1940, was fully aware of the importance which the older composer had in the so-called 'Generazione dell'Ottanta', in the revival of interest in instrumental music in Italy after the long period of its neglect, and in the 'modernism' which Malipiero represented alongside Pizzetti and Casella. It is not, however, surprising that the two had never met: since shortly after the First World War, Malipiero had jealously guarded his 'retreat' in Asolo, near Treviso, and the solitary nature of his life there was penetrated by only a few carefully chosen friends. Maderna, however, appears to have had little difficulty in becoming close to Malipiero: despite the younger musician's lack of experience as a composer (he had at this point not yet had a performance of any of his works), Malipiero took to him with enthusiasm. Although Maderna's 'official' studentship with Malipiero on the Corso di Perfezionamento per Compositori at the Venice Conservatoire was only to begin in 1942, it appears that the two musicians had been in continuous contact right from their first meeting, but on what basis, whether occasional or more regular, we can only guess.

His period of contact with Malipiero brought to the young musician influences which were to be of the greatest importance in the formation of his outlook on music. Undoubtedly the greatest influence was in bringing Maderna to a full awareness of musical history: Malipiero, like two other teachers of genius, Schoenberg and Messiaen, brought his pupils into contact with an enormous range of music, from the most ancient to the most modern, and did not restrict himself to music for which he himself had a particular affection. He insisted on a rigorous and complete understanding of the historical development of music, and encouraged Maderna, along with the fellow-students, to investigate musical history through the study of original manuscripts and treatises to be found in the Biblioteca Marciana in Venice. By this means, Maderna became fascinated with the music of the sixteenth, seventeenth and eighteenth centuries, Venetian music in particular but not exclusively: we find amongst the composers whose music Maderna was to edit or transcribe the names of Monteverdi, Pergolesi, Ziani, Vivaldi, Viadana, Giovanni Gabrieli, Perotin, Frescobaldi, Josquin, Carissimi and Domenico Belli, as well as vocal music of the fifteenth century from the *Odhecaton* published by Ottaviano Petrucci, and pieces from the *Fitzwilliam Virginal Book*. For Maderna, this was not simply a musicological exercise, but an important part of his musical personality, 'interpreting' the music of the past as much by his imaginative realisation of the original scores as by his performances of this music which became an equal feature of his concert programmes alongside the 'standard' and 'contemporary' repertoire. The direct and immediate result of Malipiero's influence on Maderna the composer can be seen in the *Introduzione e Passacaglia 'Lauda Sion Salvatorem'*, an orchestral piece which Maderna composed in 1942 which was to remain in manuscript, and was performed only once, in Florence in 1947.

Maderna wished also to continue his conducting studies at this time and hoped to take part in the course held in Siena in the summer of 1941 by Antonio Guarnieri: Guarnieri, whose strange and problematic personality has by now become almost legendary in Italy, at first refused to admit the *'ex-bambino prodigio'* to his class there, and Malipiero had to write to both Alfredo Casella and Count Chigi Saracini (founder of the Summer School in Siena, and in whose palace it was held) in order to persuade him, and the intervention was finally successful. It is interesting to note that amongst the participants in the course in Siena that summer was the young Carlo Maria Giulini. Maderna conducted some concerts during the 1941–42 season which reflected the broadening of his musical interests, including a good deal of 'earlier' music as well as modern Italian compositions, and also, in the last concert which he was to conduct before the war finally overtook his musical activities, the first performance in Italy of Anton Webern's *Orchestral Variations* opus 30.

He was called up into the Italian army towards the end of 1942, and was placed in the training-school for non-commissioned officers of one of the Alpini regiments stationed in Merano: it was in fact a particularly fortunate placement for Maderna in that the commanding officer was very keen on music, and the young recruit was immediately asked to provide a regimental march and music for various troop-entertainments. Thus, the composer's military experience was made considerably less burdensome, and in fact he was able to assume a position of some privilege, even being allowed to absent himself from duties in order to conduct concerts in Verona and Milan. Maderna's ability, acquired early in life during his years as a member of his father's band, for the composition of 'light' music in various styles, became of immediate use to him in making his military life less irksome.

He was transformed for a time to Tarquinia, and returned to Merano at the end of 1943 as a sergeant, but was then moved once more to Verona. It was during this time, when there was a general curfew in the town, that Maderna, by temperament unable to observe such regulations, would meet in the evenings with members of the Partisan organisations. He also met for the first time Raffaella Tartaglia, who was later to become his first wife: she was a graduate in languages who at that time was working for the police in Verona, but she did not share Maderna's anti-Fascist views. Possibly because of this, or because Irma Manfredi had been hiding Jews in her house and aiding their escape to Switzerland, that Maderna was arrested by the SS in February 1945: one version of this story has him escaping from a train on his way to a concentration camp in Germany, another that Manfredi's influential friends acted on his behalf. In any case, he eventually joined up with the Partisans in the mountains and was given the code-name RAS. Manfredi rented a house nearby so that he could go there to work undisturbed on his compositions in the interludes between his acts of sabotage. There is in fact no truth in Maderna's later claim that he had travelled to Russia, and no more truth in the claim reported by Massimo Mila that Maderna was made Mayor of Verona at the end of the war. He did, however, play a great part in the reconstruction of musical life in Verona at that time, helping to found the Società Musicale Pietro Marconi in order to bring concerts once more to the city.

Maderna and Raffaella Tartaglia married on 10 November 1945 but continued to live separately for a while, and he only revealed the fact of his marriage some time later to Irma Manfredi. He was offered a small teaching post at the Venice Conservatoire by its Director Malipiero, and the young couple then found a flat in that city. He appears to have paid little attention to the need to make a living: as soon as his private pupils became his friends, he ceased to ask for further payment for lessons, and his conducting engagements were not at this time sufficient to provide a regular income. He began at this time also to compose music for films and for the radio, an activity which was to be continued for some years, right up to the time when his main activities transferred to Milan and Darmstadt. He also undertook a good deal of editing and transcription of older music, including some volumes of the *Complete Vivaldi Edition* then being undertaken by Malipiero.

As far as his own composition was concerned, a *Serenata per undici strumenti* was given its only performance at the first post-war Biennale in Venice in 1946: this work has no connection with the later *Serenata No 2* composed a decade later, and has unfortunately been lost. An *Introduzione e Passacaglia 'Lauda Sion Salvatorem'* for orchestra was also given its only performance under his direction in Florence in 1947, but this work also has remained in manuscript. It was to be only from 1948 that Maderna the composer was to be fully revealed: in the Venice Biennale of that year, his *Concerto per due pianoforti e strumenti* was performed with the duo Gorini-Lorenzi, but the work was published only in 1955, in a version which differs largely from the original. Also in 1948, Maderna composed a *Fantasia per due pianoforti (B.A.C.H. Variationen)*, the first work of Maderna's to be heard in the Darmstadt Summer School in 1949, when it was performed by Carl Seeman and Peter Stadlen, and he began work on his first serial compositions, *Tre Liriche Greche* and *Composizione No 1* for orchestra, the latter performed under Nino Sanzogno in Turin in 1950.

This move to serial techniques of compositions, techniques of which he had been aware even during his studies with Malipiero some years earlier, occurred after Maderna had met Hermann Scherchen: it was Malipiero, again, who had prompted Maderna to attend the German conductor's course in Venice in 1948, but it was to be as a composer rather than as a conductor that he gained most from contact with Scherchen, the musician who had been so involved in the music of the 'Second Viennese School' right from the earliest years of the century. Scherchen suggested to Maderna that he should attend the Summer School in Darmstadt, and from his first visit there in 1950, Maderna's association with the city became almost continuous, the city in which he was to meet the young Beate Christina Köpnick, later his second wife, and the city in which he eventually made his permanent home.

During the next few years, Maderna's music began to be performed more widely, especially in Germany: *Composizione No 2* for orchestra in Darmstadt in 1950, *Improvvisazione No 1* in Hamburg in 1952, *Musica su due dimensioni* for flute and tape (the first composition in which tape and live performance were combined) in Darmstadt in 1952, and *Quattro Lettere (Kranichsteiner Kammerkantate)* also in Darmstadt in 1953. He also spent a good deal of time in Milan, and it was there in 1954 that, together with Luciano Berio (whom he had met for the first time just a year earlier) he began to undertake some 'experimental' work in the studios of RAI (Radiotelevisione Italiana), work which led to the foundation of the Studio di Fonologia Musicale, in which Luigi Rognoni and Piero Santi also collaborated, with Marino Zuccheri as technical assistant. Maderna and Berio collaborated in the first venture of the new Studio in 1954–55: this was the radiophonic work *Ritratto di Città* (Portrait of a City), which was amongst other things intended to demonstrate to the RAI authorities the possibilities of the Studio for specifically radio projects. In the course of the following years, Maderna's work in the Studio was to occupy a good deal of his time and attention: he composed, besides a great deal of 'incidental' music for the radio, some works in which he explored the new medium (*Sequenze e Strutture, Notturno, Syntaxis, Continuo*), but at the same time he continued to compose for the 'conventional' instrumental medium (including a *Flute Concerto, String Quartet* and *Piano Concerto*). He also directed many of the concerts of the 'Incontri Musicali' series in Milan and other Italian cities, concerts which were intended to introduce audiences to the 'New Music'. Maderna was not in fact employed on a full-time basis by RAI, and had to earn a living by other means, including working as an electrician and night-porter. He collaborated with Berio in other enterprises: they sometimes composed music for theatres and for the radio in a 'four-handed' manner, Berio writing the string-parts while Maderna was busy with the winds, and in the *Divertimento per orchestra* in 1957 by both composers, Maderna composed the *Blues: 'Dark Rapture Crawl'*, sections of which were to re-appear later in the *Piano Concerto* and in the 'radiophonic opera' *Don Perlimplin* based upon a play by Lorca. It was during this period, in the late 'fifties and early 'sixties, that Maderna's name began to be widely known amongst audiences of contemporary music: he taught a class in serial composition at the Milan Conservatoire in 1957–58, and visited England on several occasions to teach and conduct in the Dartington Summer School and with the BBC Symphony Orchestra in London, both at the invitation of William Glock. He was awarded the Diploma of the Accademia Filarmonica Romana in 1962, an award which somewhat amused him, as it had been denied to his beloved Mozart.

After 1963, his conducting engagements became more and more frequent and varied: he began to visit Holland frequently (mainly to conduct the 'Residentie' Orchestra of The Hague) and after 1965 also in the United States, whilst continuing to pursue most of his conducting in Germany, where he had by this time made his permanent home. The performance of his *'lirica in forma di spettacolo' Hyperion* on stage in La Fenice in Venice in 1964, with Severino Gazzelloni and Catherine Gayer accompanied by a huge machine from which electronic sounds emitted, provoked a *'succès de scandale'*: the work was later presented in different versions on stage in Brussels and in Bologna in 1968 (in the latter city interspersed between the acts of Domenico Belli's *Orfeo Dolente* of 1616), as well as numerous purely concert versions.

Three children were born to Maderna and Cristina: Caterina (born in 1955), Claudia (born in 1960) and Andrea (born in 1966), and the home which they made in Darmstadt provided the composer with a very stable and happy environment to which he could return after his many extensive conducting-tours. He was a most loving and beloved father to his children, who were brought up totally bi-lingually, and Cristina Maderna has continued to take a great responsibility for the vast body of material which Maderna left at his death, material which she gave to the Paul Sacher Foundation in Basel in 1985.

Maderna lived his last years very intensely: his conducting activity became more regular, and yet despite this and the constant travelling which it entailed, his composition did not suffer to the slightest degree, indeed, rather the reverse, as one activity seemed to provide fuel for the other. The group of orchestral works which he composed in this last period, the fruit of his belief in the continuing validity of the symphony orchestra as an expressive vehicle, arose from commissions: *Quadrivium* for the Royan Festival in 1969, *Aura* for the Chicago Symphony Orchestra, *Biogramma* for the Eastman School of Music in Rochester and *Giardino Religioso* for the Fromm Foundation all in 1972. He also composed other large-scale works at this time: a *Violin Concerto* for Theo Olof in 1969, *Grande Aulodia* for the Persepolis Festival in 1971 amongst others.

Maderna was diagnosed as suffering from lung cancer in 1972: this revelation did not deter him from living as intensely as before, and he was realistic about his prospects. He composed *Venetian Journal* in 1972 for the American tenor Paul Sperry and as a homage to his native city, and a *Third Oboe Concerto* was performed by Han de Vries in 1973, both under the composer's direction. It became clear to everyone during the rehearsals of his opera *Satyricon* at the Holland Festival in March 1973 that Maderna was gravely ill, and some responsibility for the work's preparation had to be handed to others, including the producer Ian Strasfogel and the conductor Lucas Vis.

His last concert was given in the Royal Festival Hall in London just six days before his death, and included works by Schoenberg and Bartok. He died on 13 November 1973 in the hospital in Darmstadt, having earlier in the day planned rehearsals for Debussy's *Pelléas et Mélisande* which he would have begun the next day.

Appendix III

Bibliography

ANNIBALDI, Claudio: **Maderna:** article in *New Grove Dictionary of Music and Musicians;* Macmillan, London, 1981.

BARONI, Mario, and DALMONTE, Rossana (Editors):**Bruno Maderna: Documenti;** Suvini Zerboni, Milan, 1985.

BARONI, Mario, and DALMONTE, Rossana (Editors): **Inediti Maderniani** (Essays by MAGNANI, Francesca, MONTECCHI, Giordano and ROMITO, Maurizio); in *Musica/Realtà No 10, April 1983; Edizioni Unicopli, Milan; pp. 41–61.*

BERIO, Luciano: **Un inedito di Bruno Maderna;** in *Nuova Rivista Musicale Italiana* October–December 1978; pp. 517–520.

BERIO, Luciano: **Two Interviews;** interviews with Rossana Dalmonte and Balint Andràs Varga; translated and edited by David Osmond-Smith; Marion Boyars, London and New York, 1985. Dalmonte interviews first published as **Intervista sulla musica;** Laterza, Rome-Bari, 1981. Varga interviews first published as **Beszelgetesek Luciano Berioval;** Budapest 1981.

BITTER, Christoph: **Bruno Maderna: Dirigent und Komponist;** published in sleeve-note to recording *Bruno Maderna: Ein Dokument;* Telefunken 6.48066 EK.

BOULEZ, Pierre: **Bruno Maderna: Esquisse d'un Portrait;** in *Points de Repère;* Christian Bourgois 'Éditions du Seuil', Paris, 1981; pp. 550–551. First published as **Salut à Bruno Maderna** in *Le Nouvel Observateur* 26 November 1973.

BRINDLE, Reginald Smith: **Maderna and Berio;** in *The Listener,* 10 June 1971.

ELSENDOORN, Jo: **Bruno Maderna;** article in *Opera Journal;* De Nederlandse Operastichting, Amsterdam, April 1973.

ELSENDOORN, Jo: **Bruno Maderna: een groot geniaal mensenkind, dat componist en dirigent was** and **De grijns van Vivaldi en de tedere grimlach in het oeuvre van Maderna;** in *Musiek en Dans,* Amsterdam, May 1983, pp. 13–31.

FEARN, Raymond: **Bruno Maderna: from the Cafe Pedrocchi to Darmstadt** in *Tempo* No. 15, December 1985, pp. 8–14.

FEARN, Raymond: **At the Doors of Kranichstein: Maderna's 'Fantasia' for 2 Pianos** in *Tempo* No. 163, December 1987, pp. 14–20.

GENTILUCCI, Armando: **Bruno Maderna;** in *Guida all'ascolto della musica contemporanea;* Feltrinelli, Milan, 1969; pp. 244–248.

GENTILUCCI, Armando: **Gestualità drammatica nel teatro musicale italiano nel dopoguerra** in *Musica/Realtà no. 3, December 1980; Edizioni Unicopli, Milan, pp. 81–93.*

GIUBERTONI, Anna: **Le fonti poetiche dell'Hyperion di Bruno Maderna** in *Nuova Rivista Musicale Italiana* no. 15/2, 1981, pp. 197–205.

HÖLDERLIN, Friedrich: **Sämtliche Werke;** edited by F Beissner (7 vols); Kohlhammer, Stuttgart, 1943– .

JANSEN, Kasper: **Bruno Maderna and Dutch Musical Life;** in *Donemus no. 11, Amsterdam* 1980–81, pp. 30–36.

LORCA, Federico Garcia: **Obras completas;** Aguilar, Madrid, 1960 (4th Edition).

LORCA, Federico Garcia: **Five Plays (Comedies and Tragicomedies); translated by James Graham-Lujan and Richard L O'Connell; Penguin Books, Harmondsworth, 1970.**

MAGNANI, Francesca: **Considerazioni sul rapporto fra musica e testo nell'opera di B. Maderna** in *Ricerche Musicali,* no 5, Ghisoni, Milan, 1981; Ghisoni, Milan.

MANZONI, Giacomo: **Bruno Maderna** in *Die Reihe, no 4; Universal Edition, Vienna and London, 1958; pp. 113–118.*

MILA, Massimo; **Maderna: Musicista Europeo;** Einaudi, Turin, 1976.

PETRONIUS (G. Petronius Arbiter): **The Satyricon;** translated by William Arrowsmith; University of Michigan Press, 1959 and Mentor Books, New York and London.

PINZAUTI, Leonardo: **Musicisti d'oggi: venti colloqui; ERI (RAI Publishers), Turin 1978;** appeared originally as separate interviews in *Nuova Rivista Musicale Italiana.*

PINZAUTI, Leonardo: **La Lezione di Maderna;** article in *Nuova Rivista Musicale Italiana, July/September 1980, pp. 393–403.*

STRASFOGEL, Ian: **Nieuwe impulsen voor het muziektheater;** in *Opera Journal,* published by De Nederlandse Operastichting, Amsterdam, 1973.

STEINITZ, Paul: **Bruno Maderna's 'Greek Lyrics';** in *Musical Times,* March 1965, page 186.

WEBER, Horst: **Form und Satztechnik in Bruno Maderna's Streichquartett;** in *Miscellanea del Cinquantenario; Suvini Zerboni, Milan, 1978; pp. 206–215.*

WEBER, Horst: **Maderna: compositore veneziano; in** *Musica/Realtà* no 12, December 1983; Edizioni Unicopli, Milan, pp. 31–40.

Komponisten des 20, Jahrhunderts in der Paul Sacher Stiftung; published in 1986 to accompany exhibition held at the Kuntsmuseum, Basel, 25 April – 20 June 1986; includes essays on Maderna by BITTER, Christoph and MILA, Massimo.

Appendix IV

Complete List of Compositions Including Discography

The discographical details are presented here take account of all the recordings which it is possible to trace, whether issued as commercial recordings or recordings of first or other performances which are still housed in the archives of the following institutions:

IMD: Internationales Musikinstitut Darmstadt
NSA: National Sound Archive (British Library)
RAI: Radiotelevisione Italiana
CM: Cristina Maderna, widow of the composer
SWDR: Südwestdeutscher Rundfunk
NWDR: Nordwestdeutscher Rundfunk
NDR: Norddeutscher Rundfunk
SDR: Süddeutscher Rundfunk
RIC: Ricordi tape

1. *ALBA*

Composed	Probably 1937–40
Performed	—
Published	—
Text	Vincenzo Cardarelli
Instrumentation	Contralto solo, string orchestra
Duration	6–7'

2. *LA SERA FIESOLANA*

Composed	Probably 1938–39
Performed	—
Published	—
Text	Gabriele d'Annunzio
Instrumentation	Tenor solo
	Fl, Ob, C Ang, Cl, Bn, Hn, Tr,
	Timp, Cel, Hrp,
	Vln I, Vln II, Va, Vc, DB.
Duration	Incomplete work

3. *PICCOLO CONCERTO*

Composed	October 1941
Performed	—
Published	—
Instrumentation	4Fl, Ob, C Ang, Cl,

	Timp, Cel, Hrp,
	4 Vln, 3 Va, 2 Vc, DB.
Duration	Incomplete work

4. *CONCERTO PER PIANOFORTE E ORCHESTRA*

Composed	1942
Performed	Venice 22.6.42
Published	—
Instrumentation	Piano solo
	2 Ob, C Ang, 2 Bn,
	3 Tr, 3 Trb, Tuba,
	SD (snares), SD (without snares), Cym, BD,
	6 Vln I, 6 Vln II, 4 Va, 4 Vc, 4 DB.
Duration	Score lost

5. *INTRODUZIONE E PASSACAGLIA 'LAUDIA SION SALVATOREM'*

Composed	1942
Performed	Florence, 3.4.47
Published	—
Instrumentation	3 Fl (Picc), 2 Ob, C Ang, 2 Cl, B Cl, 2Bn, Cbn
	4 Hn, 3 Tr, 3 Trb, Tuba,
	Vln I, Vln II, Va, Vc, DB
Duration	*circa* 10′

6. *QUARTETTO PER ARCHI*

Composed	before 1946
Performed	—
Published	—
Instrumentation	String quartet
Duration	*circa* 10′

7. *CONCERTINO*
Probably identical with SERENATA or PICCOLO CONCERTO

8. *REQUIEM*

Composed	probably 1945–46
Performed	—
Published	—
Instrumentation	SATB solos,
	SSAATTBarB choir (variously grouped)
	8 Hn, 4 Tr, 4 Trb, Tuba,
	3 Pf, 3 Timp, SD (snares),
	SD (without snares),
	Susp Cym, Tam-Tam, Bd with Cym,
	Vln I, Vln II, Va, Vc, DB.
Duration	Incomplete work (only fragment remains)

9. *SERENATA*

| Composed | 1946 |

Performed	Venice 21.9.46
Published	—
Instrumentation	Fl, Ob, Cl, Bn,
	Hn, Tr,
	2 Vln, Va, Vc, DB.
Duration	*circa* 14′

10. *LIRICHE SU VERLAINE*

Composed	1946–47
Performed	Bonn 16.3.84
Published	—
Recorded	(Bonn 16.3.84?)
Text	Paul Verlaine
Instrumentation	Voice and piano
Duration	*circa* 16′ 30″

11. *CONCERTO PER DUE PIANOFORTI E STRUMENTI*

Composed	1947–48
Performed	(first version) Venice 17.9.48
Published	(later version) Suvini Zerboni
Recorded	(published version): NWDR
Instrumentation	2 pianos
	2 Hp, Cel, Vib, Xyl,
	Timp, Susp Cym, SD (snares),
	SD (without snares),
	Tam-Tam.
Duration	(published version) 12–13′

12. *TRE LIRICHE GRECHE*

Composed	1948
Performed	Louisville, USA, (date unknown)
Published	Ars Viva Verlag (now Suvini Zerboni)
Recorded	on disc in USA sometime in the 1950s: no longer
	in existence
Text	Greek poetry (translated by Salvatore Quasimodo)
Instrumentation	Soprano solo
	Chorus,
	2 Fl, 2 Cl, B Cl,
	Pf,
	4 Timp, 5 SD, Tamb, 2 Susp Cym.
Duration	12′

13. *FANTASIA PER DUE PIANOFORTE (B.A.C.H. VARIATIONS)*

Composed	1948
Performed	Darmstadt, July 1949
Published	—
Instrumentation	2 Pfs
Duration	*circa* 12–15′

14. *COMPOSIZIONE NO. 1*
Composed   1948
Performed   Turin, February 1950
Published   Suvini Zerboni
Instrumentation   3 Fl (Picc), 2 Ob (Ob d'amore),
                                Cor Ang, Alto Sax, 2 Cl,
                                B Cl, 3 Bn, (C Bn)
                            4 Hn, 4 Tr, 3 Tromb, Tuba
                            Vibr, Cel, Xyl, Pf, 2 Hp
                            Timp, Claves, Susp Cym, Tam-Tam, 2 SD, BD
                            16 Vln I, 16 Vln II, 12 Va, 10 Vc, 8 DB.
Duration   23–25'

15. *SYMPHONIC FRAGMENT*
Composed   1949–50?
Performed   —
Published   —
Instrumentation   Picc, Fl, Ob, Cor Ang, Cl, Cl in Eb,
                                B Cl, Bn, Sop Sax
                            2 Hn, Tr, Tromb
                            Hp, Pf
                            4 Timp, Susp Cym, 2 Tom-Toms, SD, Mil Dr, BD
                            solo Vln, Vln I, Vln II, Va, Vc, DB
Duration   Incomplete work

16. *COMPOSIZIONE NO. 2*
Composed   1950
Performed   Darmstadt, 26.8.50
Published   Ara Viva Verlag (now Suvini Zerboni)
Recorded   IMD
Instrumentation   2 Fl, (picc), Ob, Cor Ang, Alto Sax, Cl,
                                Cl in Eb, B Cl, 2 Bn
                            2 Hn, Tr, Tromb
                            Xyl, Hp, Pf
                            Timp, Susp Cym, Claves, 2 SD, Tamb,
                                BD, Maracas
                            8 Vln I, 8 Vln II, 4 Va, 3 Vc, 2 DB
Duration   12' 42"

17. *STUDI PER 'IL PROCESSO' DI KAFKA*
Composed   1950
Performed   Venice, 13.9.50
Published   Ars Viva Verlag (now Suvini Zerboni)
Recorded   RAI
Instrumentation   Speaker
                            Soprano solo
                            Picc, 2 Fl, 2 Ob, Cor Ang, 2 Cl,
                                Cl in Eb, B Cl, Alto Sax,
                                Tenor Sax, 3 Bn (C Bn)

	4 Hn, 4 Tr, 3 Tromb, Tuba
	2 Hp, Pf, Elect Guitar, Cel, Vibr, Xyl
	Timp, Tri, Susp Cym, Tam-Tam, Tamb, 2 SD, BD
	Vln I, Vln II, Va, Vc, DB
Duration	*circa* 20'

18. *STUDI PER IL 'LLANTO' DI G. LORCA*

Composed	1950–52?
Performed	—
Published	—
Text	from *'La cogida y la muerte'* by F G Lorca
Instrumentation	tenor, flute and guitar
Duration	Incomplete work

19. *IMPROVVISAZIONE NO. 1*

Composed	1951–52
Performed	Hamburg, 17–19.2.52
Published	Ars Viva Verlag (now Suvini Zerboni)
Recorded	IMD
Instrumentation	3 Fl (Picc), 2 Ob, Cor Ang, 3 Cl (Cl in Eb), B Cl, 2 Bn, C Bn
	4 Hn, 3 Tr, 3 Tromb, Tuba
	2 Hp, Pf, Cel, Xyl, Vibr, Glock
	Timp, Tri, 2 Susp Cym, Cym, Tamb, SD, Claves, BD
	Vln I, Vln II, Va, Vc, DB
Duration	11' 15"

20. *MUSICA SU DUE DIMENSIONI*

Composed	1952
Performed	Darmstadt, 21.5.52
Recorded	IMD
Published	Ars Viva Verlag (all copies now lost)
Instrumentation	Flute, Cymbal, Tape
Duration	7' 40"

21. *DAS EISERNE ZEITALTER*

Composed	1952–53?
Performed	—
Published	—
Instrumentation	3 Fl (Picc), 2 Ob, Cor Ang, 2 Cl, Cl in Eb, B Cl, Alto Sax, 2 Bn, C Bn
	4 Hn, 3 Tr, 3 Tromb, Tuba
	Hp, Pf, Xyl, Vibr, Cel, Glock
	Tub bells, Timp, 3 SD, Tamb, 8 Tom-Toms, 3BD, Cym, 4 Susp Cym, 3 Gongs, Cencerros, 3 Cast, Whip, Wood-block
	Vln, Va, Vc, DB
Duration	Incomplete work

22. *QUATTRO LETTERE (KRANICHSTEINER KAMMERKANTATE)*

Composed	July 1953
Performed	Darmstadt, 30.7.53
Published	Ars Viva Verlag (now Suvini Zerboni)
Recorded	IMD
Text	Letter of a Resistance hero;
	Business-letter;
	Kafka letter to Milena;
	Letter of Gramsci from prison
Instrumentation	Bass (or baritone) solo, soprano solo
	Fl (Picc), Cl (B Cl)
	Hn
	2 Pf, Hp, Harmonium, Xyl
	Timp, 2 SD, Susp Cym
	4 Vln, 2 Va, 2 Vc, DB
Duration	9' 42"

23. *IMPROVVISAZIONE NO. 2*

Composed	1953
Performed	Heidelberg, 28.11.53
Published	Ars Viva (now Suvini Zerboni)
Recorded	IMD
Instrumentation	2 Fl (2 Picc), Ob, Cor Ang, Cl, Cl in Eb,
	B Cl, 2 Bn
	2 Hn, 2 Tr, Tromb, Tuba
	Hp, Pf, Glock, Xyl
	Timp, Tri, Bongos, Tabour, SD, 2 Susp Cym,
	Gong, Wood block, BD
	Vln I, Vln II, Va, Vc, DB
Duration	*circa* 6' 35"

24. *DIVERTIMENTO IN DUE TEMPI*

Composed	1953
Performed	—
Published	Suvini Zerboni
Instrumentation	Flute, Piano
Duration	*circa* 8'

25. *FLÖTENKONZERT*

Composed	1954
Performed	Darmstadt, 22.8.54
Published	Suvini Zerboni
Recorded	IMD
Instrumentation	Solo flute
	3 Fl (Picc), 2 Ob, 2 Cl, Cl in Eb,
	B Cl, 2 Bn, C Bn
	4 Hn, 5 Tr, 3 Tromb, Tuba
	Hp, Pf, Cel, Glock, Xyl, Vibr, Timp, Tri
	Vln I, Vln II, Va, Vc, DB
Duration	*circa* 8'

26. *COMPOSIZIONE IN TRE TEMPI*

Composed	1954
Performed	Hamburg, December 1954
Published	Suvini Zerboni
Recorded	NWDR
Instrumentation	3 Fl, (3 Picc), 2 Ob, Cor Ang, 2 Cl,
	Cl in Eb, B Cl, 2 Bn, C Bn
	4 Hn, 4 Tr, 3 Tromb, Tuba
	Pf, Hp, Glock, Vibr, Xyl, Mrb,
	Cel, Guit, Mand
	Timp, Tub bells, Small drum,
	3 SD, 4 Tom-Tom, 2 BD, Jazz Cym,
	Gong, Woodblock, Cast, 4 Tri, Cocamba
	Whip, Antique Cymbals, Rumbaholzer
	Vln I, Vln II, Va, Vc, DB
Duration	*circa* 14′

27. SERENATA NO. 2

Composed	1954, revised 1957
Performed	Darmstadt, April 1956
	(Ars Viva Verlag version)
Published	Ars Viva Verlag version)
Published	Ars Viva Verlag; Suvini Zerboni
	(second version)
Recorded	Time Records ST 8002: cond Maderna CBS/ESZ
	61455: cond M. Panni. Fonit Cetra ITL 70031: cond
	M. Panni
Instrumentation	Fl (Picc), Cl, B Cl,
	Tr, Hn
	Hp, Xyl (Vibr), Pf (Glock)
	Vln, Va, DB (5 strings)
Duration	First version 16′;
	Suvini Zerboni version 12′

28. *SEQUENZE E STRUTTURE*

Composed	1954–55
Performed	Milan, May 1956
Published	tape lost
Instrumentation	tape-work
Duration	*circa* 3′

29. *RITRATTO DI CITTÀ*

Composed	1955 (together with Luciano Berio
	and Roberto Leydi)
Performed	RAI Milan 1955
Published	tape held by RAI
Recorded	RAI
Instrumentation	tape-work
Duration	29′ 23″

30. *QUARTETTO PER ARCHI*

Composed	1955
Performed	Darmstadt, 1.6.55
Published	Suvini Zerboni
Recorded	IMD
Instrumentation	String quartet
Duration	12'

31. *NOTTURNO*

Composed	1956
Performed	Milan, 24.5.57
Published	tape held by Suvini Zerboni
Recorded	IMD
Instrumentation	tape-work
Duration	3' 23"

32. *SYNTAXIS*

Composed	1957
Performed	Milan, 24.5.57
Published	tape held by Suvini Zerboni
Recorded	IMD
Instrumentation	tape-work
Duration	10' 57"

33. *DARK RAPTURE CRAWL*

Composed	1957 (first movement of *Divertimento per Orchestra* by Berio and Maderna)
Performed	Rome, 2.12.57
Published	Suvini Zerboni
Instrumentation	3 Fl, Cor Ang, 2 Cl, Cl in Eb, B Cl, 5 Sax, Bn, CBn 2 Hn, 5 Tr, 3 Tromb Pf, Hp, Mrb, Vibr, Cel, Glock, Elec Guitar, Timp 8–12 Va (I, II, III), 6–8 Vc (I, III, III), 4–6 DB (I, II, III)
Duration	*circa* 5' 30"

34. *CONTINUO*

Composed	1958
Performed	Cologne, 25.3.58
Published	tape held by Suvini Zerboni
Recorded	IMD Philips A. OO 563/6L
Instrumentation	tapework
Duration	8' 12"

35. *MUSICA SU DUE DIMENSIONI*
(second version)

Composed	1958
Performed	Napes, 11.6.58
Published	Suvini Zerboni
Recorded	IMD
Instrumentation	Flute and tape
Duration	(aleatoric)

36. *CONCERTO PER PIANOFORTE E ORCHESTRA*

Composed	1958–59
Performed	Darmstadt, 2.9.59
Published	Suvini Zerboni
Recorded	IMD
Instrumentation	Piano solo
	5 Fl (2 Picc), 3 Ob, Cor Ang, 2 Cl,
	Cl in Eb, B Cl, 3 Sax, 2 Bn, CBn
	6 Hn, 5 Tr (2 Picc Tr), 4 Tromb,
	Bar Tuba, Bass Tuba
	2 Hp, Mrb, Xyl, Vibr, Cel, Clock
	3 Susp Cym, Timp, Tub Bells, Cencerros,
	Tam-Tam
	8 Vln I, 8 Vln II, 6 Va I, 6 Va II,
	4 Vc I, 4 Vc II, 4 DB I, 4 DB II
Duration	*circa* 18'

37. *DIMENSIONI II/INVENZIONE SU UNA VOCE*

Composed	1960?
Performed	Milan, 9.4.60
Published	tape held by Suvini Zerboni
Recorded	IMD
Instrumentation	tapework
Duration	18' 58"

38. *SERENATA III*

Composed	1961
Performed	Venice, 16.5.61
Published	tape held by Suvini Zerboni
Recorded	RAI
Instrumentation	tapework
Duration	11' 30"

39. *SERENATA IV*

Composed	1961
Performed	Darmstadt, 1961
Published	—
Recorded	IMD
Instrumentation	Flute, other instruments and tape
Duration	tape of first, and only known, performance: 13' 44"

40. *HONEYRÊVES*

Composed	1961–62
Performed	Venice, 23.4.62
Published	Suvini Zerboni
Recorded	Time Records ST 8008
	CBS/ESZ 61568
	Fonit Cetra ITL 70007
Instrumentation	Flute and piano
Duration	6' 33"

41. *MACBETH*

Composed	Probably 1962
Performed	—
Published	—
Instrumentation	not known
Duration	incomplete work

42. *KOMPOSITION FÜR OBOE, KAMMERENSEMBLE UND TONBAND/ KONZERT FÜR OBOE UND KAMMERENSEMBLE*

Composed	1962 (*KOMPOSITION*), 1963? (*KONZERT*)
Performed	Darmstadt 15.7.62 (*KOMPOSITION*)
	Darmstadt 1963 (*KONZERT*)
Published	KOMPOSITION only on tape held by
	Internationales Musikinstitut, Darmstadt;
	KONZERT Suvini Zerboni
Recorded	IMD (KOMPOSITION)
	RCA MLDS 61005
	RCA VIC 1312 (Mono)
	BV HAAST 032-033
Instrumentation	(KONZERT)
	2 Fl (2 Picc, 2 Alto Fl), Ob (Cor Ang),
	Cl, B Cl, Bn
	Hn, Tr, Tromb
	Cel, Hp, 2 Pf, Vibr, Mrb, Xyl,
	3 Cym, 6 Gong
	3 Tri, Rattle, Claves, Sistrum,
	Guiro, Recoreco
	Naruko, 3 Bongos, Timp, SD,
	Chimes, Tub Bells
	6 Sheep Bells, 4 Small Bells, Tamb,
	6 Chinese drums, 3 Tam-Tam, 3 Tom-Tom
	2 Vln, Va, Vc, DB
Duration	KOMPOSITION *circa* 10'; KONZERT *circa* 15' 25"

43. *DON PERLIMPIN*

Composed	1962
Performed	RAI Milan 12.8.62
Published	Suvini Zerboni
Recorded	IMD

Text	play by F G Lorca; trans. Vittorio Bodini
Instrumentation	Radiophonic opera; orchestra employed:
	Flute solo
	Fl (Alto Fl), Cl, 2 Alto Sax (2 Cl),
	2 Tenor Sax (2 Cl), Bar Sax (B Cl), Bn
	Hn, 3 Tr, 3 Tromb
	Hp, Pf, Elec Guit, Mand, Mrb, Vibr
	Timp, Susp Cym, 5 Gong, Japanese Gong,
	3 Bongos, Sistrum, Claves, Tub Bells
	2 Vln, Va, Vc, 2 DB
Duration	44' 35"

44. *LE RIRE*

Composed	1962
Performed	Berlin, 28.9.64
Published	tape held by Suvini Zerboni
Recorded	IMD
Instrumentation	tapework
Duration	16' 01"

45. *DIMENSIONI III*

Composed	1963
Performed	Paris, 1963?
Published	Suvini Zerboni
Recorded	Version I: NDR (Hannover)
	Version II: IMD (called *DIMENSIONI IV*)
	Version III: NWDR (Cologne)
	Version IV: NSA
Instrumentation	Flute (and picc) solo
	2 Fl (2 Picc), 2 Ob, 2 Cl, Cl in Eb,
	B Cl, 3 Bn (CBn)
	3 Hn, 3 Tr, 3 Tromb, Tuba, Bass Tuba
	3 Hp, 2 Pf, Cel, 2 Vibr, 2 Xyl, 2 Mrb,
	Glock, 3 Tub Bells, 3 Timp
	6 Vln, 3 Va, 3 Vc, 3 DB
Duration	'Aleatoric' indicated in score

46. *ARIA*

Composed	1964
Performed	Darmstadt 23.7.64 (version with flute and chamber ensemble)
	Cologne (version with voice and orchestra)
	Cologne 16.11.64 (version with voice and orchestra)
Published	Suvini Zerboni (orchestral version)
Recorded	Version I: as part of *DIMENSIONI IV* in IMD
	Version II: as part of *HYPERION* in NSA
Text	Friedrich Hölderlin '*Fragment von Hyperion, oder Thalia Fragment*'
Instrumentation	(orchestral version):

	Soprano and flute (alto fl, bass fl) solos
	2 Fl (2 Picc, 2 Alto Fl), 2 Ob, 2 Cl,
	Cl in Eb, B Cl, 3 Bn
	3 Hn, 3 Tr, 3 Tromb
	3 Hp, 2 Pf, 2 Vibr, 2 Mrb, 2 Xyl, Cel,
	Glock, Tip, Large Gong
	6 Vln, 3 Va, 3 Vc, 3 DB
Duration	13' 45"

47. *DIMENSIONI IV*

Composed	1964
Performed	Darmstadt 23.7.64 (included *Aria* with flute)
	— (comprises **Dimensioni III** and **Aria**)
Recorded	This title is given to version of *DIMENSIONI III* plus *ARIA* in IMD
Instrumentation	Flute solo (alto, bass and piccolo)
	Fl, 2 Ob (Cor Ang), 2 Cl, B Cl, Bn
	Hn, Tr, Tromb
	2 Hp, 2 Vibr, 2 Xyl, 2 Mrb
	Timp, Gong
	2 Vln, Va, Vc, DB

48. *HYPERION*

Composed	1964
Performed	Venice 6.10.64
Published	— (comprises *Dimensioni IV*, chamber version, *Le Rire* and *Dimensioni II*
Recorded	*(Venice 6.10.64): NSA*
Text	*only text of ARIA*
Instrumentation	as in component works
Duration	*circa* 53'

49. *STELE PER DIOTIMA*

Composed	1965
Performed	Norddeutscher Rundfunk 19.1.66
Published	Suvini Zerboni
Recorded	NDR
Instrumentation	Solo Vln, Cl, B Cl, Hn
	3 Fl (2 Picc), 3 Ob (Cor Ang), 2 Cl,
	Cl in Eb, B Cl, 3 Bn (CBn)
	3 Hn, 3 Tr, 3 Tromb, 2 Tuba
	3 Hp, 2 Pf, 2 Xyl, 2 Vibr, 2 Mrb,
	Cel, Glock, Timp, 2 Tub Bells,
	2 Bd, 4 SD, 2 Tam-Tam, 3 Gong,
	3 Susp Cym, 3 Tri, Sistrum, Whip
	2 Wood Drums, 6 Hard Bells, Guiro,
	2 Narukos, Bongos, 2 Claves, Rattle,
	Castanets, Crotales, Chain,

	Chinese Drum
	6 Vln, 3 Va, 3 Vc, 3 DB
Duration	*circa* 25'

50. *HYPERION II*
Composed	1965
Performed	Darmstadt 19.7.65
Published	— (version of *Dimensioni III* with Flute Cadenzas, and *Entropia II*)
Recorded	(Darmstadt 19.7.65): IMD
Instrumentation	as component works
Duration	not known

51. *HYPERION*
(Rome 1966)
Composed	1966
Performed	Rome, 8.1.66
Published	— (version of *Dimensioni III* with Piccolo solos and *Aria*)
Recorded	(Rome 8.1.66): RAI
Instrumentation	as component works
Duration	not known

52. *HYPERION III*
Composed	1966
Performed	Südwestfunk 1966
Published	— (version of *Stele per Diotima*, Piccolo Solos from *Dimensioni III*, *Aria*, other parts of *Dimensioni III*)
Recorded	Sudwestfunk 1966 Wergo WER 60029
Instrumentation	as component parts
Duration	not known

53. *HYPERION IV*
Composed	1969
Performed	— (version prepared from pre-existing material for Italia Prize 1969)
Published	— (version of *Hyperion* (Rome 1966), *Hyperion II* (Darmstadt 1965), *Suite aus der Oper Hyperion* (Berlin) and other material)
Recorded	(Montage by Maderna of parts of previous versions).
Instrumentation	—
Duration	not known

54. *AULODIA PER LOTHAR*
Composed   1965
Performed   Venice 9.9.65
Published   Suvini Zerboni
Recorded   IMD (2 recordings)
                        CBS/ESZ 61453
                        Fonit Cetra ITL 70036
Instrumentation   Oboe d'Amore and Guitar ad lib.
Duration   *circa* 8' 25"

55. *AMANDA/SERENATA VI*
Composed   1966
Performed   Naples 25.10.66
Published   Suvini Zerboni
Recorded   NSA (Z recordings)
Instrumentation   2 Hp, Pf, Cel, Mrb, Xyl, Guitar, Mand
                        BD, Tam-Tam
                        6 Vln, 3 Va, 3 Vc, 3 DB
Duration   *circa* 12'

56. *WIDMUNG*
Composed   1967
Performed   Nürtingen, 27.10.67
Published   Suvini Zerboni
Recorded   IMD
Instrumentation   Solo violin
Duration   *circa* 10' 20"

57. *CONCERTO PER OBOE E ORCHESTRA NO. 2*
Composed   1967
Performed   Cologne 10.11.67
Published   Suvini Zerboni (Milan)
Recorded   NWDR (Cologne), RAI, SDR
Instrumentation   Solo (Musette, Oboe d'Amore)
                        2 Ob, Cor Ag, 3 Cl, B Cl
                        4 Hn
                        2 Hp, Cel, Guitar, Elec B Guitar
                        4 Drum, 2 Bongos, 2 Tom-Tom, 2 BD,
                            5 Chinese Drums, 2 Hi-Hat, Congas,
                            Sistrum, Narukas, 6 Crotales,
                            3 Wood Blocks, Cast, 5 Tri, Cenc
                        6 Vln, 3 Va, 3 Vc, 3 DB

58. *HYPERION EN HET GEWELD*
(Brussels 1968)
Composed   1968
Performed   Brussels, 17–25.5.68
Published   (Version using material of previous
                            versions of *Hyperion*, with the addition

	of new materials)
Instrumentation	as constituent sections
Duration	not known for certain

59. *HYPERION — ORFEO DOLENTE*
(Bologna 1968)

Composed	1968
Performed	Bologna, 18–19.7.68
Published	(Version of *Hyperion* whose five episodes were interspersed with the five 'intermedii' of Domenico Belli's *Orfeo Dolente* of 1616)
Instrumentation	as constituent sections
Duration	not known for certain

60. *ENTROPIA I*

Composed	1963
Performed	Hanover, 25.1.64 (as section of *Dimensioni III* Brussels, 17–25.5.68 (in *Hyperion en het Geweld*)
Published	(In *Dimensioni III*)
Recorded	included in *DIMENSIONI III* Version I: NDR (Hannover)
Instrumentation	as in *Dimensioni III*
Duration	not known for certain

61. *ENTROPIA II*

Composed	1963
Performed	Hanover, 25.1.64 (as section of *Dimensioni III*) Brussels, 17–25.5.68 (in *Hyperion en het Geweld*)
Published	(In *Dimensioni III*)
Recorded	included in *HYPERION II*: IND
Instrumentation	as in *Dimensioni III*
Duration	not known for certain

62. *ENTROPIA III*

Composed	1968–69
Performed	Berlin, 13.5.69 (In *Suite aus der Oper 'Hyperion'*)
Published	—
Recording	included in *SUITE AUS DER OPER HYPERION* (Berlin 13.5.69): NWDR (Cologne)
Instrumentation	3 Fl (Picc), 2 Ob, Cor Ang, 2 Cl, Cl in Eb, B Cl, 3 Bn 3 Hn, 3 Tr, 3 Tromb, 2 Tuba 6 Vln, 3 Va, 3 Vc, 3 DB
Duration	not known for certain

63. *GESTI*

Composed	1969 (?)
Performed	(Germany, some time after 1969 ?)
Published	—
Instrumentation	same as Entropia III (of which it appears to be another version) except that 2 flutes take piccolo, and bassoon takes contrabassoon
Duration	not known for certain

64. *SUITE AUS DER OPER 'HYPERION'*

Composed	1969–70
Performed	First version Berlin, 13.5.69
	Second version Vienna, 1970
Published	Concert versions of material from *Hyperion* works
Recorded	(Berlin 13.5.69): NWDR (Cologne)
Instrumentation	(Berlin version)
	2 Solo Fl
	1 Solo Ob (Musette, Oboe d'Amore)
	Speaker
	Chorus
	3 Fl (3 Picc), 3 Ob (Cor Ang), 3 Cl, (Cl in Eb)
	B Cl, 3 Bn (CBn)
	3 Hn, 3 Tr, 3 Tromb, 2 Tuba (Bass Tuba)
	3 Hrp, 2 Pf, 2 Mrb, 2 Xyl, 2 Vibr, Cel, Glock, Guitar, Mand
	Timp, BD, 2 Tub Bells, 2 Tam-Tam, 3 Gong, Cym, 4 Herd Bells, 3 Tri, Whip, 2 Wood Blocks, Crot, Sis, Narukas
	6 Vln, 3 Va, 3 Vc, 3 DB
Duration	(Berlin version); 38' 05"

65. *QUADRIVIUM*

Composed	1969
Performed	Royan, 4.4.69
Published	Ricordi
Recorded	NSA (2 recordings one cond Maderna)
	DGG 2531 272
Instrumentation	3 Fl, 2 Ob, Cor Ang, 2 Cl, Cl in Eb, B Cl, 3 Bn, CBn
	4 Hn, 4 Tr, 4 Tromb
	3 Hrp, 2 Mrb, 2 Xyl, 2 Vibr, 2 Glock, Cel
	6 Timp, Tub Bells, 2 Cencerros, 4 Tamb, 6 Drums, 2 BD, 2 small Bongos, 2 Congas, 2 Tam-Tam, 2 Gongs, 4 Susp Cym, 4 Cym, Crotales, Bells, Glass Rattles, 4 Tri, 4 Castanets, Whip, Claves, Narukos, Wood Block, Chinese Wood-Block,

                                  Recoreco, Guiro, Rattle
                                  24 Vln, 8 Va, 8 Vc, 8 DB

Duration	*circa* 25'

66. *CONCERTO PER VIOLINO E ORCHESTRA*

Composed	1969
Performed	Venice, 12.9.69
Published	Ricordi
Recorded	IMD (3 recordings)
	NSA (cond. Maderna)
	BV HAAST 032-033
	3 Fl (2 Picc), 2 Ob, Cor Ang, 2 Cl,
	Cl in Eb, B Cl, 2 Bn, CBn
	3 Hn, 3 Tr, 3 Tromb, Tuba
	3 Hrp, 2 Mrb, Xyl, Guitar, Mand, Susp Cym
	2 String Orchestras, each comprising:
	6 Vln, 3 Va, 3 Vc, 3 DB (5-string)
Duration	*circa* 29–34'

67. *SERENATA PER UN SATELLITE*

Composed	1969
Performed	European Space Operation Center,
	Darmstadt, 1.10.69
Published	Ricordi
Recorded	NSA
	Curci SPL 915
Instrumentation	variable, but normally
	Vln, Fl (Picc),
	Ob (Ob d'Amore, Mus), Cl,
	Mrb, Hrp, Guitar, Mand
Duration	variable, from 4' to 12'

68. *RITRATTO DI ERASMO*

Composed	1969
Performed	broadcast by RAI, 1970
Published	tape held by RAI
Recorded	RAI, CM
Text	prepared by the composer using writings
	of Luther and Erasmus
Instrumentation	tapework
Duration	*circa* 60'

69. *FROM A TO Z/VON A BIS Z*

Composed	1969
Performed	radio-presentation for Dutch radio 1969
	stage-version Darmstadt (Landestheater)
	22.2.70
Published	RIC
Text	Rebecca Rass

Instrumentation	tapework
Duration	42' 35"

70. *GRANDE AULODIA*

Composed	1970
Performed	Rome, 7.2.70
Published	Ricordi
Recorded	NSA (cond. Maderna)
Instrumentation	Fl (Picc, Fl in Eb, Alto Fl)
	Ob (Ob d'Am, Cor Ang, Mus) soloists
	4 Fl (3 Picc), 3 Ob, Cor Ang, 2 Cl,
	Cl in Eb, 2 B Cl (Cl), 3 Bn (CBn)
	4 Hn, 4 Tr, 3 Tromb, Tuba
	2 Xyl, 2 Mrb, Cel, Glock
	Timp, 2 Drum, BD, Tamb, Tub Bells,
	4 Gong, 3 Susp Cym, 2 Tam-Tam,
	2 Bongos, 2 Congas, 2 Tom-Toms,
	Castanets, Recoreco, Guiro, Narukas,
	Claves
	3 String Orchestras each comprising:
	6 Vln, 3 Va, 3 Vc, 3 DB
Duration	*circa* 24'

71. *TEMPO LIBERO*

Composed	1970
Performed	Rimini-Republica di San Marino
	September 1970
Published	tape held by Ricordi
Recorded	RAI
Instrumentation	tapework
Duration	aleatoric in performance

72. *JUILLARD SERENADE / TEMPO LIBERO II*

Composed	1970–71
Performed	New York, 31.1.71
Published	Ricordi
Recorded	NSA, BV HAAST 032-033
Instrumentation	Picc (Fl), Fl, Ob (Cor Ang), 2Cl (B Cl) Bn,
	Hn, Tr, Tomb, Tuba
	2 Pf, Mrb, Xyl, Cel, Hrp
	1 Vln, 1 Va, 1Vc, 1 DB
Duration	aleatoric sections, but *circa* 17–20'

73. *VIOLA (O VIOLA D'AMORE)*

Composed	1971
Performed	first performance unknown, but probably 1971
Published	Ricordi
Recorded	Italia ITL 70038 (Aldo Bennici)
	Finnadar SR 9007 (Karen Phillips)

	NSA (Duncan Druce)
Instrumentation	Viola or Viola d'Amore
Duration	aleatoric, but *circa* 9′

74. *Y DESPUÈS*

Composed	1971
Performed	first performance unknown, but probably 1971
Published	Ricordi
Recorded	DGG 2530 802
Instrumentation	Guitar solo (10 strings)
Duration	aleatoric

75. *SOLO*

Composed	1971
Performed	probably Royan, April 1971
Published	Ricordi
Recorded	NSA (Melinda Maxwell)
	NWDR (L. Faber)
	SWDR (L. Faber)
Instrumentation	Mus, Ob, Ob d'Amore, Cor Ang (1 player)
Duration	aleatoric

76. *PIÈCE POUR IVRY*

Composed	1971
Performed	first performance unknown, but probably 1971
Published	Ricordi
Recorded	Fonit Cetra Italia 70061
Instrumentation	Solo violin
Duration	aleatoric

77. *AUSSTRAHLUNG*

Composed	1971
Performed	Persepolis, 4.9.71
Published	Ricordi
Recorded	CM (2 recordings)
Instrumentation	Tape
	Soprano, Fl (Alto Fl, Bass Fl),
	Ob (Cor Ang, Ob d'Am, Mus) soloists
	4 Fl (2 Picc), 3 Ob, Cor Ang, 4 Cl,
	(2 B Cl), Cl in Eb, 3 Bn
	4 Hn, 5 Tr, 4 Tromb, Tuba
	2 Hrp, 2 Xyl, 2 Mrb, Vibr, Cel, Glock
	4 Gong, 3 Susp Cym, 4 Tam-Tam, Rattle,
	Tamb, 2 Bongos, 2 Congas, Timp,
	2 Wood Blocks
	24 Vln, 12 Va, 10 Vc, 8 DB
Duration	*circa* 35′

78. *DIALODIA*

Composed	1971
Performed	Persepolis, 4.9.71 (part of *AUSSTRAHLUNG*)
Published	Ricordi
Recorded	This formed part of *AUSSTRAHLUNG*
Instrumentation	Two Fl, Two Ob, or other instruments
Duration	2′ 15″

79. *VENETIAN JOURNAL*

Composed	1971–72
Performed	New York, 12.3.72
Published	Ricordi
Recorded	RAI
Instrumentation	Tape
	Tenor Soloist
	Fl (Picc), Ob (Cor Ang), Cl (B Cl), Bn
	Hn, Tr, Tromb
	Hrp, Cel, Xyl, Mrb
	Bd. Cym, Tri, Temple Blocks
	Vln, Va, Vc, DB
Duration	*circa* 25′

80. *AURA*

Composed	1972
Performed	Chicago, 24.3.72
Published	Ricordi
Recorded	NSA
	Fonit Centra ITL 70044
	DGG 2531 272
Instrumentation	4 Fl (4 Picc), 3 Ob, Cor Ang, 2 Cl,
	Cl in Eb, 2 B Cl, 3 Bn (CBn)
	4 Hn, 5 Tr, 4 Tromb
	2 Hrp, Cel, 2 Xyl, 2 Mrb, Vibr
	Timp. BD, 4 Susp Cym, 4 Tri, 4 Gong,
	Claves, Bells,
	2 Congas, 6 Wood Blocks, Rattle, Glock
	24 Vln, 12 Va, 10 Vc, 8 DB, (Strings
	divided into 6 groups)
Duration	*circa* 20′

81. *BIOGRAMMA*

Composed	1972
Performed	Rochester, USA, 16.4.72
Published	Ricordi
Recorded	NSA, DGG 2531 272
Instrumentation	2 Picc, 2 Fl, 2 Ob, Cor Ang, 2 Cl,
	Cl in Eb, B Cl, 2 Bn, CBn
	4 Hn, 4 Tr, 4 Tromb, Tuba
	2 Hrp, 2 Mrb, 2 Xyl, Pf, Vibr, Cel, Glock

Timp, 3 Tub Bells, Susp Cym, Tom-Toms,
   Bongos, Bells, Tri, Cast, Claves
2 String Orchestras each comprising:
   12 Vln, 6 Va, 4 Vc, 3 Db

Duration	*circa* 18'

82. *GIARDINO RELIGIOSO*

Composed	1972
Performed	Tanglewood, USA, 8.8.72
Recorded	Columbia Y 34141
Instrumentation	2 Hn, 2 Tr
	2 Hrp, 2 Pf, 2 Mrb, Cel,
	Timp, Congas, Tam-Tam, Cym, Crot, 2 Tri
	6 Vln, 2 Va, 1 Vc, 1 DB
Duration	*circa* 16'

83. *AGES*

Composed	1972
Performed	probably September 1972 (RAI broadcast)
Published	tape held by Ricordi
Recorded	RAI, RIC
Instrumentation	tape-work
Duration	33' 40"

84. *ALL THE WORLD'S A STAGE*

Composed	1972
Performed	as part of AGES, probably September 1972, (RAI broadcast)
Published	Ricordi
Recorded	This is a choral episode of *AGES*
Text	from *As You Like It*
Instrumentation	two S A T Bar Choirs
Duration	*circa* 5'

85. *SATYRICON*

Composed	1971–73
Performed	Scheveningen, Holland, 16.3.73
Published	Salabert
Recorded	Strasfogel: tape of first performance
	NOS TV (Holland) Radio and Television performances
	Television performances
Text	'Satyricon' of Petronius Arbiter (trans. William Arrowsmith)
Instrumentation	2 Sop, M Sop, Cont, 2 Ten, 2 Bass Soloists
	Fl (Picc), Ob (Cor Ang), 2 Cl (B Cl), Bn
	Hrp, Pf, Cel, Mrb
	3 Drums, BD, Cym, (2 Susp Cym),

                                3 Bongos, 2 Cenc, Tri, Claves
                                Vln I, Vln II, Va, Vc, DB
Duration   *circa* 60'

86. *CONCERTO NO. 3 POUR HAUTBOIS ET ORCHESTRE*
Composed   1973
Performed   Amsterdam, 6.7.73
Published   Salabert
Recorded   NSA (cond. Maderna)
                                BV HAAST 032–033
                                NOS TV (Film of complete rehearsal of work)
Instrumentation   Ob (Cor Ang), soloist
                                4 Fl (4 Picc), 3 Ob, 2 Cl, Cl in Eb,
                                   B Cl, 2 Bn, CBn
                                4 Hn, 5 Tr, 4 Tromb, Tuba
                                Glock, Xyl, Vibr, Mrb, Cel, 2 Hrp
                                18 Vln, 9 Va, 6 Vc, 6 DB
Duration   *circa* 15' (aleatoric)

87. *CONCERTO PER DUE PIANOFORTI, VIOLONCELLO E ORCHESTRA*
Composed   begun 1973
                                All trace of the work, commissioned by
                                Saarländischer Rundfunk, has been lost: the work
                                was never completed.

Index to Maderna's Works

General Index